⇉⇉-✴-⇇⇇

NAMES ON THE LAND

⇉⇉-✴-⇇⇇

Names
on the Land

A Historical Account
of Placenaming
in the United States

by George R. Stewart

FOURTH EDITION

Lexikos
San Francisco

Published in November 1982
by Lexikos, 703 Market Street, San Francisco.
Reprinted by special arrangement
with Houghton Mifflin Company.

"George R. Stewart, Jr.: A Checklist,"
by John Caldwell, *Bulletin of Bibliography,*
Vol. 36, No. 2 (April-June 1979), copyright © 1979,
reprinted by permission of the publisher,
F. W. Faxon Company, Inc., Westwood, Mass.

Manufactured in the United States of America.

Originally designed by Ray Freiman;
cover designed by Craig Bergquist, San Francisco.
Typeset in Garamond; additional composition for this
edition by Minerva's Typorium, San Francisco.
Printed and bound by Haddon Craftsmen,
Scranton, Pa.

Library of Congress Cataloging in Publication Data

Stewart, George Rippey, 1895–1980
Names on the land.

    Reprint. Originally published: 3rd ed. Boston:
Houghton Mifflin, 1967. With new introduction and
bibliography of G. R. Stewart's works.
    Bibliography: p.
    1. Names, Geographical—United States. 2. United
States—History, Local. I. Title.
E155.S8 1982   973   82-6578
ISBN 0-938530-02-X (pbk.)   AACR2

82 83 84 85 5 4 3 2 1

Contents

Contents

Contents

ILLUSTRATIONS
(all following page 250)

Author's foreword

FOREWORD TO THE SECOND EDITION

In 1956 I decided to reissue a book that I had originally completed in 1944. In those twelve years much water had flowed under the bridges—as we used to say. To be modern, a lot of atoms had been disintegrated. Yet, when I re-read the book critically, I found little to change. The use of the original plates remained possible.

With particular pleasure I am able to report that recent and detailed studies have not in any case invalidated (in my opinion) my original work, although they have often cleared up some details and mobilized additional evidence. I take up individual case in the notes.

There were, indeed, some errors in the original edition. I am only surprised that in the years during which the book has been open to criticism more errors have not been discovered. I am not surprised at having made a few mistakes, especially since they were on minor matters. After all, *Names on the Land* not only was a pioneer work but also was crowded with detail. I am, however, glad to have this opportunity of revision. I have rewritten a number of lines, and have also corrected some typographical errors. These changes have been made in the plates, without comment.

As I look back upon a book that I finished writing in the pre-atomic era, I still find it a satisfactory one to have written. I have seen it noted in print so often as a "classic" that I am beginning to believe what I read. That is one reason why I am willing to let the text stand almost as it was originally written.

Another reason is that I do not subscribe to that prevalent human belief—especially common among scholars—that a person becomes wiser as he lives longer, experiences more, and accumulates additional knowledge. If I should be writing the book now, I *think* that I could do better here and there. I don't quite like the usage of the relative pronoun, and I find a few passages that sound a little off-key as of 1957. But if I tried to rewrite it now, I think that I would only botch the job. Therefore I have adopted the device of adding a supplement.

The book was the result of a single impulse, and so, I think, it should remain. It was written at a particular time in history, and many reflections of World War II may be found in its pages—both in particular reference and in general attitudes. But, again, to attempt changes by weeding out such references and altering the attitude would only result in a weakening, and almost in a falsification, as if a man were denying his parentage. For the same reason, I have not attempted to recapture, in the additional chapters, any kind of previous rapture. These chapters have, I hope, their own virtues, which differ, however, from those of the original book.

Let me take the present opportunity to discuss a few matters which conversation and correspondence make me think of some general interest to readers.

People ask me how long the book took me. I might, with some truth, reply, "I began in 1941, and finished in 1944." I am likely to say, with more literal truth, "I spent all my life on it!" For, if some are born great and some with a gift for laughter, others are born with a love of names, and I believe that I am one of them. From early childhood I must have been laying away such information in my memory. The fact was brought out to me as I went about preparing this new edition, and, thus, refreshing my memory. In 1923, for instance, I met an old gentleman named Ashley, and in the course of a five-minute conversation he told me that his father had named Montana; in 1941 the coupling Ashley-Montana was fresh in my mind, and helped in the preparation of Chapter XXXV. To go farther back, around 1913 I read a book by Brander Mathews which quoted much of the poem used in Chapter XXXVI; about thirty years later I could go back to that book. The anecdote about Youghiogheny in Chapter XXXVII I heard told when I was a small boy, about 1902, by my uncle Robert Dick Wilson; he was an excellent raconteur for a group of children, but the point is that I forgot all the other stories he told on that occasion, except for the one about the name, which seemed to me as fresh in my mind in 1944 as it had been more than forty years earlier.

As it happens, I have written a rather large number of books, and people sometimes ask me which is my favorite. I tell them *Names on the Land,* and I think that I answer correctly. It is my favorite, I suppose, partly because I am possessed by the fascination of names, as I have just indicated. But also this book was the most difficult to conceive and to execute of any that I have done—and I have done some hard ones. Moreover, it is my favorite because I feel that in spite of the difficulties I finally came closer to attaining what I set out to do than with any other of my books.

I also take advantage of this opportunity to make an acknowledgment to the many readers of the original edition. I know that there have been many, both because the book circulated rather widely (including an Armed Services edition), and because I have received many letters, nearly all of which I have answered.

Most of these letters were complimentary, as is to be expected. A person who is bored with a book does not bother to write to the author about it. Many correspondents sent additional information, some of which I have incorporated in the notes. Other correspondents pointed out what they considered to be errors in the text, and sometimes these really were errors. Two or three correspondents were bad-tempered.

Some of them were unconsciously humorous. I remember the gentleman who had worked out a system for abolishing present placenames and substituting numeral-letter designations. Another one took me to task for my explanation of a certain stream-name, and stated that his own must be true because he had it from a man who often had swum across the river on a horse.

G. R. S.
1957

Publisher's note

IT IS natural that publishers think well of the books they issue. In this case the publisher has a nice story about how it came to do the fourth edition of an American classic, George R. Stewart's *Names on the Land.*

When in high school I first read *Names on the Land,* I immediately put it on a brief list of favorite books, the ones I would probably read four or five times. Of course, I pushed it on friends and relatives, hoping it would become one of their favorites as well. Years later, after giving away my own copy yet again, I went to a bookstore to replace it—and found it was out of print. Not then in publishing, I addressed a reprimand to Houghton Mifflin's chairman to point out their oversight. David Harris, then managing editor, sent a polite explanation: Sorry, we can't reprint it, but here's a copy from our shelf.

A fine, welcome copy it was, lacking only the author's signature to make it permanently my own. George Stewart, after four decades of teaching at Berkeley, was living not far from me in San Francisco. I wrote to tell him how I got my copy of *Names on the Land.* "It seems to prove something to effect that publishers are human," he replied, and invited me by for an autograph.

Four years later, on August 22, 1980, George R. Stewart died. Only weeks later I joined Tom Cole in forming a new publishing firm, Lexikos ("of words" in Greek). I proposed that there was scarcely a more significant and worthwhile book for our first list than this book "of names." Besides, being only human, publishers may as well print what they admire.

He, Houghton Mifflin, and Mrs. Theodosia Stewart were all agreeable to Lexikos' producing a fourth edition. Wallace Stegner, Stewart's friend and colleague in history and fiction for forty years, said he would write an introduction. John Caldwell, librarian of Augustana College, Rock Island, Illinois, and his publisher agreed to let us reprint his complete Stewart checklist.

We attempted to locate any material the author may have intended for another revised edition. Irene Moran and Estelle Rebeck at the Bancroft Library, University of California at Berkeley, searched the Stewart papers in vain. We concluded that the author had committed any additional material to his authoritative lexicon, *American Placenames*.

And so here is *Names on the Land,* returned to print for both my bookshelf and a new generation of readers.

We wish to thank Mrs. Stewart and Wallace Stegner; Marcia Legru at Houghton Mifflin; Sandra Conrad of F. W. Faxon Company; John Caldwell; James D. Hart, Irene Moran, and Estelle Rebeck of the Bancroft Library; and, of course, David Harris.

And we want to express appreciation to our sales force, the unsung "book travelers" who roam the American land, braving icy winds and congested downtown streets and other hazards on their way to bookstores to sell this and our other books. They are: *in the South*—George Scheer, Joe Agnelli, Sam Montgomery, and Roger Sauls, of George Scheer Associates; *in the West*—Roger Moss, William Webb, Robert Arnold, John Little, Richard Detrano, Anne Summers, and Joe Cain, of Wilcher Associates; *in the mid-Atlantic states*—John E. Leibfried, Jr.; *and in the Midwest*—Jay Ide, Jack L. Eichkorn, William D. McGarr, and Julie Ellis, of J. S. Ide Associates.

Alan Magary

[xiv]

George Stewart and the American Land

Introduction by Wallace Stegner

OF GEORGE Stewart's twenty-eight books, I find that I have seventeen on my shelves. Some of them I have read only once. Eight of them I have just re-read, to remind myself of George's historical and fictional methods. Three or four of them I read all the time, and refer to, and quote, and steal from, and couldn't get along without.

This morning, exactly a year after his death on August 22, 1980, I am tempted to think of him as a writer who during his life received less attention than was due to him; and that temptation, born of friendship and the respect I had for him, is not entirely without justification. He was a much more important writer than the general public knew.

His interests were essentially regional, and his books reflected his interests, and so his readers and his reputation tended to be regional also. He hit only a few of the jackpots by which writers become famous or notorious. His private life was serene and his habits scholarly, so that he made no copy for the gossip columnists. He would not have known how to behave if he had been lionized. His approach, whether to history or to fiction, was the reverse of sensational. He was thorough, objective, judicious, all qualities that are likely to get a man ignored in the book-news media. Personally and artistically, his impulse was to efface himself. And he never in his life wrote a book that capitalized on a fad or tendency. His books were totally his own. He never went for an audience; he let it come to him.

Nevertheless, it would be doing him and his reputation a disservice to call him an ignored or overlooked writer. He had his modest share of the rewards and notice by which serious readers and critics and colleagues, the durable audience, pay their respects to substance and worth.

In 1938 the Commonwealth Club of California awarded him its Gold Medal for *East of the Giants,* a novel that is a paradigm of California history from Mexican colonialism to American statehood. In 1936 it had given him its Silver Medal for *Ordeal by Hunger,* the story of the Donner-Reed party. Properly, the medals should have been reversed, for *Ordeal by Hunger* is the more enduring book, but never mind. The point is that the Commonwealth Club, which gives recognition to California writers, recognized him twice, and early, as a California writer of stature.

Stewart's greatest popular success came with the novels *Storm* (1941) and *Fire* (1948), both Book of the Month Club choices and both best sellers. Twenty years after *Fire* an altogether different sort of book, the study of waste-disposal problems entitled *Not So Rich as You Think,* received the Sidney Hillman Award medal, though it was enough ahead of its time (a common weakness of Stewart books) so that it did not become a major document in the environmental movement. In 1972 the California Historical Society presented him with its Henry R. Wagner Award medal in recognition of his long and distinguished career as an interpreter of California history. Walkers along the sea on Thornton State Beach, south of the San Francisco city limit, will find a trail dedicated to him. And in the latter years of his life he was honored by the United States Board of Geographical Names, the Association of American Geographers, and the American Names Society for his work on place names.

All of which is to say that for nearly fifty years he has been a name, a presence, a quietly distinguished part of San Francisco's distinguished literary tradition. If they heard less of him in New York, and if he was never elected to either the American Academy of Arts and Sciences or to the National Academy and Institute of Arts and Letters, why that was their error and their loss. Equivalent achievement, if he had lived on the east coast, would have insured his election thirty years ago.

For there is no way around those several books, adequately recognized or not, which many of us find indispensable. *Ordeal by Hunger* is *the* history of the Donner party, which closed in tragedy the first act of the American occupation of California, and it is not likely to be replaced by any future study. *The California Trail,* though it was written to order as one of a series, is the best single-volume history of the overland migration to California, and is likely to remain so. And *Names on the Land,* a unique book, is the only study we have of how we went about putting our marks on the unnamed continent, and in doing so both added ourselves to the continent and added the continent to ourselves. It can be read as a gloss on Robert Frost's poem "The Gift Outright," with its theme of a people "possessing what we still were unpossessed by," and how we learned to give ourselves "to the land vaguely realizing westward."

George Stewart testified that of all of his many books he liked *Names on the Land* best. As usual, his judgment was sound. That book best expressed his interest in history, his curiosity about the web of organizational structures by which we not only create our institutions but leave tracks and names behind, the sociological and psychological and verbal impulses that permeate and direct such a massive and unpremeditated act as the investment of a continent. Habit, fashion, accident, ritual, poetry, humor, all played a part in the naming, and the naming process—as Stewart saw when no one else did—subsumed our history as a people. Nobody ever wrote such a book as *Names on the Land* before, nobody has written one since.

Besides those three that I could not do without, there are

many other books of solid worth and astonishing originality. For those who have missed him, here is the record:

Seven novels: *East of the Giants, Doctor's Oral, Storm, Fire, Earth Abides, Sheep Rock,* and *The Years of the City.*

Four biographical works: *Bret Harte, Argonaut and Exile; John Phoenix, Esq.; Take Your Bible in One Hand: The Life of William Henry Thomes;* and the Plutarchian *Good Lives.*

Four histories: *Ordeal by Hunger, The California Trail, Committee of Vigilance,* and *Pickett's Charge.*

Four books on names and naming: *Names on the Land; American Given Names; American Placenames, A Concise and Selective Dictionary;* and *Names on the Globe.*

One book more or less unclassifiable, that I shall call historical anthropology: *Man, An Autobiography.*

A study of waste disposal: *Not So Rich as You Think.*

A study of the loyalty-oath controversy on the Berkeley campus in the 1950's: *The Year of the Oath,* done in collaboration with others.

Three books that can be loosely labeled "description and history": *U.S. 40: Cross Section of the United States of America; N.A. 1,* a two-volume guide to the North-South Continental Highway; and *American Ways of Life,* made up of lectures Stewart gave in Athens during a year as a Fulbright lecturer.

A handful of lesser books, spin-offs of Stewart's lifetime interest in western history and western writers.

It is a formidable life-work, no part of it trivial or hasty, the best of it solid, lively, eminently readable, eminently dependable, and at least one book of it unique. Almost all of it is focused on California, most especially the Bay Area. Of the seven novels, only *The Years of the City* has a non-Californian locale. Of the histories and biographies, only *Pickett's Charge* and *Good Lives* concern themselves with non-Californian people and events. Even *Names on the Land,* though like the two highway-guide books it ranges across the whole continent, has a strong list to westward, partly because the American people flowed that way, partly, one is sure, because George Stewart's own inclination was westward.

He was a Californian by adoption, as are millions of others, but of long standing. Born in Sewickley, Pennsylvania, in 1895, he was brought to Southern California in 1907, at the age of twelve. Except for his years as an undergraduate at Princeton and as a graduate student at Columbia, he was a California resident the rest of his life. Azusa and Pasadena shaped his boyhood, and a single year as a graduate student at Berkeley in 1919–1920 shaped his career, for it put him under the tutelage of Chauncey Wells, who taught him to love literature and writing, and Herbert Bolton, who introduced him to California history.

Something, perhaps the conviction of his Vassar-graduate mother that the East could teach him more than Berkeley could, sent George after one year to Columbia, where he received his Ph.D. in 1922. His dissertation was—of all things—on "Modern Metrical Techniques as Illustrated by the Ballad Meter," an inoculation that clearly did not take. A year as an instructor at the University of Michigan, during which he became engaged to Theodosia Burton, the daughter of the university's president, gave him his teaching apprenticeship. When the job at Berkeley for which he had been aiming opened up, he took it, and a year later brought his young wife west on the first of many cross-country trips, and they settled where he belonged. They never left.

The first writing project he involved himself in, a comprehensive study of the Gold Rush period, very quickly proved too big even for young ambition. It finally reduced itself to Stewart's first book, the biography of Bret Harte, which, fragment or not, is still the authoritative biography. But having been cut back, the Gold Rush theme began to grow again. It was never really abandoned, only divided into manageable portions, and much of what Stewart wrote later was part of it or an extension of it. The Donner Party book, the California Trail book, the history of the Committee of Vigilance, the biographies of Harte, John Phoenix, William Henry Thomes, and (in *Good Lives*) of John Bidwell, are all related to it. So, in part, is *East of the Giants.* So are most of the editions of early diaries that Stewart prepared, with introductions, for the Bancroft Library, the California Historical Society, the Book Club of California, and other organizations. In addition, much of that part of his work which is fictional, not historical, is set in the corridor between Donner Pass and San Francisco. Donner Pass, George used to say, was *his* pass. He invented it.

In a career as coherent and as disciplined as this, it is hard to tell cause from effect. Did California history interest George Stewart because it demonstrated the strains and lesions, the violences and disintegrations, the difficult improvisations, of a society in the process of being transplanted, mixed, and reconstituted? Or did he acquire his interest in the processes of social organization and accomodation through his long study of the California frontier? It hardly matters which way we read it, but it is of the highest importance that we do not overlook those social processes, whether disintegrative or integrative, for they are central to book after book, both historical and fictional.

Thus (a word it is impossible to avoid in speaking of George Stewart, for being a man of precise and logical habits he himself found the word "thus" inescapable) the novel *East of the Giants* traces, through the lives of Juan Godoy, Judith Hingham, and David Melton, the formation of a California civilization. The Spanish and American traditions struggle and partly mix, the Indians are suppressed, the dynamics of the Gold Rush modify and end lives and change ways of living, one kind of life declines and another shapes itself to replace it. The emphasis is less on individuals than on forces; what matters at least as much as the fates of Juan, Judith, and David is the emergence of a new society.

Thus *Storm,* and after it *Fire,* celebrated the anonymous and overlooked but indispensable agencies that a later California has evolved to deal with the strokes of nature, acts of God, that threaten its orderly procedures. Any challenge to man's domination of nature and nature's forces and nature's creatures brings out the human counter-forces. (One feels that if George were alive now he would be tempted to write a novel about our mobilization against the Medfly). Disrupt the anthill and the formic specialty forces swarm out to deal with the intrusion. Stewart had a great respect for the skill and organization of those forces, whether he expressed them as Weather Bureau people in *Storm* or Forest Service people in *Fire,* or as telephone linemen, bulldozer skinners, switchboard operators, or any other element of the complex web our society has woven and which, in both critical and routine situations, it helplessly depends. The people in these two novels especially hardly have identity apart from their jobs and their social organization, but civilization, Stewart more than suggests, would be utterly impossible without their skills and the structures that put them to work.

Thus *Sheep Rock* shows people conditioned by the city adapting their lives and feelings to a harsh land and climate and a fragile ecology, modifying their imported habits in order to live and come into harmony with this environment that accepts them only on sufferance. Twenty years before the Seventies made it fashionable, Stewart was writing an "environmental" novel about return to the land, and speculating on what such a return would do to human beings both socially and psychologically.

Thus *The Years of the City* chronicles the founding, flourishing, decline, and fall of a Greek colonial city, such a city as Paestum or Sybaris, planted on the frontier of the Italian boot, where the gibberish of the barbarian natives is full of sounds like *ibus* and *orum.* Different though it seems from the bulk of Stewart's work, it is actually a logical extension of it; it simply moves the frontier and its problems 2500 years closer to the dawn of civilization. Stewart was led into it by his year on a Fulbright lectureship in Greece—carrying, as he said with amusement, culture back to Athens.

Thus, as *The Years of the City* tells the story of a rise and a fall, *Earth Abides* tells of a fall and a rise, or at least the first steps of a rise. Science fiction of a kind, it imaginatively examines the consequences of a world-wide pestilence that wipes out all but a few pockets of the immune. Characteristically, it is the East Bay from which we witness the end of the world. In the beginning, and for some years after, Isherwood Williams and the handful of other survivors who gather around him are able to scavenge a good and easy living simply by breaking into the stores and using the buildings and equipment and power left behind by the suddenly-stopped high energy civilization. Ish himself, an educated and thoughtful man, has the enduring hope of being able to re-constitute that civilization: the symbol of his hope is the great University of California library, intact and silent, which holds the seeds of everything the survivors need to know. But as the years pass, supplies and know-how dwindle, fires and earthquakes destroy buildings and streets, animals go wild and become dangerous, gasoline and guns and ammunition and canned foods and all the other left-overs are no longer available, the automatic hydroelectric power plant stops and all stoves and refrigerators with it. Item by item the old civilization is relinquished. They sink always deeper into simple tribal ways, live by hunting and gathering, dress in skins, re-invent the bow and arrow, evolve superstitions and myths. In the minds of children who never knew it, the past barely exists as a large vague Before. They cannot be made to hold still for education, they never learn to read and write. Indescribably long and dim, the future stretches ahead, awaiting the once-in-a-century lucky accident or man of genius who will move it a millimeter closer to a new cycle of development and accretion, add one small increment to a new racial memory, new arts, new sciences, religions, technologies.

Earth Abides is a fascinating book, as compelling in its development as *Robinson Crusoe.* It is very shrewd in its knowledge of how long, slow, and painful is the development of civilization; how dependent upon perception, invention, luck, cooperation, organization, memory, communication; how vulnerable. Stewart sought scientific advice from colleagues at Berkeley while writing the novel, but one feels that his study of the California frontier had suggested to him most of what he needed to know. As a historian of civilization he had a fair idea of how law and justice might evolve, and how harsh they might be when sheer survival made them necessary. He probably already had in his mind the history of the San Francisco Committee of Vigilance, of which he would later write. In imagining how, forced back to primitive tribal circumstances, people would react to shortage, hardship, threat, competition, he had the whole history of the American frontier for a model. He had already written one version of it in *East of the Giants,* and would shortly write another in *Sheep Rock.* And in his second book, in 1936, he had traced a social disintegration all the way to bestiality and cannibalism.

All those books, diverse in subject, are closely related in theme. Whether they are about storms or forest fires in the Sierra or about a poet being spiritually acclimatized in the Black Rock Desert or about the fate of a Greek city in the sixth century B.C., they reflect the same informed, retentive, curious, speculative mind. The theme never strays far from an examination of the bonds that hold human beings together in families, tribes, cities, or civilizations—how they are forged, how they hold, how they break, how they may be renewed.

In almost every way—in subject, in method, in attitude—George Stewart was about as far as he could get from the rebellious and dissatisfied stance that in the 20th century we have come to associate with writers. Changes in society did not fill him with despair or indignation—he expected them, his cyclic view of history incorporated them. He was not agitated about such clichés as "post-Christian man," or "post-industrial man." As he indicated in *Man: An Autobiography,* on the long curve of human development such deviations didn't even show. He took the long view, with a vengeance, and he was remarkably free of both Chicken-Littleism and personal spite against the universe.

"Poet and precisionist," his friend Joseph Henry Jackson called him. Precisionist he was, but if poet, then a very apollonian poet, more an old chief than a young warrior, more on the side of wisdom, restraint, negotiation, and compromise than of intransigence and direct action. His defect, or advantage, was that he had studied history. He would have agreed with Robert Frost that there are no new ways to be new. He would have appraised every latest revolutionary discovery in the light of the long slow ages. And he had a constitutional inability to be emotional, partisan, or rabid. His impulse was precisely the other way: to be judicious, to examine evidence, to hold his fire, to be wary of taking either offense or sides.

That impulse reveals itself in nearly all his works, but is most evident in the works of history which touch on topics the historians have chosen to quarrel about. In fact, whenever he came across such a topic, Stewart had an inclination to get all the witnesses together, read all the papers, and see if he couldn't straighten the quarreling factions out.

Take, as an example, the cannibalism of the Donner Party, and in particular the character of the German Keseberg, whom the conventional historians have made a scapegoat and a ghoul. Of all the members of the party, he is the least easy to love. He fell further into bestiality, he survived longer, he partook of more man-meat. He was reported to have remarked about Tamsen Donner that she was the best he ever ate, he was suspected of killing a child who was put into his filthy bed in that filthy hut on Donner Lake.

But Stewart, pondering the disintegration of human beings under the harshest conditions, noting how sociability and comradeship gave way to suspicion and quarrelsomeness, and quarrelsomeness to murder, and murder to heightened suspicion and hostility; and how shrinking supplies led first to hoarding and then to heartlessness and then to cannibalism and then to the toasting of the hearts of dear relatives over the fire—noting moreover how nearly every member of the party who survived, survived by eating the dead to some extent—is willing to give Keseberg the benefit of the doubt. He understands the effects of starvation, hardship, solitude; he knows how a man under those circumstances could be crazed and irrational; he believes that many men, in the same circumstances, would show no better than Keseberg did. In that dreadful tragedy he chooses to find no scapegoat, though he finds several heroes.

Or take the Committee of Vigilance, often described by the historians as outlawry in the name of law. Without condoning or softening the harshness of those hangings, Stewart never forgets the provocations, the arrogance of the lawless Sydney Ducks, the venality of some parts of the apparatus of justice. As evidence of the curious sort of impersonality in the Committee, and its lack of a lust for power, he notes the fact that with the city more or less in its hands, the Committee of Vigilance voluntarily disbanded. Stewart does not exactly condone vigilantism; he simply reports the facts of the history of this example.

Or *Pickett's Charge,* the only historical work by Stewart which deals with events outside the bounds of California. Pickett's Charge was the climax of the climax, the key episode in the key battle of the Civil War. As a battle in which the omniscience of General Robert E. Lee came into serious question, Gettysburg, and especially Pickett's Charge, has been interpreted and re-interpreted by historians north and south. Stewart wrote his book, characteristically, to try to clear the air.

He did it in his customary fashion, from the evidence, impartially and at times skeptically reviewed. He is neither protecting nor attacking reputations, he is only looking at the interpretations put on events by people who *may* have been protecting or attacking. But no one reading his meticulous gun-by-gun, regiment-by-regiment, yard-by-yard report of the charge is likely to come out denying that Lee made a mistake, that with this last great Napoleonic assault he proved Napoleonic tactics outmoded, that some of the outfits both Union and Confederate that were accused of panicking did indeed panic (though with provocation), and that others similarly charged have been wronged by history. In short, if anyone wants to know about Pickett's Charge at Gettysburg, and how to interpret it, this is the history book to look into.

There is another kind of history to be examined in George Stewart's work—not the kind that makes a judicious review to eliminate partisanship and weigh evidence and separate facts from prejudice and determine what truly happened in some given situation, but the kind that nobody ever noticed, or noticed so partially that its importance was never made clear. We come to that in *Names on the Land*.

"Once," Stewart begins, "from eastern ocean to western ocean, the land stretched away without names. Nameless headlands split the surf; nameless lakes reflected nameless mountains; and nameless rivers flowed through nameless valleys into nameless bays." Like many of the ideas that he hammered into books, that one is a commonplace—the sort of commonplace we never think to examine, also the sort of commonplace which, looked at steadily, begins to glow with strangeness and wonder.

After millennia of occupation by Indian tribes, after the surges of European exploration and imperial wars, after the rise of the mongrel American republic which took over most of what the empires had quarreled over, that blankness was filled. ". . . The names lay thickly over the land,

and the Americans spoke them, great and little, easily and carelessly—Virginia, Susquehanna, Rio Grande, Deadman Creek, Sugarloaf Hill, Detroit, Wall Street—not thinking how they had come to be. Yet the names had grown out of the life, and the life-blood, of all those who had gone before. . . . In older countries the story of the naming was lost in the ancient darkness. But in the land between the two oceans much of the record could still be read—who gave the names and when, and even why one name was given rather than another."

In Europe, not only the origins but the meanings of many placenames have been lost. In a continent as new as North America, both are still traceable, or at least guessable. Placename societies, placename books and magazines and monographs, have been engaged in that work for a long time. But not until Stewart did anyone look at the subject curiously and steadily enough to see the historical and psychological, the sociological and ethnic, patterns of naming, and to clarify our history by clarifying those patterns. *Names on the Land* is not a book of placenames—Stewart did that later in the dictionary of American placenames he produced for the Oxford Press—but a book on the ways in which names are given. A book, that is, about people and cultures, and the changes that have happened to them since Spanish ships made landfall in the Indies, a book about the ways in which cultures agglomerate and spread, and swallow other cultures or are swallowed by them or fuse with them, a book about the ways in which a not-too-promising primate has marked the world with his footprints.

The ways are most various. Thus (Stewart's keyord again), Juan Ponce de Léon named Florida from the double fact that it seemed a flowery land and that he reached it only six days after the Easter of Flowers. Plain observation and an imported religious tradition fused to make a name that future generations accepted without question. Europeans of whatever nation had a strong impulse to impose upon the new continent names they had known in the old, either

[xxvii]

names of kings and queens and great men whose backing they had or desired, or names of counties and towns where their affections were rooted. Thus all the Bostons and Pomfrets and Portsmouths and Plymouths in New England, thus New England itself (and New Spain, New Galicia, New France, New York, New Amsterdam, and in a secondary ebbing sequence, New Mexico, New Harmony).

Catholic invaders planted innumerable Old World saints on the New World, Catholic and Protestant alike borrowed from (and bowdlerized) Indian names. Heroes of sorts left their names (Houston, all the Washingtons, all the Lincolns, all the MacArthur Boulevards and Kennedy Airports). Tribes of natives were acknowledged—Massachusetts, Manhattan—and chiefs who were roughly handled in life were made immortal in the placenames of the society that overcame them—Pontiac, Seattle, Chicago.

What Stewart understood was that nothing is comprehended, much less possessed, until it has been given a name, either casually as in Bear Creek (the creek where someone saw or shot or was attacked by a bear), or formally as in El Pueblo de Nuestra Señora la Reina de los Angeles de la Porciuncula. Coming at different times, from different branches of European culture, we brought different languages, different habits, different preoccupations, to our naming practices, and we heard the native tongues in different ways and translated native names differently. Moreover, mapmakers back in Europe often created or perpetuated error, simply because they did not understand or could not read the maps and descriptions from which they worked. Champlain's Frenchmen discovered and named a little river flowing into Lake Champlain, calling it "La Mouette," the Seagull. But a mapmaker misread it, seeing *l*'s where *t*'s should be, and made it into the meaningless word Lamoille. Though the headwaters of one branch of the Lamoille flow out of a pond on a Vermont farm I have owned since 1938, I confess it did not occur to me to wonder what the river's name meant until *Names on the Land* informed me that it meant nothing.

A thing that fascinated Stewart, and will fascinate anyone who submits to his book, is the variety of origin, and hence of naming practice, that Europeans brought to this country, and the ways in which America worked on those names, naturalizing and changing them. What determines whether a new town named for its founder shall be Louisburg or Louisville or Louistown or Louiston? Why does Pittsburgh have a terminal *h* and Harrisburg none? Those fashions—and they *were* fashions, dictated by the temporary dominance of Scotch, French, German, or English populations—are duplicated in our own time by the often-emetic fashions current among subdividers, who think a town called Hills or Ranch or Cove will sell better than one tagged with the once-classy *-ville*.

And not only place names, but generic nomenclature, common nouns designating common geographical features, underwent change. What in New England became known as a *brook* was in Pennsylvania known as a *run*, in New York as a *kill*, in the southeast as a *branch*, out west as a *creek*. Somehow we developed a way of changing a word like "mountain" depending on whether it came before or after. Who makes us say Sourwood *Mountain*, but *Mount* Washington? Our American ears.

When James Fenimore Cooper, in *The American Democrat*, castigated his compatriots for saying *kew*cumber instead of the proper and elegant *cow*cumber he was not keeping up with his own country. Inexorably the new continent with its new conditions, climates, diets, freedoms, worked on language as on everything else. What in Europe had been called an *elk* acquired the Algonquian name *moose*. What in England had been a *stag* or *red deer* became an *elk*. The English word *master* became progressively more unpopular until it all but died out, and was replaced by the Dutch word *boss*. What had been a *porch* showed signs of becoming a *stoop*, and down south a *gallery*, and in New Mexico a *portal*. European *ripples* became American *riffles*, with

[xxix]

a subtly altered meaning.

As with the language at large, so with the specific function of language known as placenames. Much is revealed about our background by whether we call a shallow stagnant lake a *pond* or a *slough* or a *swamp,* whether we call a shallow dry watercourse a *swale* or a *gully,* a *wash* or a *coulee.* Every regions has its native terms; every ethnic group that ever came to America has contributed nomenclature. Every historic conflict or movement of people, every change of climate and habitat, as when settlements moved from the forests through the oak openings out into the open grasslands, has enforced the borrowing of local native nomenclature or the invention or adaptation of imported terms.

Which is to say, our history, or tradition, the story of our five-hundred-year love/hate struggle with the North American continent, are there in the names we have put on the land. "Bury my heart at Wounded Knee," says a poem by Stephen Vincent Benét. Yes. Or at Spuiten Duyvil, or on the banks of the Picketwire, or on Año Nuevo Island, or in the Wah Wah Mountains, or wherever American energy has intruded and American feet have trod. *Names on the Land* will suggest plenty of choices.

For *Names on the Land,* even more than other books by George R. Stewart, is provocative in the best sense. It makes a reader look at things he has taken for granted, it stretches the mind with analogies and possibilities, it is made luminous by the learning brought to bear upon a single aspect of our incomparably complex heritage. It is never guilty of losing sight of the forest while concentrating on the trees. Though he was a master of detail, never losing one, never forgetting its importance, Stewart makes details serve the large and steadily-seen ends with which he began. As historian or novelist, anthropologist or pundit of place-naming, he is consistently an expositor and defender of the human capacity for cooperation and organization and long memory which flowers as civilization. His books teach us who we are, and how we got to be who we are.

[xxx]

NAMES ON THE LAND

Name, though it seem but a superficial and outward matter, yet it carrieth much impression and enchantment.
—Francis Bacon

Chapter I ⟨ Of what is attempted in this book

ONCE, from eastern ocean to western ocean, the land stretched away without names. Nameless headlands split the surf; nameless lakes reflected nameless mountains; and nameless rivers flowed through nameless valleys into nameless bays.

Men came at last, tribe following tribe, speaking different languages and thinking different thoughts. According to their ways of speech and thought they gave names, and in their generations laid their bones by the streams and hills they had named. But even when tribes and languages had vanished, some of those old names, reshaped, still lived in the speech of those who followed.

After many centuries a people calling themselves Americans held the land. They followed the ways of the English more than of any others, especially in their speech. Yet they gathered together in their blood and in their manner of life something of all those who had lived in the land before them. Thus they took as a heritage many names of the past. Adding more names, they gave to their children with every generation the heritage richer than before.

A few hundred were great names, known to all Americans, of states and cities, mountains and rivers. But most of them were little names, known only to those who lived near by, of ponds and swamps and creeks and hills, of townships and villages, of streets and ranches and plantations, of coves and gulches and meadows. These little names arose by so many thousands that at last they were numbered by millions.

Thus the names lay thickly over the land, and the Americans spoke them, great and little, easily and carelessly—Virginia, Susquehanna, Rio Grande, Deadman Creek, Sugarloaf Hill Detroit, Wall Street—not thinking how they had come to be. Yet the names had grown out of the life, and the life-blood, of all those who had gone before. From the names might be known how here one man hoped and struggled, how there another dreamed, or died, or sought fortune, and another joked, twisting an old name to make a new one—Providence and Battle Mountain, Hardscrabble, Troy, Smackover, Maine, Elrio, Pasadena, Troublesome Creek, Cape Fear, Nashville, Lincoln County, Fourth Crossing.

In this heritage of names the Americans were fortunate, for in general the names were good, and they were closely bound with the land itself and the adventures of the people. In older countries the story of the naming was lost in the ancient darkness. But in the land between the two oceans much of the record could still be read—who gave the names and when, and even why one name was chosen rather than another.

This is written, then, as the story of that naming—how the great names, one by one, came to stand large on the maps, and how the little names in their thousands arose on the tongues of the people, after the varying customs of time and place, of blood and language.

Chapter II ⟨ Of the naming that was before history

IN THE distant past, then, the land was without names. Yet the nature of the land itself prefigured something of what was to be.

Where jagged mountains reared up along the horizon, many names would describe shapes, but in a flat country names of other meanings would be given. Where most streams were clear but one ran thick with reddish mud, a man coming to that stream would call it Red River, whether he said Río Colorado, or Rivière Rouge, or Bogue Homa, or blurted syllables in some now long-forgotten tongue. Since alders first grew close to water and desert-cedars clung to hillsides, they predestined Alder Creek and Cedar Mountain. Long Lake and Stony Brook, Blue Ridge and Grass Valley, lay deeper than tribe or language; the thing and the name were almost one.

No one knows when man came, or who gave the first names. Perhaps the streams still ran high from the melting ice-cap, and strange beasts roamed the forest. And since names—corrupted, transferred, re-made—outlive men and nations and languages, it may even be that we still speak daily some name which first meant "Saber-tooth Cave" or "Where-we-killed-the-ground-sloth."

There is no sure beginning. At the opening of history many and various tribes already held the land, and had given it a thin scattering of names. The names themselves can be made to reveal the manner of the earliest naming.

Once, let us say, some tribesmen moved toward a new country, which was unknown to them. Halting, they chose a good man, and sent him ahead. This scout went on, watching not to be ambushed or get lost, knowing he must report shrewdly when he returned. First he skulked along the edge of a big meadow, where he saw many deer. Then he came to a stream where he noted some oak trees, which were uncommon in that country. All this time he was skirting the slope of a great mountain, but because he was actually on it, and because the trees were so thick, he did not think of a mountain; and, besides, it made no difference to him one way or the other. So he went farther on—through a little swamp, and to a stream which he crossed on a beaver-dam. This stream was the same as the one where the oak trees grew, but he had no way of being certain, and besides it did not matter

[5]

at all—each crossing was a thing in itself. He went on, through a narrow defile with many tall rocks, which he knew would be an ugly spot for an ambush. Going back, he noted all the places in reverse, but did not actually bestow any names on them.

When he told his story, however, he unconsciously gave names by describing places, such as the big meadow and the stream where the oak trees grew. He did not speak of the mountain, because the mountain was everywhere and the whole country was merely its slope; and he did not speak of the deer in the meadow, because he knew that deer are at one place for sun-up and another for nooning, so that only a fool would try to distinguish one meadow from another by mentioning them.

The others listened to his words, nodded and questioned and remembered; they knew that they would have no other knowledge of the next day's march, and that life and death might hang on how well they remembered his landmarks. So they thought to themselves, "big meadow," "stream where oak trees grow," "stream with a beaver-dam," and the rest. When they went ahead into that country, they recognized each place as they came to it.

Then, when they lived there, they used the descriptions first, saying, "There is good fishing in the stream where oak trees grow." But soon they said, "stream-where-oak-trees-grow" in one breath, and it had become a name.

The first simple names were like sign-posts, noting something permanent and easily recognized, something to distinguish one place from other places—size, or shape, or color, or the kind of rocks or trees found there. After the tribe grew familiar with the region, such sign-post names were no longer much needed, and as the people began to have memories of what had happened here or there, names of another kind sprang up.

At some stream, perhaps, a hunter saw a panther drinking in broad daylight, and killed it with a single arrow. This was a matter of wonder, and people began to say: "the stream where the panther was killed." After a few generations the actual story may have been forgotten, but the name retained. In the old Choctaw country there is still a Quilby Creek, from their words *koi-ai-albi*, "panther-there-killed." Far in the Southwest a ruined pueblo is Callemongue, "where-they-hurled-down-stones." But the name is the only testimony; no man knows the story of that desperate siege, or who hurled down stones at what besiegers.

Not all these adventures need have been real. If a young man saw a vision, what happened to him then may have been as vivid as the killing of a panther. Or he may have thought that his dream made manifest the world of spirits. So in the country of the Sioux many places had the suffix *-wakan,* and among the Algonquians *-manito,* to show that a presence haunted them. The Cherokees had a belief in a race of huge snakes. Each was great as a tree-trunk, horned, with a bright blazing crest. Even to see one was sure death. Where they were thought to lurk, in deep river-pools and lonely passes in high mountains, the Cherokees called *Where-the-Uktena-stays.*

From visions or from often-told and much-distorted exploits came a few mythological names, although sometimes the story arose later to explain an unusual name. The Abnaki of the far Northeast told of the giant Glooscap. Once he pursued an enormous moose, killing it finally close to the shore of the ocean. There they pointed out a ledge of rock which at one stage of tide looked much like a moose's rump, and so was called Moos-i-katch-ik. To reward his dog, Glooscap threw him the entrails. These became a reddish rock known as Osquoon, "the liver," and a vein of white quartz, Oolaghesee, "the gut."

If a tribe lived in the same region for many generations, the name-pattern grew more complex. The land itself might change. Stream-with-a-Beaver-Dam might fill with silt and become a mere swamp, so that the beavers no longer lived there. The dam itself would be grown over with trees and bushes. After the dam became indistinguishable, the name was actually misleading. Then it might be changed entirely, but a traditional-minded tribe would sometimes keep the old name, as in a modern city Canal Street may remain after the canal has long been filled in.

Language also changed with the generations, and names more rapidly than the rest of language. A lengthy descriptive name of

[7]

an important place was said so often that it was likely to be clipped and slurred. Before long, it sounded like words having some other meaning, or else like meaningless syllables. The tribe had no written records to show what the name should be. Eventually some story-teller might build up a tale to explain the new name. Thus Allegheny seems most likely to have meant "fine river" in the language of the Delawares, but they later told a story of a mythical tribe called the Allegewi who had lived on that river until defeated by the all-conquering Delawares. More often, when a common name became meaningless, the Indians, like other people, merely accepted it—"Just a name!"

A tribe entering a new country also faced, unconsciously, the problem of what to name. In even a small area there were thousands of "places." But the Indians had no written records, and the ordinary man could not well burden his memory with more than some few hundreds of names. The corn-growing Pueblos, who seldom wandered far from their villages, placed their names thickly. In a nomadic tribe, like the Pawnee, the ordinary man may not have known very many more names than a Pueblo farmer, and they were scattered thinly over a range of several hundred miles.

The more distinct a place was, the more likely an Indian was to name it. A small lake set cleanly in the forest was a thing in itself, as individual as a person; so was a small island, or a single up-standing rock.

Also, the more useful a place was, the more it was frequented, and the more it needed a name. If a bay had a mud-flat with a fine oyster-bed and another without any, there was no need of wasting a name on the useless one.

On both counts, mountains generally went unnamed. They were huge and vague; they mingled one with another, and faded off into their own shoulders; no one was really sure just where a mountain began. Some high peaks served as landmarks, but most mountains in themselves were of little use. An Indian might have names for the game-haunted glades on the slope, and for the lakes

and streams where he fished—but no name for the mountain itself. Most of the resonant Indian names of high peaks were placed
there later by white men.

Rivers were closest of all to the life of primitive man. In a dry
country they supplied the water of life itself. If a tribe knew the
use of canoes, the rivers were the highways. To nomads wandering across country, rivers were barriers to be crossed. Everywhere
they furnished food—clams, turtles, and frogs; catfish and perch;
in their season the salmon and shad and alewives crowding up
from the sea. Game trails led to the water, and the hunter lay in
wait by the drinking place. First of all, any tribe named the rivers.

But a well-known river seldom had the same name throughout
its course. Crossways, a river was cleanly set off, but lengthways
it was like a mountain in having no limits. A tribe often had no
idea where its rivers came from or went to. In thick forest country a primitive Indian knew the river only at the spots where trails
touched or crossed it. Each of these spots was for him a place in
itself, and the flowing of the water from one to another was of no
importance. If later he learned to use canoes, he was then likely
to name every reach and rapid and bend—a very practical procedure, since a single word then identified both the river and the
place on the river.

Anything as large and vaguely marked off as a region or territory, most Indians did not name at all. The place where a certain
tribe lived was known after that tribe, and if they shifted ground,
the name shifted with them.

Names also were affected by the absence of any "Indian language." To say that a name is Indian is even less than to say that
it is European, for among the tribes the languages differed much
more than English from French, Dutch, or Russian. Because of
this multiplicity of languages a large river or lake usually had several totally different names, which might or might not have the
same meaning in translation. This was also true of tribal names.

When the white men arrived, the pattern of Indian naming had
grown somewhat complex. Here and there, as with the pueblo-

dwellers of the Southwest and the Iroquois of the Northeast, tribes had lived for many generations in the same country. With them, many names had become meaningless, or referred to some forgotten incident. Most tribes, however, were apparently newcomers in the regions where they lived. Their legends told of migrations; their names were simple and understandable. Many tribes shifted during historical times. Far from being universally very old, many Indian place-names are recent. Some make reference to pigs, cattle, gunpowder, drunkenness, or something else of which they were ignorant before the coming of the whites.

The Europeans constantly made mistakes about Indian names, in form, and in application. They thought in terms of kingdoms and provinces, and failed to realize that Indians thought in terms of tribes. They assumed that a river or a lake had the same name everywhere. They failed to conceive the vast differences between languages of near-by tribes. They were used to names like Cadiz and Bristol which had long since lost literal meaning, and so they were likely to use a name as a mere counter, applying that of a river to a bay, or that of a tribe to a lake.

Our heritage of Indian names is rich and treasured—twenty-six states, eighteen of the greatest cities, most of the larger lakes and longer rivers, a few of the highest mountains, and thousands of smaller towns and natural features. Other names are translations of the Indian words. But merely to tell what such names mean literally or may possibly have meant to some long-vanished tribe is to miss most of the flavor. The meaning of a name is more than the meaning of the words composing it.

Arizona and Connecticut, Seattle and Des Moines, Niagara and Potomac—all these are Indian, or once were. But the white man reshaped and reapplied them, adapting them to his own language and ways of thought, until sometimes the names became more European than Indian. The story of each name is different—sometimes simple enough, as with Chesapeake and Massachusetts; sometimes very strange, as with Oregon. Such stories can best be told in connection with their later history rather than their first origins.

Chapter III ⟨ How the first Spaniards gave names

In THE twentieth year after the New World was first discovered, Juan Ponce de León sailed from Puerto Rico with three ships "to win honor and increase estate." He steered northwestward, past many islands already known and named. Running before a fair wind, on Easter Sunday, which in Spanish is called "of flowers," Don Juan and his men saw a little unknown island. They ran for three days still northwest, and then for two days westnorthwest. At last on Saturday they saw land ahead. They sailed, for what was left of that day, along the coast, seeking a harbor. Toward nightfall, they anchored off shore.

Then, as Herrera the chronicler wrote the story, they named that new land. And this is a moment which all living there now should remember, for then first a lasting name was given by men who came from overseas, on the evening of April 2, 1513.

Don Juan looked ashore, and with him were his pilot and captains, his shipmen and soldiers, and also perhaps his great wardog Becerrillo whom the Indians feared more than ten Spaniards, so that he was carried on the roll with the rank of crossbowman. But there was no priest with them to say what saint's day it was. The sails were furled on the yards, and the ship rode at anchor, dipping to the swells.

Then, as so many would do in later centuries, Don Juan gazed into the sunset, wondering what lay there. He knew that this was no mere key or sandbank, for he had sailed along the coast all afternoon, and he still saw the land stretching far off, a low plain broken by groves of trees, green with April. He thought it some large island like Cuba—but he did not know its real greatness.

Since he had not yet landed, he could not know what the Indians called that country, and in his impatience he wanted a name at once. Doubtless then he thought of many names, as a man does at such times. He might have called it for some place in Spain, perhaps New León after his own province; or he might have thought of honoring the King, or some saint. So, it would seem, as he hesitated in his own mind, or talked with his captains, he saw that one particular name was twice suitable. For, he remembered, the season was still that of Our Lord's Resurrection, only six days after the Easter of Flowers. At the same time, he thought that the green land toward which he now looked was at this season a flowered land. That there might be no doubt in the future, Herrera later wrote in plain words that Juan Ponce de León gave the name "for these two reasons." Thus they named it Florida.

Afterwards other captains coasted west and north from where Juan Ponce had sailed. All of them gave and recorded names. The King himself so instructed some of them in their commissions: "Arrived there by good providence, first of all you must give a name to the country as a whole, and to the cities, towns, and places," or again: "First you must name all the cities, towns and places which you find there." The King's lawyers who wrote these commissions believed that naming was part of holding empire, that no one could well lay claim to a nameless city, and that a province without a name was hardly a province at all.

As for the kind of names they gave, Herrera wrote:

It was the custom of those who discovered new lands to give their own names to the rivers, capes, and other places; or else the name of the saint on whose day they made the discovery; or else, other names, as they wished.

Some of those other names were for places in Spain such as Cape Trafalgar, but more common were those which, like the names of the Indians, were at first really descriptions like pilots' memoranda—Point of Reefs, or Canebrake Cape, which is still Cape Canaveral.

Also, like the Indians, they gave names because of some incident. Thus, at a little island Juan Ponce's men took one hundred and seventy turtles, and so called it Tortugas, a name which still survives, and is of oldest record of any of our present names after Florida.

Very commonly the voyagers learned, or thought they learned, names from the Indians. There was a special reason for this, because every Spaniard had the hope of discovering some rich kingdom. To bring back only his own names showed that he had found little of importance, but a strange and high-sounding roll of cities and provinces raised hope that somewhere in Florida was another Mexico or Peru. So arose the tale of the great kingdom of Chicora with its twenty-one provinces, all bearing such fairy-tale names as Xapira, Tanaca, Xoxi, and Guacaya.

With Indian names in general these first Spaniards did what all people do when hearing words in a strange language. They wrote down sounds which most nearly approximated their own speech, and so most of these names, like Chicora, looked more Spanish than Indian. Herrera noted this practice also: "The Spaniards never were bothered about a little change of the name," and he tells of a place they first called Gualé, and then changed to Gualape, which was more like their own language.

The Spaniards, with their love of pomp and solemnity, sometimes took possession of a new country with high formality, even spending the greater part of a day in the ceremonies. They set up a cross, and held mass; the soldiers paraded and fired guns. The captain drew his sword and defied the world to deny the right of the King of Spain to all that region. Then he performed symbolic acts of ownership, throwing stones and hacking trees with his sword. The rites of taking possession made use of a particular name for the country, and sometimes water was taken from the ocean or a river, and poured upon the dry land as a kind of baptism.

While various voyagers were still exploring Florida, the great Cortés conquered Mexico, and his captains pushed on till they reached the Pacific. From a strange tale heard on that coast, far to the south, arose a second great name.

One of the captains, about the year 1530, sent back a report of what he had heard from some Indians. There was an island off that coast, they said, and many of them had been to it. (Here perhaps they wet their lips lecherously.) This island was inhabited wholly by women, except when men were brought to it to do what must be done if any land is to be peopled; it was, these Indians asserted, very rich in pearls and gold, and was without Christian faith.

In those years, it happened also, there was a popular romance called *The Deeds of Esplandián,* telling of wonders and feats of arms even greater than in the conquest of Mexico. Among much else it told of an island near the Indies, peopled by women, "without any man among them," who lived in the fashion of the Amazons. In that island there was no metal but gold, and gems were "like stones of the field for abundance." The queen of this island was Calafía. She came once to fight against the Eastern Emperor, but was twice vanquished, by arms and also by love. That romance was long and strange, but hardly stranger than what happened with the name.

This is that story, as well as it may be put together, remembering always Herrera the chronicler, who with his usual interest in such matters took the trouble to record that Cortés "placed this name upon it."

We must look at the great and terrible Cortés, Marquess of the Valley, where he rules in state over Mexico, with dark-skinned slaves to serve him, among his captains and guardsmen, and his scribes and chaplains. Then before him comes the messenger, and a scribe reads the report of Amazons and pearls and gold.

Now the great Cortés had seen many strange sights in this New World, but he remained hard-headed. The new story was not for any sensible man to believe. As he listened, the Marquess thought, or someone reminded him, of that island in romance, so much resembling this one. Then unbending a little, perhaps he chuckled in his beard and said, "Yes, this must indeed be the island of *California!*"

And, we may well imagine, even the guardsmen smiled, and the captains and scribes all laughed politely, as one does when a great man jests.

In 1535, Cortés himself sailed into the South Sea and came to a land which was thought to be an island, and found it barren, with no Amazons or gold, and only a few pearls. He called it Santa Cruz in his report, and for that reason many have doubted Herrera's testimony that he called it California. But it is one thing to jest among one's own retainers, and another to report to Charles V, King and Emperor: "I have discovered California!" The King's lawyers would shake their heads, and all the Marquess's enemies would whisper: "Truly, he is far gone, and not to be trusted much further. 'Discovered California!' Next he'll claim the Earthly Paradise."

As to what the name may mean, fine theories take it back to Latin or Greek or Arabic, but the writer of the romance was obviously a man of imagination, and for all anyone knows he may have made up the name from some chance combination of syllables which came into his mind at the time. In any case, to track every word to its deepest lair is not the work of a book on how names were given, but of a dictionary of etymologies.

No matter whether Cortés or someone else placed it, whether in hope or in irony, the name stayed firmly upon that "island," which was really the tip of a long peninsula.

There was a Portuguese named Juan Rodríguez, but men called him Cabrillo, "little goat." In the conquest he served as a master of crossbowmen. Bernal Díaz, no man to praise lightly, called him "a good soldier." Later he followed the banner of Pedro de Alvarado to Guatemala, first as a captain, then as commander of ships on the Pacific. After Alvarado fell in battle, the viceroy Mendoza sent Cabrillo northward with two ships in the year 1542.

He and his men sailed along that barren coast of California, and the name sailed north with them. They reached farther than any man had gone before them. At last they came to better country, and anchored in a great closed bay. They called it for St. Michael the Archangel because they had come there on the eve of his day. (But now men call it San Diego.)

Then, if Cabrillo had been a politician or a man ambitious for himself like most explorers, he might have considered that he had left California behind, and so have given some new name of his own to the country. But since he was a straightforward and good soldier, he kept the name, and carried it north with him as far as he sailed. This was not because he lacked imagination, for in his choice of names he showed more of it than most of the Spaniards.

Northward of the bay, Cabrillo and his men sighted two islands, and named them after their two ships, San Salvador and Victoria. They named the Bay of the Smokes because of the many fires to the inland, and then the Town of the Canoes because its people came out in fine canoes. On October 15th they named an island San Lucas, for the physician, because it was close to his day. But on St. Luke's day itself, October 18th, they saw a rocky headland cutting the sea like a galley's prow, and so named it Galley Cape.

That year the storms came early. A great northwester threw them back from the cape, and they sheltered behind a little island. Landing and taking possession in the King's name, they called it Posesión. While they were there, the Indians attacked, and leaping from a boat to rally his men, Cabrillo fell among the rocks and broke a limb. Then, though the stormy weather was upon them, and though he himself was still in pain, Cabrillo tried once more. He rounded Galley Cape, and on Saint Martin's Day saw high mountains with the sea beating at their feet, and named them for that saint who parted his cloak with a beggar. That night a great storm struck and drove the voyagers northward in peril of death. For two days they saw neither land nor sky, and then sighted a bold coast with the surf breaking so high "it was frightful to behold." They found there a long point running out to sea, and named it Cape of Pines. Then they ran south before a

[16]

northwest wind, to the island called Posesión, to lie in harbor until the storms were over.

There, on the third day of the new year, Cabrillo died of that broken bone which would never heal. His men buried him on that little island, but no man knows his grave; and they changed the name from Posesión to Juan Rodríguez, after their leader, for that was his name, though called Cabrillo.

Yet, along that coast, not one of all Cabrillo's namings survived. Even the little island Juan Rodríguez is now called San Miguel. Still, the story of his voyage and his namings is worth the telling, that he may stand for all those who voyaged bravely and gave names to capes and harbors and islands, only to have others replace them. To establish names in the new land was not easy. Of all the hundreds which during a half century the Spanish voyagers strewed along the coasts, east and west, only a few survived. Like the seed on stony ground, they struck no root. Where now has vanished that rolling name El Río del Espíritu Santo? Where is the land Amichel that Francisco de Garay went forth to conquer? And Chicora with all its twenty-one provinces?

They have gone, along with the great river Jordan. Ayllon's ship-pilot named that river, after his own name, although he must also have known the river of Palestine. During a half century that name was famous, but now no man knows certainly which stream it may have been.

Those who went inland did no better. Coronado, far in the Southwest, searched for Cíbola and Quivira, and found an endless plain and so many hump-backed cattle that only the Lord God himself, as owner of all, could count them. During a full century Cíbola and Quivira were as well-known names as Florida and California, and then they slowly disappeared. De Soto, in spite of all his wanderings, left no name to be remembered by. Narváez met disaster and death, but from his expedition into Florida one great name originated. This was of the town to which the Spaniards marched in the hope of finding much gold there. They found only a poor Indian village called Apalchen. Later Spaniards remembered this name, and in various spellings it got upon the maps to designate the vague and mountainous interior. Finally it came, changed in form to Appalachian, to mean the mountains themselves.

Why so many names vanished is not hard to explain. A name could live only in continuing tradition, and a mere notation upon a map or in a journal—no matter how high-sounding—was only a hope of the man who wrote it. When exploration was not followed by settlement or by frequent voyages, the map might be pigeon-holed and its names forgotten. Even if the next voyager took a copy of the map along, still he could not reckon longitudes at all and even his latitudes, taken with astrolabe or back-staff, were many miles astray. So he would often think that he saw new capes and entered new harbors, not those already named. Also, most explorers for their own glory wished to bring back to the King some tale of new lands rather than to say only, "I voyaged where Spaniards had already been and given names." So most of them gave new names, or picked up another set from the Indians, and let the old ones die.

After Narváez and De Soto had left their bones in Florida, the Spaniards came to call it "the worst land the sun shines on," and for twenty years paid it little attention. Then the great Admiral Coligny tried to make it a colony of France, and in 1562 sent some Huguenots under Jean Ribaut. These Protestants had no reverence for the saints, and they wished even the names to show that they were planting a New France. So along that coast where the rivers run east to the sea they named the streams for the rivers of France that flow west to the sea. First they called one the Seine, "because at the entry it is as broad as from Havre to Honfleur"— then Somme, Loire, Charente, Garonne, and Gironde. Where they settled, they called the harbor Port Royal and the fort Charlesfort, in loyalty to their King; and for the same reason they called another place Fort Caroline. Thus the French first planted that name on that coast, where it still is, but not from their naming. Port Royal alone survived.

For, in the third year of the colony, Don Pedro Menéndez de

Avilés came to drive out the heretics and retake the coast for King Philip. Since the French looked for attack only by sea, Menéndez marched through the swamps and took Fort Caroline at dawn, and killed all the French except women and children. A little later, Jean Ribaut and some shiploads of Frenchmen were wrecked near by. Of these, Menéndez put aside only Catholics and musicians. The others he made first surrender, and then they were led, more than four hundred of them, to a place among the sand dunes and their heads cut off. Even the men of Menéndez were aghast, and called it Matanzas—the place of slaughter. The horror of the deed made men remember the spot, and that is still its name.

This same Menéndez was a very pious man. His namings show how new customs and ways of thought make new names. The earliest Spaniards sometimes had no priest with them at all, or if they had, they paid him no more attention than was necessary. Thus not so many names were religious. But later, there were more priests, and at the same time the Wars of Religion had made all men fanatics. So there were more saints' names and others such as Holy Cross and Immaculate Conception.

Menéndez gave the names of saints even to his forts. In 1565 he reverently named St. Augustine, because he had sighted land on the day of that gentle bishop.

Thus, during a half century after Ponce de León the Spaniards voyaged by sea and marched by land, but they placed only three names which in later years would stand large on the map—Florida and Apalchen to the east and California to the west. Here and there some smaller name lingered, but if the future in that land held little for the Indian names, neither did it for the Spanish.

Chapter IV ◖ Of English, Spanish, and French in the same years

THE English came late, but stayed longest. Since they, in the end, took the land and spoke their language there, all before their coming was only a prelude. Though many places already had names, the English rejected most of them, and gave new names of their own. Those they adopted, they reshaped to suit their own tongues. Even that first name Ponce de León had given, pronouncing it Florída, the English came to call Flórida.

Once before, a thousand years in the past, the English had come from the east by sea to another land. There they found the Britons, and from them they took some names—of the older towns, London, Lincoln, and York; of rivers, like Thames, Avon, and Severn. But the English kept mostly to themselves, warring against the natives. As they drove the Britons westward, they gave names of their own to their kingdoms and villages, and to hills and islands and little streams. In their ancient language they said *ness* for cape, and *mere* for lake, and *ey* for island, and from such words they made many simple names, like Sheerness, Grasmere, and Anglesey. Like all peoples they gave many names to mark the place for what it was—Blackburn, "black brook"; Oxford, "ford for oxen"; or Woolpit, "wolf-pit," where someone had dug a trap for wolves.

They had, more than most tribes, a sense of the individual and his property. Where a man settled and held land, they often named the place after him, as with Croxton, "Croc's settlement," and Chelmsford, "Ceolmaer's ford." Natural features of the land even came to be Bawsey, "Beaw's island," or Lilbourne, "Lilla's brook." When a man settled a farmstead, doubtless putting up a stockade and holding it as a frontier post with his sons and retainers, the English made a name with *-ing,* so that Birmingham was "the settlement of Biorma's people," and Reading, "Raeda's people." Since the English had a strong sense of the permanence of things, such names endured after everyone had forgotten all about Biorma, and did not even remember that the name referred to a particular man, or that Raeda had probably been a chieftain nicknamed "Red" because of the color of his hair.

So they named the land, and lived in it through centuries when no names needed to be given, except here and there for a new village or castle or street. The language changed. Men forgot many meanings, and lost much of the primitive feeling that a name should naturally describe the place. New forms arose and words came in from other languages—*cape, point, creek, meadow,* and many others.

When, a second time, the English sailed westward, and came to a low coast with broad river-mouths, and went inland to seize and settle, they took with them many of these new words. Also, they were used to living in a country where most names had no meaning to the ordinary man, and they had no strong tradition or fixed habit of naming. The customs which grew up in the New World, where many names were needed quickly, were therefore sometimes different from those by which England had been named centuries earlier.

In 1584 Sir Walter Raleigh got from Queen Elizabeth a patent to settle lands in the New World. His patent gave no instructions about giving names, for to the English, unlike the Spaniards, the matters of naming rested upon common custom and usage, not the orders of kings' lawyers.

That same year, Sir Walter sent Captains Amadas and Barlowe exploring. Running prosperously westward, they sounded one day in shoal water and smelled a smell as sweet as if they had been in some delicate well-kept garden—and so knew they were not far from land. With this good omen they sailed on, keeping watch, and saw a coast. (And the day of that landfall was to be a famous one in the land, being July the fourth.) They entered into a wide sound, and explored among its islands. They gave some English names, since forgotten, but more often they asked the Indians, as well as they could for want of language, how the places were called. From that summer's voyaging three names remained.

One was the island Roanoak, as they spelled it, meaning perhaps "place of white shells." That island now is Roanoke, and from it the name has spread to a river, and a county, and many towns. This, it would seem, was the first of all the Indian words which the English took over.

Also they wrote down the names "Chawanook" and "a goodly river called Neus," and still we find there the rivers Chowan and Neuse.

From that first voyage, however, sprang one still greater name. When the captains returned, their report went to Sir Walter, and he took it to the Queen. In it they wrote the name of the whole country as Wingandacoa, and of its King, Wingina. Then, it may be, that spelling spurred the Queen's thought, and she remembered her own virgin state, which her poets celebrated. Also, that far-off, sweet-smelling land lay untouched and virgin, waiting to be possessed. So while Sir Walter stood by to approve and applaud, the Queen remembered her Latin, and spoke a word of proper form for the name of a province, which was a "virgin-land." Thus when the account of the captains came to be printed, the sentence ran "The king is called Wingina, the country Wingandacoa"—but also was added, "and now by her Majesty, Virginia." This was the first name given by the English, though in form it was pure Latin.

The next year Sir Richard Grenville (who later in the *Revenge* fought the Spanish fleet off Flores) sailed to Virginia to plant the colony. His ship was embayed behind a long spit of land, and some of his men fell into terror of being wrecked in the surf. So they called it Cape Fear, and the name remained. Thus the first two names the English planted on that coast commemorated virginity and fear, although neither was a commodity held in much repute among those sea-dogs.

In that same voyage Sir Richard anchored at a place called Hatrask by the Indians. Later it came to mean no longer the anchorage or inlet, but moved south to the point of the sand-spit, and became Cape Hatteras.

Those that Sir Richard left at Roanoke, exploring, came to the northward upon a town called Chesepiook. Though the meaning of their other Indian names is scarcely to be known, this one is plain Algonquian, *che,* "big," and *sepi,* "river," with an ending "at." The English after their custom took it merely as a meaningless label of a town or tribe. They soon transferred it to the broad bay north of the town, so that the bay is called Chesapeake, a name meant for a river.

Sir Walter left a colony upon Roanoke, but King Philip sent his Armada, and while England fought for life, she could spare no captains to sail westward. When at last a ship came again to Roanoke, no colony was there, and history records that all that labor came to nothing. Yet from it we at least take seven names—Roanoke, the rivers Chowan and Neuse, Cape Fear and Cape Hatteras, Chesapeake, and (greatest of all) Virginia.

In those same years the Spaniards, far to the southwest, were reaching northward from Mexico. There they established a name which was to outlive Spanish rule.

First to come to that northern region had been Coronado, but after his time no Spaniards for many years marched so far again. Still, province by province, the frontier crept north from Mexico. During those years the Spaniards began a new way of naming. They called the whole country Nueva España, "New Spain," and its new provinces they called by similar names—Nueva Viscaya, and Nueva Galicia, and Nuevo León. In all these lands they hunted for another treasure of Montezuma.

There was Francisco de Ibarra, a great seeker after gold mines. In 1563 he went far to the north, and, guided by an Indian woman, came near a large town. First he sent some of his men to spy on it from the hills. They came back and told him that people were working in the cornfields, well dressed in colored cloth, like Aztecs of Mexico. Creeping up in the night, Ibarra himself came so close that he heard drums beaten, "as men beat drums in Mexico." He stole off under cover of darkness, for he was afraid to attack such a town with only a few men and their horses travelworn. But when he returned south, Ibarra boasted that he had discovered a New Mexico.

Doubtless, like others, he stretched the tale, and certainly the land of which he told was well south of that one now so called. Yet men remembered the name Nuevo México, though not at first as that of the region which Coronado had once conquered.

Of all countries, few have known more trouble in the naming than that one. Coronado had given and recorded many names of villages, and had known the whole region as Tiguex. So it stood for many years on the maps. Then, in 1581, those known as the Nine Companions went north. Though they must have heard of Tiguex and Nuevo México, they called the country San Felipe, and its river Concepción, and gave names to streams and mountains. Also they named fifty-three villages, sometimes recording Indian names, but generally "because of ignorance of the language of the people" giving them names of towns in Spain or New Spain, or calling them after the nature of their sites.

The next year, nevertheless, Antonio Espejo, native of Córdoba, rode north: "to the Provinces and Settlements of New Mexico, which I named New Andalusia, in Honor of my Native Land." The river he called "of the North," Río del Norte, and for the third time he gave new names to the towns. He named also many streams and camping-places, sometimes for saints, sometimes for the way they looked, sometimes for what happened there. Thus one place he called El Mal Bebedero, "the bad drinking-place," because the horses going to drink there fell into the river and swam across to the other side. But his names were forgotten.

At last in 1598 Don Juan de Oñate came with power from King Philip to conquer and hold. Halting at the river-bank, he performed most elaborate rites of taking possession. There was a sermon, followed by formal ceremonies involving both clergy and laymen, and in the evening a comedy was presented. By all this pomp Oñate put it beyond all doubt that the King's power was declared over "all the Realms and Provinces of the New Mexico."

With the name thus at last settled, the expedition entered into the country, fording the river at a place called in plain fashion, El Paso del Norte, "the crossing of the River of the North." Years later a town grew up at the ford, and the town at last became a city called merely El Paso.

Of the river itself, Oñate wrote: "It springs and flows from the north, and thus takes its name, and it turns to the east, and there is called Río Bravo." Those who later lived by its banks in New Mexico called it merely Río Grande, for to them it was the "big river." The Mexicans still call it Río Bravo.

Oñate marched on into the land, and gave new names which were not like any given before him. (Only, through all this naming and renaming, the Indians held fast to many of their own, like Acoma, and Taos.) On one day Oñate came to a pueblo called Teipana, and his men were half-starved. But there they got supplies of corn. So they called it Socorro, "succor," and still the sleepy little town between the river and the dry mountains bears that name unchanged in a single letter after three and a half centuries.

On one of his journeys Oñate and his men marched westward. Leaving behind them the high-set Hopi towns, they came to a river. They called it Colorado, "red," because, as Father Salmerón wrote with priestly caution, "the water is nearly red." This river in its lower course the Spaniards had already named Buena Guía, and Tizón, but these names did not prosper. Colorado was a word of common speech, comfortable to the tongue and fitted to the stream. It spread and became the name of the greater river and the greatest of all canyons. In the end the first-named tributary became only the Chiquito, or Little Colorado. But the name itself had many adventures, until after two centuries and much strife it became at last the name of a state—and even then its adventures were not ended.

[25]

As his capital Oñate founded a city in a high valley between mountains. To fit with its dignity and his own love of pomp, he named it sonorously La Villa Real de la Santa Fe de San Francisco, "The Royal City of the Holy Faith of Saint Francis," but it was shortened to Santa Fe.

After the galleons of the Armada were splintered hulks on the Irish headlands, the English came on again. In the second year of the new century, Captain Gosnold sailed to what was called "the north part of Virginia," and with him went Gabriel Archer, gentleman. Though most of these early voyagers were bluff, blunt seamen, Archer loved words and names, and to play with them, like a man who wrote sonnets, and read *Euphues,* and bandied quips at the Mermaid Tavern. The others might be good at seamanship and swordplay, but of Archer it was written also, "he glorieth much in his penwork."

So, in his story of that voyage, the names were like raisins in pudding—many and tasty. Savage Rock was the first, "because the savages first showed themselves there"; yet there is a pun in the name and a touch of poetry. Shoal Hope, Tucker's Terror, Point Care, Dover Cliff, Gosnold's Hope, Hill's Hap, and Hap's Hill—they are not in the run of common naming. Hope was an old word meaning "bay," but the pun is there, none the less. Tucker was a seaman who went into a panic when the ship almost struck a shoal, and the name was taken (as Archer put it with fine understatement) "upon his expressed fear." Hap means "good luck," and Hill was probably another seaman. So the little island "called by me Hill's Hap" may have been discovered by Hill. Hap's Hill was another island, somewhat matching it, so called, "for that I hope much hap may be expected from it." But why not simply Hap Island?—except that Archer loved to play with words, and having invented Hill's Hap could not resist Hap's Hill.

From Archer's fine fancy probably sprang Martha's Vineyard. The voyagers, to be sure, found many grapevines on a little island, but that would mean usually Vine Island. Wild grapevines make a vineyard only in a poet's world. As for Martha, Captain Gosnold had a baby daughter of that name, but no one has explained why she should have been coupled with "vineyard." There is also a Biblical memory of the industrious Martha and another about laboring in the vineyard—but that is a long bow for any man to pull. Most likely, the name records some little incident or joke among the voyagers themselves, on which Archer's fancy seized. The first "Vineyard" was a small island south of the present one, but the name shifted to the larger island. Hap's Hill and the other fruits of Archer's wit were lost.

The other chief name surviving from Gosnold's voyage was not of Archer's type, though he records it. On May 15, 1602, he wrote: "Near this cape we came to anchor in fifteen fathoms, where we took great store of codfish . . . and called it Cape Cod."

Nine days before Gosnold sighted Savage Rock, Sebastián de Viscaíno had sailed from Acapulco far in the south, and thus it happened that well-known names on both coasts arose in the same year.

Viscaíno commanded three vessels, with the *San Diego* as his flagship. They had slow sailing, and when Gosnold was already at Martha's Vineyard, the Spanish ships were only off the tip of the long California peninsula. At last, when the days were growing short, Viscaíno came to a harbor which he boasted "must be the best in all the South Sea." There, on November 12th, he went ashore together with the officers, the priests and most of the men. Mass was celebrated in honor of St. Didacus, whose day it was, and who in Spanish is called San Diego. In life he had been a Spanish friar of the fifteenth century, and the great King Philip himself became devoted to his memory. At the special urging of the King, Didacus was canonized in 1568. All things worked together—a Spanish saint, his day, and the King's own devotion. Then also, the flagship bore the same name, and many seamen have been pleased to use the names of their ships. So they called the place San Diego.

As with most places which he reported, Viscaíno did not really discover this fine bay, for it was the same that Cabrillo had named San Miguel. Since Cabrillo's names were still marked on the charts, the viceroy had ordered Viscaíno to use them, but like other voyagers he wished to have credit for new discoveries.

As he sailed still farther north, Viscaíno showed himself wholly without imagination. He looked in the calendar, or else he asked one of his Carmelite friars, and then he named the place after the saint of that day. So, even without the log-book, a historian can trace that voyage by the names given.

On November 25th he named an island for Santa Catalina, who is St. Catherine, patron of Christian philosophers. Three days later it was time to name San Pedro. This was not the day of the great St. Peter, keeper of the keys, but of a lesser one, martyred in Constantinople. So it went along the coast. December 4th was the day of Santa Barbara, who is patron of artillerymen and all those in danger of sudden death. Then on December 8th, day of the Immaculate Conception, the voyagers saw that headland breasting the sea like a galley's prow which Cabrillo had aptly named Galley Cape. But Viscaíno displaced that fine name, and, lacking imagination of his own, called it Conception.

Farther north, the mountains called Santa Lucía were for December 13th, and that Sicilian maiden, commemorated in the Canon of the Mass. Farther north still, a high headland reaches seaward like a claw; there the wind blows always and the surf breaks high, and the sea-lions in their hundreds lie rolling in the swells. Though it is a fearful and magnificent place, Viscaíno thought of no better way of naming than by the calendar—to call it after the Three Kings who came on Twelfth Night to adore the Child in the manger. So it still remains Point Reyes.

Two names of Viscaíno were different. He called a fine bay Monterey, after the name of the viceroy who had sent him on the voyage, and near by his friars named the Carmel River, after their own order.

Thus Viscaíno sailed, and wiped out the names given by that good soldier Cabrillo, who had died there on a little island, sixty years before. But Viscaíno was no man to die on a quest, rather one to plan a retreat before advancing. As the man was, so were the names—pious, but colorless, lacking fire. And when he departed from piety, he curried favor with the viceroy by naming Monterey.

Nevertheless, the names were hallowed ones, so that the fathers who came later preserved them in reverence. San Diego and Santa Barbara became the names of missions, and then of cities. Many people praise those names of the Spanish saints, and call them poetic—such people as think first of the soft play of the vowels or like a name which seems strange and distant. But the deepest poetry of a name and its first glory lie, not in liquid sounds, but in all that shines through that name—the hope or terror, or passion or wit, of those who named it. The second glory of a name, as with Marathon or Valley Forge, springs later from the deeds done there.

Though the French had no luck where they met Menéndez, yet far to the north they voyaged prosperously. They gave many names there, but most of them were in the land which they came to call Canada.

First of all those Frenchmen had come Jacques Cartier. His names were of Canada, except one. For, as it happened, on August 7, 1535, he was voyaging along a dangerous coast, and his ship was caught in a "stormy and contrary wind." He ran before it, and by good chance found anchorage in a bay full of islands, passages, and entrances, so that a ship was safe. Then in thankfulness and piety he named it after St. Lawrence, whose day it was. That name spread far. First it was only the anchorage; soon it covered the whole gulf. As men sailed to the head of the gulf and entered its great river, they called that also St. Lawrence.

After Cartier, the Frenchmen waited many years, and then, two years after the naming of Cape Cod, the Sieur de Champlain came to the same coast, and gave three names still remembered.

One day, sailing, he saw an island "very high and prominent," and called it therefore Isle Haute, "high island." Sighting another island with lofty summits, most of them bare of trees, he named it Isle des Monts-deserts. Again, his men ascended a river, and came to a place where streams flowed into it from both sides, forming a cross; so they called it Saint Croix, "holy cross."

Champlain made many journeys far inland to the north. Once in 1609 he came southward with the Hurons, and fought the Iroquois on the shores of a long lake. This was a famous battle, for at the firing of the French hand-guns the Iroquois fled in panic. So, as Champlain wrote carefully, as if disclaiming to name anything for himself, "This place where this attack was made . . . was called Lake Champlain."

The English ships came again from the east, and this time the colony was not to fail. On April 26, 1607, they sighted land, and "entered into the Bay of Chesupioc." Among those colonists were two captains who would give more names to the new country than any Englishmen before them. The one was that same fantastic Gabriel Archer, and the other was plain John Smith.

On the next day the colonists launched a shallop, and went searching for a river-mouth where they could anchor the ships, but found only shallow water close to shore. Then toward night, as their chronicler wrote,

We rowed over to a point of Land, where we found a channel, and sounded six, eight, ten, or twelve fathom; which put us in good comfort. Therefore we named that point of land Cape Comfort.

No one knows, but the name has the ring of Archer's naming, who elsewhere named Point Care, and Careless Point. It was like him, too, to call a "cape" what was only low land, but soon it became merely Point Comfort.

On Wednesday the company set up a cross at the southern entrance to the Bay, and named it Cape Henry, "in honor of our most noble Prince." (John Smith later claimed the suggestion of the name.) This was the Prince of Wales, who died young, leaving the far off cape, and a county called Henrico, as his chief memorials.

The next place named was Archer's Hope, and who so named it we need hardly wonder. Though the word should mean a bay, this was a point of land, and the name showed Captain Archer's hope that the town would be founded there.

On a Thursday, May 14th, the company landed elsewhere, began the plantation, and called it Jamestown, "in honor of the King's most excellent majesty." The great river there, they called King's River, but the men most often called it Powhatan's river, because that was the name of the country among the savages, and of their greatest chieftain. After many years it came to be James River, because that was the King's name and because it flowed past Jamestown.

After they had labored a week at the new town, Captain Newport took twenty-three men with the shallop, and went to discover the head of the river. With him went both Smith and Archer, but Archer wrote the journal. Also, to his delight, he gave the names, noting down often, "This place I call . . ." Of his names, Turkey Isle, on which were many turkeys, was the only one after the fashion of common men. The rest were Poor Cottage, Arahatec's Joy, Powatah's Tower, Mulberry Shade, Kind Woman's Care, Queen's Bower, and Careless Point.

What would the land be now, if such names had lived and set the fashion? Though raisins are tasty in pudding, nothing but raisins might turn the stomach. But in the common speech those names had no vigor. What man with a beard could say such fine-spun silken terms without cursing afterwards to clear his mouth? Thus in the end men said Mulberry Island, not Mulberry Shade. And Poor Cottage they soon called Port Cottage, as if trying to make better sense. Thus men would not follow Gabriel Archer (who gloried in his pen-work), and name their land as a poet might fashion rhymes for his mistress's eyebrow.

As for John Smith, his own name was common, and also the names he gave had the common touch, when, in 1608, he voyaged twice around that bay which he spelled Chisapeack. In his namings, as in much else, he might be called the first American, and his two voyages give a demonstration in miniature of the way names were placed across the whole continent.

First, in an open boat with fourteen comrades, he steered north from Cape Henry, and came upon some islands. These he called Smith's Isles. Like most men he was no more modest than need be, and if men had not named places for themselves, the land would have been far differently named indeed.

Coming to the point of land opposite Cape Henry, he called it Cape Charles, "in honor of the worthy Duke of York." But also the name was good because it was a counterpart—Henry facing Charles, brothers and princes, and so both easier to remember. And thus many men since that time have given names in counterpart.

But a good captain shares with his men, and so the next to be named was Keale's Hill, doubtless because during his trick as look-out he had first seen it. And though that hill "was but low," yet Richard Keale must have felt warm toward his Captain for that courtesy, and was perhaps the better soldier in the days that came. Also perhaps he felt that by naming he cheated Death, as long as men in that far land would say his name for a hill, which is a monument more lasting truly than bronze—not knowing that the name, like so many others, would soon be forgotten. So Captain Smith went, on that voyage and the other, naming here a point of land for one man, there an island or a bay for another.

Also, as future explorers would do, he gave names in other ways. He named Willowby River after the place where he was born, and also complimenting Lord Willowby, "his most honored good friend." And again he wrote, "That place we called Point Ployer, in honor of that most honorable house of Mousay in Britanny, that in an extreme extremity once relieved our Captain." So also many other men would do in the future, honoring their birthplaces and friends, and paying debts of gratitude.

He gave other names because of incidents. Caught cheerlessly on a low island during two days of wind and rain, he fancifully called it Limbo, after the ante-room of Hell.

One day, off the mouth of a river the boat grounded upon a

shoal. While waiting for the flood-tide to float them, the men saw many fish among the reeds, and "our Captain sporting himself by nailing them to the ground with his sword set us all a-fishing in that manner." Then Captain Smith speared a strange fish, and as he drew it from the sword, it stung him with its tail in the wrist. First a little blue mark showed, and in four hours the arm swelled to the shoulder and was tense with pain. All thought him dying, and by his order they dug his grave on an island. Thereupon he soon felt better and by the end of the day he made his supper of the fish that stung him! "For which we called the Island *Stingray* Isle after the name of the fish." And even yet the end of land where the Rappahannock meets the Bay is Stingray Point. So also across a continent places would bear names because of some adventure.

Again, Smith went to explore the Rappahannock, and he wrote:

There it pleased God to take one of our Company called Master *Fetherstone,* that all the time he had been in this Country, had behaved himself, honestly, valiantly, and industriously; where in a little Bay we called *Fetherstone's* Bay we buried him with a volley of shot.

The name was forgotten, but even in this, John Smith did as later men would do, not copying him, but merely thinking the same thoughts for the same reasons. From Fetherstone's Bay west across a continent and down through the centuries, men were to stand uncovered by a fresh-dug grave, then name the place for the lost comrade, and go on.

The farthest known of the names that Captain Smith brought back from those voyages were the Indian names of the rivers, and the greatest were Patowomek, and Sasquesahanock. Now they are Potomac and Susquehanna, but no one is sure what they mean, except that Smith made them out to be the names of tribes living there. So also in later years men called many rivers by the names of tribes.

Thus Smith and Archer gave names. As the names differed, so

did the men, and they were always enemies. Archer soon died in Virginia, but Smith lived to give an even greater name elsewhere. Most of those who followed may be called the Sons of Smith, for in their naming they were simple, or used only a touch of fancy. But here and there some Sons of Archer gave names, such as Storm King Mountain, and Vishnu's Temple. In the end some of these names became even trite, as with Lover's Leap, and Bridal Veil Falls, and Inspiration Point.

A letter went back to England to the most elegant and learned Dudley Carleton (M.A., Oxon.), and so he became the first Englishman to sneer at American names. He wrote with ready quill:

They have fortified themselves and built a small town which they call James-town, and so they date their letters: but the town methinks hath no graceful name.

Still he harped on the name even in his postscript:

Master Porie tells me of a name given by a Dutchman who wrote to him in Latin from the new town in Virginia, Jacobopolis, and Master Warner has a letter from Master George Persy, who names their town James-fort, which we like best of all the rest because it comes near to Chemes-ford.

So the cat was out, and it appears that Dudley Carleton had no better standard than that all names should be as much as possible like English names. Did he wish, Virginians, to shackle your minds, so that your names should only be stale and second-hand! If Jamestown was to be Chelmsford, should the broad Potomac flow gently to the name of Thames, and Point Comfort colorlessly echo Dungeness, and Chesapeake be the Wash? The date of this letter was August 18, 1607, about three months after the founding of Jamestown.

Thus early, the more insular of the English began to carp, and such judgments were to be frequent in later centuries. But this book will pay them no more attention, because they all followed the stupid pattern set by Master Dudley Carleton. They assumed that the traditional names and ways of naming of the little island were the only proper ones. They made no allowance for different landscapes and racial strains, or for new ideals and an ever-flourishing imagination. They argued much, however, for "good taste" and for linguistic purity, as was natural for the inhabitants of a country blessed with Maidenhead, Fryup, Sizergh, Great Snoring, Shitlington, and Ashby de la Zouche.

There was one other great name given in those first years of Virginia. As governor came an English baron who took his title from Ware in Hertfordshire, and was called in French fashion Lord de la Ware. In 1610 Captain Samuel Argoll, sighting the coast somewhat northward, found a wide entrance, and named its western cape for the governor. From this came Delaware Bay, and since the bay, unlike Chesapeake, had only one great river, the name spread upward.

Chapter V ⟪ Of Charles Stuart and some others

IN THOSE years the land to the north was as yet little known. It was no languorous Virginian coast with muddy wide creeks reaching far inland, but there the surf broke white against rocky headlands, and the farther hills were dark with spruce and pine. Off shore, men took cod by the boatload. As yet this land had no certain name, though, as voyagers had come and gone, it had borne many names vaguely, of which the first was Vineland and the most famous, Norumbega.

Even before Columbus, as the saga tells, Eric the Red sailed west from Iceland, and came to a coast far northerly, where he explored and gave names. When he came to colonize, he called it Greenland; "Because men would the more readily go there if the country had a good name." Thus first of all men in the western lands, Eric named for good omen, and from him stem all those who have given names like Richfield, and Mount Pleasant, hoping to lure settlers.

Eric's son was Leif the Lucky, who sailed south. To each part he gave, as he told, "a name after its nature"—here Slateland, because of the slabs of slate, and there Woodland, because of the forests. When he found vines, he called the place Vineland. So from Leif stem all those who have looked straight before them and given names like Black River and High Rock. Thus across all the land have passed the Sons of Eric, and the Sons of Leif. But the name Vineland was forgotten.

At last, about that year when Cortés marched on Mexico, some voyager sailed along that coast and wrote upon his map the name Arambe. Of all names none is more mysterious, for no one knows what language it is or why it changed so easily. Soon it was written Oranbega, and then Anorabega. Then, like Quivira, it stood in tall letters on all maps as Norumbega, and tales were told of a rich kingdom and a high-built city. Those tales were easy to believe, because men could see the name on the map, and just as men cannot imagine a great city to exist without a name, so they hardly believe a great name to exist without a city. But those who went searching found neither a city nor even the foundation-stones where one had been. So, as the hopes died, the name died too. No one knows whence it came or whither it vanished. Yet, though mapmakers scratched it out, the poets remembered it as a ringing word to adorn an epic. So John Milton wrote:

Of Norumbega and the Samoed Shore.

Even still it stays a little in men's memories—a name and, beyond that, nothing. As legend and poetry, like Armageddon and Atlantis, and Lyonesse, like El Dorado and Quivira, so too lingers Norumbega.

John Smith was not the first Englishman, by far, to sail that coast. Yet to him it remained to give a lasting name.

In 1614, six years after his voyages around Chesapeake Bay, he came to the northern coast with a company "to take whales, and make trials of a mine of gold and copper." Both these failing, the voyagers spent the summer fishing and trading for furs. As he sailed among the islands and past the capes, Smith noted the bearings and made a map, writing on it chiefly the Indian names. He could find no certain name for the whole region—"this part of America hath formerly been called Norumbega, Virginia, Nuskoncus, Penaquida, Cannada, and such other names as those that ranged the Coast pleased."

But to write on his new map "the North Part of Virginia" was colorless, and Canada was a French term, and Norumbega was discredited, and the others had little standing. So, having noted that a part of the coast looked like Devonshire and trying for a better name, Smith must have remembered that already the New World had a New Spain and a New France. Also he knew that far to the west "the most memorable Sir Francis Drake in his voyage about the world" had placed the name Nova Albion. So on his map Smith wrote boldly New England.

He called his book of that voyage *A Description of New England,* and in it used the name many times, so that it became known. Besides, it was a good name to Englishmen, and by itself seemed a title to the country, against the French and Dutch. And so, only six years after that voyage, King James wrote in his charter granting that land: "The same shall be called by the name New England in America."

One other great name came of the voyage, for in the book Smith wrote Massachuset as an Indian town. Though Smith may not have known it, the meaning is fairly clear, being the tribal name Mass-adchu-seuck, "big-hill-people," which in English ears was blended with the name of the place, Mass-adchu-ut, "at-big-hills." Smith made of the Indian word an English plural to indicate the tribe, and so came Massachusetts.

This then was the work of John Smith in the naming of the land. Besides lesser ones, he took from the Indians the three great names—Potomac, Susquehanna, and Massachusetts—and he named New England. So it was written of him with true prophecy:

> Then after-ages shall record thy praise,
> That a *New England* to this Isle didst raise.

Yet indirectly his work was not quite done. For, when he came to publish his map, he saw that most of its names were uncouth; moreover, like a good Englishman, he wished to win favor with a prince. So he wrote,

I presented this discourse with the map to our most gracious Prince Charles, humbly intreating his Highness he would please to change their barbarous names for such English, as posterity might say Prince Charles was their Godfather.

In that year Charles Stuart was sixteen years of age, and heir-apparent since the death of his brother Henry. The request pleased him, and indeed of all the English monarchs this Charles showed most care about names. Since he and his brother already had capes in Virginia, he wrote his sister's name upon a point which men call still Cape Elizabeth. Where Smith had written Cape Tragbigzanda for the fair Turk who had loved him, the Prince wrote his mother's name, Anna. Another cape he named for his father James. (But this one did not survive, for men still call it Cape Cod.) After himself, the Prince named Charles River.

Following Smith's suggestion, the Prince scratched out the barbarous words, and for Sowocatuck he wrote Ipswich; for Passtaquack, Hull; for Accomack, Plymouth—and so with others.

To the hills he gave names such as Cheviot and Snowdon. And since he was also a prince of Scotland, he wrote the River Forth on a great stream, and an inland town on that river he called Edinburgh and its port Leith. Having placed some thirty names, he gave the map back, and Smith wrote in smaller letters his own name and those of his friends and patrons upon lesser islands and points and bays.

The engraver drew the map with the inscription *New England* and the note "The most remarkable parts thus named by the high and mighty Prince Charles, Prince of Great Britain." But of these names only four lived—Cape Elizabeth and Cape Ann, Charles River and Plymouth. For the men who settled New England bore no love to the House of Stuart and would rather displace those names than keep them. Yet in the end Prince Charles accomplished more than he had even hoped, for though the Puritans did not keep his individual names, they followed him in that new fashion of giving English names to Indian towns.

Then in 1620 the Pilgrims came in the *Mayflower,* and, hard-pressed by the winter storms, anchored inside Cape Cod. They sent out men in a shallop, and these men came back with reports of a good bay, and brought the ship there to anchor. Then, you may read, they called the place Plymouth—because (some say) their charter was under the Plymouth Company, or because (others say) old Plymouth was the English port they sailed from. But, more truly, they never named the place at all, for it was named already by Prince Charles, and any man who knew his letters could see it plain upon Captain Smith's map of New England. (Yet no matter who named it or why, that name was to become a folk-tale and a legend, as Jamestown would never be. So it was to spread from sea to sea and become the name of many towns.)

In the first hard years, those at Plymouth had all they could do to hold their own against sickness and starvation. So they spread about little, and gave few names. But others still came to the coast, anchoring behind the islands and at the river-mouths, fishing, and trading beads and baubles for pelts of beaver and otter. Since these men were merely traders and fishermen, they cared little about giving names, but took them over from the Indians. These words were mere clutters of strange sound to English ears, and the English tongues corrupted them again, so that soon not even an Indian could be sure what some of the names had really meant. But at least we know that those tribes gave names to each part, and not, like the English, to the river as a whole. So, if a ship-captain at the river-mouth asked the name, an Indian would only think of the place where he then was. Thus, when they can be translated at all, those rivers most often bear the names of some lower part, such as Kennebec, "long reach," and Penobscot, "at the sloping rock."

Among those fishermen were some who landed, built huts and put up frames for drying cod. This was at a place which Prince Charles had called for Barnstaple, but the fishermen cared little for princes, and kept the old name, Naumkeag.

Then in 1629 a godly company with ministers of the Gospel came there from England, and began to think of a new name. For certainly, though a heathen word might serve for a river or island, it would not be proper for a town where Christians were to live and found a church. It might even be dangerous. For who would be sure but that every time a man spoke it he unwittingly invoked the power of Hobbomocco the Indian devil? (And in those years a man lost in the forest reported that he had heard great roarings, which must either be from a lion or a devil. But since no one had seen lions in that country, a devil was thought more likely.)

Nevertheless, there was difference of opinion about changing the name. Some of the learned men reported that Naumkeag, though the Indians might say it meant "place of eels," was really Nahumkeick, corrupted Hebrew meaning "comfort-haven," left there perhaps in the wandering of the ten lost tribes.

In the end the safer counsel prevailed. Someone in his Bible read words which he interpreted in terms of their own founding of a church in a new land. In the opening verses of Psalm 76 we still may find:

> In Judah is God known: his name is great in Israel.
> In Salem also is his tabernacle, and his dwelling place in Zion.

And since the word also meant "peace" and was of good omen, they named their new town Salem.

But across the narrow bay was a rocky headland, where some of the fishermen settled, calling it Marblehead. For in those days the English had no word *granite,* and all hard rocks were called *marble.* So in later years piety stood opposite worldliness, even in the names; as a Marbleheader once declared candidly: "Our ancestors came not here for religion. Their main end was to catch fish."

Just as that Marbleheader said "main," so people in general used the word very commonly instead of *great* or *important.* In particular, they said either "the main sea," or "the main land" to denote the open ocean, or the continent as against the off-shore islands. Meaning either, they often said merely "the main," so that one could "sail the Spanish main," or "land upon the Spanish main." There were places of that name, in that meaning or some other, in France, Ireland, and Virginia. In both the Shetlands and the Orkneys the chief island was Mainland. As with most names in those times, the spelling varied—every man to his fancy.

In a New England charter of 1620 the lawyers wrote "the country of the Main Land," words which suggest a general description rather than a name. Two years later, however, a charter was granted to two old sea-dogs of the Royal Navy, Sir Ferdinando Gorges and Captain John Mason, and in it the word had certainly ceased to be a description. Dated on August 10, 1622, the charter declared that "all that part of the mainland" the grantees "intend to name The Province of Maine." Some have thought that this name arose because of the greater number of islands off that northern coast, which made men have more reason to speak of "the main." Others have tried to connect it with the Province, or County, of Maine in France. But again, *main* as equaling *chief* or *important* would have been of good omen, if a little boastful. Moreover, about 1611 Captain Mason had served in the Orkneys, and must have known the name as used there.

Nothing is certain, however, because the two partners failed to record what was in their minds, and very likely, as often happens with names, many reasons mingled. Perhaps they agreed upon the name, but for different causes, or even in the same mind the motive may not have been single.

However it may have been, the name was not well fixed, and when a part of the land fell to Captain Mason alone in 1629, he called his share New Hampshire. This was because, though born in Norfolk, he had lived mostly in Hampshire and registered himself as of that county when he entered Oxford University. Yet that same year, the name was changed in another charter to Laconia. Though this did not live long, it is memorable; for in it the English first brought to the new land the name of a Greek or Latin place. Also the name was a pun, and Gorges himself wrote: "Laconia, so called by reason of the great lakes therein."

Thus all the northern part of New England had many names, but had no sure name for many years.

Just as Gorges and Mason had obtained lands, so Sir Robert Heath, the Attorney General, asked for lands far to the south. The King graciously granted the petition, and in turn, doubtless, Sir Robert asked that the new province bear the King's name. Charles in Latin is Carolus, and from it an adjective may be derived. If this adjective is placed with some noun such as *terra* or *provincia,* it takes the feminine form.

The King was pleased, and with his usual attention to such matters he established the name in the stately language of a charter granted in 1629:

[42]

Know that we of our free grace, certain knowledge and mere motion do think fit to erect the said Region, Territory and Isles into a Province, and by the fullness of our power and kingly authority for us and our heirs and successors we do erect and incorporate them into a province and name the same Carolina.

Three years later Lord Baltimore obtained a grant to the north of Virginia, and of that naming a record lingered. His Lordship, the story runs, drew up a draft of the charter with his own hand, but left a blank for the name. He wished it to be Crescentia, for he was a Son of Eric and wanted his colony to be known as one which was crescent, or growing. Perhaps, knowing the King's interest in giving names, he did not make the suggestion openly, but waited his chance.

The King saw the blank space, and asked what name should be put there. Lord Baltimore, with a courtly flourish, replied that he desired to have it called something in honor of His Majesty but that he was prevented of that happiness because a province in those parts was already called Carolina.

Then for a moment, as sometimes happens in the great affairs of men, all the question hung in balance. A name which is now cherished and rich in tradition might never have existed at all. Instead, songs might have been written of "My Crescentia," and hearts might beat stronger at the sound. But Charles I at least was consistent. Men have called him tyrant and fool, but even his enemies have granted him the domestic virtues. He had already established the names of his mother and sister upon New England capes, and so naturally he now thought of his wife, Queen Henrietta Maria.

Before Lord Baltimore had a chance to make his real suggestion, the King said, "Let us, therefore, give it the name in honor of the Queen. What think you of Mariana?"

His Lordship could only acquiesce in honoring the Queen, but still trying to attain Crescentia, he said cogently that no man who loved the King could like the name Mariana, because of the Spanish Jesuit so named who had written the well-known work against monarchy. But all this craftiness accomplished was that the King proposed Terra Mariae, or in English, Maryland.

So in Latin charters the name stood as "Terra Mariae, *anglice,* Maryland," and the King made known, "so we name it and so we will it to be named in the future."

Chapter VI ❰ How the Massachusetts General Court dealt with names

---

In the end, the men of Massachusetts Bay set the pattern of names for New England, and fixed the habits—though not so much the men in general as their rulers. In those times the ministers and wealthy men commanded, and the agency of their ruling was the Massachusetts General Court. No matter was too great or small. If a man lost a hog, or blasphemed Christ, or lay with his neighbor's wife—the Court considered, and its word was as the King's law, or (some said) the law of God.

In 1630 the men of this new colony took possession. The wording of their charter as to boundaries showed that the matter of names again had bothered the lawyers:

between a great river there commonly called Monomack river, alias Merrimack river, and a certain other river there called Charles river, being in the bottom of a certain bay there commonly called Massachusetts, alias Mattachusetts, alias Massatusetts bay.

As for the previous naming of settlements in New England, the holders of the new charter could see that it followed no system, but mingled English, Indian and Latin forms. Such variety might be good enough in a country where all men were thought equal, so that one man's name was as good as another's. But the Massachusetts General Court held no such theory of equality, and like all autocratic governments loved uniformity and system.

In its second meeting, on September 7, 1630, the Court took up the matter of names. No record was kept of the debate. Yet one can well imagine something of what was said then, which in itself may have been the gist of discussions in the preceding months.

"My masters," a member might say, "this matter of naming, though it seem little, is not so. For, though that beggarly player Will Shakespeare has flippantly asked in his lascivious play 'What's in a name?' yet have Plato, and the learned Lord Verulam said otherwise. And let us remember that what we now do (being so early done, and thus setting precedent) may determine much to be done in years or centuries to come throughout this plantation of ours, the bounds of which stretch from sea to sea."

Then perhaps spoke one trained in the Inns of Court:

"The Law is silent on this matter of naming. But already it is close to a half century since the English came to America—how have they given names?"

"In many ways," said another. "Too many! Often places bear the names of persons. As Ovid has written of that sea:

Icarus aequoreas nomine fecit aquas.

So too with Jamestown in Virginia."

"I like it not," said another. "It is not seemly that we, the first men of the state, should name towns after ourselves, and neither that towns should be named after lesser men. And as for naming them for the King or some great lord—"

But there he stopped, not wishing to speak too much; all knew what he might have said, for in that Court none loved the Crown too well, or the great lords, except for a few who were Puritan.

"There is a way of naming," said one, "which seeks to give pleasant names so that more men will come, and there shall be more wealth in trade."

"A huckster's way!" cried a minister. "The Lord's own shall not attract the ungodly seeking riches. But rather let us, like those men of Salem, plant here a New Canaan, and call our chief city Jerusalem, and our other towns, it might be—Sharon and Shiloh."

"Nay," said another. "Many think that Salem is presumptuous. And surely, the New Jerusalem is not of this world!"

"What?" said another, with grim humor. "And would you call the gallows-hill Golgotha?—But for me, I like the way of the Plymouth people, to live in a town with an English town's name, and thus truly to plant a New England.

"And why only for towns!" cried one. "Let us also plant here the other names of England. When we raise our eyes to the hills, let us look to Chiltern and Cotswold as our fathers before us! Let the Charles be called Thames and the Merrimack some other English name!"

But then one learned in law said sharply. "Is this wise talk? Merrimack and Charles are named in our charter. If we alter those names, we alter our own landmarks. What else changes, those two must stand forever!"

Then one may have spoken for names like Marblehead which described the places, and another for reviving the glory of the ancients as with Laconia, and a third may have wished to keep the names of the Indians, remembering the counsel of Origen the Church father, "Alter not the barbarous names."

But in the end, the Court spoke:

"It is ordered, that Trimountain shall be called Boston; Mattapan, Dorchester; and the town upon the Charles River, Waterton."

Thus in that second meeting the Court began to plant the names of England in New England, and unknowingly made certain that such names would spread over a vaster land than anyone there imagined.

Yet the hearts of men are subtle, and a minister may act for more reasons than he admits even to himself. Boston was indeed the name of a Lincolnshire town from which many of the colonists had come, and according to Thomas Dudley, the Lieutenant-Governor, it had been informally chosen for the chief settlement even before the meeting. But Boston also honored the Earl of Lincoln, a great Puritan lord, whose steward Dudley had been for nine years, and whose daughter had been the wife of Mr. Isaac Johnson, another member of the Court. Of the second-named town, an early annalist wrote:

Why they called it Dorchester I never heard; but there was some of Dorsetshire, and some of ye town of Dorchester that settled there, and it is very likely it might be in honor of ye aforesaid Revd. Mr. White of Dorchester.

As for Waterton, though there was one in Yorkshire, the Massachusetts town was also named descriptively, since it was close to the river and had much water about it.

Also the Sons of Eric may say that by giving English names the Court showed itself no bad promoter. Old names are easy to remember. Besides, an Englishman reading them would think of settled towns, but reading Nasnocomacack or Sowacatuck, would imagine bristling forests and wild beasts.

From its first decision the Court never altered, and with almost no exception the manner of naming ran in this way: First, men went with their families, built houses, and settled lands, calling the place as the Indians had done. When the settlement grew stronger, the Court made it a town, and gave it an English name, sometimes of a city, but oftener of a little village or even of a field. The Court wasted no words, and offered no reasons—for none could call upon it for a reason. "It is ordered . . ." was enough, and so we read: "The name of Wessaguscus is also changed, and hereafter to be called Waymothe," or "Wessacuercon is allowed to be a plantation . . . and hereafter to be called Neweberry." The same happened if the place had some English name given by the firstcomers; so Bare Cove became Hingham. But the stubborn fishermen of Marblehead kept their first name. Yet the Court was

not tyrannous, and often the name given was at the petition of
the inhabitants themselves, at least of their minister and others
whose word the Court respected:

In answer to the petition of several inhabitants of Misticke side, their
request is granted, viz., to be a distinct town of themselves, and the
name thereof to be Maulden.

Most often the settlers asked for the name of a place where
some of them had lived, and since the minister was their most
respected man of all, many towns took their names from his old
home, as with Lynn, and Rowley, and Haverhill.

Cotton Mather summed up the situation well enough, when he
wrote:

for as there are few of our towns but what have their *namesakes* in
England, so the reason why most of our towns are called what they are,
is because the chief of the first inhabitants would thus bear up the
names of the particular places from whence they came.

In changing one name, the Court paid a debt of honor, though
the record reads merely, "It is ordered, that Aggawam shall be
called Ipswitch." Yet in Governor Winthrop's journal under
August 4, 1634, the note stands:

At the court, the new town at Agawam was named Ipswich, in
acknowledgement of the great honor and kindness done to our people
which took shipping there.

Another place which had already the good name of New Town,
the Court changed to Cambridge because of the college founded
there. If anyone wonders why the name was not Oxford, he
should remember that Cambridge was the more Puritan of the
two English universities, and that John Harvard himself had
studied there. Besides, Cambridge was in east England where
most of the settlers had lived, and many more names were taken
from Suffolk and Essex and the near-by counties than from other
parts.

When the War came in 1642, the men of Massachusetts felt their sympathies with Parliament, and gave the names Reading and Hull, which were places where the Roundheads had won success. This was also the time of the naming of Manchester, though it was then only a village far in the northwest of England; but the Duke of Manchester commanded the army of the Parliament.

Only Roxbury seems to have had a purely descriptive christening. As William Wood wrote: "Up westward from the town it is something rocky; whence it hath the name Roxberry." Many towns, however, echoed an English name for descriptive reasons. Medfield was a meadow or "mead-field," and was thus first spelled, but there was a Medfield in Suffolk. At Springfield there may have been a spring in a field, but it was also a little place in Essex where William Pynchon had lived. Charlestown was on Charles River, but there were many English Charltons, and that was the first spelling in Massachusetts. With another town the Court spoke out plainly:

the name of the place may be Suffield (an abbreviation of Southfield) it being the southermost town that either at present is or like to be in that country, and near adjoining to the south border of our patent.

But the spelling was that of a Norfolk village. Yet here the Court for once was wrong; that town was not within their patent at all, and now it is named by opposites, being the most northern town in Connecticut.

Only one town which the Court named in those early years bore a name of wholly different type. In the year 1635 the record reads: "There shall be a plantation at Musketequid . . . and hereafter to be called Concord." Why it was thus called, no one now knows; some think it was for a peaceful settlement with the Indians or between two factions of the settlers, and others think it was in hope of future amity. (This was not the first of such names, for already the Virginians had named Hope-in-Faith, and Fort Patience.) The naming of Concord almost set a fashion, for

[49]

in the next year a settlement petitioned to be called Contentment. But the Court ordered it to be Dedham.

Yet, though so many families came from the eastern counties, there was nowhere in Massachusetts, and is not to this day, a Saint Albans, or Bury Saint Edmunds, or any other town named for a saint. Such names smelled too much of papistry. Once Governor Winthrop journeying to Plymouth came to a place which some simple fellow had called for himself Hue's Cross:

the governor being displeased at the name, in respect that such things might hereafter give the Papists occasion to say that their religion was first planted in these parts, changed the name, and called it Hue's Folly.

With Boston, however, the Court had thoughtlessly erred a little, for in England that town took its name from Saint Botolph. So in later years the divines had this matter on their consciences, and even disowned the saint. Thus Cotton Mather wrote:

Old Boston, by name, was but Saint Botolph's town. Whereas thou, O Boston, shalt have but one *protector* in heaven, and that is our Lord Jesus Christ.

The Court named no towns for men, except for one like Manchester where the name of the man was the same as an English town. Once the people of a place known as Nashaway petitioned, and the Court decreed "at the request of the inhabitants," that it should be called Prescott. That was the name of several English villages, but one of the chief men of Nashaway was a certain Prescott, and it would seem that he thus tried slyly to have a town named for himself. But the Court soon saw the trick, and in the end the place became Lancaster.

Also the Court would not have liked Prescott if it had known the word to mean "priest's cottage." But though they were learned in Latin and Greek and Hebrew, the rulers of Massachusetts knew little of the roots of their own language, and the names of most English towns were to them merely counters without meaning. So probably they never realized that Braintree might be "Branuc's tree" and some shrine of the heathen times, and they did not consider whether there was really a "crooked brook" at Woburn, or a "lake" at Lynn, or whether Dorchester was rightly "the camp of the fist-play." Yet sometimes they must have done better than they knew at description, for there may well have been a "beaver-stream" at Beverly. But generally the sites of the places had little to do with the naming of the towns.

When the Court came to form the first counties, it borrowed again from eastern England—Essex, Middlesex, Norfolk, and Suffolk, properly arranged, with Norfolk to the north. (In political shuffles this county ceased to exist, and in 1793 a new one was carelessly named Norfolk, though it lay south of Suffolk.)

Plymouth Colony followed the same ways of naming, not quite so strictly. So Scituate kept the old Indian name, meaning "cold brook." In another town the minister chose a name from Scripture, meaning "the Lord hath made room," as it was written of the patriarch Isaac when he removed from the land of the Philistines: "and he called the name of it Rehoboth; and he said, For now the Lord hath made room for us, and we shall be fruitful in the land."

Even perhaps before the settlement of Plymouth, the English had known of a river lying farther to the west. Again, it would seem, some shipmaster anchored at the river-mouth, and, as best he could, talked with the Indians. They gave the name of that part where the tide washed back and forth, which meant to them "long estuary," and to this they added an ending which meant "at." The name sounded to the English in such a way that they wrote it down at first as Quinetucquet or Quenticutt. Finally they wrote it Connecticut, although no one knows who first put in the extra *c,* or why—for none who have lived there, Indian or English, have pronounced it. Perhaps some half-wise town-clerk first so wrote it, trying to relate it to the English word *connect.*

Later, when Englishmen came from Massachusetts to settle the rich lands by that river, they naturally called their three settlements after English towns—Hartford, Wethersfield, and Windsor. When these towns leagued together, they gave no name to their "one public State or Commonwealth," referring only to the three towns upon the River Connecticut. But people soon came to call that whole region by the name of the river—for it had no other. (Thus the precedent first was set that a state should bear the name of its chief river.)

In 1635 other Englishmen came under a patent held by many lords and gentlemen, among whom were Lord Say and Sele, and Lord Brooke. These newcomers built a fort at the river-mouth, and for its name they ran together the names of those two lords, so that it was Saybrook. This also set a precedent, since it was the first time that men made a new name in the land by putting together old names or parts of them.

In Connecticut, as in Plymouth, one town kept an Indian name, by a strange manner. First it was called by such a name as Naramake, and on English tongues this came to be Norwaak, and soon was spelled Norwalk. Then men thought it wholly English, as if it might be a name like Norwich. Finally, someone made up a story to explain the name, saying that it was because the first comers had bought of the Indians as much land as would lie within one day's "north-walk" from the Sound.

But most of the western towns took English names, and, as in Massachusetts, sometimes with double meaning. Thus, New Haven was at once a "new harbor" and an English village, and so with Middletown, Fairfield, and Farmington.

Most of all, in the renaming of a place called Naomeage, the men of Connecticut showed how they, like all the New Englanders, thought about naming towns. To this place they decided to give a great name. So, on March 11, 1658, instead of merely writing, "It is ordered . . ." the Court passed a resolution which showed clearly that the process of naming was neither accidentally determined nor lightly considered:

Whereas, it hath been a commendable practice of the inhabitants of all the Colonies of these parts, that as this Country hath its denomination from our dear native Country of England, and thence is called New England, so the planters, in their first settling of most new plantations have given names to those plantations of some Cities and Towns in England, thereby intending to keep up and leave to posterity the memorial of several places of note there, as Boston, Hartford, Windsor, York, Ipswich, Braintree, Exeter.

Having thus stated its precedents, the Court went on to justify itself in what other colonies might have termed presumption, in seizing a name which would rate highest of all for advertising:

Considering that there is yet no place in any of the Colonies that has been named in memory of the City of London, there being a new plantation within this Jurisdiction of Connecticut settled upon the fair River of Monhegin, in the Pequot Country, it being an excellent harbor and a fit and convenient place for future trade, it being also the only place which the English of these parts have possessed by conquest, and that by a very just war upon that great and warlike people, the Pequots, that therefore they might thereby leave to posterity the memory of that renowned city of London, from whence we had our transportation, have thought fit, in honor to that famous City, to call the said plantation, New London.

The river at New London, by counterpart, became the Thames, which is "England's richest treasure." But the New Englanders, in spite of what they did with town-names, never made it a practice thus to transfer the names of rivers and hills.

In those years the rulers of Massachusetts persecuted Roger Williams because he was not altogether of their opinion, and spoke too boldly, and said the King had no right to give away the Indian lands. Fearing worse things, he fled into the snowy forest by an Indian path, and came to his friend Massasoit. All winter he lived in the forest for conscience sake. But in the fair month of June in 1636 he came to some lands on a bay, and his good friends the sachems of the Narragansetts gave him a place to live there. Then, as he wrote in later years, "having in a sense of God's merciful providence unto me in my distress called the place Providence, I desired it be for a shelter for persons distressed of conscience." And so it remains, proudly to be borne by a great city, being no common name, and no common consecration.

When Providence came to be a colony, however, its rulers followed the custom of echoing English towns, in evidence, as they once resolved a little cautiously, "of our unity and likeness to many parts of our native country."

While much was happening in the south and west of New England, there was little either of settlement or of naming in the farther north. Sometimes men referred to the nearer region as Laconia, but more often only as the settlements on the Piscataway; the four towns there lived to themselves. As for the name New Hampshire, no one paid it any attention, and there was no government in that name.

With Maine the case was nearly as bad, for in a later grant Sir Ferdinando Gorges named it New Somerset after his own county in England. But King Charles disliked New Somerset, though no one knows why, and in a grant of 1639 he spoke so sharply that it is a matter of wonder, unless he himself had had something to do with the original naming:

And We do name, ordain, and appoint that the portion of the mayne land and premises aforesaid shall forever hereafter be called and named the Province or County of Mayne and not by any other name or names whatsoever.

Even this did not establish the name, for in the years afterward the sovereignty of the North was changed, and the new rulers gave new names to strengthen their title.

When the founders of Massachusetts Bay first got their charter from the Plymouth Company, it allowed them all the land from the Merrimack to the Charles and three miles beyond, north and south, and everything east and west from sea to sea. But whether from carelessness or from craftiness the wording ran, not merely "river," but "or of any or every part thereof." Perhaps no one gave the matter much thought, for in that wild land a little more or less made slight difference. (So we may read of two neighbors who were measuring their boundary through a salt-meadow, and one of them growing tired, cried out, "Hang it, a pox on't, here is marsh enough for us all!") Also the English lawyers would have thought of the name of a river as fixed and allowing no alteration, and would not have known the uncertainties of a new land.

During some years no one considered the boundary, and then the rulers of Massachusetts Bay began to be ambitious. In 1638 they sent Goodman Woodward, Mr. John Stretton, with an Indian, and two others (paying them five shillings a day apiece) "to lay out the line three miles northward of the most northern-most part of Merrimack." Thus sent and paid, no man was likely to find that the source of the Merrimack lay to the south. Instead, the scouts traced the river far north to where it flowed from a large lake, and the Indians said that this was the same stream. When the scouts asked why the different reaches of the river were differently called, the Indians said that was only for the places on the river-bank, and it was all the Merrimack. But this was not so, and most likely the Indians were trying to please their English friends, or else there was a misunderstanding, or someone merely lied. On the Charles, however, the Massachusetts men traced the water farther and farther to the south, naming it always Charles River, until they came to the last little rill.

Then in the next year the men of Hingham in Massachusetts Bay claimed a certain meadow on the boundary-line and drove stakes to mark their claim. But the Scituate men of Plymouth came and pulled up the stakes. Since the two colonies had always lived in peace and friendship, the Courts appointed an arbitration. In that meeting the Massachusetts men told about "Charles River" and the Plymouth men were astonished. For, as Governor Bradford wrote, in indignation mixing his grammar, "that every runlet or small brook, that should, far in the land, come into it, or mix streams with it, and were by the natives called by other and

different names from it, should now by them [of Massachusetts]
be made Charles River or parts of it, they [of Plymouth] saw no
reason for it." Also, he thought that the sellers who were first in
the land should know better what was the Charles River than the
buyers who came later. But the Massachusetts men stood upon
the wording "any or every part thereof." Also they showed that a
line drawn east and west from that farthest point to the south
would bring the town of Plymouth under the rule of Massachusetts. All this appalled the men of that older but weaker
colony, and in the end they were at such disadvantage that in
saving the roof over their heads they granted the other claims.
Thus, because they had not looked carefully into the name, the
men of Plymouth were shut in, and lost their western lands; and
in the end they became part of Massachusetts.

After two years more the Massachusetts Court pushed its claims
to the north because of the name Merrimack. By drawing a line
east and west on the map three miles north from where the river
flowed out of the lake, they thought that their claim took in all
those northern towns. There they met no trouble. Those towns
were weak and needed protection; so they joined gladly with the
stronger colony. Thus by juggling with names Massachusetts Bay
widened its grant from thirty-seven miles to nearly a hundred.
Then the Court ordered all the northern towns to be joined in one
county "called by the name of Yorkshire," and the names Maine
and New Hampshire, like Norumbega, no longer lived, and
seemed likely never to live again.

The northern settlements were mostly called for English towns
already, but one of them bore the lovely name Strawberry Bank,
"so called by reason of a bank where strawberries was found in
this place." The people, there, however, were Sons of Eric, and
besides they wished to be in fashion. So they asked for an English
name which would also serve for advertisement:

Now your petitioners' humble desire is to have it called Portsmouth,
being a name most suitable for this place, it being the river's mouth
and a good harbor as any in this land.

Thus the strong will of the Court helped establish custom. Both together wiped out the Indian names and the names describing the land. Consciously, town by town, the colonists planted a New England. So the proud Cotton Mather wrote:

Well may New England lay claim to the name it wears and to a room in the tenderest affections of its mother, the *happy Island!*

Chapter VII ❬ How the people began to give names

WHEREVER men live, there must be a hundred or a thousand little names to every great one. In the South and in New England the ways of giving the little names were often the same, but they also were different in some ways.

Most important of all, the Virginians had no policy or system of naming, so that their names from the beginning grew more naturally, and were more adapted to the country, and more various. Even their names of towns and counties sprang rather from the people than from the government. For these reasons there was no marked cleavage between such names and those of natural features, as there was in New England.

In Virginia men settled chiefly, not by towns, but by plantations. At first the word, as it was used also in New England, meant *settlement,* or *colony.* Later it meant a place where several men had their tobacco farms, or where one large landholder had a grant from the Company. When several plantations had developed in the same region, the governor bound them together under the old English term *hundred.*

Since no one had thought out any system, the name of a plantation or hundred sprang sometimes from location, as with Upper Hundred and Nether Hundred, or more often from a landowner, as in Digges-his-Hundred, and Lawnes Plantation. Sometimes it was borrowed from England, as with Isle of Wight Plantation, which gave its name to the county. Again it was for good omen, as with None-Such, because its planters felt that there was "no place so strong, so pleasant, and delightful in Virginia." And Bermuda Hundred was in remembrance of those who were wrecked in Bermuda, from whose story some think that Shakespeare wrote *The Tempest.*

Since a man generally named his own plantation, there arose a variety and originality such as New England lacked—a touch of wit or irony, a pun, an alliteration. So came Chaplin's Choice and Jordan's Journey, Flower dieu Hundred, Argall's Gift and Martin's Brandon. Thus the Virginians brought to the New World a touch of Elizabethan fancy.

Also two brothers named Newce came there to make a plantation. Once before, in Ireland, they had founded a town, naming it Newcetown, where it still stands. So now to their second settlement they gave the name New, and since it had an anchorage, they called it Port, and it became New Port Newce. The brothers were unfortunate, and men forgot them soon; but men remembered Captain Newport, who had done much to found Virginia. So they began to think and write Newport's Newce, perhaps even to confuse the second part with Neuse River. Then in trying to make sense they wrote Newport News, and so it remained. Thus with men and names, as with fishes in the sea, the greater often swallow up the smaller.

When the Virginians took an English name, it was usually not from a place, as in New England, but from a member of the royal family, or some nobleman. So they named a town in Greek form Henricopolis from Prince Henry, though it was soon shortened to Henrico. Some of them indeed even tried to replace the Indian names of the rivers with royal names, changing Rappahannock to Queen's and Potomac to Elizabeth.

When the first counties were formed in 1634, they took the names of settlements already existing. These in turn had come chiefly from the royal family, but Accawmack and Warrosquyoake were Indian, and Warwick River used indirectly the name of a nobleman.

As the counties show, Virginia kept Indian names for the settlements a little more than New England did, but there was definite feeling against them. In 1619 the inhabitants of Kiccowtan petitioned the House of Burgesses "to change the savage name," and the settlement was accordingly called Elizabeth City. Warrosquyoake County took a plantation-name and became Isle of Wight after only three years. Accawmack shifted to Northampton in 1643, but a section of it was restored as Accomac twenty years later.

In any new country the actual settlers must establish many names for the smaller features of the land itself. No one bothers usually to record the giving of these little names. Sometimes no man by himself learned or bestowed or invented the name, but, as with the Indians, it grew by usage. Thus, when swine were brought to the new plantations, the custom was to keep them on low-lying islands. There they needed no fences, for they would not swim willingly; they also found good rooting, and some protection from wolves and thieves. Then at first men spoke perhaps of "that isle where we keep the hogs," but soon they said, as it still stands in the records, "the Isle of Hogs," and at last Hog Island.

The men who came to Virginia were English, speaking English, and having no desire to vary from the old customs. Yet even in spite of themselves, the nature of the land itself and their new ways of life caused them to change—in the ways they gave names, as in much else.

In naming rivers, they followed ancient custom. Since they were

Europeans, they looked upon a river as being in some way a thing in itself, a not very logical belief which may have originated from the idea of a river-god. So the Virginians did not adopt the Indian system of calling each section of a stream by its own name, and when they came to a place where two rivers joined into one, they picked out the branch which seemed more important and gave it the name which the lower stream already bore. Because of such reasoning, they believed that somewhere would be found the head or true source of every river. By thus naturally following the European custom they set a precedent for all their descendants who took the frontier westward.

The domination of the river in their thought showed in various namings. Almost immediately they divided their whole country along the line of the James, calling the north Popham-side, and the south Salisbury-side, both from English gentlemen who were patrons of the colony. Later settlements grew up along the lines of communication offered by the easily navigated streams. Charles River and Warwick River were the names of two of the first counties. The Virginians thus fell easily into the habit of calling a whole region by the name of its river, and that custom was to mean much in the distant future.

In other ways, the Virginians soon changed the English system of stream-naming because of their manner of approach. At the beginning they entered into many broad tidal streams. Each of these they naturally called a river. Following the channel, they came to where at last the tide reached no farther and the current flowed always one way. They called this still the river. A smaller stream where the tide washed back and forth they called a creek, as in England. Following up such a creek, they came also to a place where the water flowed always one way, and since it seemed the same, they kept the same name for it. Thus a creek came to mean a flowing stream, although in England it meant, and still means, a tidal channel. But sometimes at the end of the tide they spoke of the stream as a rundle or run. Then soon they came to think of the river as being the largest, and the creek as smaller, and the run as the smallest of the three. Perhaps also they needed three grades of distinction because they were living on a continent, not an island. A Virginian creek was likely to be larger than an English river.

As for *brook,* it became soon a strange, far-off word, read in books, as when one heard in church, "The hart panteth after the water-brooks." And children, wonderingly, asked their mothers what a brook might be.

Also those English always went upstream first, for they came from the sea. Going thus upstream, they thought of a river as a tree—first a single trunk, then splitting into branches. So they called any little stream a branch, especially in low country close to tide where the streams had little current and could not so well be called runs.

From England also they brought three good words—bog and fen and marsh—but they rarely used them. Instead, from the Indians they took *pocosin.* But another word they used was *swamp,* which was not then common in England, except in rustic dialects.

Another manner of speech also arose from the country. There the tide ran far up in many creeks with the land in narrow strips between, but often wider near the river before the creeks divided. Then, as a point may be called a head, they called the narrower part a *neck*. In the end any land between two arms of water was a neck.

With words like creek and swamp and neck, the English coupled another word to distinguish one from another, as the Indians had done, and the Angles and Saxons long before in England. So by size came Big Creek, and Little Creek, and by color Black Creek, and from the kind of bottom Mud Creek, and Sand Creek. If tributaries came in from opposite sides at the same place, it became Cross Creek. Or, if a great ash tree or a rock marked the crossing, it might be Ash Creek or Rock Creek.

Men also named places for what happened there, as in Stingray Isle. So, after good hunting, they might call a stream Turkey Creek, or Possum Creek, or Raccoon Creek. Here again the names differed from those of England, because such beasts had never lived there for the Angles and Saxons to hunt.

Then, too, just as people take their names from places, places take their names from people, especially in countries where the idea of private ownership is strong. So in Virginia many streams, as well as plantations and towns, were called after men who lived there, sometimes Indians, more often English.

Very soon also, the faster because there was little reading and writing, names changed in speech until they often really became new names. This happened more commonly with the long Indian words. Thus a small bay was first called Powhatan, from which it may be traced through the spellings Poetan, Portan, and Purtin, until it finally was written as Putin. Sometimes the process followed what is known as folk-etymology; that is, the people made over a strange name into something which sounded better and gave some semblance of sense. This was the process by which Poor Cottage became Port Cottage. There was also a stream spelled Quiyoughcohanock; first shortening it to Quiyoughc, the Virginians seem to have made that into White Oak, and there is still a creek so called. Near it is also Chippokes Creek, sometimes called Chip Oak, although there is no such tree.

The common people in New England also went about, giving the little names as they wished, with no one telling them how or how not. Being English, they were much like the Virginians in their ways, but they differed here and there because the land itself was different, and the Indians used another dialect, and they themselves came more from eastern England. Since there was little travel back and forth between the South and New England, the differences tended to increase with time.

As the Virginians were a river people, so the New Englanders were a salt-water people, and gave more shoreline names. If any great headland showed the trend of the coast and was a landfall for fishermen standing in from the banks, they called it a cape. But juttings-out of land which were of note only to coasting sailors, they called points. For this reason the points bore later and more homely names, sometimes as if named by farmers instead of sailors, as Cornfield Point and Calfpasture Point.

There were more capes in New England than in Virginia, partly because the coast was bolder. But also there was an Indian word *kepan* or *kuppi* meaning a closed-up passage. So the first settlers learned to say Kepaneddik and Kuppaug, and people later wrote the words as Cape Neddick and Cape Poge.

Like the Virginians, the New Englanders also said *neck*, sometimes perhaps because they took over the Indian word *naiack*, "point" or "corner," from which came also Nyack, and Nayaug. (So also men may have come to say "that neck of the woods.")

In their words for streams, the New Englanders differed most from the Virginians, and were closer to the ways of England. Their coast rose more sharply from the sea, and so had fewer long tidal channels. Doubtless for this reason the New Englanders did not come to use *creek* for a running stream. At first they sometimes said *beck*, or *runlet*, or *riveret* for a small stream, but the common word was always brook, as in eastern England. They never learned to say *run*, and if a Virginian came there and asked where he might find a *branch*, they told him to look at the nearest tree.

For a lake or pool, they said *pond*, which was a common word in eastern England. This was the easier also because the Indian word *paug* was much like it. But they often doubled the words, saying Mashapaug Pond, which is really to say Big-pond Pond. Also of this common name they made sometimes Marshpaug, as if it were so called for being marshy.

Like the Virginians they also used that rustic word *swamp*, and less often *marsh*. But the Indian word *paug* was sometimes *baug* as in Quinebaug, "long pond." Since a marsh often resembles a pond, for this reason perhaps the New Englanders kept the old word *bog*, though the Virginians lost it.

The New Englanders borrowed many names from the Indians, but not so many as they might have. The Indian words were long and strange, difficult both to say and to remember. Sometimes, even when they learned the Indian name, they changed it, as with a stream: "called in the Indian tongue Conamabsqunooncant, commonly called the Duck River."

Most of all, the New Englanders took their little names from those settlers who lived there or owned the land, as the Virginians did also. Thus there was one George Bunker, constable of Charlestown, and by that name a hill was called.

Like everyone else, they often called places for how they looked. In those days, eye-glasses were new and uncommon, and men were quick to note that something had two large ends and a narrow strip between. Thus came Spectacle Island and Spectacle Pond.

Also, sugar was then no common food, and even in England men sweetened mostly with honey. The sugar that men knew came in the form of a large cake, sticking up to a high rounded point at the end. So, within two years after Roger Williams had come to Providence, men had named a Sugar-Loaf Hill not far off. From that first hill the name spread, until it was so common that men could even say "a sugar-loaf," meaning merely that kind of hill. As the years passed, sugar grew cheap, and its form changed; it came to the table in bowls, and no longer stood in the middle, like a jutting-up mountain above a plain. But still men said Sugar-Loaf Hill, though they did not know why, and though the only loaf-sugar they had ever seen came in small cubes. Thus the name may outlast the thing.

So also even in the earliest days, men began another custom of naming which spread far. For, as they walked or rode from one place to another, they gauged the distance by stream-crossings, naming Three-mile Brook, or Ten-mile River. Then the name spread up and down along the stream, and later perhaps the old trail was no more used. But by way of the new trail the distances were different, and so the name lost its meaning. Yet often it remained, for names remain in spite of meaning—not every Smith is a worker of metal, or every Fletcher an arrow-maker.

Of all names for streams the commonest in Massachusetts came to be Beaver Brook and Mill Brook. In trade the beaver was most desired for its fur, and moreover it was not like other animals, here now and gone again; but like man himself the beaver was a builder of dams and canals and towns, to be plainly seen. So even Winthrop the Governor, journeying out from Boston in his second winter, gave that name, because "the beavers had shorn down divers great trees there, and made divers dams across the brook." Mill Brook also was a name to be given, because in those early days a mill marked off one brook from another.

As all men do, they also named places for what happened there. Once, as it came about, when there was war with the Pequots, some men worked in a meadow by Saybrook. But the Indians came suddenly upon them. Nevertheless, all escaped except one. The Indians took a godly young man named Butterfield. For that, it was called Butterfield Meadow. The next year, as Governor Winthrop wrote the story, some English killed six Indians and took two, who were sachems. A little later (since this was a war as if against the Canaanites, with little quarter given) having come near a certain point of land, they beheaded the two sachems. Then with a grim pun they called that headland Sachem's Head, and so it still is.

Yet life was not always stern. Once two men disputed over a boundary-line, and came to an open quarrel. Then there was much loud shouting of threats and great sword-brandishing, but in the end neither had stomach for a fight. So the neighbors in jest called it Bloody Point, though no blood was shed there—and so it too remains.

Also in high spirits or in jest many other names were given—Cotteril's Delight and Dog's Misery and Labor-in-Vain Creek and Mad Mare's Neck. Also, even in those early years, they loved to parody the names of their towns to make fun of those who lived there. So the men of the other towns said that Boston was Lostton. And once the men of Beverly asked the Court for a new name, complaining: "because we being but a small place, it hath caused on us the constant nickname of Beggarly."

Sometimes for humor and sometimes by ignorance they also made English names of the Indian words, by folk-etymology. Moskitu-auke, "grass-land," became Mosquito Hawk. Nama-auke, "fish-place," was first Namerack and then Namalake, until by some great twist it was at last Mayluck. So Piscot River became Piggsgut, and then Pigsty; and Pashipscot soon was Sheepscot, and Oxopaugsaug became a jocular Oxyboxy.

Thus it was with names in those high days when the Church ruled and the Court spoke the word in New England. In those times the rule was so strong, and all men were so much of the same thoughts, that the names even seemed to form a pattern, and though much has changed since then, even still some of that pattern remains. First, from Penobscot to Housatonic, stood the Indian names on the greater rivers, and also on the large lakes and ponds. So even yet, if a man looks at a smaller map, he thinks that most of the names in New England, except of towns, are Indian. But this is because only these first-named and larger features are shown upon the smaller maps. Next, to form the pattern, were the names of towns and counties, on which the Court had placed the names of England. Then finally came the many smaller streams and ponds, the lesser hills, points of land, swamps, and meadows. These were neither Indian nor brought from England, but were simple names given by the people, and were English because that was the people's speech.

With all such smaller names, the custom of the English, north and south, was to give them little attention, but to let them arise as needed, by chance. Indeed the King's law took no note of the names of natural features. In England they were mostly established before the kingdom itself, neither by act of Parliament nor by the King's will, but by common usage. So when early charters and deeds in the colonies referred to a town or county or other creation of government, they used merely the name; but with a river or hill they often inserted the formula "commonly so called" as if recognizing that the authority of the name rested upon the usage of the people.

Chapter VIII ❨ How names were symbols of empire

Wₕᵢₗₑ Virginia and New England were growing strong, the Dutch also had come to that coast, and founded a colony, and given names.

In that middle region the first great name began, like many others, somewhat mysteriously. About the year of the foundation of Jamestown, it seems that some English voyager entered into a broad bay and sailed northward a few miles to where it narrowed and was more like a river-mouth. He learned some names from the Indians, and on the map which he drew up, he wrote Mannahata to the west of the river-mouth and Manahatin to the east.

Two years later Henry Hudson entered the bay, guided probably by a copy of that map. On September 2, 1609, before dawn, they on the *Half-Moon* saw a great fire, and when day broke, the beauty of that landfall was such that Robert Juet of Limehouse, who kept the log, seems to write poetry:

> Then the sun arose,
> And we steered away north again,
> And saw the land from the west
> By north to the north-west by north,
> All like broken islands.

They sailed far up the broad river, but strangely (so far as the record stands) they gave it no name, and Juet wrote merely "the River," as if all others were nothing by comparison. He mentioned the naming of only one place on that voyage, and that was to commemorate a dead comrade:

An Englishman, named John Colman, with an arrow shot into his throat . . . whom we carried on land and buried, and named the place after his name, Colman's Point.

But later men knew it as Sandy Hook.

Also Juet wrote down, as if quoting from the map, "that side of the River that is called Manna-hata," and so the tradition of the name was passed on. What the words meant can hardly be known for certain. The placing of Manna-hata and Manahatin on opposite sides of the river was not in the ordinary run of naming, and may show that the explorer was only trying to indicate the Indians inhabiting both banks. If so, the names may be only variants of the well-known tribal name Mohican, sometimes spelled Manhecan or Manahegan, in itself meaning "wolf." Two hundred years later some Indians said Manhattan meant "where we all got drunk," because someone gave the Indians rum at that place—but this was merely a fanciful, though pleasant, legend. If it is not a tribal name, the best theory seems to be that it means "hilly island."

Hudson was not one to be remembered by the names he gave, but soon after him came Dutch skippers who were better at that work, especially Adriaen Block whose own name remained on Block Island. He was shipwrecked on Manhattan, but built himself a little vessel, which he aptly christened *Onrust*, "restless." Then in 1614 he sailed through the strait to the east of the island, and named it Hellegat, "hell passage," because of the dangerous tide, and also after a channel in Holland. But some have joked that this was an inept name—for the road to hell is broad and easy.

Block sailed on into the sound beyond Hellegat. Since he had the advantage of a small craft, he explored inshore, and worked his way some distance up the largest stream, which he called "Fresh River" in distinction from that at Manhattan, because the tide did not penetrate it far. Sailing farther eastward, he discovered before long that he was in the open ocean again, and had thus proved that the land which he had kept to his starboard was an island. Probably by means of his reckonings he worked out its dimensions, and so called it "Long Island," which is not a name to be given by anyone actually looking at the island, but is very obvious to someone who has calculated its shape or drawn it on a map.

Block explored still farther east, giving Dutch names. Some of these places already had English names from Gosnold, but Block paid no attention to them, either unknowingly, or else purposely, in order to strengthen the Dutch claim to the coast.

After their captains had reported, the States General in 1614 followed the fashion of the time by formally naming the region New Netherland. Soon afterward men went out to build trading-posts.

The Dutch were used to sailing the inland channels of their own country. In New Netherland also they kept close to navigable water, and as in Virginia most of the names were strung along the courses of the chief rivers. Farthest north and east was "Fresh River," which the English called Connecticut. Farthest south was "South River," which the English called Delaware. In the center was the river where Hudson had sailed.

For this greatest of the three, the Dutch fumbled over a name. Officially it became Mauritius, which was the Latinized form of the name of the Dutch Prince, Maurice of Nassau, for whom the stream was also sometimes called Nassau River. It was often known as the North River in counterpart to the South River. From the island or tribe it was Manhattans River. Because of some legend of early Spanish discovery another name was River of the Mountains, usually in a French form. But most commonly the Dutch who lived there called it simply the Great River. So a Dutch mapmaker, when the settlements there were forty years old, wrote Groote Rivier, and then added four other names. But one name the Dutch never used was Hudson River.

The whole failure of the river to be securely named shows how an original uncertainty of naming leads to more uncertainties. If Hudson had christened it simply and appropriately, the matter would probably have been settled, once for all. But as time went on, there was even more uncertainty for his river than for the Rio Grande; and to this day, like the Rio Grande, it has two names—Hudson to the world, but North River to many of the people of Manhattan itself. In Dutch times also arose the habit of calling the tidal channel on the other side the East River, and ever since that time inquisitive people have inquired why the river balancing that one on the west should be called, not the West River, but the North River.

Usually, however, the Dutch were practical in their naming, and like the Indians considered that the various parts of the river should have secure names even if the whole did not. To a boat-man the stream could be simply "The River," but he needed terms for every section, to locate himself, or give directions, or to gossip about past voyages. In the very first years, before 1625, the skippers named every reach and point, so that still along that river men say names ending in *rack* and *hook*, like Claverack, "Clover Reach."

With the Indian names the Dutch did as all the others had done, making the words over to be more like their own language. So arose Hackensack, and Poughkeepsie, and Scheaenhechstede (which became Schenectady) looking enough like Dutch to deceive an Englishman.

With Hopoakan-hacking the Dutch went even further. This was a place across the river from Manhattan, meaning in the local dialect "at the place of the tobacco-pipe." But Hopoakan sounded like the name of a village in Flanders, and there were also Dutch people of the name, one of whom came to New Netherland as a schoolmaster. So the name soon came to be, and remained— Hoboken.

With their towns and villages the men of New Netherland followed no system. Often they used names from the old country, as with their chief settlement, New Amsterdam. So they also transplanted Breukelyn, Vlissingen, and Haerlem.

Sometimes the name arose from the landholder. One settler was Jonas Bronck, a Dane, who had a farm just north of Manhattan. From him men came to speak of Bronck's River. Also apparently they said "the Broncks," as men say in English "the Smiths," meaning where the Smiths live, and so came the Bronx.

Still a little farther north was the settlement known officially as Colen Donck, "Donck's Colony." But this Adriaen van der Donck bore a courtesy title "Jonkheer," meaning about the same as "Squire." By that title his tenants usually addressed him; before long they began to call Colen Donck merely "the Jonkheer's," and so came Yonkers.

In later years there grew up a legend that these early Dutch were dull-witted and ox-like, notable mainly for baggy trousers. But more truly those first Dutch were as wild a crew as any that ever landed in Virginia, and they looked upon the New Englanders as parson-ridden snivelers with no appreciation of rum or a bawdy song or an Indian wench. Their word *gat* which they used so freely for "channel" or "passage," meant also "hole" in its most derogatory sense, so that a map of New Netherland must have impressed a contemporary Hollander as of a peculiar pungency. They named a Hoeren Eiland in the Fresh River, and a Hoeren Kill on South River. A tradition is preserved about the naming of the latter, and though it may not be wholly correct, it shows what the next generation thought a likely story:

These men or traders came ashore with their goods, where they traded with the Indians and frequenting so much with the Indian women, till they got the country duties, otherwise called the pox, and so they named that place Whore-kill, that is in English the Whores' Creek.

This writer told also of another name on the South River:

remembering (I suppose) how they had been served at the Whore-Kill, they went some ten or twelve miles higher, where they landed again and traded with the Indians, trusting the Indians to come into their stores ashore, and likewise aboard of their sloop drinking and debauching with the Indians till they were all at last barbarously murdered, and so that place was christened with their blood and to this day is called the Murderer-kill, that is, Murderers Creek.

[71]

And so to *this* day also there is on that coast a stream called Murderkill River.

During those first years there was peace between England and the Netherlands, but in America the Dutch and English were always in dispute. The English claimed that the Dutch were interlopers. The names became tied up in this dispute, each side maintaining its names to be the older ones. In mentioning the three great rivers the English said carefully Connecticut, Hudson, and Delaware, and even for small places the names were often different.

Thus it was with a place the Dutch called Rodenberghen, "Red Hills." It was settled by some English who called it New Haven. Later, some of the English settled still closer to New Amsterdam, and the General Director and the Senate of New Netherland formally protested in a Latin letter haughtily addressed to the "Governor of the place by us called the Red Hills in New Netherland (but by the English called New Haven)." The protest continued on the grounds that "you and yours have of late determined to fasten your foot near Mauritius River in this Province." It was dated, "August 3, 1646, New Style."

The English replied in Latin also, not even unbending enough to use the same calendar, on "August 12, 1646, Old Style." With more sophistication in diplomacy than one would expect in a newly settled village, the New Haven men took up the matter of Mauritius River, writing, "We do truly profess we know no such river, neither can we conceive what river you intend by that name." Then they added, as if in perplexed afterthought: "unless it be that which the English long and still do call Hudsons River."

Nevertheless the Dutch claims were troublesome. If the two countries had been actually hostile, a mere question of legality would have made little difference. But with England and the Netherlands friendly at home, the men of southern New England must always have feared that after some twist of international politics they would find themselves surrendered to Dutch rule by the home government. Anything they could do to bolster the legality of their settlement would be useful. Sovereignty of uninhabited or un-Christian lands was generally held to rest upon discovery, and the language of the names of a region was often cited as proof of discovery by that nation.

At the very height of the controversy, on March 13, 1644, without preamble or explanation, the Court of Providence Plantation ordered, "that the island commonly called Aquethneck, shall be from henceforth called the Isle of Rhodes, or Rhode Island." To re-name an island by official act was not according to English custom anywhere, and to give it a name drawn from the Mediterranean was doubly strange. But De Laet, a Dutchman writing in 1630, had made mention of a "little reddish island" in that vicinity, and the Dutch may thus have had a common name Roode Eyland, without any *h,* before 1644—as they certainly had soon afterward. Because of this they could taunt or threaten the English who lived there, saying that the Dutch title was better because of the name.

Then some Englishman may have read in Hakluyt's *Voyages* how Verrazano had sailed along that coast in 1524, long before any of the Dutch. Verrazano had written vaguely of an island "about the bigness of the Island of Rhodes." From this passage the English may have seen how they could play the Dutch a trick. For, if they boldly took the Dutch name with a little change of spelling, they could then say to them: "You did not give this old name at all, but we merely use the one that Verrazano left here."

The Massachusetts General Court, however, which looked upon Providence Plantation as "the sink of New England," seemed to regard the new name as presumptuous, and usually spelled it Road Island, as if it were merely an island with an anchorage for ships, in spite of the act establishing the spelling.

After Gustavus Adolphus had made his pikemen and musketeers the best of Europe, Sweden became a great power, and in the reign of the famous Queen Christina began to think of colonies. Thus in 1636 one wrote: "The English, French, and Dutch have occupied large tracts of land in the New World. Sweden ought no longer to abstain from making her name known in foreign countries." So in 1638, by arrangement with the Dutch, one of the Queen's captains sailed into the Delaware (or South) River, landed colonists, and immediately made the name of Sweden known. For, as soon as some land had been purchased from the Indians, a pole was set up bearing the royal arms, and "with a salute of cannon, followed by other formal ceremonies the land was called New Sweden."

At first the Swedes paid little attention to names, but trusting to their peace and friendship with the Dutch and English, and their own strength in arms, they merely took over many of the Dutch names, and even used the name South River, translated into their own language as Södre Revier. Their chief fort they named Christina after their queen, gallantly firing off more cannon when they named it. Across the river from Fort Christina they built Fort New Elfsborg, naming it from a famous fortress in Sweden.

In their ways of naming they differed little from either the Dutch or the English. They took over Indian words, spelling them to look Swedish. They called places for animals or birds they saw there, and also for some fancy they named Camel Creek, Dragon Creek, and Ostrich Creek, though except through a rum-born imagination they certainly saw none of those creatures there.

Often they made over the Dutch names into a kind of half-Swedish, as with Aleskins Kijlen. This was formed from Swedish *aleskins,* "eel-skin," and Dutch *kill,* "creek," and at the end the Swedish article *-en,* so that the whole was roughly "the eel-skin creek."

Before much time had passed, both the Dutch and the English began to look on the last-comers as intruders. The truculent and hard-fighting Swedes at first cared little about the ins-and-outs of precedence. When a Dutchman once urged claims of priority, the Swedish governor replied cavalierly that doubtless also the Devil was the first proprietor of Hell, but he had admitted others later. Nevertheless the Dutch continued to say that there were many places in that region still bearing Dutch names, "which sufficiently shows that the river belongs to the Hollanders, and not to the Swedes."

As the Dutch grew stronger and less friendly, the Swedes saw their mistake, and began to call the stream New Sweden River or Swedes' River. So it then had three wholly different names, depending upon whether the Swedes or Dutch or English were talking, and each governor in his correspondence with one of the others put first the name on which his own claims were based, and then added "called by you . . ." with diplomatic formality.

At last in the year 1655 the famous one-legged governor of New Netherland, Peter Stuyvesant, led a Dutch army to the South River, and forced the Swedes to surrender. Soon afterwards, Fort Christina was given a Dutch name, Altena. There was no more heard of New Sweden or of New Sweden River. But the Swedes who had come there as settlers still remained, speaking their own language and calling many places by Swedish names. The Dutch made no attempt to wipe out these lesser names. So they remained, and in the end, by strange and devious ways, a few came over into English.

As the years passed prosperously, New Amsterdam grew to be a compact little Dutch town on the southern tip of Manhattan. Around the fort, the governors granted private holdings in a roughly rectangular pattern. In 1656 the town had 120 houses, and streets were ordered to be "set off and laid out with stakes." These streets had no names, and when the notaries made out a deed, they still had to describe what was meant, as, "the path that Burger Jorisson made to go down to the strand." In 1657 there was a city ordinance about dumping garbage, and its wording shows that the streets were still nameless. Within a year, however, the Council took action, for in 1658 the notaries began to mention streets by their names, and New Amsterdam thus became the first of our cities to have regularly named streets.

Most of these names were simple, merely describing what was there already, such as Bridge Street and Marketfield Street, which thus translated remain still. Another was Pearl Street, but it is harder to explain. Perhaps it means that there they opened oyster shells looking for pearls, or perhaps it is some corruption of *pier,* since it was then along the waterfront and a pier had been built there in 1648.

From the Dutch, however, arose one other name of a street, which was to be far known and often repeated in other cities until it became a symbol, now of power, now of glamour, now of wickedness. The story of that street and of its name might almost stand for the whole history of the nation. First it was an Indian trail leading down from the north through the forest. Close to the lower tip of the island it turned west a few rods, and came to the river. Off that spot the Dutch ships rode at anchor, and the Indians brought their beaver-skins for trade. So the Dutch came to call that trail the Beaver Path. When they settled on the island, the Dutch built their fort just south of where the Beaver Path turned, and cleared a space at the turn, for convenience in trading and to open a field of fire for their guns. This space was not so much like a market-place or square as like a wide road. When the streets were named, a small lane became "Beaver Street," and still remains so. The wide road north of the fort became Heeren Straat, "Lords' Street," in honor of the Lords Directors of the colony. But the people commonly called it simply what it was— Breede Wegh, "broad way."

Another informal Dutch way of speech turned into a name famous in finance. At the same time, its manner of shifting shows how a name may possibly spring from more than one origin. When a fortification was built across the island, the street running along its inner side became officially the Cingel, "Encirclement." But off the end of this street was a *waal,* "anchorage." In addition the fortification itself was much like a *wal,* "wall." Still another common word in New Netherland was *Waal,* "Walloon," because some of these people had been among the first settlers, leaving their name on Waalen Bogt, "Walloons' Bay." Because of the anchorage, and perhaps also for the other two reasons, the Dutch came to speak of that street as De Waal.

Finally, England and France drew together against the Nether-lands. Then the New Englanders grew even bolder against the Dutch, and in 1663 those who had crossed from Connecticut and settled on the eastern end of Long Island moved suddenly against the Dutch towns of the western end and took them over. Immediately they gave them the names of English towns.

In the end Colonel Richard Nicolls sailed with an English fleet, and anchored before New Amsterdam in the year 1664. Against the guns of his four frigates the matters of names and first explorers were of no strength, and old Peter Stuyvesant was short of all munitions except courage. Since he had no means to fight with, he could only surrender. By that very act the three great rivers became for certain, Connecticut, Hudson, and Delaware. On that same day, also, Colonel Nicolls declared New Netherland and New Amsterdam both to be New York.

The end of those old names may be seen in the dating of the letter which the Town Council wrote that very day to their Lords Directors in Amsterdam. First they told the strength of the English in ships and men, to whom were joined "a party of new soldiers both from the North and from Long Island, mostly our deadly enemies." Then they told of their own weakness. At the end they wrote pathetically: "Since we have no longer to depend on your Honors' promises of protection, we, with all the poor, sorrowing and abandoned commonalty here, must fly for refuge to Almighty God."

And signing themselves "your sorrowful and abandoned subjects," they dated the letter "Done in Jorck heretofore named Amsterdam in New Netherland, Anno 1664, the 16th September."

Chapter IX ❨ The History of New York

Wʜᴇɴ Colonel Nicolls changed New Amsterdam to New York, he thought of the noble Duke, his patron. He must also have known the shire and ancient city of England, but to him the name was merely a symbol for man or place, devoid of further meaning. In a history of naming no more need usually be said. Yet now and then, to taste the full richness we should go to the most distant origins. This, then, is the story of the name New York, as language and history reveal it. . . .

First of all, we begin with the yew-tree. It grew in ancient Britain and was called *eburos* in the Celtic language. Yew-trees were sometimes sacred to a god. Again, some ancient Britons bore the name Eburos, perhaps because of living near a yew-tree, just as we still have Mr. Pine and Mr. Birch.

In the course of time a village took its name either from a yew-tree, perhaps a sacred one, or else from a man called Eburos. With an ending to indicate a place, the village was Eburacon.

It grew to be important, as towns then went in Britain. Eventually the Romans conquered it, and in their records the name at last stood surely in the light of history in the Latinized form, Eburacum.

The town soon came to be the chief Roman city of northern Britain, headquarters of the Ninth Legion. Two generations later, the tribesmen rose in revolt and wiped out that legion. But the Romans came again. The Sixth Legion took over at Eburacum, which finally became a well-Romanized city with walls still traceable. Through three centuries the city prospered, and during that time the name changed somewhat, as names will in three centuries. Even the Latin scribes shifted the spelling to Eboracum, and the half-Romanized townspeople in the streets and market-places came to call it Evoroc. Then finally a hard-pressed Emperor withdrew his troops, and the Anglian pirate-ships felt their way up the broad river.

Those conquerors talked a dialect of early English, and neither Eboracum nor Evoroc was anything to them except a rattle of unfamiliar syllables. They transformed the name so that it seemed more familiar and made some sense, just as their descendants a thousand years later would be doing with Indian names. Its first part sounded to the Angles like their own *eofor;* they combined this with a common word *wic,* which resembled the British *-oc.* Thus they got Eoforwic, "wild-boar place." This was by no means the equivalent of Pigtown, for the boar was a highly respected and dangerous wild animal, much more feared than the wolf or the bear.

Eoforwic it was for another three centuries, and then history repeated itself. This time the year was 865, and the new conquerors were Danes under the sons of Ragnar Lothbrok. In their ears the last syllable of Eoforwic was much like their own word *vik,* "bay" or "inlet," from which they themselves were called Vikings. On their tongues Eoforwic became Yorvik, and in the course of a generation or two wore down to York.

About a century later the English reconquered the city, but the descendants of the Danes continued to live there, and their short, convenient name eventually came over into English.

Thus the name York originated, but to explain how it came to be applied as New York is still more of a story, involving a lusty young English king and a buxom low-country princess.

In 1319 when Edward of Windsor, eldest son and heir of Edward II, was only seven years old, negotiations for his marriage were already under way. An alliance with the Count of Hainaut (in what is now Belgium) was politically desirable, and the Count had several eligible daughters. But the continuation of the English dynasty was important, and the question arose as to whether these daughters would be likely to supply heirs. In modern times a competent neutral gynecologist would be called in, but in the absence of specialists the delicate task was entrusted to the Bishop of Exeter, as a dignitary combining priestly decorum with worldly wisdom. His report upon one daughter was presented under a careful title: *Inspection and Description of the Daughter of the Count of Hainaut, Philippa by name.* The description began systematically at the top: "The lady whom we saw has not uncomely hair." It went on, omitting little:

Her neck, shoulders and all her body and lower limbs are reasonably well shaped; all her limbs are well set and unmaimed; and nothing is amiss so far as a man may see. Moreover, she is brown of skin all over.

With a certain relief, however, we read at the end: "the young lady will be of the age of nine years on St. John's Day next."

Still, the careful English statesmen hesitated, and in some later year apparently they sent as another deputation a bishop and certain "lords temporal." In Hainaut these were admitted to a chamber "privy and secret." There (hidden perhaps like Polonius behind the arras) they observed the Count's five daughters "disheveled," which means literally "with their hair down." Afterwards the ambassadors consulted together, and the Bishop spoke out roundly, "We will have her with the good hips, for she will bear good sons." These "pleasant words" of the Bishop tickled the temporal lords, and they joked at him over his "mickle skill" about women, declaring he must have had "right great experience."

The ambassadors reported favorably upon the well-hipped Philippa, and when Edward was only sixteen, they were married.

Queen Philippa vindicated the Bishop's knowledge of womankind. In two years an heir arrived, a fine boy, known to history as the Black Prince. Philippa continued to show her mettle, bearing seven sons and five daughters. The great number of heirs proved in the end an embarrassment, and incidentally became involved with the naming of New York.

For, like other people, kings wish to set up their children in the world, and Edward always cultivated the grand style. He set out to find dukedoms for his sons. There happened at this time to be no noble family holding a title from the great northern city and county, and the King was thus able to preempt it for his fifth son, Edmund of Langley, whom he created the first Duke of York.

From these numerous sons of Philippa sprang eventually the Wars of the Roses. The Dukes of York became kings, and when the Tudors overthrew the Yorkists, the title had such regal suggestions that it was retained for the royal family, as a convenient honor for the second son.

In the seventeenth century, this title was bestowed upon James, second son of Charles I. This James proved a far from exemplary prince. He was bigoted and stupid, and as a libertine was even more unblushing (at the same time less witty) than his brother Charles II. He was not without talents, possessing some military skill, and fathering twenty acknowledged children.

While the noble Duke was thus engaged, New Netherland was growing prosperously. In 1664 easy-going Charles granted it to his brother the Duke, and Colonel Nicolls took possession. Perhaps he had had private instructions from the King or the Duke, or perhaps he sought only to pay a bit of obvious flattery, but in any case he lost no time in renaming it.

It may still be asked why the name was New York rather than simply York, after the usual custom of the English. But the town was already called New Amsterdam, and so probably by analogy it became New York.

Thus it came about that the town at the end of the Beaver Path drew its name from the Celtic word for yew-tree, but more immediately from a not-at-all-admirable duke.

Chapter X ❴ Of the French

AFTER the Sieur de Champlain had fought the Iroquois in that famous battle, he gave no more memorable names. He kept to the north, for the Iroquois always fought the French. Thus during a time so long that the first children born in Canada grew to be tall Frenchmen who had never seen France, the French established only five names which would be great in the land to the south.

First, they came to the lowest of the lakes which are like inland seas, and knew it as the Lake of the Onondagas after the Indians living there. But in the end they took a name from the language of the Hurons, in which a lake was called *ontara*. To this word the Hurons added the ending *-io,* which might mean "good," or "large," or "beautiful." So arose Ontario, meaning vaguely "fine lake."

Next the French voyaged by canoes up a river, and crossed a low divide, and came downstream to a lake so large that for a while they called it merely Mer Douce, "Freshwater Sea." Later they called it the Lake of the Hurons, because their friends the Hurons lived there. But this name was French, not Indian, and meant a miner or any kind of rough peasant. Also it was like the word *hure,* which meant the bristly head of a wild boar. Father Lalemont thought the French gave that name to the first of the tribe they met because the Hurons cut their hair to form a bristling crest, and therefore looked like boars.

Beyond and above this lake the French also heard of another one. So they called it Lac Supérieur, "Upper Lake," as if only two lakes were concerned. The English later took the name over without translating it, and so they thought it had another meaning, as one of them wrote: "Lake Superior . . . is so called on account of its being superior in magnitude to any of the lakes on that vast continent."

Now and then, however, the French made some brief truce with the Iroquois, and during one of these times a French priest came to an Indian town called Ongniaahra, "point of land cut in two," because it stood near Lake Ontario, where a wide river cut through the land. Farther up this river, the Indians said, was a waterfall; but the priest did not go to look at it, probably thinking all waterfalls were alike. The French remembered the name of that town, and called the river after it, and later the waterfall. But they twisted it on their tongues until it became Ongiara and finally Niagara.

Also the French as early as the time of their coming to Niagara had heard of another lake to the south, though for fear of the Iroquois none of them went there for many years. They called it often Lac du Chat, "Lake of the Cat," because the Indians south of it were known to them as the Cats. Some of the French thought the name arose because of the many wildcats in that country, but it was really because that tribe like many others called themselves after a beast which they held sacred. They might better have been termed the Panthers, for in their own language they called themselves *Yenrish*, "it is long-tailed," in that roundabout fashion setting off the panther from the smaller lynxes and wildcats with short tails. These tribesmen, like the panther, were subtle and fierce warriors.

At last in 1653 there was again a truce with the Iroquois, and a black-robed priest went to live among them. There he made a few converts. Also, that winter, the Iroquois danced about the kettle, preparing themselves for combat, and the father, hoping thus to divert war from Canada, promised that the French as their share would put gunpowder under the kettle. So all the upper tribes of Iroquois—Senecas, Cayugas, Oneidas, and Onondagas—went to fight the Panthers, and many were killed on both sides, or captured and burned. In the end, the Iroquois, who were more numerous, drove the Panthers back upon their stockaded town and besieged it. Then an Iroquois who was newly baptized shouted out presumptuously to the Panthers, "The Master of Life fights for us! If you fight against him, you are lost!" But the besieged answered back boldly: "Who is this Master of our lives? We know none but our own axes and right arms!" Then the Iroquois attacked, but were driven back again and again. At last they brought up their canoes and using them as shields reached the stockade; then leaning their canoes like ladders, the warriors of the Onondagas scaled the stockade. Thus they entered the town, and within it (as the reverend father wrote): "They made such slaughter of women and children that in places there was blood knee-deep." Thus the Panthers were broken, and the survivors were scattered or led captive. Yet, as may happen with a brave but vanquished people, though they were destroyed, the name lived on. The French shaped Yenrish into something easier to pronounce, and thus men still commemorate the undaunted Panthers when they say Erie.

Afterward, however, the Iroquois again made their raids northward, and in the years when the English and Dutch and Swedes were naming the lands farther south, fear of the Iroquois kept the French close to their own stockades.

At last in 1659 the wars in Europe came to an end for a while, and France under Louis, the Sun-King, stood gloriously as the first among kingdoms. Then, since there was for the moment no glory or power to be won in Europe, the French turned to the west. For, certainly, when all Europe acknowledged the power of Louis, it was not fitting that Frenchmen scarcely dared plow their own fields for fear of a few rascals of Iroquois. So new governors, and priests, and soldiers went to Canada, and the orders were to spread the rule of France. In a few years the French reached out farther than in all the time before, and suddenly many great names began to be spoken.

The French who journeyed to the west in those years were of

three kinds; so they gave names of three kinds—for names are always shadows of the men who give them.

First among these explorers went the men born in Canada, French and half-breeds, called "forest-runners." They were simple men, and when they named a place, they used simple words, calling it Green Bay, or Big River. But these men also knew the languages of the Algonquins and Hurons; so more often they took over the Indian names.

Along with the forest-runners went the priests, and like priests everywhere they loved the names of saints. So still from their naming we find here and there a St. Joseph, or St. Ignace, or St. Anthony. But the priests also, being missionaries, came to know the Indian languages, and so they too used the Indian names.

With the others went also the officers and gentlemen of France, who sought to win fortunes and serve the King. They liked best to give names flattering and honoring the King and his ministers. But they also, like the others, mingled with the Indians.

So in the end it worked out that of many great names which the French then established only two were French in language. No one can say always what Frenchman first used those names. The forest-runners could not write at all, and so perhaps a name was already well established before some priest or officer put it on paper. Sometimes also the name was known by report even before any explorers had reached so far.

Thus as early as 1640 there were tales of the Eriniouai. By better report it was written later as Aliniouek or Iliniouek. But anyone knowing the language would see that the last of that word was only an ending, and the root of that tribal name was Ilini, of which the meaning was simply "man." The French added s to make a plural, and finally it became even more French-looking as Illinois. Of these people one of the first of the French to visit them wrote: "To say 'Illinois' is as much as to say in their language, 'the men,' as if the other savages were to be thought mere animals."

Then the French began to call the fifth of those great lakes the Lake of the Illinois, because that tribe then lived on its western shore. This name did not last long, because the tribe shifted hunting-grounds. So the lake came to be called merely Michi-guma, meaning "big water," though there was also a tribe of that name. Later a priest called it St. Joseph, and a gentleman called it Dauphin, but in the end Michi-guma became Michigan, and survived. The name Illinois, however, followed the tribe, and the French applied it to the southward-flowing river where the tribe afterwards lived.

There were also some rivers that took their names by descrip-tion. One was in the Iroquois language from a word meaning "road," or sometimes "river," to which was added as in Ontario the ending "fine." The French wrote the whole word as Ohio.

Another was a smaller river which took its name from the "good land" there, in the Algonquian language, Milo-aki. After many shifts of spelling it became Milwaukee.

Almost at the southern tip of the Lake of the Illinois, also called Lake Michigan, a low and swampy plain stretched away between two small rivers. In early summer that plain was pink with the blossoms of the little wild onions growing there. So the Algonquian-speaking Indians called it "onion-place." To the French this became Chicagou, and they used it for the name of one of the rivers. In 1688, when there could hardly have been doubt about the meaning, a Frenchman wrote: "We arrived at the place called Chicagou which, according to what can be learned about it, has taken this name from the amount of garlic growing wild in that vicinity." Two other early Frenchmen also mentioned the onion or garlic in that region.

A great city took its name from this place and that river became for a while very odorous; so jokes were made about the origin of the name. It happens also that in the Algonquian language words related to that for *onion* or *garlic* apply also to the skunk, and certain kinds of bad-smelling filth. So some said that the city was really Skunk-town, or something worse. Then the city's defenders raised the claim that the sounds really meant anything strong, so that the city was Strong-town. Actually the meaning of Chicago seems better settled than almost any other early Indian name, be-cause the Frenchman took the trouble to record it. Since he wrote so early and since wild onions grew there, he can scarcely have been mistaken.

During these years the French hunted for a passage to the South Sea. They often asked the Indians, and some of the Indians told them tales of a "great water" farther to the west. The Algonquins who had fled west to escape the Iroquois also reported about 1659, as a priest wrote down the story, "a beautiful river, large, wide, deep, and worthy of comparison, they say, with our river St. Lawrence." Since the priests wrote these reports in French, no one can be certain what words the Indians used, but being Algonquins they most likely said *miss* for "big" and *sipi* for "river." Finally, in 1666, though no Frenchman had yet been there, a priest wrote down, "the great river named Messipi."

There was a Frenchman named Louis Jolliet, Canadian-born and skilled at voyaging. Also he had gone to school with the Jesuits, and been to France for study, so that men called him Sieur Jolliet. Thus, all in one man, he was something of forest-runner and priest and king's officer. In 1669 he went to the farther lakes, and on his return led the first French party through the narrow passage from Lake Huron to Lake Erie. After that time the French knew that place as the "strait," and the English preserved the word as Detroit. Three years later, Frontenac the governor fittingly chose Jolliet to discover for France the river Messipi.

There was also a priest, a black-robed Jesuit named Jacques Marquette, who served in the mission at Michilimackinac, where he heard tales of that great river far to the west, and grew eager to go there and preach the gospel.

Then, on December 8, 1672, Jolliet came to the mission with orders that Marquette was to be the priest to go on that expedition. At that news Marquette was overjoyed, and since it was the day of the Immaculate Conception, he placed the voyage under the protection of the Blessed Virgin, "promising her that, if she gave us the favor of discovering the great river, I would name it Conception."

They wintered at Michilimackinac, and then in May, 1673,

when the ice was gone from the lake, they set out to the west, across the open water, in two birch-bark canoes. In the one went Marquette with three boatmen, and in the other Jolliet with two, for he himself took his shift at the paddling. This was a famous expedition, and from it also came back more of our great names than from any other voyage.

First they followed the northern shore of what they still called the Lake of the Illinois. Then they entered that arm of water which was known, after the Indians living there, as the "Bay of the Stinkers." But this name perplexed the French, for they could not notice that these Indians smelled any worse than the others. So Marquette thought the name might come because of the odors from the swamps. But also the French called it Baie Verte, and the English kept this name as Green Bay. The reason for it was, as some said, that when voyagers left Michilimackinac at the end of winter and followed the lake-shore south to this bay, they found the leaves green on the trees by the time they arrived there.

At the head of this bay the voyagers brought their canoes into the river then known as Mascoutens for an Indian tribe, and now called Fox for a tribe that came to live there later. Going upstream, they passed through lakes and swamps, and after a portage came to a west-flowing river. There, from their Indian guides, they heard the first of the great names which were to spring from that voyage, and recorded it as Mescousing, or Mesconsing. What it means, no one can be sure, but soon the French spelled it Ouisconsing, and in English it became Wisconsin River.

At last, near the middle of June in 1673, they came to the great river, which was already known by name. They wrote the word as Mississipi. But Marquette, it would seem, called it also Conception, and Jolliet called it Buade, after the family name of Count Frontenac, the governor. Thus all at once the river had three names—an Indian name for the boatmen, a religious name for the priest, and a political name for the officer.

During eight days they paddled down that river, seeing no trace of man. Then they made out some tracks on the water's edge. They landed, and Jolliet and Marquette followed a path to a village. There they found some of the Illinois, of a branch called Peouarea. But soon this tribe migrated back to their old lands farther south and east, and took their name there as Peoria.

As it seems, although the record is far from clear, the explorers heard from the Peouarea of another tribe living farther inland on a river, and called Moingouena. Afterwards this stream came to be Rivière des Moingouenas. But the forest-runners liked always to shorten names, and so they made this into Rivière des Moings. Still later, others thought it was really "river of the monks," and so it was written Des Moines. This was the third great name of the voyage.

Still paddling downstream they came in a few days to a wide river pouring in from the northwest, very muddy and swift. From some Indians they learned its name as Pekitanoui, or "muddy." On their maps, Jolliet and Marquette put down the name of various tribes living along its course, as they must have learned them from Indians near the mouth. Among these tribes were the Ouchage and the Messouri. Afterwards the French called that river by the name of the first of these tribes, changing it to Osage. But finally that became the name of a smaller river, and the greater one became Missouri. As to its meaning, *miss* may mean "big." But whether the whole name means "big muddy," or "big canoes" or something else, is a matter of doubt.

At the mouth of that river the Indians told also of other tribes, and the names of three of them stand on the earliest maps as Maha, Kansa, and Ouaouiatonon.

Of the first came Omaha, meaning "upstream people." For, in their legends, these tribesmen told that once they came from the west to the banks of the great river. There they divided. Those who went to the south called themselves Quapaw, or "downstream people," and the others took the name oppositely.

To Kansa the French added an *s* for a plural, and so got Kansas, first for the tribe and then for the river. But the meaning is lost, except for guesswork. This tribe, from 1601, had been known to the Spaniards as Escansaques, but the tradition of the name followed the French form.

Ouaouiatonon, it would seem, the French treated in another way. They dropped the ending, which may have meant only "tribe" or "people." Then they had left a strange word of vowels —Ouaouia. This, passing through many spellings, became Iowa.

Still paddling on, the seven voyagers in their two canoes came to a river flowing in from the east. For this they kept an Indian word Ouaboukigou, which some think means "shining white." Soon the French shortened it to Ouabache, and the English made it Wabash. But this was the same stream which higher up was already called Ohio. Then, as often happens when two ends of a river are discovered and given different names, men used both for a while, but in the end one was victorious, and the other became the name of a tributary.

At last in the month of July they came to a village and tribe called Akansea, and near it another great river flowed in from the west. Jolliet called the river Bazire after a friend who was a fur-trader in Montreal. But in the end it took its name from the tribe. The French soon spelled the name Arkansa, and making a plural as with Illinois and Kansas, they wrote Arkansas.

Then from Akansea the seven voyagers turned back, fearing that if they went farther south they might fall into the hands of the Spaniards. They returned by way of the river of the Illinois, and hauled their canoes across the portage called Chicagou. So it may be this last also should be counted among their names.

Thus Jolliet, Marquette, and five boatmen, though they voyaged only during one summer, set down more of our great names than any other explorers. Ponce de León himself left only one, and some notable voyagers like Cabrillo and Hudson left none at all. Even John Smith, for all his journeys, may be credited with only four. Yet in this single summer these Frenchmen set down ten great names, or eleven, if Chicago is counted. These names survived so well, because other Frenchmen followed soon afterwards, and the tradition was never lost. Also, all the names were drawn from the languages of the Indians; priests and gentlemen tried to replace some of them with religious or political names, but the Indian terms served as a common ground for all the French.

As to the meanings, they are more uncertain even than is usual with Indian names, for they were mostly tribal. Such names for tribes were often so old that they had lost all sure meaning. In any case, to the Frenchmen who established the names, they meant nothing except that a certain tribe lived there. (So in a modern city a district may be called Irishtown because some Irish once lived there. But why the Irish themselves were first so called is another matter.)

These, then, are the certain names of that summer's voyage, which now stand upon rivers and states and cities—Wisconsin, Peoria, Des Moines, Missouri, Osage, Omaha, Kansas, Iowa, Wabash, and Arkansas.

After they returned from the village of Akansea, Jolliet went on to report to the Governor in Montreal, with the maps and his journal in a little strong-box. But when he was within sight of the town, the canoe overturned in La Chine Rapids, and all except Jolliet were drowned, and the box was lost. So what we know of that voyage comes from the record of Marquette, and from what Jolliet put down from memory. Jolliet's later service took him northward, and he never returned to that western river.

As for Père Marquette—after the return he fell sick, and remained among the Mascoutins. In the next November he started south again to establish a mission. Though he was taken with a bloody flux upon the journey, he came at last to some of the Illinois, and lived with them a few days. On Easter he took possession of that land in the name of Christ, and called his mission there for the Immaculate Conception, as he had promised. Then, still weakening, he set out upon his return with two boatmen.

They came to the Lake of the Illinois, and while they were journeying along its eastern shore the boatmen despaired of his life. He prepared holy water for his death, and talked with them of how he should be buried. As they were thus voyaging, the father saw a little river flowing into the lake and by it a hill. On that hill, he told his men, they should bury him. But the men pushed on, hoping still to save him and not wanting to halt so early in the day. Then, as at the will of God, a contrary wind came up, so that the boatmen had to put about and enter the river. By that water-side Père Marquette at the age of thirty-eight made ready for his death—he who had voyaged to far Akansea and written down so many names that would resound in the future. And there at last he set out peacefully upon a longer voyage.

His two men buried him devoutly, ringing a little bell as he had told them; and they set up a cross. After two years some Christian Indians came there, and took up his bones, and brought them to holy ground in the Mission of St. Ignace. But they did not take away that memory, and voyagers by the lake-shore remembered the little stream. So, even yet, it is called Père Marquette River.

There was also Robert, Sieur de la Salle, a man like Sir Walter Raleigh, more famous than fortunate. He built forts and gave names; but his forts crumbled, and generally his names were forgotten.

Four years after Père Marquette had died by the little river, La Salle built the first ship above the falls of Niagara. He sailed gallantly along Lake Erie and through the strait already called Detroit. On August 12, 1679, he entered a smaller lake between the two greater ones. He, or his priest Father Hennepin, called it for Sainte Clare, the maiden of Assisi and follower of St. Francis in poverty. This name still lives, though the English have made it St. Clair.

La Salle gave one yet greater name. For, as he explored for France, he came to see that the vast central region was nameless. As yet it was called only Florida, or more vaguely still, Quivira; but these were Spanish. Canada and Nouvelle France were names only for the North, and moreover (since he wished to be the ruler of the new region) La Salle could not well call it part of Canada. He knew that Jolliet had called the region of the upper river Frontenacie for the Governor, and that the Governor had thought better to place his own name upon Lake Ontario, and to compliment the minister Colbert by changing Frontenacie to Colbertie. But La Salle was no man to think in terms of governors or even of ministers, and felt rather that this vast new country was of royal rank. So he took the name of the Sun-King, and adding a suffix, wrote in a letter of August 22, 1681—Louisiane. When he reached the mouth of the Mississippi on April 9, 1682, he erected on a post the royal arms, and "in the name of the most high, mighty, invincible, and victorious Prince, Louis the Great, by the Grace of God, King of France and Navarre, Fourteenth of the name," he took formal possession of that country Louisiane.

The story of the Mississippi is enough to be told by itself. What name it may first have borne is lost beyond any searching. Even when it still flowed from beneath the vast northern ice-cap, men may have lived on its lower course, and called it White River or Milk River, as men still call streams which bear in their water the fine glacier-silt. But tribes came and went, leaving no record. So the earliest certain names are those that the Spaniards wrote down.

First of the Europeans, in 1519, Pineda coasted the gulf-shore and afterwards on maps stood the name of the river Espiritu Santo, "Holy Spirit." But no one can be sure what river this may have been, whether the Mississippi, or some bay. Or it may be that this name was scarcely more than a guess; for from so much land it would seem safe enough to assume that somewhere a mighty river must flow out.

First of the Europeans who surely saw the river were De Soto and his men in 1541. De Soto gave it no name that we know of, for he was not a man who cared about naming. He seems rather to have been content with the old name Espiritu Santo, and his men called it most often simply Río Grande, "big river." When his scribes, however, inquired its name of the Indians, they found that it had many. This was only to be expected, for there were many tribes living near such a long river, and they spoke different languages. Also, like other Indians, they may have had a name for every bend and reach. So the scribes wrote down that it was called variously Chucagua, Tamalisieu, Nilco, and Mico, and that at its mouth it was called simply The River. We know also that it has been called Okachitto, Olsimochitto, Namosi-sipu, Sassagoula, and Culata.

But far to the north in the land of lakes and wild rice lived the tribes who spoke the widespread Algonquian language—Chippewas, Miamis, Outagamis, Illinois, and many others. Along the edge of their country flowed a branch of the river, and though there it was much smaller, yet it was still the largest stream that those northern tribes had seen. They differed a little in their speech; some said Kitchi-zibi, and some Mis-sipi, and others Misi-sipi. Whatever they said, the meaning was plain, for among their commonest words was that meaning "big," and in differing forms it still stands, not only in Mississippi, Michigan and Massachusetts, but also probably in Missouri. Moreover, *sipi* was plainly "river," and it also may be found in Chesapeake. This then was the word that the French heard, variously sounded as they passed from tribe to tribe.

Yet there was no just reason why this name as said by these northern tribes should have displaced all the others, and even caused the smaller branch of the river to be held the chief one. This came about more by accident. For, when Jolliet and Marquette first approached the river, they had as guides two Miamis. Then, as they passed farther and farther down the river, they thought of it as having still the same name, though the Indians living there might not have recognized the words. Even when they passed the mouth of the great muddy Pekitanoui, they considered that to be only a tributary, not stopping to think that it might be longer than the branch called Mississippi, and in some other ways too a greater river. So, because the explorers first voyaged *down* the river, the northern name spread along it clear to the mouth. But if the explorers had come from the south, they would naturally have called the river by some southern name. When they reached the forking, they might have taken either to be the main river. Or, the lower stream and each of the upper branches might have been known and named separately by overland travelers before their joining was learned. Then, as has happened with other rivers, there might have been a different name for each of the three, and men would have said that the lower river was "formed by the union" of the two upper branches.

Even after it was well known, the name Mississippi did not certainly establish itself for some time. Jolliet had called it Buade; and Marquette, Conception. Frontenac and La Salle tried to make it Colbert. A few years later, others called it Louisiane, and St. Louis. But perhaps because they could not agree, finally they all used the Indian name that came from the far north.

When the English approached the river, they called it sometimes Malabanchia. This was a Choctaw name, "place of foreign speech," and was used because of the French living upon it. But in the end the English also said Mississippi.

Chapter XI ❨ How the Spaniards named another kingdom

Frst of all, in 1541, Coronado's men knew the name of some Indians called Teyas, living on the plains eastward. Now and again in the next century some Spaniard heard vague stories from the north and east of a people so called who were ruled by a king, and a few adventurers went in that direction to trade for skins or hunt for pearls in the river-mouths. Then in 1683 seven Indians from the east came to the Spanish governor at El Paso to ask for missionaries and for help in a war. These emissaries talked much of the tribes to the east, and particularly of what the Spaniards understood to be "the great kingdom of Texas." That realm was so rich (said these poor wanderers from the cactus-plains) that there the people even fed grain to their horses! Also, it was close to Gran Quivira, so that the people of the two kingdoms visited back and forth almost every day. By this time the Spaniards had heard too many such stories to get greatly excited. Nevertheless, the Governor sent an expedition, which did not find Quivira or even "el gran Reyno de Texas."

In the next year La Salle landed on that coast, and the Spaniards became concerned for their sovereignty. They began to take more interest in the region, even after they knew that the French colony was broken up. In 1689 a Spanish expedition arrived at a village where the Indians came out to meet them in peaceful fashion, calling "Techas! Techas!" This proved to be a greeting which meant "Friends! Friends!" From that time on, the Spaniards realized that Texas was not really the name of a kingdom or a tribe, but was this greeting, which was also used for a group of allied tribes who spoke this word among themselves and so were known as "Texas" by some of the neighboring Indians. But by this time the idea of the "great kingdom" had taken some hold on the imagination. Though the priests and soldiers who went into the country knew that it was really a salutation rather than a tribe, the governors in the official letters continued to use Texas. Also, out of jealousy of the French, the Spaniards began to explore that country, and so the name was established.

As usual, each of the Spanish explorers was more likely to give his own names than to find out what the places had already been called, and so the names were often changed. As always, the Spanish took naming seriously. Thus, when Don Domingo Terán set out, he received a list of seventeen official instructions for the expedition, and the thirteenth was: "The said governor shall give names to such important places, rivers, and woods as have no names."

Terán set out in 1691 across Texas, and in his company was the friar Damián Massanet. Terán not only obeyed his Instruction No. 13, but even went far beyond it, giving a name to every place he reached, although it may have had a known Indian name and been already named once or twice by preceding explorers. At the same time Fray Damián kept a diary, and in it he recorded a complete series of his own names, nearly always different from those of Terán. The result was perhaps the greatest confusion since the Tower of Babel.

One of the very few places upon which Terán and Massanet agreed was a small river which they reached on May 13, 1691. This was the day of Saint Anthony of Padua, the famous Franciscan, who is always ready to aid the pious in the finding of lost articles. So the stream was called San Antonio. The name remained upon the mission later founded there, and from the mission sprang a city.

Chapter XII ❨ When King Charles came to his own

WHILE the French and Spanish had been exploring far to the west, the English had established themselves more firmly along the coast, founding new colonies and absorbing the old Dutch and Swedish settlements.

The government which the English set up in what had been New Netherland interfered little with local customs. The change of New Netherland and New Amsterdam to New York was necessary as a symbol of the English rule. But Colonel Nicolls effectively changed only one other name. This was of the second Dutch town in importance. Its official name was Fort Orange, but the people called it commonly Beverwyck, "Beaver-town," because it was the depot for the inland fur-trade. Nicolls took the Duke of York's Scottish title, Duke of Albany, and from this beginning the name Albany spread also to many other places.

This second title almost gained even greater fame, when Nicolls applied it to the region west of the Hudson, in the Latin form Albania. There, however, it was suddenly wiped out with the news that the Duke had granted that region to his two friends Lord Berkeley and Sir George Carteret. The latter was of the island of Jersey, and to the Duke himself that name also was of good omen, since he had once found asylum there during the troubled times of the Civil War. Accordingly the charter was made to read: "which said tract of land is hereafter to be called by the name or names of New Cesarea or New Jersey."

The seat of government for the new colony drew from the same island, again with double origin. First, there was Carteret's wife, in spite of her royalist connections, a Puritanical lady. Samuel Pepys went to dine with the Carterets one day in 1666, and afterwards wrote in his diary:

She cries out of the vices of the Court, and how they are going to set up plays . . . She do much cry out upon these things, and that which she believes will undo the whole nation.

But second, there was an island in Jersey, a fortress on a half-tidal island, and Carteret had held it gallantly for six weeks against the Roundhead besiegers. It too was a name of good omen. So, most likely with reference both to Castle Elizabeth and to Lady Elizabeth, the new town took that name.

Most of the settlers who came into New Jersey at first were from New England, and they brought with them their own habit of naming towns. They thus founded Shrewsbury and Monmouth, and of greater note they transplanted Newark. In later years some thought that this name was to be taken as two words, to show that there the pious settlers planted a New Ark of the Covenant, but more likely they followed only the common custom of echoing English towns.

These New Englanders also established their own ways of naming, so that even yet in northern New Jersey there are Stony Brook, Beden Brook, Bound Brook and others; but in southern New Jersey such streams are known as runs or creeks.

Almost by accident the grant to Carteret gave rise to still another colony. New Jersey extended only as far as the Delaware, but west of that river lay most of the old Swedish settlements. Since their conquest by Peter Stuyvesant, the Dutch had ruled them as part of New Netherland, and although they were beyond the legal limits of the Duke's patent, Colonel Nicolls did not admit the claims of Maryland and Virginia. Instead, even after losing New Jersey, he governed them still as an isolated bit of New York. The region could no longer be called New Sweden, and the Dutch had known it as the settlements on South River. By the analogy of this Dutch usage, the English began to refer to it by their own name for the river. As early as 1665 it was definitely known as Delaware, and thus became the second colony to take its name from a river. In later years this little strip of land was joined with a larger neighbor, but it never quite lost the tradition of independence and name, and in the end both were preserved.

In this little region also occurred what was perhaps the first instance of a practice which was to spread far. In the earliest years the rough Dutch fur-traders had called a stream Hoeren Kill, and the equally masculine English who followed them had taken this over as Whorekill. Such a name was good enough as long as only fur-traders lived there, but when time came for a more respectable settlement, no decent woman wished to live at a place so called. So it was re-named Deal after an English town. Thus, when the frontier was still within earshot of Atlantic surf, restraint of language began.

During the long years of the Commonwealth, the Massachusetts General Court had ruled as it wished at home, and had also bullied the neighboring colonies. To the north it had annexed the old lands of Gorges and Mason and organized them into Yorkshire County. But with the conquest of New Netherland, the situation changed. Massachusetts and Connecticut, the most king-hating of the colonies, came suddenly to hold the weakest position of them all.

In 1665 three King's Commissioners began an investigation. Though the Court kept up a bold front, its situation was perilous. In June the Commissioners entered Yorkshire, and made quick work of the Massachusetts jurisdiction. Their first report read: "another province called Yorkshire now, by the Massachusetts, under whose government we found it, formerly called the Province of Maine." Then on June 23, as if in symbol of a world gone topsy-turvy, the clerk of the local court turned his book upside-down and began to make his entries working from the back forwards, and writing "Province of Maine" by order of the King's Commissioners.

The Commissioners then went farther south, and on July 16th addressed a letter from "Pascataquay River." This was the region which the rulers of Massachusetts had annexed by virtue of their interpretation of "Merrimack River," at a time when no one could well argue with them. Now the situation was reversed.

The local inhabitants were hard pressed. They had no quarrel with Massachusetts, but their land-titles might be forfeited unless they could make their peace with the King. So at this time the old name given by Captain Mason was brought out of hiding, and in a petition to the King on July 20, 1665, some of the local men referred to themselves as "inhabitants of New Hampshire."

Massachusetts fought stubbornly, however, for more than ten years. In 1677 the case was finally brought before the Lords Chief Justices in England. The chief legal point at issue was the old question of the definition of "Merrimack River." The decision as rendered, however, seems to indicate that the Justices hardly took the trouble to listen to the long arguments, but voted on a political basis. Massachusetts was in bad odor, and almost rebellious against the Crown. So the sharp dealing of the Massachusetts Court against Plymouth Colony at last met with poetic justice—Maine was confirmed as against Yorkshire.

In the end, however, Massachusetts won a substance of victory by purchasing the Gorges patents. Naturally, no attempt was made to change the name, and under the restored rule of Massachusetts the northern country continued to be Maine.

Maine was thus finally fixed in 1677, fifty-five years after the Gorges and Mason charter, and thirty-eight years after Charles I had flatly ordered it to be known, "not by any other name or names whatsoever." Along the Piscataqua the decision was delayed for still two more years. On September 18, 1679, however, Charles II set the Great Seal upon a proclamation declaring "ye towns of Portsmouth, Hampton, Dover, and Exeter" to be "The Province of New-Hampshire."

Purely as a matter of names, the result in the North was good. New Hampshire was a little cumbersome, but like New Jersey and New York it preserved historical and sentimental bonds with the mother country. And certainly to have had one large region called New York and another Yorkshire would have been perpetually a nuisance.

Charles II, unlike his father, was a confirmer of names, not a bestower. In 1663 he re-granted the territory which his father had given to Sir Robert Heath, using the same name Carolina. The proprietors were nine English gentlemen interested in the new colony as a business venture, but their names were placed in flattery upon counties, and bays, and broad rivers.

There was George Monk, for instance, second son of a small gentleman, a professional soldier with a talent for making himself indispensable, and picking the winner. In the stream of a troubled time he steered among the currents so well that in the Carolina charter he stood, forsooth, "George Duke of Albemarle, Master of Our Horse and Captain General of all our Forces." And so the broad waters of Albemarle Sound stretch off mile after mile, though George Monk never sailed them.

So also it was with Lord Anthony Ashley Cooper. Where a ship-captain saw two rivers flowing into a bay, he called one the Ashley and its twin the Cooper. And the others too—Clarendon,

Craven, the Berkeleys, Carteret, Colleton. You will find their names along that coast, and not the names of the folk who lived there, and came to love the land, and were buried in it.

But for the chief settlement of Carolina, they took the King's own name, and called it Charles Town.

Before many years had passed, the northern settlements of Carolina were divided in government from the southern. Then it would have been better perhaps if one section had taken a new name, but Carolina was established in the charter and a different name might have endangered the title. So about 1690 men began to write North Carolina and South Carolina, and thus rather cumbersomely the names remained.

In the early spring of 1681 England was in an uproar. The cry was "No Popery!" and newly elected members of Parliament rode through the shires with their armed servants behind them. Men whispered not too softly that the son might go the way of his father.

But Charles II was too good a politician. First of all, he summoned Parliament to meet at Oxford, removed from the London mob. Also he knew accurately enough just how far the English people could be pressed. Nevertheless, Charles must have been worried, and have felt the need of something to take his mind off his troubles.

He left London for Oxford, spent the week-end at Windsor, and was probably still there on Monday. On that day, March 14, 1681, an English gentleman of somewhat unusual stamp waited upon him with a matter of business, the settling of a claim against the Crown in exchange for some American land. The gentleman's name was William Penn.

The King's private opinion of Penn can hardly be known. Charles was never a fool, and so doubtless had a respect for Penn's courage and honesty. But their ideas about life were wholly opposite, and Charles must chiefly have regarded Penn as an obstinate and humorless enthusiast, wearing eccentric Quaker clothing, preaching in the streets to the rabble, and lying sometimes in jail.

Nevertheless Penn would write off a debt of £16,000 for some lands, and a charter had been prepared. As with Maryland, it would seem, the space for the name had been left blank, to be arranged between the Crown and the proprietor.

William Penn in his dull Quaker clothes stood before the King's secretary, and the name he proposed was New Wales, because the lands were said to be hilly, like Wales.

But the Secretary was himself a Welshman, and doubtless no lover of Quakers. So he refused to put down New Wales. Instead then of taking the matter to the King over the Secretary's head, Penn amicably suggested Sylvania, a Latin form meaning "forest land." This name, like New Wales, was what was to be expected of Penn, for as a Quaker he was no respecter of persons and could not suggest a name honoring any person, even the King.

The Secretary, as the story can be put together, took the name in to the King; and the King, who had made many a better witticism in his day, then perpetrated what seems to be a rather dull practical joke. When the charter came back, the name was Pennsylvania.

Good Mr. Penn was shocked, even appalled, "lest it should be looked upon as a vanity in me." He stood no longer on ceremony with the Secretary, but demanded to see the King. He came to the royal presence, but his honest indignation beat in vain against the nonchalant manner of Charles, backed by the power of the Crown. "He said it was past," wrote Penn later, and that he "would take it upon him." But also, always the gentleman, Charles was polite enough to give a hole for escape by saying that the name was really in honor of Penn's father, the Admiral.

Far from satisfied, Penn retired. Knowing his way about in the courts of kings, he tried offering an undersecretary the magnificent sum of twenty guineas to alter the name in transcript. That the undersecretary remained virtuous in a Court where virtue was not much regarded is good evidence that the name came directly from the King, so that no secretary dared tamper with it.

Penn withdrew in defeat, and wrote immediately to a friend. His pleasure at the fulfillment of his grant was soured with the appalling accident of what had happened to the name, and his account broke down in grammar and logic. He wrote: "The King would give it in honor of my father," and in the next sentence declared contradictorily that Pennsylvania should be taken to mean "high or head woodlands," since *pen* in Welsh means "head"—"as Penmanmoire in Wales, and Penrith in Cumberland, and Penn in Buckinghamshire."

Thus the name was established, though the spelling might vary a little. Most men will agree that the outcome in the end was good, for New Wales is not so original or poetical a heritage as Pennsylvania.

Since he thus met humiliation over the name of his whole colony, Penn perhaps came to pay more attention to the other names. It may be argued that in the end he had more influence than John Smith or any other man, early or late.

First of all, he considered a name of the chief city, for from the first he planned this to be no small clearing in the forest, but the capital of a great province. So it needed a name befitting its dignity, and the ideals upon which he founded it. Since Penn was a scholar in the classics, he may have known the city of Asia mentioned by Strabo and Tacitus, taking its name from a king Attalus, surnamed Philadelphus, "the brother-loving." Even more certainly Penn knew that St. John in Revelation had written of that city as sheltering one of the most faithful of the seven churches which were in Asia: "for thou hast a little strength, and hast kept my word, and hast not denied my name." But most of all Penn must have thought of the literal meaning of the Greek *philadelpheia,* as St. Paul used it in Romans: "Be kindly affectionate one to another with brotherly love." So he took that word in its Latin form, doubtless remembering also the city of the faithful church, and perhaps the brother-loving king as well. Later he wrote:

And thou, Philadelphia, the virgin settlement of this province, named before thou wert born, what care, what service, what travail has there been to bring thee forth!

Thus through centuries of public war, and private bickering, the name of that city "brotherly love" remained to hold aloft the ideal of its founder.

With what seems almost another echo of Revelation, Philadelphia was laid off four-square, like the heavenly Jerusalem. With Quaker honesty, the streets crossed at right angles, and since they were fixed and regular from the beginning, they called for names. Even on the original plan the two axial thoroughfares were written in as Broad and High. So matters stood officially until Penn himself came there in 1682. Already many houses had been built, and since most of the streets had no official names, people had naturally begun calling each after the most important person who lived there and had built the largest house. But this would never do in a Quaker town, where there was to be no respecting of persons. Thereupon Penn established a system of naming which was to sweep across the continent.

Beginning at the eastern boundary he simply called the first street, First Street. And so he went successively, making the numbers into names. This was in harmony with the customs of the Quakers who even called Sunday, First Day.

To distinguish the other streets, Penn chose a system of naming which also avoided reference to persons and accorded with the Quaker love of botany. He took, as he wrote, "the things that spontaneously grow in the country." Some of these names were later changed, but enough of them survived to make the famous rhyme for remembering the order:

> Market, Arch, Race, and Vine,
> Chestnut, Walnut, Spruce, and Pine.

At the very edge of the town-plot, Penn wrote of "a large Front-street to each river."

But for some reason the people in Philadelphia did not keep the original name High Street, and soon changed it in popular usage to Market.

Thus in 1682 was established the basis of the most far-reaching and typical habit of American naming. Philadelphia became not only a city, but the mother of many cities. The Americans, though far from an orderly people in everything, loved the orderly system of streets intersecting at right angles, and they carried it everywhere, even imposing it upon hilly sites to which it was not suited. Along with the plan went the naming, so that most American towns show numbered streets in one direction, and named streets in the other. Very often also the names are tree-names, and even in the far-distant deserts, towns were laid out with streets called Chestnut, Spruce and Vine, though such plants never grew there.

Also many towns have a Market Street, and if any town "fronts" on water, even a canal, there is likely to be Front Street. Sometimes even that name will occur, though there is nothing for it to front on, just because that is known as a good name for a street.

In his counties and county-towns Penn chose to echo English names, in the fashion of New England. But he went even further, and usually made county and town parallel those in England. So one of his "three lower counties on the Delaware" became Sussex, and its town, which had been Whorekill and then Deal, became Lewes, which was also the county-town of Sussex in England. Penn established the custom so firmly that until the Revolution every Pennsylvania county, except Philadelphia, bore the name of an English county, and many of the towns took the names of English county-towns, as in Berks County with its seat at Reading.

But Penn himself loved all men, and did not exclude the Indians. He was not repulsed by the Indian names of hills and streams, and perhaps by his example they were well preserved in Pennsylvania. In 1683, a century before men began to turn toward the strange and primitive, he wrote the first praise of Indian names,

Octorockon, Rancocas, Ozicton, Shakamacon, Poquerim, all of which are names of places, and have a Grandeur in them.

Also in Pennsylvania was published in 1692 the first of the

many poems which would try to invoke the magic of American names. Though Richard Frame was only an unskillful versifier, yet he deserves a little memory for that first trial:

> Philadelphia, that great Corporation,
> Was then, is now our choicest Habitation.
> Next unto that there stands the German-town,
> Also, within the Country, up and down,
> There's Haverford, where th' Welch-men do abide;
> Two Townships more, I think, they have beside:
> Here's Bristol, Plymouth, Newtown, here doth stand,
> Chester, Springfield, Marple in this Land,
> Darby, and other famous habitations,
> Also, a multitude of New Plantations.

Thus in the reign of Charles II, new great names arose, until twelve colonies and the Province of Maine were well established. In addition some cities and all the great rivers and capes and bays and islands of that coast had their names. Inland, the French had scattered names as far as Lake Superior and Kansas and Arkansas, and the Spaniards even farther to the southwest.

Since 1607 almost every year had seen the establishment of some new great name. In 1681 La Salle first used Louisiane; within a year Pennsylvania and Philadelphia were established; about the same time the Spaniards were beginning to use Texas. But the next two generations of men were to give few great names; instead they would fill in with thousands of little names, and establish new habits.

Chapter XIII (How the names became more English and less English

AT FIRST all the thin scattering of names along the eastern coast had been Indian; later many had been Dutch and Swedish; then after the English occupied the country, they made the names over to fit English speech. Yet when it was all done, the names had begun to have a flavor of their own, so that an Englishman must have felt that he was neither quite at home nor quite in a foreign country. Though the people still thought of themselves as English, the names showed that they were beginning to be Americans.

There are three ways by which a name can pass from one language into another. The English in those years used all three, though in differing proportions depending upon whether they were taking over from Dutch, or Swedish, or some Indian language.

With the Indian names, the simplest way was to listen to the sounds, and then pronounce them and write them down. It was not so simple as it might seem. Those languages had many sounds which were unknown to the English ear and tongue, and so the English could pronounce only what they *thought* they heard, or their own sound closest to it. Then, in writing the names, they made still more changes, because few of them knew much about spelling.

At best the English form of the name was only a doubtful replica of what the Indian name had been, and often the one was hardly recognizable in the other. Sounds like *l, n,* and *r* were especially easy to confuse. The famous Merrimack was also written Monumac and Molumac, each of the three yielding a different meaning, and from these basic forms an almost endless number of different spellings was produced. No single spelling could be declared correct Indian usage, because their languages were not written; no single spelling could even be declared correct English usage, because standardized spelling had not yet been established. If the Indian word passed through a Dutch or French form, the confusion was made the worse. As a result, for the older Indian names, it is often easier to find different spellings than to find two alike. Dozens of forms exist for such names as Milwaukee and Iowa, and an industrious scholar has listed 132 for Winnipesaukee.

Since the settlers were not skilled in the processes of language and had little interest in the whole matter, they frequently heard the strange names, not as mere sounds, but as equivalents of English syllables or whole words. Thus arose the second way of taking over names, known as folk-etymology.

Its varieties and shifts were almost without end. Sometimes part of a name was taken over by sound and part by this attempt at sense, to produce hybrid-looking words like Kingsessing, and Westkeag. Sometimes folk-etymology transformed Indian words into what looked like good names drawn from England—Lamington, Pompton, Walpack, Aughwick, and Wantage. Sometimes the result was a name in another foreign language, and so came Jamaica on Long Island. Sometimes a clerk gave the name a classical form, writing a kind of nonsense Latin—Octorara, and Quisquamego.

Often the process of folk-etymology must have been conscious, and its aim have been humor and the general jollity of life. Thus arose, north and south, a whole group of rollicking names— Ticklenaked, Rockawalking, Longacoming, Cheesequake, Down Sockum, Hoss-goin'-over, 'Scape-Whore, and Neversink.

The third way of taking over Indian names was to translate them boldly into English. This could occur only after Indians and English had learned to talk to each other, and so it happened chiefly where the two races mingled freely. Since Penn was always friendly with the Indians, there still exist translations by the dozen for creeks and runs in Pennsylvania.

A single name in Pennsylvania came over in all three ways. At that place there was one of those rare openings in the forest where the buffaloes, it was believed, "left the face of the country as bare as though it had been cleared by the grub-axe." The Indian word itself survived in Chindeclamoose Run; by clipping and folk-etymology it became Moose Creek; and in translation, Clearfield.

The Dutch names went the way of the Indian. The English in general held the Dutch language little better than Iroquois or Mohegan, and thought it a speech for merchants and traders, a kind of snorting and comical English dialect. Gentlemen learned French as part of their education, but not Dutch.

The New Netherlanders themselves continued to speak Dutch, but most of them could not read or write. When written or printed, names appeared mostly in an English text, and so they were rapidly absorbed into that language.

Many Dutch words for places were so much like the English that they came over easily—*kreek* to creek, *nek* to neck, *vlachte* to flat. With a change of suggestion, *bosch,* "wood," shifted to *bush,* and *hoek,* "point," to *hook.* *Gat* was sometimes translated as "hole" or "passage," and sometimes came over as *gate.* So people still say Sandy Hook, and Hellgate, and call a grove of maple-trees a sugar-bush. In the same way, half translating, half taking over by sound, the English made Antonies Neus into the jocular Anthony's Nose.

Other words the English never accepted. Even the very common *kill,* "stream," they usually took as part of the description, so that we have doublings like Bushkill Creek, and even Kill Creek. In the same way Waalen Bogt doubled to Wallabout Bay.

Some of the names came over with little change, as Tenafly from *thyne-vly,* "garden valley." But a surprising number were transformed.

On the Jersey side Achter Cul, "Back Bay," became Arthur Cul's Bay, but ended in double confusion as Arthur Kill. Along the Jersey shore one early Dutch map apparently bore twice the simple pilot's note *barnde gat,* meaning an inlet where surf was breaking. When the map was prepared for a book, the engraver took these as proper names, and entered them both as Barndegat. One of them became Barnegat, and the other was partly translated, partly mistranslated, as Bear Hole.

Up the Hudson, *tarwe,* "wheat," seems to have worked into Tarrytown. On the Delaware *Bompties Hoek,* "Little-Trees Point," became Bombay Hook in the mouths of passing deep-sea sailors who were more familiar with ports of India than the Dutch language.

On Long Island, Vlissingen became Flushing, the name by which the English already knew that town in the Netherlands. Vlachte-bosch, Greene-bosch, and Midwout were taken over or translated (it is impossible to say which) as Flatbush, Greenbush, and Midwood. Amersfoordt, also from a town in Holland, was man-handled into a thoroughly anglicized Amesford.

The village across the East River from Manhattan was Breukelen, another name drawn from the Netherlands. It was often Brookland, but seems to have felt the influence of such New England town-names as Brookline and Lynn, so that it ended as Brooklyn.

On Manhattan Island, Haerlem suffered merely a minor change of spelling. Deutel Bogt was "Wedge Bay," perhaps for its shape, but turned naturally into Turtle Bay. *Kolk,* "pond," passed into Kollick, and then became Collect Street, as if it were a place where water collected. Krum Marisje, "little crooked marsh," became Crummashie, and eventually gave its name to Gramercy Park.

The Dutch names of the streets mostly survived in translation or anglicized form. De Bouwerij, "the farm," became the Bowery. Breede Wegh came over easily into Broadway. Waal, no matter what its origin may have been, inevitably was absorbed to a common English word, and ended as Wall Street.

Along the Delaware the Swedish names also lingered. But the

Swedes had always been few, and even from the beginning they took over many names from the Dutch.

The name of the queen, Christina, remained on a stream, but shifted into Christiana. Their Fort Elfsborg became Elsinboro Point. By translation Hwijte Leer and Rödhleer became White Clay and Red Clay, and remained upon two little streams. Folk-etymology took over with the name of another stream to which the Swedes had given the common name Skillpadde, "turtle." As early as 1683, the English were writing this as Skilpot, and finally it became and remains, in a desperate attempt at sense, Shellpot Creek.

From the earliest times there had been men of different nations who came to the new colonies merely as individuals, such as Jonas Bronck, the Dane. Another of these was Augustine Herrman. In 1661 he became the first naturalized citizen of Maryland, and Bohemia River remained after him to commemorate his native rountry.

After the settlement of Pennsylvania, such immigrants came faster than ever, until in some parts they outnumbered the English. The effect on names was small, for these people never held the reins of power, and so lived in towns and counties with English names, and gave their own only to some of the villages and townships and smaller features of the land.

When they had a chance, these new immigrants usually transplanted the names of their homeland. So, from the Welsh Quakers, arose that strange little cluster in the rolling countryside beyond Philadelphia—Bryn Mawr, Cynwyd, and others. The French Huguenots brought New Rochelle to Long Island Sound, and some Swiss founded New Bern in North Carolina.

All these were few compared with the Germans who flooded into Penn's new colony. First they settled near Philadelphia, and the English called their village Germantown. Soon they spread into all the back-country beyond the Welsh townships. They kept their language tenaciously, but they left less mark upon the names than might be expected. Even the counties of the Germans were

York, Lancaster, and Berks. For the streams and hills of that region the ruling English generally either took over Indian names or established their own, but some German names also survive, as in hills called Kohlberg or Kirchberg, and a stream known as Hazelbach Creek.

A little later came German-speaking enthusiasts of strange religious sects, to find toleration under Quaker rule. Of all the colonists, they were fondest of Biblical naming, and from them sprang Ephrata, Emaus, and Nazareth. A few years later, when some of them migrated to North Carolina, they settled Salem, and Bethabara, and Bethany.

In 1741, some of these pious folk under their leader and bishop Count Zinzendorf began a settlement in wild country along a river in Pennsylvania. In that wilderness, on Christmas Eve, a Sunday, the little company drew together in the first house that had been built, to hold Holy Communion and keep the vigil of Christmas. At the end of the service, between nine and ten of the winter evening, the Count led them into a stable which had been built near by—for was not the Prince of Peace born in a stable? There, deeply moved, they sang a German hymn:

> Not Jerusalem, but Bethlehem—
> Of thee cometh what me rejoiceth.

So they gave that name Bethlehem to the little new village, and by one of the worst ironies of naming it grew into a smoky city, renowned for the making of cannon and armor-plate.

Also among the non-English immigrants may be counted the Scotch-Irish, who brought with their scanty baggage (as has been said) three things of different worth to the new country—whiskey, the Presbyterian Church, and independence from Great Britain. They were lean fighting-men whose ancestors in Ireland for three generations had known what it was to face "the wolf and the wood-kern." A shrewd Pennsylvania governor settled them beyond the Germans, "as a frontier, in case of any disturbance." Also they settled in New England far to the north, along the

Merrimack. Since they spoke English, though with a little northern burr, they established no new habits of naming, and took over
the ways the English had already begun. Moreover, they were not
a very sentimental people, and of one name alone they seem to
have been proud. That was of the city which they had held
through one of the famous sieges of history, until at last King
William's ships broke the boom, and came sailing up Lough
Foyle. The young man who saw those ships from the cathedral
tower and fired a gun to signal the relief came years later as Pastor McGregor to settle in New Hampshire, and the town there
too was named Londonderry. That same name or its shortened
form Derry was scattered across Pennsylvania and even farther
west—in that name was the glory of the Scotch-Irish.

Thus while the English were making over the Dutch and
Swedish names, other un-English names were arising. Though no
one of these new peoples alone had much effect upon the map, all
together they broke up the English dominance. So began that
never monotonous pattern of names of many languages which,
with its evidence of toleration, is a chief glory of our heritage.
Thus within the limits of a single Pennsylvania county bearing
the English name Lancaster are townships named Caernarvan and
Brecknock for the Welsh; Manheim and Lititz for the Germans;
Colerain and Donegal for the Scotch-Irish; and New Holland for
some wandering, homesick Dutchman.

Mere spelling also sometimes worked to make the names less
like those of England. Each man spelled much as he pleased, on
the principle expressed by Mr. Weller: "It depends upon the taste
and fancy of the speller, my Lord!" Sometimes one variant of a
name happened to survive in England and another, usually more
phonetic, in the colonies. Thus Hartford differs slightly from
Hertford and Topsfield from Toppesfield. From the written forms
alone, people would hardly recognize the twinship of Pomfret
with Pontefract. Yet the American forms had as good ancestry as
the British. The same process was at work when some Yorkshire
Quakers settled in New Jersey and called the place Burlington.

This name spread extraordinarily in later years, but without a single example of the English form Bridlington.

In Maryland also a patent was made out as early as 1677 for a place to be called by the common English name Burleigh. Later it was spelled Berlin, although still accented on the first syllable. So also the towns in New England thus spelled and pronounced were more likely from some Burland or Birling, for not until well after 1700 did the Prussian capital grow to be a place of enough importance to be well known in the colonies.

Sometimes of course the spelling must have been from sheer ig, norance, as when an irritated New Jersey clerk made a note in the record, "I have followed the method in the original, though in some places non-sense and false orthography." But even Governor Dongan and the Assembly of New York, when they established a county in honor of the Duchess of York, were merely following the preferred usage in spelling it Dutchess.

In naming streams and hills the English-speaking colonists differed little in their mental processes from either the Indians or their own ancestors. Having killed a wolf, any of them might call the place Wolf Meadow. But even here arose a difference between the old country and the new. An early Saxon used *leah* instead of *meadow,* and in the course of time his originally plain name became unintelligible as Woolley. Thus in America the new names were open and understandable, like Wolf Meadow, but in England most names like Woolley had no meaning to the common man.

Also in America the land itself was different. There were few barren uplands to be called *moor* or *heath,* and so in most of the colonies those words became merely bookish. The English *ford* implied a civilized passage of a stream, almost guaranteeing safety. The American term became *crossing,* which suggests wading, ferrying, or swimming—cross as you can. At deeper crossings a ferryman might settle, and then on the opposite side the traveler stood hallooing until he was heard. Thus the name Hallowing Point began. Also in the deep forest, *clearing* soon became a common word, or *deadening,* if the trees had merely been girdled. Along the looping lowland rivers of the South they began to say *bluff,* and its counterpart, *bottom.*

Thousands of names arose from plants. To identify a stream-crossing, an oak-tree or a patch of wild onion was as good as a sign-post—permanent and conspicuous. But such a name could be useful only in a region where that plant was not too common. In a country where pines grew everywhere, every stream would have pines along it, and Pine Creek would be as little distinctive as Water Creek. Thus Maple became commoner as a place-name in Pennsylvania and Virginia, where maples were a little unusual, than in New England. Such names rarely sprang from incidents, because a man does not often have an adventure with a tree.

The oaks and wild-onions yielded to cornfields. The blight took the chestnut-groves that the ax spared. Only men graying at the temples remember the generous spreading trees, and the prickly burr with the sweet little nuts in the velvety pocket. But still, in half the counties from Massachusetts to Carolina, a Chestnut Hill stands as the monument to that brave upland tree.

Like plants, a few wild animals were of use as sign-posts, most notably the beaver. Another was the playful otter whose name so commonly remained on Otter Creek where he once built a slide in the clay-bank for his amusement. Often, such names noted the sign rather than the actual animal, as with Beaverdam and Bear Wallow.

In contrast to plants, however, most wild animals moved about constantly, and made themselves as inconspicuous as possible. They therefore were of no use as sign-posts. But men have adventures with animals, and most animal-names arose in that way. They marked where someone encountered or killed or hunted that animal in such a way as to be worth remembering. For this reason, the name was often Buck Run, or Doe Run, instead of Deer Run. The commoner the animal, the more chance of a memorable encounter; but the rarer the animal, the more reason that the encounter should be remembered.

When such a name did not arise from an incident, it often, as with a plant, showed rarity rather than abundance. In every low-land southern stream the alligators floated lazily. They were dull and worthless, neither much feared nor much valued, too common to matter. An Alligator River is in northern North Carolina at the very edge of their range, where they were rare enough to be noted.

The plants of the colonies were not much different from those of England, but the animals differed more. Skunk, coon, moose, possum—even the names were Indian. England had never known the rattlesnake, alligator, and panther. Even wolf and beaver had become words only in England, and the bear was a chained and captive thing to be matched against dogs in the bear pit. So the animals made the names still more different from those of England.

Sometimes the animal-names are misleading. For that gaunt wader of the northern lakes, the first English used the established word, *elk*. Later, they took the Algonquian *moose,* and shifted *elk* to what the first colonists had called *stag* or *red deer.* "Red deer," wrote John Lederer in 1672, "for their unusual largeness improperly termed elks by ignorant people." In most places both kinds of larger deer were rarer than the smaller, but the killing of a large animal was more noteworthy, and so in some regions place-names in Elk or Moose exceed those in Deer.

The skunk apparently impressed the colonists rather less than might be expected. In the primeval forest the animal may have been very rare, and the early English, accustomed to the high odors of Elizabethan London, did not find the skunk so offensive as men of more degenerate days. Some of them even praised his musky smell.

So, according to his imprint upon the folk-imagination, every animal and bird left his mark upon the map. Like the chestnut-tree, some of them have vanished. Few remember the common little parrot of the Carolinas, and we think of the parrot as a tropical bird. But here and there lingers some feature called Parroquet. So it was also with the wild pigeons. "Pigeons that fly together in thousands," wrote a Dutchman, "and sometimes ten, twenty, thirty and even forty and fifty are killed at one shot." Where they roosted, their numbers broke limbs from the trees. Not one is left, but here and there a Pigeon Roost or Pigeon Creek survives.

Not all animal-names were for animals. A settler named Fox might leave his name upon a hill or stream, and Baer could easily shift to Bear. Where a few Indians lingered after the rest of the tribe had moved westward, the place often became Indian Creek, but one of the Indians might be called Red Bird, or Buffalo, and his name survive after he was forgotten.

Not only from animals and men, but also from the works of men, the country was named. Mill Creek was the commonest of all; in Bucks County, Pennsylvania, there were six. A bridge was often noteworthy enough for the naming of Bridge Creek. As iron-smelting began, other streams and hills were identified as Furnace, and Forge, and even Ironworks, or Limekiln.

Not all incidents sprang from animals. No one knows who first named a Troublesome Creek, or why. But it filled a need, and the name went west into the forest. In Virginia alone there were three of them.

There was conscious art also, usually with a touch of humor. Some poet, or jester, named True Love Creek, because "the course of true love never did run smooth"—or "straight," as some prefer it. There was also a river in Virginia with an Indian name written by Captain Smith as Mattapanient. By 1654 it was written Mattaponie, and a little later as Mattapony. Then some early eighteenth-century wit named its four branches the Mat, Ta, Po, and Ny, and the story was coined that the name of the whole river had arisen like the river itself, by the joining of its four tributaries.

The need of many names in the new country was so great that they constantly sprang from other names. First, let us say, a hunter killed an elk at a stream, and remembered the place as Elk Creek. The rise beyond the stream became almost automatically Elk Ridge, and an open space was Elk Meadow. Settlers coming later called the region Elk Valley, and the village became Elk Crossing. A higher settlement was called Head of Elk, and a tributary stream, Little Elk Creek. Thus from one name a dozen often sprouted, like a cluster of grapes on a single stem.

Sometimes the original name suggested different ones. In Hell-gate two rocky shelves came to be known as the Gridiron and the Frying-Pan. On the Delaware coast a small stream was known as Dragon Creek, and a tributary was called St. George. So everywhere, by counterpart, Big was likely to suggest Little; and Red or White, some other color.

The period after the founding of Pennsylvania was a time too for filling in with the settlement of towns. Few great cities were founded, but with the springing up of hundreds of villages new habits of naming began. Already, in the older colonies, many people were two or three generations removed from England, not new-landed immigrants, homesick for hedge-rows and thatched cottages.

Nevertheless, the habit of naming towns for English towns remained for a while, especially in Massachusetts. The planting of Worcester in 1684 showed it still continuing. A tradition lingered that this name was a gesture of defiance against Charles II, to preserve in Massachusetts the name of that city where he suffered defeat and afterwards had to flee across the southern counties, doubling like a hunted fox. But Worcester in England was a good royalist city, not a symbol of Puritanism. If it was reproduced in defiance, the gesture was a very timorous one indeed. More likely it was thought only another good English name.

Even after the royal governors came into power under the new charter, the roll of Massachusetts towns continued with Tiverton, Harwich, and Attleborough in 1694, all good names of England. The old system, however, at last began to weaken. Pembroke in 1712 echoed the name of a Welsh town, and also may have been partly named for the Earl of Pembroke, then a member of the Privy Council. Rutland in 1714 was for a county, not a town. The system finally cracked in 1715. In that year Hopkinton was founded on land purchased by a bequest left to Harvard College by Edward Hopkins, and the town was expressly named, "to the perpetuating the memory of the pious benefactor." But by this time the practice established in 1630 had lasted eighty-five years, and had made certain that the names of English towns and villages would be repeated abundantly all the way across to the Pacific.

In Connecticut the old system began to break in 1695 with the Biblical name Lebanon. Mansfield, in 1702, set a precedent by being named for Major Mansfield, one of the chief landowners. In 1703 a new town set off from Milford merely took the name New Milford, thus becoming a grandchild of Milford in England. In 1708 a town was organized on land granted to volunteers in King Philip's War, and was called by a coined name, Voluntown. Thus Connecticut—stiff-necked, eccentric, and provincial, though wholly English in blood—began before the more cosmopolitan Massachusetts to proceed American-fashion by utilizing home-products and eschewing imports.

Over all New England, however, a drift resulting from the political organization was slowly taking the names more unlike those of the mother country. The New England town was generally large in area. New settlements usually sprang up in addition to the original one; these were all considered part of the same town, and so used its name with some distinguishing word, usually of location. Thus arose a distinctive feature of New England, one which troubles an outsider and makes him think that the Puritans suffered from a poverty-stricken imagination. In Massachusetts, Northampton was founded in 1656, and within its limits the full geographical quota grew up—Southampton, East-hampton, and Westhampton. In Connecticut, Woodstock spawned not only North, South, East, and West Woodstock, but also Woodstock Valley and Woodstock Hill. Other villages added the boastful Center. Often the later settlement surpassed the original one, as Newburyport eclipsed Newbury. Many of these villages became towns in their own right. On the occasion of their incorporation they sometimes took wholly new names, but more often not. Occasionally the name was a compromise as in Westfield and Westford, originally the western parts of Springfield and Chelmsford. In Massachusetts alone some twenty-five independent towns and many dozens of villages came to bear these derivative names.

In the middle and southern colonies the incorporated town was of less importance than in New England; the county was often the first to be organized. As always, the names reflected the difference. A southern seaport bears the name of an English county because the county was first organized as Norfolk, and the town merely echoed the name. In New England the town would have been founded as Norwich, and the county perhaps called by the same name, just as Plymouth County copied the town instead of being Devon. So predominating was the southern county that its chief settlement and seat of government usually took that name, merely adding Court House. The few formally founded southern towns were named generally from some governor, proprietor, or royal personage.

In this fashion the most notable foundation of the early eighteenth century conformed. Maryland had always been a colony of scattered plantations; Governor Andros noted in 1678: "Maryland, populous and strong, but do not live in towns." The colony was actually in want of centers of trade, and the government made several efforts to found one. Each of these towns took the name of the proprietory family, and promptly died. Finally, the Assembly in 1729 incorporated in Baltimore County another town of the name, but according to southern custom bearing a suffix to distinguish it from the county. As was usually to happen in later days also, the addition was sluffed off, and Baltimore City remained as Baltimore. At the time of its founding, the county of the same name was seventy years old.

This same period saw also the first important town founded as a business venture, and named for the founder. In the history of naming there was much classical and European precedent. Emperors and kings had named cities for themselves. Legend had busily supplied so-called eponymous heroes where none existed of record; everyone believed that Romulus had founded Rome, and many accepted the story that London preserved the memory of King Lud. In the southern colonies some plantations bearing the owner's name had turned into villages, but the actual founding and naming of a town for oneself was strangely lacking throughout the first hundred years of settlement.

In the early eighteenth century, however, conditions were changing and the American business man was beginning to emerge. One of these was William Trent. He was a Scottish immigrant, who with good Scots industry rose to be prominent in Pennsylvania and New Jersey. In 1714 he bought land at the head of navigation on the Delaware, a shrewdly chosen site. On the New Jersey side he laid out a town, and offered lots for sale. Perhaps he believed that his own name, as that of a successful business man, would inspire confidence in investors; in any case, it became Trent's Town, and soon, Trenton.

In spite of these exceptions, the general rule in the southern, and even in the middle colonies, was that towns were not formally founded, but emerged from mere settlements. The town plan still shows the difference. In New England the central common gives evidence of a planned settlement, but elsewhere the town still shows in its street-lines how the original houses strung along the pack-horse trail, or converged upon some fork or cross-roads or "Five Points," or clustered at a river-crossing.

The names showed the same distinction. The English town-names of the North told at most that the settlers came from some certain part of England. But in the other colonies the names of the little straggling settlements were closer to the land. Sometimes an Indian name of the place was kept, as with Yeopim, one of the first towns of North Carolina. Lewis Turnout and Smith's Turn Out in South Carolina seem by their names to show that they were once literally what has since become that good American phrase: "a wide place in the road." Such names for towns often show a mingling of poetry and grotesquery—Little River, Meadows of Dan, Pine Flats, Forks of Buffalo, Gum Fork, Happy Creek, Locust Hill. Often, too, they showed the actual reason for existence of the settlement—Medlar's Mill, Dare's Wharf, Principio Furnace, Harper's Ferry, James Store. Rolling Road in Maryland preserved the record that through it once ran a track along which hogsheads of tobacco were rolled to the landing-place.

The early plantation names were often colorful, not without a touch of humor—All That's Left, Orphan's Gift, Trouble Enough, The Widow's Last Shift, Hard Bargain. Often they included such words as Folly, Chance, Hope, and Adventure. Chance survives as the name of a village in Maryland, and Charlie Hope in Virginia. Their roll might be called by the dozen—Peace and Plenty, Ending of Controversy, Bowman's Folly, Bachelor's Hope, Oxon Hall Manor, Shepherd's Delight, Want Water, Pleasant Hill, Violet Bank. Many of these early plantation names vanished, but a few survived as towns.

Sometimes the village sprang up around a little country church. Perhaps the first sermon was preached in the open air to the apt text of Joshua, 18, 1: "And the whole congregation of the children of Israel assembled together at Shiloh, and set up the tabernacle of the congregation there." Then, as happened in New Jersey, it might be called Shiloh Church, and the name survive as a village. Thus, and not originally from towns, began many of the Biblical names of the South—Bethesda, Bethany, and Zion. From little congregations in the wilderness came also such names as Chapel Hill and Church Creek.

Other men, especially in the middle colonies it would seem, liked better to gather at the tavern, and from these sprang villages called Traveler's Rest and Boyd Tavern. Relay in Maryland preserved the memory that the stage-horses were changed there. The tavern names usually represented something which could be painted on a sign for travelers who could recognize pictures better than letters. The names of the towns preserved the same pictorial virtue—Cross Anchor, Rising Sun, and Blue Ball. Most of all in the rich country behind Philadelphia the taverns flourished and the pictures painted on their signs survived as villages—Bird-in-Hand, Broad Axe, Compass, King of Prussia, Red Lion, White Horse.

Thus, gradually in New England, more rapidly in the other colonies, the names of towns came to be no longer the names of England.

In a small village it is enough to say that a man lives "by the church," or "just at the top of the hill." (Thus indeed many men came to be called Church or Hill.) Most of the colonists were from small English villages, and so had little feeling that a street needed a name.

New Amsterdam had established the first regular system of named streets. Philadelphia seems to have been second. Boston lagged. The town itself grew up with notoriously little plan. The King's Commissioners reported in 1665: "their streets crooked, with little decency and no uniformity." A government which gave no thought to the streets themselves would hardly think of the need of names. In the famous Possession Book of about 1645, Sudbury and Spring were mentioned as established names, but other streets had to be identified by tedious descriptions: "a highway of 24 feet between the house of Daniel Travers and William Copp, touching on the north corner of Elder Copp's house." Inevitably, however, people in common speech began to give names for mere convenience, usually fixing upon some easy feature of reference—Fort Street, Cove Street, Water Street.

Finally in 1708 action was taken. Some of the homely names already established by custom were preserved, such as Frog Lane and Milk Street. Other streets received the names which might be expected in any English city of the time—King, Queen, Prince, Marlborough for the current hero.

In general, however, the early colonists brought with them no tradition, and so street-names in the end differed more from England than those of towns or natural features. The common name for the chief street of an English town is High, arising not usually from the idea of height, but of importance. High Street became fairly common in the older towns along the Atlantic coast, but failed to be established in tradition. By the time streets were being generally named, *high* had come to suggest only a built-up way or a road following a ridge. Instead, after a village had more than one street, the villagers began to speak of the chief thoroughfare simply as "the main street." This petrified into Main Street, and in the end became a symbol of the small town itself.

Other names arose in various ways. Mere folk-custom often resulted in official recognition of such names as School, Church, Meeting, Chapel, Mill, Court, and Bridge Streets. Royal titles and symbols were everywhere popular, even in New England—King, Queen, Prince, Princess, Duke, Orange, Hanover, Crown.

In any early settlement the radiating roads were naturally called for the town to which they led, and these names often remained upon the streets. In Hartford, thoroughfares known as Wethersfield, Bloomington, New Britain, and Farmington still lead out toward those towns. But the same road in Wethersfield has reversed the name, and become Hartford Avenue. On the other side of Wethersfield it emerges as Middletown Avenue, which again arrives in Middletown as Hartford Avenue, the less important Wethersfield being ignored. Passing through Middletown as Main Street the thoroughfare continues toward the next town as Saybrook Road.

In Providence, Hope and Peace Streets harmonized with the name of the town itself, but this was exceptional. There seems also to have been little attempt to echo the street names of the English cities, although in New England especially some such effort might have been expected.

All names tend to repeat themselves. Just as an original Troublesome Creek was passed on to others, so certain names became conventional for streets. Most strikingly, the streets of the larger towns were echoed in the villages of the vicinity, even though incongruously. Tremont Street in Boston fittingly recalled the original English name of the settlement and its three hills. But Tremont Street in many smaller towns was only an aping of Boston. Broadway radiated out from New York, along with Wall Street. Pearl Street spread over Connecticut and reached as far north as New Hampshire. But most of all the Philadelphia pattern of street-naming went on to the west.

Thus in that long period of steady development the names became more English as the strange Indian and Dutch and Swedish words were made over, but in most other ways the names became less like those of England.

->>>->>>->>>->>>->>>->>>->>>->>>->>>->>>->>>->>>-❊-<<<-<<<-<<<-<<<-<<<-<<<-<<<-<<<-<<<-<<<-<<<-<<<-

Chapter XIV ❰ How they took the names into the mountains

DURING half a century, there were no new colonies; then in 1732, the fifth year of King George II, the last of the thirteen was merely called in its charter, without explanation: "The Colony of Georgia in America," thus taking the King's name with a Latin ending.

About this time the frontier began to reach the mountains. First of all went the hunters and Indian traders, but their namings often failed to be written down and preserved. Next went most often the surveyors, and the giving and recording of names came to be part of their profession. Their work was to determine the boundaries between colonies, or lay out the lines of grants. With both, they made maps, and wrote on them the names of streams and other easily recognizable features, such as outstanding or strangely shaped hills. By reference to these, other men could locate the surveyors' marks. Once thus written on a map, a name became involved with land-titles, and had a fair chance to survive.

One of the most famous surveys was that of 1728 to settle the boundary between Virginia and North Carolina, an expedition rendered the more notable because of the *History of the Dividing Line* written by that sprightly Virginian, Colonel William Byrd of Westover.

The surveying party was a cross-section of colonial society. Some Sapponi Indians went along as guides. From them the scale ranged upward through hunters, ax-men, horse-tenders, and surveyors, to the chaplain and commissioners, reaching the pinnacle in Byrd himself—planter, gentleman, wit, gallant, scholar in Latin, Greek, and Hebrew.

From the very beginning the controversy grew out of a name, and like that involving the Charles and Merrimack it illustrates how little the English government understood the difficulties involved with names in a new country. In 1665 the northern boundary of Carolina had been fixed by reference to Weyanoke Creek, located only as lying "within or about the degrees of 36 and thirty minutes northern latitude." The region of the boundary lay in the vicinity of the Great Dismal Swamp, and was not attractive. Before it was settled, tradition had lapsed. As Colonel Byrd put the matter: "In the long course of years Weynoke Creek lost its name, so that it became a controversy where it lay." Recourse to old-timers merely resulted in the usual split: "Some ancient persons in Virginia affirmed it was the same with Wicocon, and others again in Carolina were as positive it was Nottoway River." The difference was a strip fifteen miles wide, extending in theory three thousand miles to the other ocean.

The commissioners finally agreed upon an interpretation, and with a point on the Atlantic coast thus settled, they set out to run the survey due west. The first 125 miles passed through country which was sparsely settled and already named. The surveyors entered in their notes such common backwoods names as Blackwater River, Jack's Swamp, Beaver-Pond Creek, and Pigeon-Roost Creek. Nut-bush Creek was the last of these, and Byrd entered the next stream as Massamony, "Paint-Creek," "because of the great quantity of red ochre found in its banks." At that point the surveyors had apparently passed beyond the frontier of settlement and established English names, but were in a region familiar to their Indian guides. Within the next thirty miles, four more such Indian names were taken over. In this same sector, also, Byrd recorded their first giving of a name. It was October, and the ducks were flying south. The surveyors came to a small stream where they saw many ducks of a kind called Blue-Wing, and using a phonetic spelling of the word, Byrd noted from that incident, "we gave the name of Blewing Creek, because of the great number of those fowls that then frequented it."

On October 7th the Carolina commissioners, deciding that the line had been carried far enough, turned back, and took with them all the Indians except Ned Bearskin. Apparently he was no longer familiar with the country or its names. After Hico-ottomony Creek, surviving as Hyco, the surveyors bestowed English names liberally.

Most of them were of the common stock of the frontier— Buffalo Creek, "so named from the frequent tokens we discovered of that American behemoth"; Cane and Lowland Creeks by obvious description; Miry Creek, "so called because several of the horses were mired in its branches"; Crooked Creek, because in running the east-west line they found themselves forced to cross it several times; Mayo and Irvin Creeks in honor of two of the surveyors; Tear Coat Camp, an often-recurring folk-name, because of the rough thickets surrounding it; Cockade Creek, "because we there began to wear the beards of wild turkey-cocks in our hats."

Occasionally they indulged a little fancy, as with Matrimony Creek (doubtless suggested by Massamony), "called so by an unfortunate married man, because it was exceedingly noisy and impetuous." But the worldly-wise Colonel added, "though the stream was clamorous, yet, like those women who make themselves plainest heard, it was likewise perfectly clear and unsullied." In similar ironic mood they named one small mountain The Wart and another The Pimple because neither was of much size in comparison with the greater ones in the distance.

Now and then Byrd's own vocabulary was in evidence. The packers and ax-men, when naming a stream "by reason of the multitudes of water-falls," would have used the folk-name Falling Creek. Cascade Creek sounds like the Colonel himself.

The most successful name of this expedition was also probably his. The despairing lover in English folk-lore might die of a broken heart but did not resort to jumping from a precipice. As a student of the classics, however, Byrd was familiar with Sappho's leap from the Leucadian promontory. On October 25th, he wrote: "The air clearing up this morning, we were again agreeably surprised with a full prospect of the mountains." One of them toward the south was very high, and "the west end of it terminated in a horrible precipice, that we called the Despairing Lover's Leap." This Carolina cliff was thus probably the first spot in America to be called by a name upon which the folk-imagination quickly fastened.

It spread from coast to coast. Even Louisiana, the flattest state, has several. Lover's Leap may be anything from a little clay bluff to a typically grandiose Californian example insuring a good thousand feet in the clear. Local legend sometimes reports, half-heartedly, the story of a lover, usually an Indian girl. But even the tellers of the stories seldom show conviction, and it would be difficult among our hundred or more Lover's Leaps to find a single one from which a lover ever jumped. Often, like Byrd, the namers seem only to suggest that here would be a good place to take off, if anyone wanted to.

The fascination of a high place and the prevalence of a similar Indian folk-tale may have aided the popularity of the name. Certainly the alliteration made it stick easily in the mind. Any alliterative coupling is likely to be often repeated—Roaring Run, Crooked Creek, Hungry Hill, Robbers' Roost, Devil's Den, Hell's Half-Acre.

Colonel Byrd made another excursion to look at some lands. In his journal for September 19, 1733, he wrote:

The heavens lowered a little upon us in the morning, but, like a damsel ruffled by too bold an address, it soon cleared up again. Because I detested idleness, I caused my overseer to paddle me up the river.

On returning home, he and his surveyor indulged in some fancy:

We laid the foundation of two large cities. One at Shacco's to be called Richmond, and the other at the point of Appomattox river, to be named Petersburg. . . . Thus we did not build castles only, but also cities in the air.

As regards the names, however, he need not have been so modest. Petersburg made use of an already established Peter's Point, although Byrd may also have enjoyed using the name of the Russian capital recently built up by Peter the Great from the marshes along the Neva. Richmond he is thought to have named from some fancied resemblance of its site on the James to that of Richmond on the Thames, which he had known during his long residence in London. Both names survived and were copied for many other towns.

Farms were beginning to fill the coastal plain and the rolling country behind it. On the western horizon, many men besides Colonel Byrd saw the higher mountains, "like ranges of blue clouds." Needing a name before they got close enough to see the green of the trees, men began to say the Blue Ridge.

Stretching a thousand miles north and south, they had no general name, and were often called merely The Mountains. They were too huge for any man to see at one time. So, coming to some particular part, men called each differently. Sometimes they learned an Indian name such as Kittatinny, "big mountain." But the Indians had few names for mountains, and so their names for streams often did double service, as with Allegheny. So it was too with the Dutch Catskill, "Cat's Creek," so called probably because someone saw a wildcat there. Everywhere rivers were likely to be named first, and then mountains to take their names from rivers, and seldom the reverse.

The English needed words for mountain streams. When Marlowe wrote:

How they took the names into the mountains

By shallow rivers, to whose falls,
Melodious birds sing madrigals,

he suggested, not a roaring cataract, but something gentler. Thus the first English used *fall,* in America, to mean almost any place where the surface of the water was broken a little. But when they came among the dashing streams of the mountains, they saw real waterfalls, and needing a new word for a mere swift place, they used *ripple,* which after a while became *riffle.*

They still advanced upstream, and so said *branch* sometimes. But that remained mostly a tide-water word. In the hills, when men came to a place where they looked ahead and saw two streams flowing together, their minds worked in different ways. If one stream was much larger than the other, they might keep the old name of the lower course for that stream, and call the other by a new name. But it was hard to think of new names. So, if the main stream was Sandy, they might call the smaller one Little Sandy. This also was easier to remember. When the two streams coming together were of much the same size, the place might be called the Forks of Sandy, and one stream the North Fork, and the other the South Fork. And sometimes, using a different figure of speech, they said North and South Prong.

Men using canoes also developed some new words. When they came to a riffle and were forced to carry their canoes around it, they called that a carrying-place. The smooth stretch above a riffle, they called a stillwater.

Those who traveled by land needed words for low places through mountain barriers, for there was no common English word. In New England, men came to say *notch;* in the other colonies, *gap.* Sometimes the gap or notch was named first because it marked the road, and was more important than the mountain that merely towered above it.

One of the many men who went into the mountains was Asa Kinsman. His could be the story of hundreds. He piled his goods on a cart, yoked his two oxen, and went with his wife to take up land. At some place where the rough track branched, he went right instead of left. When he came at last to a settlement, they told him that his land was off to the northwest over the trackless mountains, and that he must return and take the left-hand fork. But he was of that stubborn breed which will not turn back on the traveled road. He found a low place between mountains, and cut himself a road with his ax, and took his cart through. So men called it rightly Kinsman Notch, and later, Kinsman Mountain.

The English even took sea-coast words into the mountains. *Flat* had meant low land by the sea, as men still say *tide-flat*. But it became a level spot on the side of a mountain. *Cove,* which had meant a little bay, came to be used for a valley shut in among hills.

Most mountains were so shaped that they were easily called by the old word *ridge*. But the English had no word for a mountain standing up sharply by itself. So they began to say *knob*.

Individual mountains got their names in the usual ways, by description, or incident, or ownership. Most of these mountains had thick forest all the way to the top. But some were higher or more wind-swept, or more rocky, or had perhaps been cleared by fire. These grassy-topped or rocky-topped mountains stood out sharply among the others and were good landmarks. In all the colonies they were most often named Bald Mountain, sometimes Bare Mountain, occasionally Naked Mountain. In some regions the name became so common that any such summit was simply called a *bald*. Later, after the forests had been cleared, these mountains were not so individual, or sometimes the trees grew on a burned summit. Then, because the sounds were the same, men often wrote Bear Mountain. So there is no way of telling which it first was, but there are so many more of these than of mountains named for other animals that most of them were probably Bare Mountain.

Men found the mountains strange, and sometimes fearsome. In one way the names reflected this sense of awe. The English did not often name rivers for streams of England or of the Bible. But mountains were constantly called for Biblical mountains.

Mount Sinai, where the glory of the Lord was like devouring

fire, was too fearful a name to be lightly used. But of the others there were many—Mount Carmel and Mount Horeb, where the prophets dwelt; Mount Nebo, where Moses died; Mount Ephraim, Mount Gilead, Mount Hermon, Mount Moriah, Mount Pisgah. Thick-forested with chestnut and spruce and maple they echoed the names of those far-off desert peaks. Even Mount Zion was not too holy. And from the Mount of Olives, where Christ had walked, came more than one Mount Olive on whose wooded slopes no olive trees had ever fluttered their little gray leaves.

From Biblical usage also sprang perhaps another strange custom, that Mount should precede and Mountain should follow. Thus they said Mount Tom, but Black Mountain.

As the English worked into the mountains, they began to have new experiences. In England they had known mostly a well-watered country where streams ran throughout the year; but in certain parts the people had found need of the name Winter-bourne to denote a stream which ran only in winter. New England and all the tide-water country had been well watered, and so the tradition of Winterbourne was lost, along with the word *burn*. Later, when the colonists entered the mountains, they came to a region where the water ran off quickly from the steeper slopes. Then it happened, especially toward the south, that in some hot August or September hunters or surveyors came to a stream-bed where no water ran among the boulders. This was a matter for wonder, and all such matters for wonder create names. So men spoke of Dry Run, or Dry Creek, or even Dry River, although the name was a contradiction in itself. Perhaps the stream ran water during ten months; even so, it often kept the name Dry. Thus arose another difference between the countries. Winter-bourne noted the presence of water, but Dry Creek arose from the opposite point of view and emphasized its absence.

Also, like Colonel Byrd, all who went westward had heard tales of the great buffalo. In every glade they looked for the shaggy beast with the ponderous head. Where they first saw him or his traces, they often called the place by that name. So, right across Virginia runs a line of buffalo names. Eastward there are none, for there the buffalo had not come. Westward such names are fewer, for by the time men had reached those regions the buffalo had ceased to be a novelty. But north and south, from Buffalo Branch in Augusta County to Buffalo Springs in Mecklenburg, that line of names still shows where our ancestors first came to the range of the buffalo.

As they entered the mountain-country and passed through it, they began to find other strange traces, and not of beasts. Perhaps a Kanawha squaw nursed a blue-eyed papoose, or in a Twightwee village a crucifix hung by a lodge-door. Then the Englishmen looked at each other, and sometimes they gave a name. Even on the sea-coast it had been heard before—French Harbor, French Watering-Place told where strange ships once dropped anchor. Far in the north, above Winooski River, French Hill marks off the inland frontier. That stream itself was once called French River, because along it the French with their Indians marched upon the English settlements. In Massachusetts a hill and three streams may be called from some colonist named French, or may mark where a raiding partisan led his painted warriors. The line swings around the Iroquois country, but French Creek in western New York shows the route of King Louis's men southward from Lake Erie. Among the mountains the name runs on toward the south until at last, far in Carolina, the Broad River flows off toward the Atlantic; but over the ridge the westward-flowing stream is the French Broad. If the fortunes of battle had proved different, the western stream might have been La Grande, and the eastern La Grande Anglaise.

Chapter XV ⟨ Of the years when they fought the French

ON A winter night in 1690 some French and Indians surprised the frontier village of Schenectady, sacked and burned it, killed sixty people, and carried off twenty-seven captives. From that time, for three-quarters of a century, the frontier knew only war and the threat of war, and for a while war seemed to dominate even the giving of names.

In 1699 the French began to colonize again on the Gulf near the mouth of the Mississippi. They founded a fort in the country of a tribe who had long been known to the Spaniards as Mauvila. The French made the name over into the form of a French word as Mobile. On a river near by they found some Indians who called themselves "thicket-clearers," meaning perhaps that their ancestors had learned to cultivate land. The French wrote of them as the Alibamons, and called the river by that name.

At last in 1715 old King Louis died, and in the infancy of the new King, the Duc d'Orléans became regent. The Scottish promoter, John Law, won his ear with grandiose schemes for money-making, and a great company was organized to found a colony on the Mississippi. Since the project had the Regent's support, the chief city was to be called Nouvelle Orléans, taking its name from his title and from Orléans on the Loire. Like Philadelphia it was named before it was born, and even before the location was fixed. The founders voyaged along the river, looking for a suitable place for the settlement and the name. Finding one, they founded the city in 1718.

Far off to the west the French also established two great names, and the Spaniards, one.

Hunting everywhere for precious metals, as they always were, some Spaniards about 1730 came upon what seemed the greatest find ever made. Gigantic nuggets of pure silver lay loose upon the ground near a desert spring; one of them was reported to weigh three tons. It was a freak of nature, and after the surface was cleared, no great ore-body could be located. But the memory of the first rich finds made the place famous. As a name, the Spaniards took the simple description in the Papago language, "little spring"; fitting it to their own pronunciation, they wrote it down as Arizona.

Only a few years after this Spanish naming, two Frenchmen called Mallet, brothers, went well up the Missouri River, and wintered there. Starting out with some Indians across-country in the spring, they came to a broad, shallow river. It differed from most rivers because it did not flow in a distinct valley or even between high banks, but seemed to spread out almost level with the plain. The Indians therefore called it in their language, *ni,* "river," and *bthaska,* which gave the idea of spreading flatness. The Mallets translated this as Rivière Plate, but spelled it Platte, and in that form it survived for the river. But from Ni-bthaska a greater name was to arise.

Also the French ascended the rivers beyond Lake Superior and found still more lakes. In that region they came to know the Crees, who told them of some mountains farther to the west. The Cree name for them was either the word meaning *stone* or one much like it. But Stony Mountains is hardly a reasonable distinguishing term, since high mountains are generally stony or rocky. So the explanation is possibly different. Between the Crees and the mountains was the tribe called Assinaboins, friends and allies, from whom the Crees had probably heard of the mountains. But in the Algonquian languages *assin-* is the general root meaning "stone." The Assinaboins took their name from it, and in later years the English often called them the Stonies.

Whether the Crees meant really Stony Mountains or Assinaboin

Mountains, the French understood the first. An Indian drew a map on which the name was written in French as the Mountains of the Shining Stones, as if taken from crystals or gems. Because of this, they were sometimes called by the fine name Shining Mountains. But more often the French wrote Montaignes Rocheuses, and the English took this over as Rocky Mountains.

During these years the French, like the English, filled the map in with hundreds of little names in all the usual ways. Even more than the English, they liked to clip the long Indian names, saying Pè for Peouarea, Moin for Moingona, Ark for Arkansas, and Ka for Kansas. So it happens that the Kansas River is still commonly called the Kaw, and from a phonetic English spelling of the phrase "Aux Arks" came Ozark.

One early French party wrote down a Choctaw word: "a deadwater which the savages call bayouque"; from this came *bayou*. The same party in 1700 ascended the Mississippi, giving many names. They came to a place called Istrouma, meaning "red post," because one had been fixed there to mark the boundary between the hunting grounds of two tribes. The French translated Istrouma as Baton Rouge.

At this same time some English captain entered the river, and careened his little ship on the bank of one of the many bends. While his crew was thus momentarily helpless either for flight or defense, a party of French came down the river. The two countries were then temporarily at peace, but the French leader boldly approached the English captain, and demanded what he was doing in the Mississippi—didn't he know that the French were established there? The Englishman was overwhelmed. All he could do was to sputter that he knew nothing about it. He got under way as quickly as he could for the mouth of the river, cursing the French as a nation and as individuals. The incident so amused and pleased the French that they always remembered the place as *le Détour à l'Anglais,* or the Englishman's Bend. Slightly mistranslated it survives as the town of English Turn.

Once more, as had happened with the Dutch and Swedes,

names themselves became symbols of empire. Thus a French priest reached far back to the times of Jean Ribaut, and claimed the whole country for France, by such evidence:

The kings of France named these lands Carolina and New France before the English gave them names—after their fashion of causing to be forgotten the names which the French had given them.

On the other side, Sir William Johnson came to a beautiful northern lake among mountains which the French had called St. Sacrement. To replace this name—doubly odious as both French and Romish—he called it Lake George: "not only in honor of His Majesty, but to ascertain [by which he meant *make certain*] his undoubted dominion here." So also Englishmen spoke and wrote of Lake Ontario and the Welinis instead of Lake Frontenac and the Illinois. In the end sometimes the English form survived, sometimes the French.

Then, year after year, by the lake-sides and at the river-crossings, the red-coated British and the kilted Highlanders fought the regiments of La Sarre, and Languedoc, and Guienne, and the Royal Roussillon. And on their flanks fought their colonials and red tribesmen. Here and there still are names that echo that fighting. Artillery Cove is on Lake George where Montcalm disembarked his cannon, with Bloody Pond close by where corpses of some Frenchmen once were thrown. Another name there preserves a mistranslation; in French it was Chevelure, or Scalp; but the English rendered it Crown Point.

In a great smoky city far over the mountains men still say Grant's Hill and Forbes Street, though few remember why. But the first is the hill where Major Grant's Highlanders and colonials camped on a September night of 1758, trying to surprise Fort Duquesne—and met defeat themselves. But Forbes Street marks the final victory, for it follows the line of the road which the Scotch general had cut through the forest to capture the French fort, and which the colonials called Forbes' Road.

The skirmishing all along the frontier left its names. One is a tributary river far north on the Connecticut. When the Indians fell upon Deerfield in Queen Anne's War, they carried off the captives toward Canada, and among them the pastor John Williams. On the bank of that little river, in the wintry forest, he gathered the remnant of his pitiful flock about him, and took for his text Lamentations, 1, 18: "Hear, I pray you, all people, and behold my sorrow: my virgins and my young men are gone into captivity." Men, remembering later, called it Williams River.

So also, some captives, making their way back from Canada, were starving. Then in a meadow they saw a horse. Thinking themselves far in the wilderness, they believed the horse must belong to some Indian, and in desperation they shot and ate it. Afterwards they soon came to the first of their own towns. But the place where they had shot one of the townspeople's horses was remembered as Horse Meadow.

Far to the west a creek flows into the Ohio River, and from it a city is called Wheeling—a name which seems as much English as Barking or Reading. But it is really *wil-ing,* "place of the head," because, as the Indians reported, a captive had been put to death there, and his head stuck upon a sharpened pole.

Farther south is a stream called Tug Fork. In the spring of 1756 four hundred Virginians and Cherokee allies set out to take revenge on the Shawnees for some border raids. The names along their route of march ring like an American saga—across New River below the Horse-Shoe, down to Wolf Creek, over to the Bluestone, to the head of the North Fork of Sandy, and down to the Burning Spring. (This last was so called because a strange gas bubbled up through it. You could light this gas with a firebrand, and it would burn until the wind blew it out.) At the spring they killed and ate two buffaloes, and hung their hides on a beech tree. They went on, but having used up their provisions, they had to retreat, and were starving when they got back to the Burning Spring. So they took the buffalo hides from the beech tree, and cut them into thin strips like bootlaces, which were called *tugs.* They roasted these at the fire, and ate them. From this, men told the story, the stream was named. (Yet there may have been another reason, at least to reinforce the first. In the Cherokee language *tugulu* means the fork of a stream, and other streams not far off are called Tug. Also, farther south, there is a river called the Tugaloo.)

There are many legends about names—some fanciful, some foolish. A few touch poetry, and one of these springing from the wars should be told. From it may be seen how close to magic is the power of a name in men's minds. This is a well-attested story, explain it as one will.

In the Highlands, in those days when great-sword and dirk were above any law, a certain Duncan Campbell, laird of Inverawe, sat in his hall, and there came a loud knocking at the gate. A stranger of another clan stood there with a bloody kilt; he had killed a man in a fray, he said, and came to seek refuge. The Campbell promised to protect him, and swore it on his dirk, and hid the slayer. The pursuers soon came, and said, "Your cousin Donald has been murdered, and we are looking for the murderer." But he remembered his oath above the law of blood, and without lying he said he could be of no help.

That night, in a dream, he saw his murdered kinsman and heard him cry in a hollow voice, "Inverawe! Inverawe! Blood has been shed. Shield not the murderer!" But Duncan Campbell of Inverawe stood by his pledged word. A second time the vision came, and then the third time it cried like the ghost of Caesar, "Farewell, Inverawe! Farewell, till we meet at Ticonderoga!" The Campbell, awaking, knew that he had heard of his death-place, but there was no such name in Scotland.

Later he took King George's commission with a Highland regiment, and rose to be its major. Here indeed there is no mere legend, for Major Duncan Campbell of Inverawe came with the Black Watch to America, and all that happened afterwards is sure in the record.

When he heard that the attack was to be against Ticonderoga, he knew that his hour had come. But his brother officers conspired against him, and said, "This is not Ticonderoga; we are not there yet; this is Fort George!" and he was surer of himself.

Then in the night he saw the murdered man again, and knew that they had lied.

(Yet the name itself is only a simple one in the language of the Mohawks, "between two lakes." And many died that day, men who had seen no visions, as men always die when a stupid general flings them against an unshaken fortress.)

Even the stone they raised above that grave seems to make a question of the name:

Here lies the Body of Duncan Campbell of Inverawe, Esq., Major to the old Highland Regiment, aged 55 years, who died the 17th July, 1758, of the wounds he received in the Attack on the Retrenchment of Ticonderoga or Carrillon, on the 8th July, 1758.

A war is always more than the battle-front, and so all over the colonies the wars affected the names. More and more towns and counties were named for governors and ministers of state. These men became symbols of national power and unity, although they were often little men in themselves.

Such a one was Spencer Compton. A favorite of George II, "neither suited to become a leader of men or a framer of measures," he rose to power. Nobody remembers Spencer Compton, but a town in Massachusetts and cities of Delaware and North Carolina take their names from his title, Earl of Wilmington.

So it was with the others, those periwigged lords of London, who wore their laces and took their snuff and kept their mistresses, and in an unheroic age conducted the affairs of state on the principle, "Every man has his price." You will find their names and titles from Maine to Georgia—Sunderland, Walpole, Litchfield, Hardwicke, Bedford, Halifax, Pelham, Newcastle, Carlisle, and the rest. What most of them ever did for the colonies to deserve so much as the naming of an out-house would be difficult to discover.

With the royal governors the case was better. Many of them labored hard, and their names were deservedly bestowed. Eight Virginia counties bear such names.

During the wars the royal family also became even more a symbol of the nation. Georgetown vied in popularity with Kingston. Between 1720 and 1765 fifteen Virginia counties took their names from branchings of the royal family tree. Of these, the strange new names Brunswick, Hanover, and Lunenburg celebrated the King's German titles, which were popular elsewhere as well. King George County was for the first of the German kings. Caroline County honored the Queen of George II. His eldest son, Prince of Wales, had a portion in Frederick County, and his third son a double portion in Prince William and Cumberland. Amelia and Louisa were his daughters. Orange honored his son-in-law; Augusta, a daughter-in-law; Prince Edward, a grandson. Finally, Charlotte and Mecklenburg loyally recorded the marriage of George III to Princess Charlotte of that German duchy.

The same queen won further immortality by Mecklenburg County in North Carolina with its county-town Charlotte. The royal names indeed became highly popular for towns and streets. Fredericksburg in Virginia was laid out in 1727, and took its name from the Prince of Wales. In spite of a revolution its chief streets are still William, Edward, George, Hanover, Charlotte, Amelia, Prince, Princess, Caroline, and Sophia. These names with the addition of King, Queen, Duke, and Crown came to form a conventional name-pattern, still well preserved in such cities as Alexandria and York. New England followed the fashion, and even in the heart of notoriously anti-royalist Connecticut, Meriden and New Haven still preserve some good royalist street-names.

The royal influence, acting chiefly through the increased influence of the governors, effected nothing short of a revolution in the customs of naming throughout most of New England. In Massachusetts the naming of new towns became a prerogative of the Governor himself. Doubtless he was subject to local pressure and tactful palm-greasing, but certainly the old system of the General Court went completely to pieces. The governors built their political fences by giving names in honor of the royal family, or the ministers of state, or even influential local gentlemen. A superficial continuity was preserved by the accident that English names and titles were often taken from towns, so that it may be a matter of argument whether Acton was named for an English village, or a certain baronet, or some other person of the same name.

Connecticut alone stood out against the new fashion. Of forty-six towns founded there during the reigns of the first two Georges, not one can be definitely shown to be named for any Englishman —prince, lord, or commoner. In Connecticut the old system of re-producing the names of English places continued strongly. As more and more people were native-born, however, the practice became less exact and somewhat bookish. Towns began to take the names of counties, as with Cheshire, Cornwall, and Kent. The religious revival known as the Great Awakening had a reper-cussion in the four towns—Goshen, Canaan, Bethlehem, and Sharon. Connecticut also carried on the tradition of Saybrook and Voluntown by coining Harwinton from syllables of Hartford, Windsor, and Farmington. Thus even under the stress of the war years, Connecticut went its own stiff-necked way.

The kings and lords were mere symbols of nationality, not heroes in their own right. But the people also sought heroes in an age which had few. As yet, like colonials everywhere, they lacked heroes of their own. Smith and Standish were not yet much re-membered, and the frontiersman was only a whiskey-drinking Scotch-Irishman of the back counties.

In 1745 William Pepperell, born in Kittery, led a New England army against the French fortress of Louisbourg, and captured it. He returned as a military hero. The King made him a baronet, and Massachusetts honored him with a town, but such examples remained rare.

A hero of any colony was a foreigner, viewed with suspicion by men of twelve colonies. A native Englishman had a better chance of being accepted everywhere. Each successive general who came to beat back the French and Indians had his chance, but most of them were not of heroic stuff. Lord Jeffrey Amherst, however, was remembered in three towns and a Virginia county, besides a college and a college-song. Wolfe was the most brilliant and heroic of them all. He won Quebec, and death in the hour of victory. All England bowed to his memory, but he made strangely little impression upon the thirteen colonies. The grantees of a town in New Hampshire named it Wolfeborough, hot on the news of victory. Otherwise, only an occasional street commemorated him.

One British admiral, by little more than mere accident, gave rise to a great and often-repeated name. When an attempt was to be made against Cartagena in the Spanish colonies, a young Virginian received his captain's commission with the colonial troops. The expedition met disaster, chiefly because of the incompetence of its high commanders, but the Virginian survived fever and bullets, and returned home to his plantation overlooking the Potomac. As a young man will, he made a hero of his commander, even though Admiral Edward Vernon had done little to deserve such loyalty. So Lawrence Washington called his plantation Mount Vernon, and died a few years later, leaving the land and its name to his younger half-brother. Thus the name of a blustering and not very competent British officer spread from ocean to ocean.

In that time, however, there was a greater Englishman than Vernon or Wolfe; more than any other man, he broke the grip of France. So it is fitting that his simple commoner's name should stand upon a greater city than any called for a George or Frederick.

Far to the west at the forks of the Ohio, the French had built Fort Duquesne. Braddock marched, but met defeat and died saying, "Who would have thought it!" Then the testy Scot, John Forbes, tried his hand. It was largely a Scotch affair, that second advance. Many of the British troops were Highlanders, and the colonials were mostly Scotch-Irishmen from the middle colonies. Scotch also was Sir John Sinclair, Quartermaster General, who really built the road, sending back a good Scotch requisition for "Pickaxes, crows, and shovels; likewise more whiskey." Thus aided, they put the road through, and the French evacuated Fort Duquesne. Then the English—or one had better say Forbes, the Scot—named it for the Great Commoner and called it Pittsburgh.

Any Briton might have honored Pitt, but the Scotch of it comes rather in the *-burgh*. An Englishman would have used some other suffix, as indeed elsewhere we find Pittsfield, and Pittsylvania. But a Scot remembered Edinburgh. Thus the name was doubly suitable; that town grew up as the stronghold of the Scotch-Irish, and after a century and a half they were to defy their own government over the question of a single letter rather than let their name be Germanized to Pittsburg.

There was one other hero of those years, but his way was made easy, because he was a king's son. Christened William Augustus, he was created Duke of Cumberland at the age of five, and thenceforth was known by that title. He undertook a military career. Displaying courage and being what he was, he found himself in 1745, at the age of twenty-four, no less than Captain-General in command of all the British, Hanoverian, Austrian, and Dutch troops in Flanders. He was a stiff disciplinarian—after all, he was nearly pure German by blood. On the battlefield he showed more courage than finesse. That old strategist, Marshal Saxe, beat him at Fontenoy, but it was touch-and-go that day, and everybody at least could comment on the Duke's personal coolness. He was recalled then to defend England against Bonnie Prince Charlie. Once and for all, he broke the clansmen at Culloden, and afterward he harried the Highlands thoroughly and frightfully. He was a hero for Culloden, but a reaction followed. The English had little stomach for burning and hanging after a victory, and when Cumberland came back to London, they called him "Billy the Butcher."

The colonists, however, were not so squeamish. They were familiar with Indian scalpings and torturings, and they accepted the victor as a real hero. Within a few years after Culloden there were Cumberland counties in Virginia, North Carolina, and Pennsylvania. But more important still, a certain Dr. Thomas Walker of Virginia went exploring across the mountains. He was a very loyal admirer of the royal family. He named a far-off river after the Princess Louisa, but the frontiersmen forgot what it was, and now it is called Levisa. Also on April 17, 1750, he entered in his journal:

> Still rain. I went down the creek a-hunting, and found that it went into a river about a mile below our camp. This, which is Flat Creek and some other join'd, I called Cumberland River.

The French had already named this river at its other end, but Walker's new name was English, and it spread with the triumph of English arms down the course of the stream. Soon afterwards, Walker called the chief opening in that direction Cumberland Gap. Then came Cumberland Mountains, and more counties and towns. By this time men had new heroes and had forgotten all about Prince William Augustus. Probably they did not even think of that English county, "land of the Cymri," but the name grew upon its prosperity, as a fire by its own heat. Thus Billy the Butcher, not much of a hero at best, spread himself over a whole region, including a river much greater than Thames.

When the first English had come in ships, they had entered the broad mouths of the rivers where they flowed into the ocean, and had established names accordingly—usually taking one from the Indians, or bestowing the name of some English prince or lord. But from the tidal mouth no one could tell which river was really large or small, and so it happened that the Charles in Massachusetts, and the York in Virginia, though they bore royal names, were not great rivers. But on the other side of the mountains, the English came first to the headwaters, and just the opposite sometimes occurred with the naming.

Thus it happened that there was a plain frontiersman, descendant of a Swede who had been a settler of New Sweden. This Stephen Holston was one of those who went farthest west. In 1746 he built a cabin in the mountain country, near the headwaters of a little creek, which flowed no one knew where. In the next year, when some surveyors worked in the region, they gave the name Holston Creek to that stream, because he lived there. As later men followed that stream down, they called it by the same name, and as it received tributaries and grew larger, they called it Holston River. Thus one of the largest streams of that region came to bear the name of a common settler.

So it was also with Clinch River. But Clinch was even more obscure, and no one knows even who he was, except that Dr. Walker wrote of a stream, "which the hunters call Clinch's River, from one Clinch a hunter." So also a stream which was once called Beargrass River had its name changed. With Dr. Walker in 1750 was a man called Ambrose Powell, and at a camp on that stream he passed the time by carving his name on a tree. Eleven years later a party of hunters went that way and saw the carved letters. And so that stream, which is no small one, is called Powell River.

The greatest of all those west-flowing streams of the South took its name in much the same way. This was at first known as Cherokee River, which was a good name to anyone looking at it on a map, or considering it from far off, because it flowed largely through the country of that powerful tribe. But when the traders and the hunters got over the mountains, they came first to the headwaters of the river and found the Cherokee towns, actually not on one stream, but on many different smaller ones.

It happened that one of the chief towns bore an old name of which the Cherokees themselves did not know any meaning. As early as 1707 an Englishman had written this name as Tinnase. Later, the English began naturally to call the small river there by the same name. As they went downstream they carried the name along, and as the river grew larger and larger, it was still called the Tennessee. Then again, as with the far-off Colorado, the first-named branch became in the end the Little Tennessee. The name Cherokee, however, remained official for many years. In 1754 a report came back from the frontier that the French were intending to build forts on the Tennessee. This report mystified Governor Dinwiddie of Virginia, and he wrote of it as "a river indeed I cannot find by that name on any drafts I have." But as usually happened on the frontier, the frontiersmen's name overcame the official one.

[147]

In the naming of rivers clear across from ocean to ocean there were many twists and inconsistencies and conflicts. No one ever sat down over a well-made map, and worked out a system of naming, as a man might make a plan for a town and then name the streets. But the rivers lay hidden far off in the forests, and often even the same hunters coming to a second stream-crossing would not know whether it was a stream they had crossed before, or another.

The greatest river to be thus formed suddenly is the Ohio, which begins at Pittsburgh with the flowing together of the Allegheny and Monongahela, although the latter is smaller. Ohio was an Iroquois word, and the French applied it to the whole river. But the French also, as early as 1681, recorded its Algonquian name as Olighin. Later a Moravian missionary who had lived seventeen years among the Algonquian-speaking Delawares and had had two Indian wives (so that his knowledge of the language can hardly be disputed) wrote: "The Ohio, as it is called by the Senecas. Allegheny is the name of the same river in the Delaware language. Both words signify the fine or fair river." Most likely one name was a translation of the other, but which came first would be hard to say, for there had been much shifting about of tribes before the white men came, and the legends of the Delawares told that they had once lived in the region of that river.

Later the Delawares, displaced from their eastern lands, came again to that stream. By that time some of them seem to have forgotten the meaning of the name, and they told of an ancient tribe called the Alligewi. No matter what the true meaning may be, the English traders who came to the new Delaware towns heard Allegheny for the river there, and this became established locally. But lower down, the Delawares did not live, and the English used the other name, which the French had already established on the maps. In the end, to bring reason and order out of confusion of wars and shifting peoples, a fiction was developed as with other such streams. So, even in the most official publications, we may read: "*Ohio*: river, formed at Pittsburgh . . . by the junction of the Allegheny and Monongahela rivers."

At last in 1763 peace came, and all the land as far as the Mississippi was confirmed to King George. As was natural, however, the French who lived on the east bank were still loyal to King Louis. Among them was a certain Pierre LaClede, who with others decided to move across to the west bank, hoping to remain under French rule. He obtained rights, and selected a site where, he wrote, he intended "to establish a settlement which might hereafter become one of the finest cities in America." In February, 1764, the ground-breaking began, and LaClede named the village St. Louis.

Like so many names, it may have arisen from more sources than one. The province itself, being called Louisiana, may have helped suggest it. Also, like the Georgetowns, it honored the reigning king. But also, and most certainly, it honored one far greater than Louis XV. That was Louis IX—king, saint, knight-at-arms, chivalrous victor, lover of beauty, uniting in his life all that makes for greatness, and dying as a man best dies, upon a great quest. St. Louis!—a name to be held aloft, as a symbol of what man may attain, like a battle-tossed banner on a still doubtful field!

Chapter XVI ⟨ Of a pause between wars

AFTER the French had been beaten, the King's ministers drew a line on the map beyond which the people should not go to take up new lands. But the people crossed it, nonetheless.

They went through Cumberland Gap by a narrow horse-trail which they called a *trace*. Later they cut a passage for wagons, and this was the Wilderness Road because, for a hundred miles and more, it passed through country so called, where there were no houses, and people in their weariness remembered the Wilderness where the Children of Israel wandered their forty years.

Those who passed that way were of two kinds. Some pressed on toward the rich lands westward. Others settled in a pleasant cove or by a creek, and from them sprang the mountaineers.

They are simple, plain, and English, the names of the mountaineers. They show old ways of life—Notchlog and Blaze, Stillhouse and Rockhouse, Wolf-pen and Wolf-pit. Of the same kind are Trace Creek and Road Creek, for they tell of the years when a trail or road was a matter of note.

Sometimes also there is a Schoolhouse Creek, for a school was a matter of note indeed. And the lack of them is seen in the spellings, like Kerless Knob, and Tater Knob, and Teeny Knob.

As among clanspeople everywhere, a man went by his christened name, or a nickname, more than by his father's. So arose those dozens of streams and mountains called Davy, Joe, Jake, and Jim. Rich Mountain came more often probably from some Richard than by any suggestion of wealth in a mine. Red Creek may be not from the color of the water, but (like the original Reading) from a nickname.

There are few Indian names in that country. The mountaineers had no love for Indians. Besides, being unable to read and write, they easily made the words over into a wholly English form so that even their origin could no longer be known. Now and then, however, the story of the words can be made out, as with the Cherokee *gurahi,* a salad plant, which became the name of a mountain, and later was spelled Curry He. From that, by counterpart, came Curry She Mountain.

Those who pressed on through the mountains came at last to a beautiful country, but somewhat strange. Its greatest strangeness lay in its open lands. Those men who crossed the mountains were not Englishmen who had known Salisbury Plain and the sheepwalks of East Anglia. But they were Americans (and their fathers before them) born to the forest, and knowing open lands only as little clearings, or stretches of swampy meadow too wet for trees, or as what they called "Indian old fields." So one of them wrote, "a fine meadow, about a mile wide, very clear like an old field, and not a bush in it." And he added in wonder, "I could see the buffaloes in it above two miles off."

From its openness, as was fitting, the new country was known as Kentucky, not "dark and bloody ground," but in the language of the Iroquois, *kenta-ke,* "meadow-land." From the country, the river took its name, and not the reverse, as was customary. But farther north, about the same time, a river gave its name to the region when men began to speak of the Ohio Country, or merely Ohio.

Of the heroes of the new land, the first was Daniel Boone. He and his comrades gave two names which were not of the ordinary. Once, as he slept by a stream, he dreamed that yellow-jackets stung him. When he awoke, he interpreted this to mean that he would be wounded by the Indians. The dream was so vivid that he called the stream Dreaming Creek, and it still remains so.

The other name was even stranger. It happened that Boone, though he could hardly spell, enjoyed reading. On one expedition, as he later testified, he and the others "had with us for our pleasure" a certain book. That book was one of the best of all—that which tells of travels to farther lands even than Kentucky as made by one Lemuel Gulliver. One evening in camp they were reading of Brobdingnag and its city Lorbrulgrud, but were interrupted by some Indians creeping up on them. There was a little skirmish, and afterwards one of the hunters remarked that they had disposed of the Lorbrulgruds. The creek kept that name, and with the spelling shifted to Lulbegrud it remains.

Just as the first English had found the names of England not always suiting the new land, so the English and Scotch-Irish (and the few Germans and Swedes who went with them) found that lack beyond the mountains.

First of all they needed a name for the wide treeless stretches. At first they said *meadow* or *glade,* and those are still common names there. Sometimes a man with more book-learning, like Dr. Walker, remembered the Spanish *savanna,* and others said merely *naked land.* But most of the newcomers looked at the open spaces, and thought that they were treeless because the soil was too poor. So they called them *barrens,* and a whole region took that name, "from there being little or no timber in it." Afterwards the Kentuckians found that the soil was not poor, and perhaps for this reason they took a new and foreign word from the French. In that language the word meant only "meadow," but to the Kentuckians it meant something greater, and so *prairie* has always borne a touch of strangeness and poetry. In English, *meadow* is to *prairie* as a placid cow to a shaggy buffalo-bull.

Also, the sea-coast land of unbroken forest had needed no word for isolated trees, but the Kentuckians began to say *grove,* and it grew into the pattern of names. In the end men cut down the forests and planted trees in the prairies, so that now only the names remain to show where prairie and grove once alternated.

The land had other wonders. Many fine springs of water flowed from underground, and the settlers looked on these with favor. They were no longer green Englishmen who would settle at Jamestown and drink the river-water and die of the fever; but they were men and women who had learned to be at home in the forest, and they did not stoop to a stagnant pool or muddy stream if they could help it. So they built their cabins close to springs, and that word survived in the names of their towns.

Not all the springs were good for drinking; some had films of oil upon them, and some were brackish with salt. Near these last the clay was salt to the taste, and the buffalo and deer came there in hundreds to lick it. So these were the best hunting-grounds. They were called *licks* and that name survived upon many streams and towns.

Near the licks the buffalo might even trample down all the growth. Such a place was called a stamping-ground. That too became the name of a town, and still an American may call his own particular haunts his *stamping-ground.*

By these names then you may know that new land beyond the mountains—by Glade, Prairie, and Grove, by Spring, by Lick, and by Stamping Ground.

Often enough some name has arisen merely by mistake. When the French came to Lake Champlain they called one of the rivers La Mouette, "the sea-gull." Later, a map-engraver, neglecting to cross his *t's,* made this into La Mouelle. This meaningless mistake survived, and the English further changed it to become Lamoille. So it went with a greater name.

Among the French explorers of the west was the Baron La-hontan. He was not a man of integrity, and told a tale of a certain Long River which did not exist. But he wrote charmingly, and his book with illustrations and maps was published in French and English in several editions. Most of these contained a map on which appeared Wisconsin River, spelled in French fashion Ouisconsink. But for the French edition of 1715 this map was redrawn by a careless engraver who made many mistakes with names, such as Magara for Niagara. He wrote Ouisconsink as Ouariconsint, and he also broke the word with a small hyphen because the map was crowded, and put *sint* beneath. So anyone looking at the map a little carelessly would think that there was a river Ouaricon, flowing toward the west.

Thus matters stood when in 1760 Major Robert Rogers, famous leader of the Rangers, went west to receive the surrender of the French posts at Detroit and elsewhere. There apparently he heard the old tale, often reported by the French, about a River of the West flowing to the Pacific through a break in the Rocky Mountains. The Indians with whom the French had ordinary contact could not have been so far west themselves, and they must have been telling tales they picked up from others, or else (as Indians often did) they were merely saying what they knew the white men wanted to hear. La Vérendrye, the French explorer, had known plenty about Indians and their tale of the River of the West, and he wrote: "These people are great liars," though he added hopefully, "but now and then they tell the truth."

Rogers may have believed the story, or may only have used it for his own ends; though a great frontier fighter, he was by no means trustworthy in peace. Later, being in London, in 1765, he petitioned the King to be granted a commission and funds for the discovery of the Northwest Passage by way of this river. In his petitions he would naturally try to make the story as reasonable as possible, and so he had a motive for using a more precise name than River of the West. He wrote "the river called by the Indians," and then spelled the name much as it stood by mistake on that map.

Perhaps the explanation is that some Frenchman or Englishman, remembering vaguely, had told Rogers: "I have seen on an old map a river Ouaricon, flowing to the west, by which you can pass in canoes to the ocean." (This indeed was true, for the Wisconsin served as one route by which the French reached the Mississippi and the Gulf.) If Ouaricon had been passed by word of mouth, its *c* could easily have become *g,* because these sounds are often interchanged. As for Roger's own assertion that the river was so called "by the Indians," it rests only upon his own word, which was then considered far from reliable. Besides, being a man who knew Indians, he would more likely have said Chippewas or Crees, if telling what actually happened, for he would have known that as far as language goes the word Indian means nothing. So, in his petitions to the King, Rogers wrote uncertainly—Ouragon, Ourgan, and Ourigan.

The King did not grant Rogers any money for an expedition, but sent him to command at Michilimackinac. From that post Rogers sent Jonathan Carver to explore farther west, and in 1778 Carver published his *Travels through the Interior Parts of North-America.* Like Rogers, Carver was unreliable, and some have called his *Travels* largely fiction. But he at last established the form which the name was to take, spelling it Oregon.

Over the source of this name more controversy has raged than over any other on the continent. Men have guessed wildly that it might be from the Spanish *orégano,* "marjoram"; *orejón,* "big ear," or "slice of dried apple," *origen,* "source"; or from the old kingdom Aragon. They have guessed also the French *ouragan,* "storm"; the Abnaki *orighen,* "fine"; the Shoshone *ogwa-peon,* "river-west"; the Chippewa *owah-wakan,* "river of slaves." They have also pointed out its resemblance to Orjon, a river in Tartary, and to the tribal name of some eastern Indians known vaguely as Horikans. The final absurdity is perhaps the suggestion that it originated from a wandering Irishman called O'Regan.

Most likely, however, it arose from that mistake of the map-maker which made Ouisconsink look like Ouaricon; thence it passed into Ourigan and Ouragon, and finally became Oregon.

After the French were defeated, quarrels arose between the colonials and the King's government, but some of the British supported the colonials, either from principle or merely because they were in the opposition. One of these was the Earl of Camden, Lord Chancellor, who in his judicial decisions denounced the Stamp Act as a breach of the English Constitution, and declared taxation without representation to be sheer robbery. Immediately towns named Camden sprang up in the Carolinas and New Jersey.

Men of the opposition and friends of liberty also were John Wilkes and Colonel Isaac Barré. From them came Wilkesborough in North Carolina and Barre in Massachusetts. Also a certain Major John Durkee had his son christened Barré, and his cousin Andrew Durkee named a son Wilkes. This Major Durkee founded a settlement in Pennsylvania, and either from the two boys or directly from the men themselves he called the place Wilkes-Barre. So it remained, doubly dedicated to the champions of liberty. Thus such names began to cast the shadow of what was to come.

Chapter XVII ❰ How the Leather-Jackets rode north

During all those decades of the wars, the Spanish rule in Mexico had sunk further into languor, but at last the King sent a man to stir up life. This was José de Gálvez, Andalusian-born of the fiery South, with full shares of Spanish pride and Spanish cruelty, and a triple share of restless energy. Wherever the tight-lipped Gálvez went, the land seemed to break into a sweat of energy. No careful man wished to arouse the cold glitter of his eyes, and sometimes he crossed the line of sanity, imagining himself King of Sweden or of Prussia, or even God Almighty.

Most of his energy he loosed upon the western coast. He looked at what charts and reports were available, and saw the notations of harbors with the names Viscaíno had given them—San Diego and Monterey. There was also a vaguely known bay, not mentioned by Viscaíno, called San Francisco.

It had come by its name in 1595. A certain Sebastian Rodríguez Cermeño, commanding the galleon from Manila, made a landfall far north along the California coast, and sailing southward, entered a good harbor. On November 7th, he landed and took possession. The time of the year was well past the day of St. Francis, but there was with the ship a Franciscan father, whose own name also was Francisco. This father "baptized" the land, doubtless pouring water upon it symbolically as in baptizing a child, and the bay was thus named San Francisco. The galleon itself was wrecked, but Cermeño and his men got back to Mexico in a longboat.

Seven years later Viscaíno reached the same bay, but as usual, displacing the names of others, he called it Don Gaspar, for the Viceroy. Nevertheless the name San Francisco remained, somewhat dubiously.

When Gálvez then began to look at the maps, he could not have been very certain about that bay, and in any case it seemed too far north to be reached in the first advance. So he located three places for the foundation of the original missions, and he himself decided that they should be dedicated to San Diego, San Carlos, and San Buenaventura. Then he called to him Father Junípero Serra, a Franciscan.

Serra was eager to found the new missions, but he was troubled at the names of the saints. He even braved Gálvez, and said:

"Sir, is there to be no mission for our Father St. Francis?"

Then Gálvez replied almost blasphemously, as if challenging the saint:

"If St. Francis wants a mission, let him cause his bay to be discovered, and a mission dedicated to him shall be founded there!"

Father Serra said nothing more, but he remembered what had happened.

In 1769 a Virginia county was called Pittsylvania, and a New Jersey village, Camden. In that same summer Father Serra and Captain Portolá and their men came to the bay which Viscaíno had called San Diego, and there they founded that mission on July 16th. Soon afterward, Portolá set off toward the north, overland.

Sixty men went northward, and they should be remembered— for they gave many little names, and with the help of a miracle established two great ones. At their head rode Captain Portolá with two officers, two Franciscans, six men of the Catalan volunteers, and some Indians from the Lower California missions, armed with bows and arrows, and carrying picks and axes to clear the way; next went the pack-train in four sections of twenty-five mules each, every section with its dark-skinned muleteers and its guard of leather-jackets; last, as rear-guard, rode Captain Rivera with more leather-jackets and Indians and the spare horses and mules. The soldiers were called leather-jackets because they wore sleeveless jackets of white deer-skin to deflect arrows. Their saddles had leather aprons, serving to guard the legs in brushy country. Each of them carried also a shield of bull-hide, and a lance, broadsword, and short musket. They were, as an admiring Spaniard wrote, "the best horsemen in the world." Though they had no rifles or coon-skin caps, they were as true frontiersmen as any Boone or Rogers, and from them also we take our heritage.

As they rode north, they gave good frontier names. To be sure, Father Crespi usually gave a saint's name, but nearly all those were forgotten. Even yet in California, however, men say Carpintería and Buchón, Gaviota and Espada, and Pájaro River because the leather-jackets saw an Indian carpentering a canoe, and met a chief with a goiter, or killed a sea-gull, or lost a sword, or found a stuffed bird left by the Indians. Why these names survived better than the saints' names is easy enough to see; in those years few men in California could read, and there were few maps. Names lived mostly in the memories of men. So, after a year or five years or ten, a man returning to a certain place could easily remember that here a wounded bear had mauled two mules, and it was therefore La Cañada de los Osos. But even a priest might have difficulty in remembering exactly what saint's day it may have been when they had camped there.

So they went north toward the great harbor of Monterey which Viscaíno had described, and all the while, it seems, St. Francis was looking out for his own. Thus one day Father Crespi named a stream for the Wounds of St. Francis, but he carefully reserved the name itself for the greater bay and mission. At last, already travel-weary, they came to a stream which seemed to be Viscaíno's Carmel River; they followed this to the sea, expecting to find Monterey. The latitude was correct, but they could not recognize the landmarks, though they had a copy of the description recorded by Cabrera Bueno, the pilot. So nothing was left to do but search farther north.

North they went, sick with scurvy and the flux, half-starving. But the orders of tight-lipped Gálvez drove them on. Day after day they climbed and slid, up and down the steep coastal ravines, through the thickets. They came to some great trees of an unknown kind, and called them *palo colorado,* "red-wood." It was October and the turn of the season. The ocean-fogs chilled them, and then came the rains. The tough leather-jackets—weary, ill, and hungry—rode slumped in their saddles. Portolá was ill; Rivera had scurvy and the flux together. The jerked meat gave out, and the daily ration was down to five tortillas. Some Indians gave them tamales made of black seeds, and the long-enduring leather-jackets said they were not so bad.

Finally, on the last day of October, the officers and priests came to a high summit and looked out far over the ocean. They saw west-northwest some little rocky islands, and a long point stretching far to sea, and under the point some white cliffs, and what seemed the entrance of a bay. Then some of them said plainly at last what they had suspected before, that they had passed Monterey and come to the Bay of St. Francis. "Filled with these doubts and arguments," wrote Father Crespi, "we descended from the hill, and camped."

Next day they sent scouts ahead, and then the day after, which was November 2nd, some men went deer-hunting and came back to tell how they had climbed a ridge and seen a vast water to the east! There seemed only one explanation to Father Crespi—that the Bay of St. Francis was even larger than was reported, so that this arm stretched clear to the south. So they began to call this newly seen water by the name of St. Francis, although it was really another bay, never discovered by any sea-voyagers. Even when the mistake was learned, the larger bay kept the name, and in the end the other was called Drake's Bay because some thought that the Englishman had anchored there in 1579.

Then the Spaniards and the leather-jackets and the Indians dragged back, living on game and eating their mules when other food failed. Finally they arrived at San Diego "smelling frightfully of mules."

It was all very strange. Most expeditions turned back before they had even gone as far as ordered, but Portolá and his men had pushed a hundred miles beyond, and they had all missed the land-marks at Monterey. The leather-jackets told their children (and their great-grandchildren told the same story when men were writing histories a hundred years later) that the Captain had secret orders not to find Monterey, but to go on to San Francisco. But that is only the kind of rumor that men in the ranks always tell.

The pious Franciscans, by putting two and two together, arrived at another and to them very sound conclusion. It was plainly a miracle wrought by St. Francis. Had not Gálvez as much as challenged him to show his power? And how otherwise could it be explained that so many men in their good senses could not recognize the landmarks at Monterey though they were as plain as words on paper? So Father Palou concluded: "In view of this, what else can we say than that our Holy Father evidently desired a mission at his port?"

However it came about, the name San Francisco shifted from the smaller bay to the larger, and in 1776 a mission of that name was founded there. Thus another great name was established, commemorating the gentle saint of Assisi who tamed the wolf of Gubbio, and hailed the sun as "our brother," and preached to his sisters the birds.

One other great name arose from the expedition of Portolá, but it came without anyone's thinking much about it, when all minds were set upon Monterey and San Francisco.

On August 1, 1769, the expedition was only about one hundred miles from San Diego. On that day the camp was not moved, partly that some exploring could be done in various directions, partly that the priests could celebrate, a day early, the great Franciscan jubilee of the Porciúncula, which takes its name from the tiny mother church of the Order, built upon that "little portion" of land in Assisi which the Benedictine monks gave to St. Francis, and which he dedicated to Our Lady of the Angels.

The priests said mass, and the men took communion. Three earthquakes occurred. Some soldiers went hunting and shot an antelope. Father Crespi took an observation, and worked out the latitude as thirty-four degrees and ten minutes.

Next morning, the day of the Porciúncula, they went on through a pass between low hills. They came to a river, "about fourteen yards wide," and Father Crespi noted that the place had all the requisites for a large settlement. He named the river La Porciúncula.

Perhaps for that very reason the soldiers remembered it. Or perhaps they gave no other name because nothing happened by which to remember that camp.

Until 1781 the river was generally called La Porciúncula. Then a town was founded there. Apparently the name (strange even for a river) was not thought suitable for a town, and the full title of the patroness of the church was substituted—Our Lady, Queen of the Angels, of the Little-Portion. On September 4, 1781, probably without much pomp, the new town was founded, and named in eloquent and verbose Spanish, El Pueblo de la Reina de los Angeles de la Porciúncula.

This was a long name, even for speakers of Spanish, and was rapidly simplified. The result was that the original name of the river was omitted, and even all direct reference to the Virgin. The town became simply Los Angeles, as if named for those heavenly messengers and not for their Queen.

Thus new beginnings were made in California. The fathers followed with their missions, using some of Viscaíno's saints and introducing others. But their namings there differed from the naming of missions elsewhere, because the Indian tribes were weak and had little background of stable culture. In other regions the fathers often compromised, tagging the old heathen name after the new holy one, so that they had San Fernando de Taos or San José de Tucsón. In the end the Indian half often prevailed, and the town became Taos or Tucson. But in California there were no such names of missions.

Chapter XVIII ❲ Of new names in the Land

I~N~ THE chilly darkness of the April morning they heard the command—fall out, assemble again at the drum-beat. Most of them went to John Buckman's tavern. And if they needed their ale or the hotter sting of rum, who would blame them? For they made ready to face the might of the King, and that is cold comfort, of an early morning.

They heard the noise of the hooves, and it was Thad Bowman, coming a-gallop. The drum beat, and they formed a straggling line across the green, their veterans of the French wars stiffening them. It was light enough by then to see musket-sights.

They watched the head of the column coming along the Boston road, the red of the coats against the new grass and leaves. They stood there with the battle-dryness in their mouths, and Captain Parker spoke bravely: "If they want a war, let it begin here!"

(All this was in a little village, not much noted or far known. Once it had been called Cambridge Farms, but now it was Lexington, in itself a simple name, being only "place of Leaxa's men." In Nottinghamshire it was called Laxton, but in Massachusetts men used the other form.)

Then the firing came, and men lay dead upon the grass. The line wavered and broke, and perhaps some British officer thought: "Well, that's over!"

Yet all day that news and that name spread outward from the village where women sat with their dead. Reuben Brown took the alarm west to Concord. It went east to meet the men of Salem and Marblehead, marching already. They fired . . . our men are dead . . . Lexington! A new name in the land!

[162]

At Waterton, within five hours of the firing on Wednesday, Mr. Palmer scrawled a hasty note for the Committee—"To all friends of American Liberty . . ." Israel Bessel rode west with it. The town-clerk of Worcester wrote his visé and sent it on.

In Connecticut men heard the name on Thursday, as the riders galloped. In Norwich and New London and Lyme they read the dispatch; in every town, men of the Committee scribbled endorsements. By Guilford and Branford it came to New Haven on Friday—"Lexington . . . killed six men . . . furnish him with fresh horses." On Sunday morning a rider clattered upon the cobbles of New York, and men marched in the streets shouting the new name.

The Jerseymen heard it—at New Brunswick in the dark of Monday morning, standing by the tavern door at Princeton in the sunrise. Trenton endorsed the dispatch and sent a galloper southward. It came to Philadelphia that evening—"be it known . . . alarm the country . . . have seen the dead."

Still the name hurried on. South it went, over the bridge of the Brandywine, where the water ran as yet unreddened. George Washington heard it at Mount Vernon—"Sad alternative. But can a virtuous man hesitate in his choice?" On it went, until at all the ferries and landings of the tidewater, clear to Charleston and Savannah, men had learned that news.

Still farther it went, the name of that little village. What riders carried it, no one knows. By the waters of Clinch and Holston men listened. It took the Wilderness Road through Cumberland Gap. There at last in that western land, a thousand miles from the village green, it came in June to a camp of hunters. They heard the name and said, "Let us call this place Lexington." And so they did, though four years passed before the town was founded there.

That was only the first of many. For now there was a new name in the land, and children learned it with their first words. At last the people had a symbol—not a stupid king across the ocean, but a name red with their own blood.

Lexington was the first, but soon there was a second and greater.

Once far off, when the English still were the Angles, a man called Wassa held a farmstead, and it was called Wassington. It became a village, and the knight who held lands there under King Henry II was Sir William de Wassington. Later the family name was merely Washington, and John Washington was wounded at Agincourt. One of his descendants at the eighth remove, another John, came to Virginia, and a great-grandson of this latter John was named George.

How great a man he was, or even what kind of man, is hardly now to be known. For he became *pater patriae*. He grew to be a hero and a symbol such as the English of England in all their history had never gained.

The first of the places to be named for him was on Manhattan Island, where men still say Fort Washington and Washington Heights; this was in the spring of '76. The next was a district of North Carolina. Then, so quickly that one can hardly say which came before the other, there were counties in Maryland and Virginia and towns in New Hampshire and North Carolina. After that there was no ending, for the name of the man had come to stand for the hopes of the people.

On the two hundredth anniversary of his birth the roll of these places was taken, and they were more than could be surely counted—a state, thirty-two counties, 121 cities and towns and villages, 257 townships, ten lakes, eight streams, seven mountains. Of streets there were counted 1,140, and others uncounted, and besides these there were schools and colleges, buildings, districts, monuments, ferries, bridges, forts, parks, and other features—a tribute of names such as has been paid to no other man, in any country.

Then they fought on, and the names of the places where they fought and the men who died there became names to be given to town sites not yet hewn from the forest.

They fought at Bunker Hill, calling out that first war-cry, "Don't shoot till you see the whites of their eyes!" The fame of that fight was such that even in England the name became a common one for fields. There Warren died, first of the battle-heroes, and you will find his name upon counties and towns.

From Congress and the Signers, and from local leaders came more names—Franklin, Hancock, John Adams, and Sam Adams. Virginia remembered Patrick Henry with two counties. These were not the names of far-off English lords.

After Washington and Warren came other heroes of the army —Greene, the great Rhode Islander, a tower of strength in battle; Montgomery who fell before Quebec; Knox, the gunner, that mountain of flesh; Wayne, "Mad Anthony," who led the Pennsylvania Line. There were the foreigners too—Lafayette, and Pulaski, and von Steuben. You can read all their names upon the map.

Also General Benjamin Lincoln of Massachusetts tried to hold Charleston against the British, but was taken prisoner with his army. Yet the Southerners remembered his good defense, and his name spread across the South in counties and towns, long before a greater Lincoln was known.

As was fitting in a land so dedicated, they also made a hero of one who was not a general or even a captain. That was Sergeant William Jasper, who fought at Charleston and then was killed at Savannah. You will find that name on six counties, besides towns.

Where they braved the passage of the Delaware that winter night is still called Washington Crossing. Next morning they fought the Hessians at the town which William Trent had founded, and that was the first place they ever beat a German army. Then they fought the British at Princeton. General Mercer fell there in the hour of victory, and his name came to stand upon that county. Thus the names Mercer and Princeton were twinned, and you will find them now—county and town together—far off among the mountains and even beyond the Mississippi.

Then in a dark time an often-defeated army drew back among the hills of Pennsylvania. The place of their winter-quarters had only a simple name of the country. Through a narrow valley a little stream flowed down to the river, and the people had called it Valley Creek, and at the mouth of that creek Isaac Potts had built a forge for the working of iron. But now when men say Valley Forge, they think neither of a valley nor of a forge, but of that winter when the winds from Canada swept across the bleak hills and the fires burned low, when the gaunt men stood by their colors, scarcely knowing why—except that the great Virginian held them, and somewhere through the snow-flurries a wraith of Liberty still lured them on.

There began to be talk of a French alliance; men knew that the French were sending munitions and that Dr. Franklin had gone to Paris to negotiate. At that time another great name began, and both its form and the manner of its beginning were somewhat strange.

Far off in the north was a region held in dispute between New York and New Hampshire, but the settlers who moved into it came more from Connecticut than from either of those other colonies. At last the settlers decided that the only way to insure their land-titles was to establish a government of their own and defend themselves in both directions. So they wrote a constitution, and called themselves New Connecticut. But soon afterward they changed the name.

In that country there were some low ranges called the Green Mountains, in contrast to the White Mountains farther east, which kept in translation the old Indian name, given probably because they had snow for much of the year. Some think that the name of the lower mountains was translated from the French, who would have said Les Monts Verts.

Then in 1777, with more enthusiasm for French friendship than knowledge of French grammar, someone made up the new name Vermont.

It did not escape without attack. Both New Hampshire and New York objected to the new state and its name as well, and there were various references in resolutions to "the assumed name of the state of Vermont," and "the said pretended state." People with better knowledge of language were also quick to point out that it was impossible French and if it meant anything at all was not "green-mountains," but "worm-mountain." But even the people of Connecticut had always been highly immune to what other people thought of them, and the Vermonters, being the people of New Connecticut, were doubly immune. In short, it remained Vermont.

As it happens, the best indication that the French ever said Green Mountains is the name of a little river of that country. Impossible stories are told to explain it, but it is still called Lemon Fair River, and the most likely explanation is that the strange name is only a Vermonter's attempt to render Les Monts Verts.

At last the French came. Then, after so many hostile years, the men of the white uniforms became allies, and the lilies of the Bourbons flew beside the new striped flag. So the names that had been hated became suddenly loved, and villages became Versailles or Paris. Virginia also named a western county Bourbon, and from it by the strange chance of words the name of the royal house became a word for whiskey.

From this enthusiasm for the French arose also the name of a great city. During the war some settlers came to a spot which was called from the place, the Falls of the Ohio, although that word was already changing its meaning, and some said, "There are no falls there, only rapids." In 1780 the new settlement petitioned the legislature of Virginia for regular establishment under a name which recognized the aid given to the new states by the French King. On May 14th the petition was granted, and the settlement became Louisville.

In that war, as in any civil war, there was much bitterness. Towns were bombarded and houses burned, and men were beaten, and tarred and feathered, and hanged. There arose a hatred of the British which was deep and slow to die. Yet the men who fought that war did not cast off their English traditions. Though they fought King George to the death, they rejected neither their old ways of life nor their old ways of speech.

Ten of the colonies had been named for English places or men, and six had names of royalty. But not even Georgia was changed.

Probably the new "Americans" did not keep the names out of admiration, but rather they as much as said stubbornly—"The name is ours now, no matter whose it may once have been!" Perhaps they thought that the changing of the names would have been a sign of weakness, and they did not want to admit that their names any more than their lands were held at the will of the King.

Even for towns and counties the changes were few, and expressed dislike for some particular man rather than for English names. Dunmore County in Virginia had honored the last royal governor in 1772. Lord Dunmore, driven out, vindictively bombarded Norfolk from his ships. In 1777 the county was given the Indian name Shanando, later spelled Shenandoah. So also William Tryon, Governor first of North Carolina and then of New York, became much hated for his ravaging of various towns. In New York, Tryon County became Montgomery, and in North Carolina it was abolished completely. North Carolina also wiped out Bute and Dobbs counties, and New York shifted Charlotte County to Washington, probably more to honor Washington than out of dislike for the Queen. The town of Skenesborough in New York, after Mr. Skene proved a Tory, became Whitehall. In Massachusetts three towns, all of them recent foundations, were shifted. Murrayfield had honored John Murray, a settler, who later sided with the Tories; it became Chester, in itself an excellent British name. Hutchinson, founded in 1774 and honoring the Governor, became Barre in 1776. In 1777 the people of Gageborough petitioned for a change, "because the present name of Gageborough may serve to perpetuate the memory of the detested General Gage"; the name became Windsor, taken from the town in Connecticut rather than from the royal residence.

Streets, which always shifted names more easily, showed more changes, and most of the royal names were displaced in New England. King Street sometimes became State, as in Boston. But the process was slow, and even in the end was far from thoroughgoing. A principal street in Charlotte still bears the name of that hated Governor, Tryon.

By and large, the changes of names were negligible. The evidence, for what it is worth, would support those who believe that the Revolution was fought about practical things like taxes, not about names and ideas like liberty.

Some of the new names even seem to show a wistful hope of peaceful settlement, as when a new Massachusetts town in 1778 became Foxborough, honoring Charles James Fox, who was speaking in defense of the colonies in Parliament. In the same year a Virginia county was called Rockingham after the Marquess under whom the Stamp Act was repealed.

They still fought on—at Camden, named for an English earl, and at Cowpens, which was a good frontier name meaning just what it said, and at King's Mountain, which no one bothered to change. At last the armies drew together at Yorktown, which took its name from that Duke of York who became Charles I. After that, the guns were quiet at last.

Chapter XIX ❨ America discovers Columbus

WHILE some had fought, others had gathered in a Congress to establish a government, and matters had turned out badly so far as a name was concerned. Men had often shown much care, and even had carried on disputes, about the name for a colony, or for even a little town. But they seemed to have given no thought at all to the name for the whole new country, and it grew up merely by common usage—a description, cumbersome and commonplace, like the South Fork of Big Creek.

Before the war there had been no need of a name for the colonies as a whole. Each of them had been a unit, and they stood together only as being under the Crown. But when a front was made against the King, men began naturally to speak of "the united colonies." Soon this became The United Colonies, and next The United Colonies of America, or North America. Commissions in the new army stood in one of these later forms.

Soon, however, men began to realize that, as long as they used the word Colonies, they were little better than mutineers, and their revolution lacked any show of legality. So they began to say States. Thus, early in 1776, someone writing under the name *Candidus* declared: "the American States are neither Provinces, Colonies, nor children of Great Britain."

Who first may have happened to say United States of America can never be known. A hundred people may have done so independently, because the elements of the name were all in common use. Fittingly, however, the first recorded use was from the pen of Thomas Jefferson in the Declaration of Independence: "WE, THEREFORE, The Representatives of the United States of America."

The treaty with France used United States of North America. This form was more accurate, but also longer, and never gained popularity.

The abbreviation U.S.A. soon came into use as a mark for army supplies, but was afterwards replaced by the words United States. These were branded into the stocks of muskets as a mark of ownership, and this usage may have been sufficient to establish that term rather than the equally possible America. After a soldier had stared at those words on his musket-butt through several years of campaigning, he was not likely to have any doubts as to the name of the country he was fighting for.

At the time and for the immediate ends, the name United States of America was excellent. It represented the least possible break with tradition, and thus did not unduly frighten the conservative. It raised no question about subordinating the individual states. It was even an argument of the legitimacy of the Revolution. As all these, it probably represented the astute mind of Jefferson, and his special interest in names.

As soon, however, as the emergency of the war had grown less, the inadequacy of the name became apparent. United States of America was greatly lacking in that it supplied no good adjective or term for the inhabitants of the country. It was unwieldy, inexact, and unoriginal. Although it rolled well from the tongue of an orator, not even the sincerest patriot could manage it in a poem or song.

Possibly some far-seeing federalists may also have realized already that, however good it may once have been, the name could become a political hazard. England or France, Virginia or Massachusetts—all these implied an indivisible unity. Such states could be conquered or their governments overthrown by revolution, but they could not be obviously split into components. The very plurality of States, however, was a standing suggestion that what had once been united could equally well be taken apart; in the very name, the seeds of nullification and secession lay hidden.

The chief rival name can actually be traced back a little further than United States of America. In 1775, while Boston was still under siege, Philip Freneau wrote in his *American Liberty:*

> What madness, heaven, has made Britannia frown?
> Who plans or schemes to pull Columbia down?

Perhaps Freneau himself invented the name; at least it must still have been not generally known, for he added a note: "Columbia, America sometimes so called from Columbus, the first discoverer." It was an obvious coinage by the standards of the time. Poets quite generally preferred such elegantly classical circumlocutions as Britannia for Great Britain, Scotia for Scotland, and Cambria for Wales. Some of these terms had already established themselves in English as national names, such as Russia and Austria.

Columbus had never risen as a hero during the colonial period. Great Britain had always, for political reasons, emphasized the

Cabots' discovery of North America. By the time of the Revolution, however, there was no chance that Spain would extend a claim of sovereignty over New York or Philadelphia, and the Cabots were shadowy agents of a British king, unheroic in stature. The new nation began to look back toward Columbus as a kind of founding hero.

Columbia was a happy coinage. Virginia and Georgia had already made such names familiar. It was almost everything that the United States of America was not—short, precise, original, poetic, indivisible, and flexibly yielding good adjectives and nouns. Freneau used it several times in *American Liberty,* and in the succeeding years it gradually became established in poetry. In 1786 it was adopted for the new capital of South Carolina.

The natural opportunity for a reconsideration of the name would have been in the Constitutional Convention of 1787, but apparently the troubles of the delegates were such that they did not get around to the question. Both the Virginia and the New Jersey proposals used only the shortened form, United States. There seems also to be some kind of unimaginative quality in statesmen which makes them think that a name should describe, even at the expense of being awkward. Of the two chief men who might have argued for a better name, Franklin (that old maker of proverbs) was no longer vigorous, and Jefferson was in France. So the preamble read: "this Constitution for the United States of America."

In the text, the framers generally used the shortened form, but were not consistent. As a result, the chief executive is declared to be "President of the United States of America," but is required to take oath: "I will faithfully execute the office of President of the United States." The framers thus followed the English tradition of carelessness in names.

In the course of time the new name became even worse suited to actualities. The foundation of the Latin-American republics and of the Dominion of Canada made the use of America more inept. Every "American" traveling southward soon came to realize that he must call himself "North American" or arouse antipathy.

The terms Yankee and Yank, although actively disliked by millions of people and not greatly loved by anyone, have come more and more into use.

After the adoption of the Constitution a certain amount of agitation for Columbia continued, but was ineffective except to establish a poetic substitute, and furnish the names of many counties, towns, townships, and a great river.

Shortly after 1800 a certain Dr. Samuel Latham Mitchill proposed Fredonia, a gross coupling of the English *freedom* with a Latin ending. It had some advocates, but was never a serious contender. Fredonia survives as the name of a dozen towns. Its origin, however, has been so completely forgotten that in Arizona it is locally said to come from *free* and the Spanish *doña,* and thus to mean "free woman," so called by the polygamous Mormons, although community of women has always been far removed from any doctrine of the Latter-day Saints.

After 1819 Columbus was associated with a region in South America, and was no longer available as a national name. Yearly also, the practicality of a change was becoming less. Various suggestions continued to be made, but they never attained the dignity of political issues. Washington Irving proposed Appalachia or Alleghania. Much later the initials of United States of North America were combined to make Usona.

The makeshift establishment of the national name was the worst misfortune in our whole naming-history. Its too great length has consumed paper, ink, time, and energy. Its vagueness and inaccuracy have caused incalculable misunderstanding, and bad feeling. Yet the trouble has never been acute enough to occasion an amendment to the Constitution, and any official change has become less and less likely. In the course of time the mere evolution of speech may establish some substitute, possibly a derivation of the increasingly popular Yank. Such a change is not without precedent. A state is universally known as Rhode Island; few people realize that it is still officially named under act of July 18, 1776, "the State of Rhode Island and Providence Plantations."

In spite of this history the political mind has continued to exercise its ineptitude about names. British Commonwealth of Nations is almost as bad as United States of America, and Soyuz Sovietskikh Sotsialisticheskikh Respublik is even worse. Rowland Hill remarked that he did not see why the Devil should have all the good tunes. The case is not so bad with names, but certainly the terse Axis is, as a name, much superior to its floundering counterpart, United Nations.

Chapter XX (Of the last voyagers

JUAN PONCE DE LEÓN was the first who ever looked ashore from a ship's deck at the land which was to be the United States of America, and gave a lasting name. After him followed a noble company of voyagers—Cabrillo, Gosnold, Viscaíno, Block, Champlain, and many others.

During two and a half centuries after Ponce de León, the shipmasters sailed along those shores, naming and renaming capes and bays and river-mouths. Gradually, better maps were made and settlements established, and toward the end of the eighteenth century the chief names had been fixed upon all the coasts which would later be included in the forty-eight states—except for the section northward from San Francisco Bay.

It was a dangerous coast, always a lee shore against the westerly gales sweeping across the open ocean. The surf crashed at the foot of cliffs, and the fog shut down close, day after day. So, even when a shipmaster ventured there, he kept good offing, and saw only a few dim headlands, and found no harbors. It remained a region of mystery, where some men still hoped to find the Northwest Passage.

Two beliefs were current about that coast. One was the likely enough report of a bay seen by Martín de Aguilar, Viscaíno's lieutenant. The second belief rested upon so strange a tale that it was more like a legend, although for all anyone knew it might yet turn out to be gospel-truth.

This is that tale of Juan de Fuca. In the years of Queen Elizabeth there was an Englishman named Michael Lok who told it, and Purchas printed it in his collection of voyages. The beginning rings with the true touch of the seaman's yarn, as Michael Lok, himself a voyager, told it:

> When I was at Venice, in April, 1595, happily arrived there an old man, about threescore years of age, called commonly Juan de Fuca, but named properly Apostolus Valerianos, of Nation a Greek, born in the Island Cephalonia, of profession a mariner, and an ancient pilot of ships.

One almost sees the Greek's dark eyes watching the Englishman, who has money for wine and dinner, and telling in his horrible blend of Italian and Spanish the story that will hold the interest: "Forty years . . . mariner and pilot . . . robbed and taken at Cape California . . . sixty thousand ducats . . . a small caravela and a pinnace . . . along the coast of Nova Spania and California . . . very fruitful, and rich of gold, silver, pearl."

Thus, in perhaps the very year when Shakespeare wrote *The Merchant of Venice,* Juan de Fuca, an old man and poor, sitting at a table or walking in the Rialto, told Michael Lok how in 1592 he sailed north, and just above forty-seven degrees found a broad strait, and sailed through it into the Atlantic, and then back to Acapulco in the Pacific.

Michael Lok, unlucky promoter of voyages, felt his pulse rise, and he believed again in the Northwest Passage. He had not the extra hundred pounds to bring the old Greek to England. They parted, and Juan de Fuca wrote some letters in his mingled Italian and Spanish, and then died.

[175]

Lok tried to find a backer, but the Northwest Passage was an old tale. Perhaps the London merchants jested:

"Of Cephalonia, you say?"

"Aye—"

"And that is close to Ithaca?—I remember another 'ancient pilot of ships' who told a story called the *Odyssey*. Perhaps the air of those islands breeds good sea-tales."

Yet neither Michael Lok nor Juan de Fuca lied altogether. There was such a man as that Greek pilot, and he had served the Spaniards on the western coast. Perhaps he really sailed far north on some voyage of which no log-book ever reached the Archives of the Indies. The curious truth is that, close enough to the latitude which Fuca mentioned, a strait runs eastward. A pilot sailing through this would find a broad sound beyond it, and many islands, as Fuca told. Certainly, however, no one ever sailed through that strait into the Atlantic, but that may have been what the Greek had to add to make sure of his dinner.

Seven years after they talked in Venice, Viscaíno voyaged north, and after that the coast was neglected for nearly two centuries. Even more hazily than Martín de Aguilar, men remembered Juan de Fuca.

After the leather-jackets had ridden north, the Spaniards sailed again. Pérez was the first, in 1774, and with him went Father Crespi who had been with the leather-jackets too. They gave some names, which were forgotten. In the next twenty years the Spaniards sent many expeditions under good officers who explored the coast fairly well, and one of them even found what seemed to be the river of Aguilar. But Spain was then a poor kingdom, and the charts and narratives of these officers lay unpublished. Because of this you will find few Spanish names on that coast. Almost alone, far at the northwestern corner there is a little group of names commemorating those last voyages of Spain—San Juan Island, Lopez Island, Rosario Strait, and a few others. (But Anacortes, a town on one of the islands, is not Spanish, but only a name made to harmonize with the Spanish ones. It is really for a girl named Anna Curtis.)

The first of the English after Drake to sail along that northwest coast was the great Captain Cook, in 1778, and he gave some names still used.

Where he first saw land, he called the point by a good seaman's name, Cape Foulweather, "from the very bad weather that we, soon after, met with."

By the maps Cook knew that the places farther south had mostly saints' names. Because of this, perhaps, he also began to give saints' names, but from the calendar of the Church of England. So, looking in his prayer-book, he named Cape Perpetua on March 7th, and Cape Gregory five days later. He went on, giving an English saint's name when he had no better reason, and so even far north in Alaska a cape still commemorates the Venerable Bede.

Cook also named the northwestern point of the United States. On March 22nd he saw a small opening, "which flattered us with the hopes of finding an harbour." But, as he wrote, "These hopes lessened as we drew nearer; and, at last, we had some reason to think that the opening was closed by low land. On this account I called the point of land to the north of it *Cape Flattery.*" But for some reason, foggy weather probably, Cook missed the broad passage north of the cape, and wrote scornfully of "the pretended strait of Juan de Fuca."

Nine years later, an English captain named Barclay entered it, and in 1788 Meares, still another Englishman, fixed the name. "The strongest curiosity," he wrote, "impelled us to enter this strait, which we shall call by the name of its original discoverer." Thus the ancient pilot of ships, after nearly two centuries, won his immortality, and maps still read Strait of Juan de Fuca.

Having found what he deemed the strait, Meares also went looking for the river of Martín de Aguilar. In high hopes he rounded a cape and sailed into a bay. But the breakers foamed white in a solid line ahead, and he turned back, disappointed. So he called it Cape Disappointment, and Deception Bay. Both were good names, and better than Meares knew. For really the river was there, and he himself was deceived. And Cape Disappointment still stands as the north head of the bay, a monument that not only Meares but Great Britain too was turned back disappointed.

Meares also named a tall peak Mt. Olympus for the abode of the gods, and from that touch of classical fancy the whole northwestern corner of the United States has become the Olympic Peninsula, and a state capital is Olympia.

The English explorations of the coast were naturally not for mere scientific purposes, but they also strove to take possession of the country against the rival claims of Spain, and later of the United States. As always, the establishment of a name was counted a point toward possession.

In 1791 Captain George Vancouver sailed from England for the northwest coast by way of the Cape of Good Hope. The list of his officers rings familiarly, including Joseph Baker, Joseph Whidbey, and Peter Puget. Vancouver touched Australia, then called New Holland. The incident was not without importance in our naming, for he there relieved himself of a few names which he would otherwise have felt obliged to bestow elsewhere.

On April 17, 1792, Vancouver sighted the coast of what the English still liked to call New Albion because it carried their claim of possession back to Drake's voyage of 1579. His first naming, which carried on the old tradition of the coast, was that of Point St. George, and near it, by counterpart, he named Dragon Rocks. During two months Vancouver explored industriously, and more than fifty of his names survived.

He entered the passage which he still called skeptically "the supposed straits of De Fuca." On April 30th his third lieutenant sighted a high mountain, which thus won the name Mt. Baker. The second lieutenant, Peter Puget, led an exploring party in one of the boats, and the body of water which he discovered became Puget Sound. Whidbey Island, second largest in the United States, was called for the officer who circumnavigated it.

Vancouver's namings were honest, but they struck few sparkles. He put the name of the great Lord Hood upon a minor branch of the whole network of waterways named for the mere lieutenant. But perhaps justice was better served thus, for Lieutenant Peter Puget, who had sailed there, may have deserved that particular honor more than Admiral Hood, who had not.

Vancouver must have had little sense of natural beauty. In weather which he noted as "serene and pleasant," he saw before him one of the most magnificent views in the world—a lofty white peak, of noble outline, towering far off above the blue water of the sound. Apparently quite unmoved, he merely mentioned "the round snowy mountain . . . which, after my friend Rear Admiral Rainier, I distinguished by the name of Mount Rainier."

By and large, Captain George Vancouver was a competent naval officer of the old school, as pig-headed and unimaginative as the next. These latter qualities showed in his names, and they also cost Great Britain a good slice of empire.

On April 29th, sailing north along the coast, Vancouver had experienced the novelty of sighting a sail in those deserted waters. She hoisted American colors, and proved to be a Boston ship bearing the new name, *Columbia*. The ships exchanged courtesies, and two of the British officers visited the American captain, Robert Gray. He told them of the mouth of a river which he had seen slightly to the south, but had been unable to enter because of the current, though he had stood off and on for nine days. When his officers brought back the story, the British naval captain was unimpressed by the word of a Yankee shipmaster. He himself had examined the coast, and seen no such river. Therefore there was none. Gray, he thought, might be deluded by that legend of the river, "asserted to have been discovered by Martín D'Aguilar." In the confidence of skepticism Vancouver held his northerly course, forgetting that he himself had noted brownish water some days previous. One of the world's great rivers thus escaped bearing the name of some naval captain, or second-rate lord.

The Boston captain sailed south. For once, the weather was

favorable. On May 11th, Gray saw the river-mouth from a distance of six leagues. Later in the day he took the *Columbia* across the bar, and anchored in fresh water. He sailed up the river a short distance and spent a week trading with the natives, who gave no evidence of having previously seen a ship.

Gray took possession, and on May 19th prepared to return to sea. On that day he seems to have given his names. Himself a good Massachusetts man, he called the headlands for two Massachusetts heroes—Adams's Point on the south, Cape Hancock on the north. But the latter still is called Cape Disappointment, as Meares named it.

The river itself Gray named Columbia. That was the name of his ship, but if it had been called the *Susy Q.* or the *Staghound,* as it might well have been, he would hardly have given such a name to a great river. More likely, in his naming, he sought to commemorate not only his ship, but also his country.

The name was excellent, indubitably linking the river with the United States. Even Vancouver was forced to use it, lamely adding, "so named by Mr. Gray." As long as the name could continue, it was a flag flown in the face of the British. Some indeed might call it The River of the West or the Oregon, but in American usage it must always remain the Columbia, as a symbol of empire.

In 1792 a phase of our history, begun by Ponce de León in 1513, seems definitely to end. Gray and Vancouver were the last of that great company of voyagers. Other shipmasters who came afterwards named many points and coves, but those later voyagers were traders or chart-makers rather than explorers by sea.

Chapter XXI 〔 Of ancient glory renewed

THE village of Vanderheyden's Ferry took its undistinguished name from a Dutch-descended family who owned land there. It stood on the east bank of the Hudson, some miles above Albany —a few stores and a dozen houses. Not more than fifty people called it home. Some of them, however, had ambitions for their town, and felt that it might become a notable river-port—but not as Vanderheyden's Ferry. These forward-looking citizens called a meeting for the evening of January 5, 1789, "for the purpose of establishing a name."

As with many seemingly minor affairs which in the end have great results, no record was preserved of the details of this meeting. Fewer than twenty men probably attended. Some of them were of Dutch descent, speaking thick English; others were New Englanders, who were beginning to drift across from Massachusetts. All must have been plain Americans—farmers, storekeepers, a village carpenter, a ferryman, perhaps a minister. From what happened, one would guess that a schoolmaster was present.

The meeting was not wholly harmonious. The Dutch, always conservative, stood for the already Dutch name. Ashley's Ferry was in use as an alternate, and this may have had its proponents. But Ferry implied only cross-river passage, and the new ambition was to replace Albany as the head of navigation on the river, from which boats should ply to New York City. Under the circumstances some such name as Hudsonport would have been conventional, but in that little town-meeting someone, perhaps the schoolmaster, possessed learning, imagination, and originality. He made a proposal for which he could offer little precedent. Doubtless it met objections and ridicule. Even in the end the meeting could not reach unanimity. Nevertheless it managed to take action for the village: "By a majority of votes, IT WAS CONFIRMED, that in future it should be called and known by name of TROY."

That very evening an announcement "To the Public" was written. Its excellent wording suggests that whoever had enough education to think of Troy also wrote the proclamation. The notice was inserted as a paid advertisement in the *Albany Gazette,* and the new name was launched.

Its originality and tradition-shattering quality were shown by the immediate comments of an Albany editor:

Some classical critic has perhaps thought fit so to style it, from dissimilitude, as *lucus* is derived *a non lucendo.* Some wag must surely have been playing a trick with the good people of the place, and is now laughing in his sleeve at their ignorance of ancient history. . . . I find not the least resemblance between the old city of that name and this small village.

He then pointed out in somewhat labored humor that by anagram Troy could be twisted into tyro, ryot, or Tory. Doubtless the editor thought that the village was presumptuously setting up as a rival to his own Albany, and he may also have been a friend of the influential Dutch family whose name had been discarded. The Vanderheydens indeed were huffed, and continued for some time to write, "Vanderheyden, *alias* Troy."

Possibly, as the editor suggested, the original proposal was a joke, but more likely it was serious. The rapid springing up of similar names elsewhere showed that Troy was in the spirit of the times.

In a certain sense, the custom of using classical names was as old as English settlement. Virginia was Latin in form; a girl of that name was the heroine of a famous Roman tale. Laconia echoed the name of a region in ancient Greece. In 1663 Mr. Thomas Pope had a tract of four hundred acres surveyed along the Potomac, and called it Rome; by association, a small creek became, no doubt humorously, the Tiber.

Some classical names were reproduced more or less accidentally. Mantua in New Jersey came from a local tribal name meaning "frog," but assumed the exact spelling of a city known to all lovers of poetry as the birthplace of Virgil:

Mantua vae miserae nimium vicina Cremonae.

Various towns were called Augusta from the queen of George II, but the name also echoed those Roman foundations honoring some emperor. In 1748 the Virginia Assembly authorized the town of Alexandria. The name was for the Alexander family, local plantation owners, but was also that of many ancient cities.

All these gave suggestions, but the actual habit arose after the Revolution. First of all, the Revolution had broken traditions. In the same years the Classical Revival was sweeping the country. Jefferson was only one among hundreds of plantation owners to build a house with a columned portico. Newly founded academies were spreading some knowledge of Greek and Latin. Even an unlearned man writing a letter to his newspaper might sign himself Junius or Publicola or Cato, because that was the fashion. Ancient Greece, particularly Athens, replaced Cambridge and Oxford as an ideal of culture and learning. Sparta stood for valor and moral integrity. Most of all, republican Rome was the model. Rome had austerely cast off the rule of its king, adopted republican institutions, and set out upon a glorious career. So also had the new nation.

The adoption of Troy may have genuinely amazed the Albany editor, but in the retrospect of history it is not at all surprising. The ground had been well prepared. Why Troy rather than Rome or Constantinople may be questioned. But at least, by virtue of the poets, Troy was known as widely as Rome itself. Like Sparta also it symbolized the masculine virtues. Rome had fallen into degeneracy, but Troy had been overcome only by base stratagem, and had perished nobly in flames.

Whatever the editor might think, the future was with the innovators. No fewer than thirty-one places bearing the name of Priam's city came to deck the map of the United States. Also, this action of 1789 set a precedent for the many other classical namings, which were most numerous in a part of New York not far removed.

On July 3, 1790, the year after the town-meeting at Vanderheyden's Ferry, a board of three Commissioners, plus an auditor, met in New York City. They were entrusted with the disposal of certain public lands, and on that day a region around Cayuga Lake was to be divided into townships; it was known as the Military Tract, because veterans were to receive grants there. A map of the region lay before the Board, and on it the boundaries of twenty-five townships had been drawn. Anyone thus confronted with twenty-five names to be given will normally fall into some system. He may name the places for his friends or the members of his family, or he may compliment men to whom he rests under obligation, or he may patriotically run off some roll of heroes.

On that day, as the Commissioners looked at the map, they must have seen that the body of water just to the west of their tract was Seneca Lake, and they probably knew that Seneca had been a Roman philosopher. How that name came thus to stand upon that lake is in itself a strange story. First of all, a western tribe of the Iroquois called themselves "people of the standing stone," which Champlain first wrote down as Ouentouronon. This name passed to the Mohegans. They translated it roughly into their own language and the Dutch took over this translation. The Dutch wrote it down as Sinneken, and in various other forms, and then passed it to the English. The English spelled it in many ways, and such a form as Sinnegar or Sennicky (always the frontiersman's pronunciation) would naturally have been the final result. Apparently, however, some classically schooled Englishman spelled it like the name of the Roman philosopher, and that un-English form was established. Seneca thus illustrates all three ways in which a name can be passed from language to language—by transference, translation, and false etymology.

By 1790 Seneca Lake was a well-fixed name. Also, closer at hand, Troy was established. Another influence also must have worked on the minds of those Commissioners. The day of their meeting was that just preceding the Fourth of July, and patriotism was the further suggested by the fact that these lands were to be bestowed upon veterans.

If the names of the Military Tract were given in the order of the numbers of the townships, as would seem likely, the minds of the Commissioners can almost be seen at work. First of all, a suggestion might be made that a region to be settled by veterans should bear military names. The Revolutionary generals were passed over as having been already used too often. Then perhaps with a deprecatory "Why not—" one of them suggested ancient generals, Lysander the great Spartan, for instance—especially, he might add, since it would harmonize with the classical name there already on Seneca Lake. Lysander was approved, and then Hannibal. But perhaps someone suggested that they were on the wrong road—Hannibal had fought against the Republic, not for it. Thereupon the Commissioners hit their stride with the names of the heroes of the Republic, and ran off Cato, Camillus, Cicero, Manlius, and Marcellus. After that, their republicanism faltered, and they admitted Aurelius and Romulus, emperor and king. A second wind took them through four more republican heroes— Scipio, Sempronius, Tully, and Fabius. This seems definitely to have brought them to the end of their resources, and the last ten names mingled Latin, Greek, and English, poets, philosophers, and warriors, in almost desperate improvisation. Ovid was followed by Milton, Locke, Homer, Solon, Hector, and Ulysses. Then came Dryden and Virgil, with Cincinnatus at the end for a final republican gesture.

Thus considered, the naming of the famous "classical belt" represents neither great originality nor great classical learning. Troy had given a suggestion. Seneca Lake presented ready-made the idea of using classical worthies, a practice which later namers generally rejected in favor of the Troy-tradition of classical places. The Military Tract itself suggested military names. The inconsistencies in the list imply that it was made up off-hand, by men who had little background in ancient history or literature. In using both Tully and Cicero they even named two places for the same man.

The next classical naming of importance was far in the west. On the Ohio River a town was growing up opposite the mouth of Licking Creek. That name itself was half a translation, half an adoption of the Delaware *mahoning,* "at the salt-lick." The settlement on the other side of the river took as complicated and bizarre a name as was ever coined. An *L* represented the Delaware-English Licking, *os* the Latin "mouth," *anti,* the Greek "opposite," and *ville* the French "town." The whole was Losantiville, "the town opposite the mouth of the Licking."

Such grotesquery was, however, a little too much even for the frontier. In 1790 General St. Clair, the new governor, changed the name to Cincinnati in honor of the newly formed society of that name, which in turn had taken its name from the republican farmer-soldier Cincinnatus. The form, however, continued to give trouble. A year later, John Cleves Symmes, Congressman and land-speculator, who himself claimed to have suggested the new name, wrote a letter inquiring whether the word should properly end in *i* or *a*. He added: "I have frequent combats in this country on the subject." Whether these combats were physical or merely verbal, he failed to state. In either case we may wonder at the vehement inconsistency of the frontier which almost swallowed the camel of Losantiville, and then strained at the gnat of Cincinnata-Cincinnati.

Once the precedent of classical names was established, many appeared. In 1798 Utica, New York, took its name on the suggestion of a certain lawyer, Erastus Clark. Mr. Clark was a graduate of Dartmouth College, and must have had classical training, but why he should have so loved the name of a rather unimportant city of ancient North Africa is puzzling. Most likely, he suggested it in honor of that stout hero of the last days of the Roman Republic, Marcus Porcius Cato, who was extraordinarily admired in Revolutionary times. Under his leadership Utica was one of the last cities to hold out against Julius Caesar; at its fall the hero stabbed himself in true Roman fashion, and was hence known as Cato Uticensis.

By the end of the century the naming of a town after some classical city was a well-established custom. Contrary to a common opinion, such names were not always the result of a naïve desire to adorn an insignificant backwoods settlement with a grandiloquent name. The namers often knew their classics. In 1800 an Ohio village became Athens, because a college was to be established there; Athens in Georgia was named in the next year for the same reason. Each is still the seat of a university. Corinth, the cross-roads of Greece, might be chosen for the meeting of important roads. Spartanburg County, South Carolina, honored the Spartan Regiment, which had fought in the Revolution.

Plays on words sometimes gave the connection. From a Mr. Palm the village might be, not Palmstown, but Palmyra. Media in Pennsylvania used the ancient name for the land of the Medes, but was also the plural of *medium,* because it lay at the center of a county. Then a later town, instead of being New Media, took the spelling Numidia.

Less than a year before the town-meeting at Vanderheyden's Ferry, Captain Meares had named Mt. Olympus. But just as names brought from England had seldom been fastened upon American streams and hills, so Rubicon, Tempe, and Etna, if used at all, were more often put upon towns than upon natural features. A Styx River in Alabama is said to have been named by a Virginia schoolmaster in frontier times; he was so depressed by the isolation of the forest and the darkness of the water that he called it for the river of Hades.

The classical interests of the later eighteenth century are as much part of the history of the United States as the existence of the Indian tribes or the Revolution. To maintain, as many have done, that Rome and Troy are mere excrescences on our map, is to commit the fallacy of denying one part of history in favor of another part—or else is to be ignorant of history.

The ideals and aspirations of the Americans of that period deserve their perpetuation.

⇒⇒⇒⇒⇒⇒⇒⇒⇒⇒⇒⇒⇒⇒-✶-⇐⇐⇐⇐⇐⇐⇐⇐⇐⇐⇐⇐⇐⇐⇐

Chapter XXII ❨ Of the new Nation

No LONGER, suddenly, could men call counties and towns after kings and queens, and lords. The people had cut themselves loose from what had gone before. After the Revolution came a critical period in naming, as in government—a time of new loves and new hatreds, when the brightness of new heroes moved across the land, and new ways of naming must be found.

The changes, however, came mostly in the naming of governmental units, not of natural features. Big Creek, Black River, and their like, honest folk-names but often repeated, continued to move westward. Incidents of settlement supplied most of the unusual names. Thus, three surveyors once camped by a beautiful stream in western Pennsylvania. It was called Toby's Creek, most likely not for any settler named Tobias, but from the Algonquian *tobi,* "alder-tree." As they lay in their tent at the hush of evening, they heard the clear resonant sound of the stream flowing across its riffles. One of them said it was like the note of a far-off clarion. So they called it Clarion River, and from it came a county and town.

Once a surveyor named Strange became separated from his comrades and hopelessly lost in the forest. Years later, forty miles from where he last was seen, men found his bones beneath a great beech tree. Against it leaned his rifle, the shot-pouch still dangling. In the smooth bark could still be read the carved words in plaintive doggerel:

> Strange is my name and I'm on strange ground,
> And strange it is I can't be found.

So the stream once known as Turkey Run became Strange Creek.

Even under the Confederation the problem of new states had arisen, and with it necessarily the problem of their names. With the British tradition severed, only four of the thirteen colonies offered models for the future. Pennsylvania was in harmony with the classical tastes of the period; Massachusetts preserved the memory of an Indian tribe and a bay; Connecticut bore the native name of a river. Delaware also was more associated with a river and tribe than with the little-known British lord.

The first proposal for new states was dated March 1, 1784. It was the report of a committee of three of which Jefferson was the leading member, and the document was in his handwriting. The names, probably of Jefferson's coinage, were a Greek, Latin, Iroquois, Algonquian, and patriotic miscellany. Saratoga and Washington echoed the Revolution. Sylvania was wholly classical, along with Chersonesus, Metropotamia, and Polypotamia. Michigania combined the established name for the lake with the elegance of a classical ending. Similarly combined names for rivers supplied Assenisipia, Illinoia, and Pelisipia.

This report was never adopted, and probably had little influence upon the tradition of names. It shows only what might have happened. We are prone to take our present names for granted without considering how different they might have been. What would have happened if, in those first uncertain days, some faddist had successfully initiated grotesqueries? Or if some inflexible system had imposed a strait-jacket on the future? Or if the names had been treated as political footballs, to be given by one party in power for its own ends, and then shifted after the next election? Or worst of all perhaps, if makeshift descriptions had been allowed to remain, as with the name of the whole country?

This last was perhaps the imminent danger. Thus the Ordinance of 1787 provided for three states and set their boundaries, but gave them no names. With the usual ineptitude of the political mind for naming, however, the same Ordinance established "The Territory of the United States Northwest of the river Ohio." This name was so completely bad that perhaps for that very reason it vanished finally without trace.

The clumsy error of the name United States of America indeed probably helped prevent other similar errors, and the agitation for Columbia in the seventeen-nineties had indirect good results in the state names.

Down to 1800 six new state names were fixed. A tradition was established which was not broken for three-quarters of a century, and really remained in effect, in spite of a few exceptions, throughout the whole period of the admission of states.

Vermont was the first. The name was already established, and its inhabitants claimed the status of an independent republic. They were admitted to statehood under the name which they themselves had chosen.

Kentucky was also well fixed. It had been first applied to a vague trans-mountain region, and a river. Virginia organized it as a county in 1776. By 1792 it was already sentimentally known as "Kentuck," and any attempt in Congress to have imposed another name would have stirred up a hornet's nest of local wrath.

The region to the south of Kentucky had no such firmly established name. It had been known variously as Franklin, Watauga, or the Washington District. Its chief settlements were on the Cumberland River, but the British origin of this name was against it. Since 1777 North Carolina had been organizing counties in the western lands, and had named them for Revolutionary heroes, with one exception. This last was Tennessee County, named for the river.

From the time of the first Virginia settlements, a tradition had developed for calling a region after the name of its chief river. Even in the mountains, where streams were not navigable, the frontiersmen spoke of the "settlements on the Holston," and this passed easily into "the Holston country." In the same way, people began to say "the Tennessee country," and the words "Tennessee Government" even appeared on maps before the term had legal status.

In 1796 a Constitutional Convention met in the region, and the question of a name arose. No record of the debate was preserved, but tradition holds that a young man named Andrew Jackson proposed the name. The Preamble to the Constitution read: "to form ourselves into a free and independent state by the name of 'The State of Tennessee.'" A name arising from local usage and then officially established by a local body thus again went to Congress and was accepted.

The first territory actually to be named by Congress was that to the south of Tennessee. Its western boundary was the Mississippi River, and in 1798 Congress followed the already fast developing tradition of naming from rivers by establishing it as Mississippi.

Ohio had been a river-name since the time of La Salle. The Ohio Company was organized in 1748, and the name was applied to the region about the same time. Virginia formed Ohio County in 1776. It was thus a natural choice for the name of the Territory in 1800.

Along with Ohio, the next territory to the west was organized, a vast and vague area, as yet almost wholly owned and inhabited by the native tribes. Since it was thus Indian territory, it might well have been descriptively called Indian Territory, but the classical taste of the time preferred a different form. The name itself had originated about 1765, when a company of land-speculators obtained dubious rights to a large tract of land on the east bank of the Ohio below Pittsburgh. Perhaps they knew the Spanish book *La Monarquía Indiana;* more likely they merely coined a Latin form on the model of Carolina. They called themselves the Indiana Company, and their tract became Indiana. Virginia disputed the title, and a long and famous litigation ensued, leading in 1798 to the Eleventh Amendment to the Constitution. Thus finally defeated, the Company ceased to be powerful, and the name was eradicated from its first location. For over thirty years, however, it had had a vague existence, and litigation had made it known. After a lapse of only two years it was restored, differing from Indian Territory only by a single letter.

Thus by 1800, whether consciously or not, new principles for the naming of states had been established—Congress would not coin a name or impose a strange one, but would take an already rooted name, as of a river or district, and would be guided not by its own federal power or by any fine-spun theory, but by the voice of the people of the region democratically assembled. Thus it came about that most of the names, even before they were officially established, were strongly rooted, and well on the way to becoming patriotic symbols. Also, since many of the rivers had Indian names, four of the six new states and territories had native origins, and even Indiana carried the same suggestion.

The tradition of naming counties had suffered a less shattering blow. They had always been the creations of the central authority, and the state legislatures merely took over where the colonial governors left off.

In Virginia the old system had continued in full sway with the organization of Dunmore County in 1772. In 1776, however, seven counties were formed, and in their names the break with the past was complete. Henry, Montgomery, and Washington honored recent heroes. Ohio and Kentucky were the first counties to receive Indian names in more than a century. Monogalia and Yohogania were of the curious hybrid variety beloved by Jefferson, and may have been his coinages.

The ax of the Revolution fell suddenly in other states too. Pennsylvania had held steadily to its tradition of English names until Westmoreland in 1773, the last county organized under the old government. But Washington County was formed in 1781, and the period of enthusiasm for the French produced Fayette,

Dauphin, and Luzerne. Allegheny in 1788 was the first with an Indian name.

The shock suffered by town-naming was the greatest of all, for it affected the basic manner of formation.

In early colonial times town-names had usually been formed without suffixes. Many taken from English towns and persons ended in *-ton,* or *-ham,* or *-bury,* but the colonists did not think of these as separable elements meaning "place of settlement." If a suffix was thought to be needed, usually they added *-town,* or else Town as a separate word.

In the generation preceding the Revolution the use of suffixes had begun to increase, probably because of the greater use of personal names. More and more often some man founded a town, and like William Trent, put his own name upon it. If, again like Trent, the name was short, a suffix might be thought to add dignity.

Shortly before the Revolution the two related suffixes, *-borough* and *-burgh,* had been rising in popularity. Their history was highly complicated. Their remotest ancestor began as a word among the early Germanic people, meaning a defended place, or a settlement, the two ideas being as inseparable then as they would be later on the American frontier. King Alfred, if he could have seen an early Kentucky *station,* would have called it a *burh.* The word became *burg* in German and Dutch, *borg* in Swedish. The Franks established it in France as *bourg,* and it passed into medieval Latin as *burgus.* Through the Visigoths or from the Latin it became the Spanish *burgo* and the name of the city Burgos.

In Great Britain the word assumed different forms. In the south it became *-bury,* as in Canterbury. More often in the Midlands and North its rolled *r* sprouted another syllable, and it appeared in the spelling seen in Scarborough. In Scotland, it was *-burgh,* as in Edinburgh; but there were also English towns such as Dunstanburgh, and Aldeburgh.

In America the use of these suffixes might thus theoretically have sprung from any of the European languages. The Swedes founded Elfsborg, and the French, Louisbourg. Middelburg was a Dutch town on Long Island. A further complication arose with the Dutch *bergh,* "hill," which supplied Rodenberghen, their name for New Haven. The Germans in Pennsylvania used *-burg* sometimes for their villages, and said *berg* for mountain. But a stronger German influence arose with the Hanoverian kings, especially with their titles, although those thoroughly German names were frequently spelled Mecklenburgh and Lunenburgh.

Williamsburg in 1699 seems to have been the first English town to use the suffix. King William III was Dutch, and for a town in his honor the Virginians may have thought a Dutch-sounding suffix appropriate.

Before long, legal usage had its influence. In England *borough* was employed to indicate a town formally incorporated and possessing certain privileges. But in Scotland *burgh* was the equivalent term. In the natural course of events *borough* would have become established in all the English colonies. In most of them it did, and some towns which were incorporated as boroughs used that suffix. In 1705, however, Virginia passed an elaborate act for the establishment of towns, and very surprisingly adopted the Scottish legal term *burgh.* This innovation, which was so greatly to change the American map, may be the result of the historical accident that a Scot had just been appointed Governor-General. George Hamilton, Earl of Orkney, never got round to taking over his new office personally. During those years he was also a lieutenant-general under Marlborough, and was busily employed in the vicinity of certain continental towns, such as Blenheim, Ramillies, and Oudenarde. He sent his deputies to Virginia, and doubtless one of them was a Scots lawyer.

As a result, the founders of many Virginia towns added the legal term as a suffix to some personal name. The bill of incorporation might read either with or without the *h,* but the former was probably more common.

The act of 1705 and the common presence of the *h* thus show that the chief origins of our modern *-burg* were Scottish, although it also drew support from the Dutch and Germans, and even from the French. Before the Revolution it was not common except in Virginia, but it had spread here and there to near-by colonies, and even appeared in New England. Connecticut, naturally, would have none of it, but it reached Massachusetts, with Fitchburgh in 1761.

After the Revolution *-burgh* became even more widespread. Pittsburgh, mother-city of the West, offered a precedent. Before many years had run, the word passed into common speech: "What burg do you come from?"

In contrast to *-burgh*, *-ville* was almost wholly post-Revolutionary. Charlottesville, authorized by Virginia in 1762, was one of its very few earlier appearances. Granville in Massachusetts honored the Earl of Granville, and Abbeville in South Carolina was brought over bodily by French immigrants of 1764. The suffix even had little connection with towns. Granville was a North Carolina county, and Fredericksville in Virginia was a parish. The sudden popularity can thus be simply and surely credited to the enthusiasm for the French which swept the country.

In such a foundation as Louisville, named in 1780, a French ending was naturally coupled with the name of the French king. But this was enough to give the suggestion that *-ville* might be coupled with any name.

A play upon words may have aided this feeling. In 1781 Danville, Kentucky, was founded by Walter Daniel. That he should have taken only a part of his family name is curious. A tradition about the same name in Vermont, however, connects it with a Frenchman named D'Anville. This tradition is not quite so far-fetched as might at first appear, for enthusiasm for things French ran high in those years, especially in Kentucky. Moreover, Jean Baptiste Bourguignon D'Anville was the greatest geographer of the time, and his maps were widely known. In any case, the coupling of *-ville* with a common American nickname indicates that it was completely naturalized. A curious result has been that all across the country any town in which a man named Daniel or Daniels was concerned was likely to be called Danville.

Thus in a very short time *-ville* became so well Americanized that few people thought of its ever having been anything else. The Pennsylvania Germans became unusually fond of it, so that their country is probably the only place in the world which presents such an amicable mingling of the two hostile elements in numerous names like Trumbauersville, Kleinville, and Schwenkville. Applebachsville is English, German, and French all in one. As the meaning of other suffixes faded, *-ville* was even added to produce such doublings as Sadsburyville, and Marlboroville. Its full force was exerted upon the regions settled shortly after the Revolution. In Indiana more than a hundred post-offices end in *-ville*.

No feature of American naming has provoked fiercer attack than the prevalence of this suffix. It has been called ostentatious and lacking in good taste. Very well. Good taste was sitting comfortably in New York and Philadelphia when the town sites of Indiana were being cleared. Purists, such as Matthew Arnold, have shaken their heads that an English name like Higgins should be married to a French suffix to make Higginsville. But before this marriage occurred, Higgins had become an American name. And didn't the French fight on our side? To reject *-ville* is to deny something very deeply rooted in the American past.

Along with the growth of *-burgh* and *-ville* other changes occurred. The popularity of *-town* declined. In common speech it had already come to be *-ton,* and for new settlements this clipped form was generally used after the Revolution. In South Carolina, Charles Town officially became Charleston in 1783, and there were many similar shifts. Any *-ton* along the eastern seaboard may formerly have been a *-town,* just as any *-burg* or *-boro* was probably once *-burgh* or *-borough*. This last suffix declined. Unlike *-burgh,* it was thought to be too British. After the Revolution it was less commonly used, and some *-boroughs* actually changed their names.

No effect of the Revolution upon names was more striking than that upon suffixes. The sudden extraordinary popularity of *-burgh* and *-ville* transformed forever our whole nomenclature.

Once the fashion of suffixes was established, various minor ones developed. Settlers were thought to feel the attraction of *-land* and *-field*. Possibilities of commerce were implied in *-port,* even though the river could do nothing more than float log-rafts downstream at high water.

A strange accompaniment was the tendency of certain words and names to associate with one suffix more than with another. One factor in the popularity of *-ville* was the feeling in the folk-mind that it could be aptly coupled with almost anything. It had first been joined only with people's names, but soon nothing strange was seen in Beaverville or Elkville. Rockville, Spring-ville, Plainville, and Pleasantville became common. On the other hand *-burg* was rarely combined with anything but a personal name, a restriction which partially accounts for its less frequent use. Nevertheless *-ville* was never popular in certain combinations. The commonest linkages, for instance, were Williamstown and Williamsburg. Even Williamsport was commoner than Williams-ville. Many places, moreover, were merely called Williams.

Jones tended to stand alone, or associate with *-borough* or *-ville*. Smith went with *-field* or *-ville*. Pitt usually added an *s,* and then *-burgh* or *-field*. But Georgetown was almost universal.

Women's names showed the same tendency. Jane and Mary went with *-ville*. Ellen preferred *-borough* and *-ton*. Longer names usually stood alone, but Elizabethtown was common. Ruth also was thought sufficient by itself, and so was Anna, except when joined with *-polis*.

The explanation calls for no digression into mystical values. Ease of pronunciation played a part, but more important was the earliest coupling with an important town. Thus James and *-town* were united in 1607. Ever since, when a settlement has been named for any James, the suffix was almost predetermined. Jamesburg, Jamesport, Jamesville and James all exist, but they are rare and must have been named by some rebel against tradition, or more likely because some near-by Jamestown already existed.

From *-ville* and ᐧ *burg* the Americans merely got new ways of formation. Actually to supply new names, during the years after the Revolution, they kept some old habits, and developed some new ones.

As the people went west, they took the old names along, just as their ancestors had brought them from England. Plymouth, which Charles Stuart had first placed on the New England coast, moved to Connecticut, then to the Susquehanna valley, then to Indiana. Falmouth, Richmond, and Winchester leapt the mountains from Virginia to Kentucky. Newark passed from New Jersey to Ohio, and there were many others. With the family Bible and grandmother's pewter, the names joggled with the pack-horse loads, or floated in the keel boats. Already they were a heritage, not to be abandoned or forgotten.

Whether they had once come from England, or were other names, was now no matter. They had become American. From Salem, New Jersey, they took the name to Ohio; once it may have been a name from the Bible; now it was a name of their own land. Men remembered no longer that Norwalk was Indian, or Brooklyn, Dutch. Granville in Massachusetts had honored an English earl, but in Ohio it recalled the town in Massachusetts.

In these years for the first time also the people were cut off from the history of England, and began to look back into their own. Leyden, Massachusetts, was named in 1784 in memory of the Dutch town which had sheltered the Pilgrims long before. Carver and Brewster commemorated the valiant founders of Plymouth.

In those years a hero-loving people with a new set of heroes entered a land where many names must be given. So sometimes the roll of new counties and towns and townships reads like the roll of Washington's generals. And Washington himself had more places named for him in Ohio and Indiana, where his veterans settled, than in any other states. Most of these towns, though they may have been ambitiously founded, remained only small places, and of the many Washingtons only the national capital grew to be a large city.

Its naming came about very informally. In 1791 the Commissioners wrote to L'Enfant the city-planner: "We have agreed that the federal district shall be called 'The Territory of Columbia,' and the federal city, 'The City of Washington.'" Actually, the Commissioners had no authority to name the city, but no one questioned their choice, and it was established.

Besides Washington, only three Revolutionary heroes won the honor of large cities. They were Knox the gunner, "Mad Anthony" Wayne, and Francis Nash, whom nobody remembers.

As it happened, Knox became the Secretary of War in Washington's cabinet. At that time a town in the mountains far to the south and west took his name, coupling it with the newly popular suffix to make Knoxville.

As for Wayne, he won a double right to be the name-hero of a great city. After the war, he led a campaign against the western Indians, who had already defeated two armies. There he worked out new tactics, and sent cavalry "to put the horseshoe on the moccasin." This, his greatest victory, was known by good frontier manner of speech as Fallen Timbers; the fort which was built near the battlefield took his own name. Later a town grew up, but it did not, like many towns, slough off Fort as if ashamed of its frontier origin and become Waynesborough or Wayne City. Instead, it chose to be Fort Wayne.

The story of Nash is this. On a foggy morning in 1777 General Washington launched an attack upon Lord Howe at Germantown. The sudden advance of the Continentals sent the British light infantry rolling back. Then the defense stiffened and held. Confused in the fog, the American regiments lost contact, and fired into one another. In a desperate attempt to restore the line, the North Carolina brigade pushed forward from the reserve under its youthful commander, General Francis Nash. A cannonball struck him down, and he was carried dying from the lost field. His own state honored him, and three years later a stockade in its western lands was called Nashborough. In 1784 it followed the fashion by shifting to Nashville.

In that time of rapid growth so many places had to be named

that even very minor heroes had their chance. The dangerous habit developed of thus honoring still living people. Inevitably some of these men turned out to be far from heroic in the end. North Carolina named a county for its first Secretary of State, James Glasgow. Later, he was convicted of malfeasance, and the county had to be renamed after General Greene, who was safely dead. Thomas Jefferson shrewdly decried what he called "the mania of giving names . . . after persons still living." He added: "Death alone can seal the title of any man to this honor, by putting it out of his power to forfeit it."

On the other hand, such a naming might be only too empty an honor. In 1798 the Kentucky Legislature named a county after Daniel Boone, and in the same year a tract of land owned by him was put up for sale because of his inability to pay the taxes.

Many of the new towns took their names from men who were never of heroic stature. Sometimes they were merely the original land-owners; an epitaph in the cemetery of Brownsville, Pennsylvania, sums up:

> Here lies the body of Thomas Brown,
> Who was once the owner of this town.

Sometimes also the name honored a respected local citizen or political leader. Most commonly of all, the new town was called for the speculator or promoter who laid it out.

General Moses Cleaveland, in spite of his title, was no military hero. He served as a captain in the Revolution, but won his higher rank with the Connecticut militia afterwards. By profession he was a lawyer, and a smart one. He purchased, for $32,600, two shares in a land-company with large holdings along Lake Erie. In 1796 he went with a party of surveyors to take a look at the property, and the surveyors gave his name to a location at the mouth of a little river. The General went back to Connecticut, and never visited the namesake village which grew up on the site. The spelling was later changed to Cleveland—according to tradi-

tion, because a newspaper preferred a shorter form for its masthead.

In view of the large number of disreputable people who have
wandered loose over North America, it is surprising that of the
larger cities only New York and one other bear names of dubious
import. Jonathan Dayton began life under the best auspices. His
father was a brilliant lesser commander of the Revolution. The
son, aged sixteen, finished at Princeton in 1776. Aged twenty, he
served as a captain at Yorktown. He was the youngest member of
the Constitutional Convention, was elected to Congress, served as
Speaker of the House, and entered the Senate. During this time
he had joined with three others to purchase a tract of land in
southwestern Ohio. They called the town Dayton, the other three
partners resting content with the principal streets, which still remain—St. Clair, Wilkinson, and Ludlow.

Like many brilliant young men, Dayton arrived at middle age
with achievements not quite equaling promise. He clutched un-
scrupulously at greatness, and joined Aaron Burr. The plans of
the conspiracy collapsed, and Dayton was indicted for high treason.
Though he was never brought to trial, his career was ruined.

The people of Dayton did not change the name. Perhaps, with
the short memory of frontiersmen, they had already half forgotten
its origin; perhaps they transferred their allegiance from the discredited son to the honorable father.

Of all Americans to have their names preserved in large cities,
John Young is the most obscure. He came as an early settler in
1797. Untroubled by modesty, he named the place Youngstown;
then, according to tradition, he traded a deer-skin for a quart of
whiskey, and celebrated his immortality.

He was a man of no importance. But why should not John
Young stand as a symbol? If he was a man of little note, so also
were nearly all his fellow frontiersmen. They died; their wooden
grave-markers (if they had any) rotted into dust, and they were
forgotten. But if we believe in democracy, why should not John
Young, whiskey and all, stand as their symbol, with the blast-
furnaces of Youngstown flaming to their memory?

So also Nathaniel Rochester might stand as a symbol of the solid citizen. Born in North Carolina, he did a little soldiering as paymaster. After the War, he moved to Hagerstown in Maryland. He lived there for many years, doing well in business and building a gracious house, which still stands. Aged fifty-five, he became president of the local bank. About this time he invested in lands in western New York, his most fortunate purchase being a hundred-acre lot (at $17.50 an acre) on the Genesee River. A village was laid out, and named Rochesterville. Aged sixty-six, Colonel Rochester moved there. He lived on for thirteen years, respected as the leading citizen. Decades later, when the village had become a great city conscious of its history, old men who had been boys when Rochester was still Rochesterville recorded their memories of the Colonel, white-haired but hale, digging in his garden. He still rose before dawn. Sagely, like Franklin, he told one child: "If young people let the sun get the start of them in the morning, they never overtake him during the whole day."

Colonel Rochester was not a great man. Possibly he was something better. Like John Young's, his name may stand as a symbol —for millions of honest, hard-working, moderately successful Americans. Without such men the greater heroes would have no foundations on which to build their fame.

Still another to stand as a symbol is William Paterson. Born in northern Ireland, he arrived as an immigrant in 1747 at the age of two. The family rose a little in the world, and young William was able to attend college at Princeton. He became Attorney General of New Jersey during the Revolution, served notably in the drafting of the Constitution, became Senator, and then Governor of his state in 1790. At that time plans were laid to found an industrial town, utilizing the water-power of the falls on the Passaic River, and under the leadership of Alexander Hamilton, a Society for the Establishing of Useful Manufactures was chartered in 1791. In that charter the town was named for the Governor.

Paterson himself, primarily a jurist, continued his career by codifying the laws of New Jersey, and by serving on the Supreme Court. As Young might stand for the frontiersman, and Rochester for the solid citizen, so Paterson might well be the symbol of the minor statesman. Conscientious, able, hard-working, a score or two in each generation, they make possible the maintenance and development of government.

In the first years under the Constitution a few extremists advocated a wholesale changing of names, to cut the new republic wholly away from its royalist origins, but the people in general rested content. An alteration of name indicated usually a new enthusiasm rather than an old hatred. Thus in Boston one street had long borne a wholly inoffensive and un-royal name. On February 6, 1788, a convention sitting in a meeting-house on Long Lane ratified the new Constitution, and on that same day Long Lane became Federal Street.

In New York City the royal names survived the War, and only succumbed to the excitements of the French Revolution. On February 11, 1794, a letter signed Democrat appeared in a newspaper pointing out the continued existence of such names, and calling upon "all true Republicans" to change the names of King, Queen, Princess, and Duke Streets. But *Candor* replied, citing a new and highly interesting argument:

The names of towns, cities, and streets in America are standing historical monuments; they tell us from what country, whether England, Holland, Germany, or France, the first settlers came, and the names of King and Queen street tell us we were once subject to a foreign monarch. This, so far from being a reason for abolishing the names, should be a reason for preserving them.

Pressure was thus brought upon the Council from both directions, and the names might well have remained unaltered except for other reasons.

In the earliest times New York, like most American cities, had followed the European system of having a street change its name at almost every intersection. This had its conveniences. A stranger, knowing someone's address to be King Street, could learn what section of the city was thus denoted. Arriving there he would find the street to consist of only a few houses, and so could readily find the right one. A man was usually said to live "in King Street," as if the street were a region, not a thoroughfare. Toward the end of the eighteenth century, however, the idea of numbering the houses was developed. The Americans, less bound by tradition than the Europeans, quickly saw that a multiplicity of short streets had suddenly become an inconvenience. The relative location on a long street could now be easily indicated by the number. A single name now began to stretch out perhaps for a mile or more. At the same time, a street lost its two-dimensional quality, and came to be imagined as a line, like a river. So men began to say more commonly, "on King Street."

New York, as it happened, had adopted a system of house-numbering in December, 1793, only a few weeks before the controversy about royal names developed. This lucky circumstance offered the Council a convenient escape. Late in 1794 a large number of small streets were consolidated; among them, Duke and Stone, Princess and Beaver, King George and William. In every case the new street, naturally enough, bore the more innocuous name. At the same time, however, the Council bowed to republican opinion sufficiently to change Prince to Rose, and Crown to Liberty. Hanover Street, equally royal, escaped the purge.

The name-changers, however, often met resistance. In 1753 John Harris had set up a ferry on the Susquehanna River, and called it in plain style Harris's Ferry. Thirty-two years later, he laid out the town of Harrisburg. In the same year Dauphin County was formed. The Executive Council of Pennsylvania conceived that the town also should be French, and decreed:

The name of the county town . . . is altered from Harrisburg to Louisbourg in consequence of the Supreme Executive Council of the Commonwealth so styling it.

But the days of the Massachusetts General Court were ended, and democracy was abroad in the land. Men tell that old John Harris spoke stoutly:

The members of the Council may *Louisbourg* as much as they please, but I will never execute a title for a lot in any other name than Harrisburg.

The Frenchified name remained official for several years, but in the end a stubborn local resistance carried the day.

Some sentiment for root-and-branch eradication of British names remained as late as 1800. In that year a correspondent wrote to Jefferson making some such suggestion. In his reply, as in so much else, Jefferson seems to have expressed the general feeling of the country:

I am not sure that we ought to change all our names. During the regal government, sometimes, indeed they were given through adulation; but often also as the reward of merit of the times, sometimes for services rendered the colony.

He ended with an afterthought to which the practice of the nation seems to have agreed:

Perhaps, too, a name when given should be deemed a sacred property.

Chapter XXIII ❨ Yankee flavor

DURING the eighteenth century, by some alchemy, the Puritan was transmuted into the Yankee. Separated from the other colonies by the bottle-neck of the Dutch-speaking Hudson Valley, the New Englanders went their own ways. They still said *brook* and *notch*. The Maine people developed the use of *stream*. At first perhaps this denoted the water flowing from a certain pond or lake, so that Mopang Stream was said in distinction from Mopang Pond; it came, however, to mean any flowing water, between a brook and a river in size. The usage spread into northern New Hampshire and Vermont, and emigrants took it westward into the Adirondacks. *Intervale* was another northern word. Zadock Thompson, Vermont historian, explained it with rare exactitude:

It may be derived from *inter*—within, and *vallis*—a vale, or valley; and in its specific signification, it denotes those alluvial flats, lying along the margins of streams, which have been, or occasionally are, overflowed.

Another word arose from the frustrating process of attempting to lay out right-angled plots upon a spherical earth. The surveyors were sometimes left with a wedge-shaped piece of land lying between the boundaries of two towns and not included in either. Most of these were too small and badly shaped to be incorporated in their own right. Some were annexed to the adjoining towns, but others still remain as Coburn Gore, or Million Acre Gore, possessing individuality neither by the lay of the land nor by legislative act, but as mere left-overs.

New England was little affected by *-burgh* and *-ville*. As everywhere, the majority of the town-names were commonplace, but the legends and folk-tales attaching to a few of them do much to show the nature of the people. The accuracy of a tradition may always be questioned, but the very persistence of one shows the quality of the folk-mind and suggests that, even if merely invented for one town, it may well have functioned at the naming of another.

In 1781 the citizens of a small community in Maine petitioned for incorporation, and sent their minister, the Reverend Seth Noble, to Boston on this errand. As the clerk was filling out the papers, Mr. Noble stood by, in true Yankee fashion, quietly humming a tune to himself. When the clerk suddenly asked him,

"What's the name?" he absent-mindedly thought of the tune, not the town, and replied "Bangor." The naming from a hymn-tune became a repeated folk-tale. Even one of the greatest of New Englanders gave it circulation: "named at a pinch from a psalm tune," as Mr. Emerson wrote, disparagingly.

Post-Revolutionary Vermont maintained a tradition of French names—Vergennes, Calais, Montpelier. Hector St. Jean de Crèvecoeur, author of *Letters from an American Farmer,* used an Anglicized form of his family name to christen St. Johnsbury.

Illogically, as the religious fervor of the Puritans declined, Biblical names grew more numerous. Perhaps they began to seem less holy. Goshen and Canaan and Sharon might even be good for advertising, vaguely suggesting rich valleys flowing with milk and honey. Bozrah in Connecticut may also have brought to mind good pasturage from the mention of its sheep by the prophet Micah. On the other hand, its inhabitants braved the full-fledged threat of Jeremiah, 49, 13:

I have sworn by myself, saith the Lord, that Bozrah shall become a desolation, a reproach, a waste, and a curse.

As the story runs, however, the name sprang from still another quotation. In 1786 the district applied for incorporation and asked to be called Bath. The rustic who presented this petition was dressed in some parti-colored homespun so strange as to cause someone to quote the query of Isaiah, 63, 1:

Who is this that cometh from Edom, with dyed garments from Bozrah?

And so the Assembly, in acknowledgment of an apt quotation, rejected Bath, and substituted Bozrah.

The re-naming of a certain town in Vermont shows that such affairs did not always pass without heat. It had been granted as Wildersburgh in 1780, but the name became unpopular. A town-meeting to replace it met in 1793. Various names were proposed, but the running was soon limited to two. Captain Joseph Thomson strenuously contended for Holden, in honor of the town in Massachusetts which had been his former home. Mr. Jonathan Sherman was equally vehement for Barre, because he had come from Barre, also in Massachusetts. The argument was so hot that someone proposed a settlement by combat. The champions readily agreed.

The meeting then adjourned to a new barn-shed with a floor of rough hemlock planks. Space was cleared, and a pole was leveled waist-high. The combatants were to fight with their fists across this pole; but if one should knock the other down, he might follow up his advantage in any way he could.

Like two ancient warriors, they squared off—Thomson to lay on for Holden; Sherman, for Barre. Thomson was the more powerful; Sherman, the more lithe. After a little sparring, Thomson with a mighty blow knocked Sherman to the floor, and then leaping upon him began to pummel his head and face. But the supple Sherman squirmed so elusively that many of Thomson's blows merely barked his own knuckles on the hemlock floor. And all the while Sherman was working his own fists adroitly from beneath. Suddenly Thomson groaned, and his blows grew weak. Sherman, throwing him off, sprang to his feet and claimed the victory by shouting in exultation, "There, the name is Barre, by God!"

This particular story was transmitted through the village doctor, an eye-witness. He may even be called a participant because, next day, he had to use his professional skill to extract from the victor's back and buttocks the hemlock splinters they had collected while he was writhing on the plank floor.

Less authenticated but even more illustrative of the folk-mind is the naming of Canton. Realists may point out that by 1798 the China trade had made Yankees familiar with the name of the most frequented far-eastern port, and also that *canton* was used in France and Switzerland to mean a district. According to the tale, however, Canton was named at the instance of a prominent citizen, who maintained that his Massachusetts town was antipodal to the Chinese city. Actually, such an opinion was startlingly wrong. No two places in the northern hemisphere could be antipodal. Even if Canton was thought to be the corresponding opposite spot in the northern hemisphere, the calculation was still 1300 miles in error. The name, however, rapidly became popular.

Canton in Ohio was settled by New Englanders in 1805, and the name has spread to twenty-three states. Several of them tell the same story to explain their naming. The very perversity of the story is almost an argument for it. It seems just what a crotchety Yankee of 1798 would be likely to maintain. Moreover, the folk-mind is never scientifically exact. American children (and probably most American adults) still believe firmly that if they dug straight down through the earth, they would come out in China. Actually, they would emerge in the southern part of the Indian Ocean, west of Australia.

>>>-->>>-->>>-->>>-->>>-->>>-->>>-->>>-->>>-->>>--✵--<<<--<<<--<<<--<<<--<<<--<<<--<<<--<<<--<<<--<<<--<<<

Chapter XXIV ❲ How they took over the French names

In 1803 a Corsican adventurer signed away a province, and put an end at last to La Salle's old dream of French empire along the Mississippi. The Americans swept across the river. They kept the spelling of St. Louis, but pronounced it in their own way. Nouvelle Orléans they half translated as New Orleans. From Louisiane of the French and Luisiana of the Spanish they made a strange mingling to produce Louisiana.

What happened to the French names west of the river was nothing new. During a century the speakers of English had been encroaching on the territory where the French had first explored and settled. On the whole, the changes of names were fewer than commonly occur with shifts of sovereignty and language. The French had used many Indian words, and these came over easily into English, because they seemed native to the country, even though many of them, like Illinois, had French spelling and pronunciation. Also, the English had looked upon the French as worthy rivals, and considered French the language of culture and diplomacy. Many British officers spelled French as correctly as they spelled English. So the British had made no wholesale corruption of French, as they had done with Dutch, which they neither knew nor respected. Later, the Americans held the French as their dearest friends. So most of the greater lakes and rivers kept names which the French had given them, and in the midland country we still have good French spellings, except for lack of an accent here and there—Detroit, Fond du Lac, Racine, Eau Claire, Prairie du Chien, Lac qui Parle, Baton Rouge, and many others.

The smaller names, as always, suffered the most. Many of them were not printed upon maps, but circulated only by word of mouth, and so shifted easily. Sometimes they were translated, as when Le Sault de Saint Antoine became Saint Anthony Falls. Many French words were so much like some corresponding English word that one easily passed into the other. Bleu often became Blue, whether by translation or by change of pronunciation. Sometimes such a shifting amounted to a mistranslation, as when a river called Boeuf for the *boeuf sauvage,* "buffalo" was changed to Beef River.

As always happens with words which pass chiefly by speech, many of the lesser names took new forms. Sometimes the shift was within the French itself. St. Cosme, an early traveler, left his name on a river-point; when he was forgotten, the French themselves made it Cinq Hommes, "five men."

More often the transformation occurred in the shift between the two languages—sometimes from mere ignorance, sometimes doubtless for humor. A single word might take different forms.

Marais Salin, "salt pool," became Marie Saline, but Marais d'Osier, "willow pool," shifted to the semblance of a Greek name and remains as a town called Meredosia. Terre Bleue, "blue earth," became Tar Blue, and Pomme de Terre, "earth-apple," became Pumly Tar. But Terre Noire, "black earth," shifted into Turnwall. Mauvaise Terre, "bad earth," changed to Movestar, and doubtless children are already calling it Movie Star.

The early French traveled much by boat. Sometimes trees uprooted in freshets jammed together at some narrow or shallow place farther downstream, forming a dense tangle and blocking the passage as completely as a waterfall. The French called such a place an *embarras,* "obstruction," and many streams were distinguished as "aux embarras." This name proved almost as much a difficulty to speakers of English as the original tangle of trees had to the boatmen. One became merely Embarrass River; others were translated as Floodwood and Driftwood; another wore down into Zumbro; still another under classical influence became Ambrosia.

Occasionally the French name was transformed into sheer nonsense, as when Ile aux Galets, "pebble island," became Skilligallee. But typically the new name was a kind of striving after sense which would seem almost pathetic, if it did not so carry also the touch of primitive humor. St. Joachim became Swashing Creek. A lake called *du Chemin* because a trail passed it, became Dishmaugh. Rivière à Fèves could have been translated as Bean River, or if it was really Rivière à Féviers it would have been Locust-tree River. But the Americans pessimistically called it Fever River. Louse Creek would only be mystifying, if it were not known to stand for L'Ours, "the bear."

Many French proper names were taken by the English for something else; contrariwise, many French common words turned into English proper names. François became Franceway. Des Ruisseaux, a family name, passed through Dairysaw, and ended as Darysaw. Glaise à Paul was merely "Paul's lick." After the simple meaning was forgotten, attempts to make sense of it took it through Glazypool, Glazypole, Glazier Pole, and Glacierpeau.

Finally it was standardized as Glazypeau, and thus remains on a creek and a mountain.

Darden, another proper name, yielded Dirty Creek, but the real French word *sale,* "dirty," turned into English as Sally. Bois Brûlé, "burnt wood," shifted spelling as if it had been named for someone called Bob Ruly.

The list runs on indefinitely. Nowhere did the unlettered frontiersmen, both French and American, have a better chance than along the Arkansas River. The French themselves may have altered *Duc de Maine,* name of a ship as well as of a nobleman; it passed through many forms, arriving finally at Dugdemona. In that region also, L'eau Froide, "cold water," became Low Freight, and Chemin Couvert, "covered road," became Smackover. With such names folk-etymology became veritable poetry. They might well be declared national property, to be preserved like peaks and waterfalls for the perpetual delight of all lovers of names.

By these names you may know where the Frenchmen passed— boatmen and forest-runners, King's officers and black-robed priests. The Americans took them over, not knowing what they meant, using them only as counters, and so you will find them still, coupled with River, or Bay, or Point. *Glaise,* they said for a salt-lick, and thus came Auglaize River, "at the salt-lick." *Marais* they said, not for a marsh, but for a pool. *Vase* was their word for swamp or muddy place, and so came Auxwasse River. Where, canoeing on a lake, they left the shore and steered across the mouth of a bay for the point on the other side, they called it a *traverse.*

They said *grand* for big, and the Americans took such names over, though the word had a new meaning in their speech, and Grand River would never be the same as Big River.

Sable was their name for a sandy point or a stream with sandy bottom; *roche,* for rock; *saline* for a stream with brackish taste, flowing from a salt-lick. *Rouge* meant a stream with reddish water; *vermillon,* not the color of the water, but a stream where the Indians dug red clay for their war-paint.

Raisin they said for the wild-grape. Like *grand* the Americans took this word, though its meaning was different, and they made it a battle-cry: "Remember the River Raisin!"

They gave these names and many others, but more than by all the names given one by one, the French changed our heritage by leaving new general terms. They furnished *portage* and *rapids* and *prairie*. Along the Mississippi *bayou,* which had first passed from Choctaw to French, passed over into English. So also the boatmen of New France did not say *chenal* for a river-channel, as a Parisian would, but they said *chenail,* and the word in English became *sny*.

Another change came about because the Virginians first took the names over from the French. The New Englanders had said *pond* usually and *lake* rarely. But in Virginia there were few bodies of water to be called either lakes or ponds. So the Virginians easily took from the French the habit of saying *lake,* and in all the great valley, and farther to the west also, *pond* is seldom used except for something so insignificant as hardly to have a name at all.

The French manner of speech worked in subtler ways too. In England itself men had usually said River Thames and River Severn. But in the colonies they had used the common order of words, saying James River or Black River. Even when they occasionally borrowed a stream name from England, they reversed it as with Severn River in Maryland. The French also used what seemed to the Americans the wrong order of words, and generally they changed it. But here and there, where the French were firmly rooted, the old names survived. Thus there is still River Rouge near Detroit.

Since *lake* was even more a French word than *river,* the Americans always said Lake Superior and Lake Erie, using the French order of words when they took over French names. With lakes which were still to be named, a curious custom arose. A small and unimportant one was called merely Round Lake or Smith Lake, but a large or famous one would be called in the French fashion, Lake Tahoe or Lake Mead.

Chapter XXV ❨ Of Mr. Jefferson's western lands

M<small>R</small>. T<small>HOMAS</small> J<small>EFFERSON</small>, like other Virginia gentlemen before him, having made a purchase of western lands, sent some agents to look over the property. Since his was the largest such purchase ever made, the work of his agents attained corresponding fame, and is known as the Lewis and Clark Expedition.

On May 14, 1804, the two captains with their company began their ascent of the Missouri River, and immediately started to give names to every namable stream, hill, or point which seemed not to possess one already. Probably they did more naming than any other explorers who ever traveled within the territory of the United States. Yet only one great name arose from Lewis and Clark, and even most of their smaller ones were destined to perish.

Nevertheless, by looking at their work, we learn the ways in which thousands of creeks and hills were named on unrecorded occasions by hundreds of hunters, emigrants, and land-viewers. The men who pushed out into the current of the great muddy river were ordinary Americans of their day. Only Captain Lewis could have been called educated, and even he was a poor speller. Captain Clark was frontier-bred, and his misspellings at times approached the inspired. The rank-and-file were volunteers from the regular army along with some young Kentuckians, a few French frontiersmen, and Clark's Negro body-servant. The two captains doubtless decided upon most of the names, but as in western expeditions generally, there was a good deal of democracy, and one name at least was decided by popular acclaim.

In two respects the namings showed an unusually conscious selection. There were almost no repetitions, and the more commonplace terms were avoided. The journals of the expedition did not record a single Sandy Creek or Rock Creek. They did not admit Sugar-loaf, Beaver, or Deer. The use of Corvus for Crow showed a fixed policy of avoiding the ordinary. Their Rivers-across was doubtless a conscious substitution for the ordinary Cross Creek. Such originality indicated a certain national point of view which Jefferson himself might well have suggested.

As far as the Rocky Mountains, the explorers passed through country in which French trappers had already named the more important streams. Lewis and Clark learned these from Drouillard and their other Frenchmen, and recorded them, sometimes in translation. Thus Yellowstone originated from Roche Jaune, in turn probably a translation of its Minnataree name Mitsiadazi.

In the motives behind their own namings, the explorers followed the conventional American habits, even when avoiding the conventional names. They described, as in Scattering Creek, Crooked Falls, and Diamond Island. They often displayed touches of descriptive fancy, as in Bald-pated Prairie, so called from the bare hills surrounding it. Notimber Creek was an example of that rare type of naming by negative. Unwittingly, on May 8, 1805, the explorers used a descriptive which itself would become conventional in the future. "The water of this river," wrote Lewis, "possesses a peculiar whiteness, being about the colour of a cup of tea with the admixture of a tablespoonful of milk." Without knowing it, they were looking, and were the first Americans so to look, upon water which had flowed out from beneath a glacier, and bore suspended the whitish silt. Lewis added: "From the colour of its water we called it Milk River."

Any token of Indian occupation was good for a name—Stone-idol, and Sticklodge. Goat-pen indicated where the Indians had built a corral for trapping antelope, which were usually called "goats" from the French *cabri*.

Any incident of the voyage was also likely to suggest a name. Council Bluffs was a record of the meeting between the explorers and some Ottoe Indians. Good-humored Island wrote into the journals another encounter which ended happily. Caution Island corresponded with the entry in Clark's always bizarre spelling: "Observed great caution this day, expection the Seaux intentions somewhat hostile." Colt-Killed Creek and Hungry Creek, close together, told their own stories.

Some places were named for the presence or abundance of a plant or animal; others, for an incident in which an animal figured. Once, as the crews were laboring up some rapids, they were amazed to see a mother elk and her calf come swimming gallantly downstream: "hence the name Elk rappids which they instantly gave this place."

When some member of the party supplied an incident, his name was often given to the place. Floyd's River recorded the only death on the expedition. Reuben's Creek was named because "Reuben Fields, one of our men, was the first of our party who reached it." Field's Creek was for the same man. Where another man wounded a large bear, the stream became Gibson's Creek. In the end, almost every man had left his name somewhere, many even twice.

Not being Quakers, the two captains remembered themselves. The great southern branch of the Columbia became Lewis River, and an almost equally notable stream received the name of Clark.

Not being Catholics, they paid no honor to the saints' days, but Independence Creek commemorated July 4, 1804. Sunday Island recorded where they camped upon that day, and Birth Creek was to celebrate Captain Clark's anniversary.

Following a tradition as old as Jamestown, they honored their patrons. A large stream became Jefferson's River, and others listed the members of the Cabinet—Madison, Smith, Gallatin, and Dearborn. Clark remembered his sister with Fanny's Island, and his future wife with Judith's Creek; he named Martha's River, "in honor of the Selebrated M. F." Captain Lewis commemorated his own lady-love with even more flourish:

I determined to give it the name, and in honour of Miss Maria W—d, called it Maria's River. It is true that the hue of the waters of this turbulent and troubled stream but illy comport with the pure celestial virtue and amiable qualifications of that lovely fair one; but on the other hand it is a noble river.

In still further compliments to the President three tributaries of the Jefferson were called Philosophy, Wisdom, and Philanthropy—"those cardinal virtues which have so eminently marked that deservedly selibrated character through life."

The current classical furor and the love of the republican heroes may account for Pompey's Pillar, now so called. Captain Clark merely recorded: "This rock which I shall call Pompy's Tower is 200 feet high and 400 paces in secumpherance."

Of the many dozens of names planted by Lewis and Clark all the way from the mouth of the Missouri to the mouth of the Columbia only a few survived the turbulent years between exploration and permanent settlement.

In the next season after the return, the Spanish fur-trader Manuel Lisa led an expedition up the river, and Drouillard accompanied him. But Drouillard was French, and probably knew or cared little about the names which his American captains had given to every little creek. Several other old Lewis-and-Clark men returned to the mountains at various times, and through them the tradition of a few names survived. As might be expected, these were mostly of the larger rivers, which were important enough to be remembered. Even some of these lapsed for a while, and were restored later from the written records. Clark Fork was at various times known as Bitterroot, Deer Lodge, Hell Gate, Missoula, and Silverbow. Floyd's plainly marked grave (ghost-fearing Indians must have avoided it) preserved that name upon the stream. Milk River probably survived because it was too apt to be easily displaced. Pine Island also, marked by a large pine tree, was another signpost name which might well have been given again by later comers even if the original naming had been forgotten.

Most of the names, however, were simply overwhelmed by a flood of commonplace frontier terms. Happily, Judith River and Maria's River survived. Martha's River became the Big Muddy.

Jefferson's River survived as Jefferson, and with equal luck the names of his cabinet members all survived. With strange inconsistency, Clark Fork finally remained, but Lewis River soon became the Shoshone, from the Indian tribe who lived along it. It survived, however, as the Snake, not because it was twisty as a snake or because it was notable for snakes, but because Shoshone could be thus translated.

Saddest of all was the fate of the cardinal virtues. Philosophy River degenerated into still another Willow Creek; Wisdom, into Big Hole River. Philanthropy River came to be known as the Passamari, its Shoshone name, and was called more commonly, by translation, the Stinking-water. Under the refinements of civilization this was altered to Ruby River.

Although Lewis and Clark explored a region where ten states would be later established, not a single state name stemmed from their expedition. They originated only one nationally known term. On first starting out, they used *prairie* for open country. This word, however, indicated an area definitely bounded by forest. When the explorers came to a region where treeless country stretched off to the horizon, they apparently began to feel that *prairie* was hardly suitable, and they wrote of the "great plains," which became the Great Plains.

The ordinary Westerner, however, was not so sensitive. *Prairie* meant open country to him, and he was not particular whether it was a mile or a thousand miles across. So the cowboy lamented:

Bury me not on the lone prair-ree

without bothering about what the word may have meant to his Kentucky ancestors.

Chapter XXVI ❲ Of the dry country and the farther mountains

AFTER Lewis and Clark the next to come were the trappers and fur-traders who were called "mountain-men." Then for the first time men who spoke English lived in dry country.

It was a far-stretching treeless land where the short grass rippled under the west wind, a topsy-turvy land of volcanic rocks and salty water bubbling from boiling springs, where rivers grew smaller as they flowed from their headwaters. At noon, mirages wavered above the sage-brush, but in the dawn a man looked out and saw pine-trees on the mountains farther off than he could walk by nightfall. The bare mountains themselves stood up along the horizon like dry fangs. Among all the words of a language which forest-dwellers had spoken for a thousand years, there were no names for such a country.

So they used old words with new meanings, or borrowed from their French comrades, or in New Mexico took over words from the Spaniards, who themselves had come from a dry land.

To describe arid country they took the old word *desert,* changing its meaning. For, as the word itself shows, it meant once merely a deserted place; thus as John Smith wrote:

The most of this country, though desert, yet exceeding fertile; good timber, most hills and dales, in each valley, a crystal spring.

In the early colonies when a man said "the desert" he meant merely that no one lived there, more likely because it was a swamp with too much water than a region lacking water. But in the dry lands of the farther west, water was life, and an uninhabited place was a desert because it was dry.

The old meaning, however, lingered in people's minds. When men talked of the Great American Desert, they may have meant sometimes only to describe a vast uninhabited area. But the new meaning suggested endless sand dunes which only camels could cross. As time passed, the new meaning displaced the old, especially in the eastern states, where men saw no deserts and imagined them worse than they really were. So the Easterners thought of deserts as sands beneath a blazing sun, but the Westerners, who made their peace with a new country, knew that deserts were of many kinds, and were even friendly enough to a man who knew their ways.

The trappers also brought in many other words. From their own language they took *wash* for the dry bed of a stream, and *waterhole* for a pool of standing water too dirty and stagnant to be called a spring. But by *hole* used alone they meant a secluded mountain valley, which their grandfathers would have called a cove.

In the forests men had followed Indian trails on foot, but in open grass-country they moved faster, on horseback, and often followed no trails. A man in such country always had to watch against wandering across from the headwaters of one stream to those of another, because he might pass into a different region and be lost. So men marked especially the ridge parting the waters of two rivers and called it a divide. The line parting the waters of the two oceans became the Great Divide.

Many of the trappers were Frenchmen of the old settlements. Their *mauvaises terres* for a region cut by ravines, hard to travel, was translated into terse English as *badlands*. From the French also came *butte* for a sharp hill rising from a plain, and *coulée* for a stream bed, and *park* for an open valley among mountains.

The western mountains also were different from the eastern ones. They were not long ridges, but rose into points. There was no ordinary English word for such a mountain; not even *knob* would serve. So the *pic* of the French trappers brought *peak* into common speech.

The Americans already had two words for a passage through mountains, but in the western land they developed a third. *Notch* and *gap* were good words for a sharp break in a single ridge, but they implied something that might almost be looked through. In the greater mountains of the West a trail might twist and turn for many miles before at last topping the ridge. So the trappers, hearing *passe* in Creole French, began themselves to say *pass*.

The trappers also went southward and over the mountains to Taos and Santa Fe. There they learned from the Spaniards. In *mesa,* originally "table," they got a word for a flat-topped hill with steep sides, or a flat shelf at the base of a mountain. The Spaniards also had a word meaning pipe or cannon, and in Mexico they had come to use it also for a narrow watercourse among mountains. The trappers needed such a word; they took over *cañon,* and spread it across all the West as *canyon*.

These mountain men, seeking the beaver, gave few great names. The larger rivers had been named already. The regions they called by the names of the Indians living there—the Blackfoot Country or the Snake Country. In comparison with the size of the West they gave few names, for they themselves were few, and were wanderers. Such men did not bother to name every little stream and hill, for they could not remember them from year to year, even if they gave them. Like all nomads, they scattered their names frugally—remembering surely the greater streams, and the holes where they wintered and made rendezvous, and a few buttes and peaks which served as landmarks.

With canyon and pass and their other words, they coupled simple names to distinguish one from another. Black, white, and red were the colors of the mountain men. They used the names of animals often—beaver, elk, buffalo, and sheep. They spread across the West the names of three trees.

This is the story of those trees, as you will find them again and again on Cottonwood Creek, and Cedar Mountain, and Pine Mountain. When you see cottonwoods, that dark green line across the desert, you may know that they stand by a stream, or else you can get water by digging in the sand beneath them. When you see the scrubby cedars upon a hillside, the chance is not so good, but there may be a spring in one of the gullies. But the pines grow only on the higher mountains, and when you see pines, they will not be so far from a running stream or at least a little water in a pool.

Their names were homely and short—Mud Creek and Dry Creek, Sand Creek and Rock Creek. If the water smelled too much of sulphur, they called it Stinking Spring.

They rarely departed into fancy, but as always when simple people give names, there was now and then a touch of poetry. Such a one was Bitter Creek for water too strong in alkali. But when a stream flowed untainted, they might give it that loveliest of names—Sweetwater.

They could often use mountains as signposts; those great bare mountains took many strange shapes. In the East there had been Round Top, and Haystack, and Sugarloaf, but in the West many more arose, so that a man could tell what mountain it was by merely looking at it. Thus came Saddle Mountain, and Broken Top; Castle Peak, Court House Rock and Chimney Rock, Pillar Peak; Two Top, Dome, and Coffin. So also came The Rabbit's Ears and The Deer's Ears, and Mulehead Butte. Since the forces of nature saw fit to leave many hills in the shape of a woman's breast, those simple men knew no reason not to name them so. The French said *mamelle* and *teton* as common words, and the Americans named Nipple Butte and Tit Butte. But a sharply up-standing rock might have a correspondingly male name.

Like all the others, the mountain men left their own names on the land. Bridger's Butte, where Jim Bridger built his post, still looks down upon the highway to the West. Ogden's Hole has become Ogden, the city. John Day, who went mad; Bill Williams, who ate man-meat; Beckwourth, the mulatto; Sibylle and La Bonté, the Frenchmen—you will find them all on the map. One of them was Joseph Walker, who led Bonneville's men to California, and became a river and a lake and a pass. There was also Jedediah Smith, to whom the lure of far places was like bugles calling, until the Comanches killed him; but he left his name far off on a river in California. So they went—Sublette and Ashley, Carson, Greenwood, Jackson, and Hoback; on stream and canyon and pass they left their names, and afterward came counties and cities.

Though they took Indian wives and knew the speech, the mountain men used few Indian names, and those which they took they often translated. This was perhaps because the land had few people for its size. When the trappers came to a stream, they might find no Indian there to tell them the name; or, since languages differed, two Indians might give different names. Some of the larger rivers took their names from the tribes living there, after the tradition which went back as far as Potomac and Susquehanna. Thus from the branch of the Pawnee known as the Wolf tribe came in French the Loup River, and from another branch called the Republicans came the Republican River.

The trappers also, French and American, twisted the Indian names by mistake or for humor. The tribe called by some such name as Yamhela yielded Yamhill River. A tribe farther south in the Oregon country was the Ku-kwil. Of this the French trappers made Coquille, and they put that name upon a river as if because a "shell" had been found there. Perhaps a different sounding of the same tribal name gave rise to Coquin, both for the Indians and another stream. Later the Americans translated the French as Rogue River.

Three famous names defy sure explanation. The mountains known as Siskiyou probably arose from a Cree word for "bobtailed horse" which had come into the Chinook trade-language. As one story goes, a bob-tailed packhorse was lost there in a snowstorm in 1828. But another story would have the name to be the pronunciation of the French *six cailloux*, "six stones," a name given on account of some landmarks. Coeur d'Alene means "heart of awl" but fails to make sense, and all explanations are far-fetched. Pend Oreille, on the other hand, is not even good French. It may have been given to some Indians who had ear-ornaments, but if so, the name must have been clipped from *pendant d'oreille* even by the French themselves. All three names may well be transformations of now-forgotten Indian words, but their uncertain origin has not prevented their being placed upon rivers, lakes, mountains, towns, and counties.

The life of the mountain men was adventurous, and many of their names sprang from incidents of hunting and of Indian fights. George Ruxton, the dare-devil British officer who lived for a while in the mountains, noted that many creeks bore "familiar proper names, both English and French." He added, "These are invariably christened after some unfortunate trapper, killed there in an Indian fight, or treacherously slaughtered by the lurking savages."

The many streams called Cache Creek recorded a place where furs and trade-goods were carefully buried to await their owners' return. Cache la Poudre River was more explicit of the memory that gunpowder was hidden there. Malheur River was the "river of misfortune" because a cache made there was discovered and stolen by Indians.

Not far from the Malheur, the Owyhee River commemorates a curious detail of history. After trading-posts were established on the Pacific Coast, a few men were brought there from the Hawaiian Islands. In 1819 some of these Kanakas went with the first trappers to penetrate the Snake River country. On a far-inland stream two of these wanderers were killed by Indians. The Owyhee River records their death in a form which was common for the island now spelled Hawaii.

A name commemorates the famous, but melancholy and sinister, tale of Hiram Scott. He fell ill, and his treacherous comrades abandoned him. With grim will-to-live he dragged on for sixty miles, until at last he died at the foot of some upstanding hills along the Platte. That next summer the very men who had abandoned him returned that way, and found his remains. The place is still Scott's Bluff.

The Russians also came for furs. In the summer when Napoleon marched against Moscow, Ivan Kuskoff brought south from Alaska one hundred Russians and eighty Aleuts to hunt the sea-otter. On a barren shelf between the mountains and the surf, they founded a post north of San Francisco Bay. At the end of three months they finished the stockade of redwood with block-houses at the corners. Then, eight days before the French batteries opened at Borodino, they named their new post, asking divine guidance.

They wrote various words upon pieces of paper, and put them into a vessel standing in front of the image of the Savior. One of them drew out a lot, and the name written on it was not a common word in the speech of hunters, but was from the formal language of poetry, meaning a Russian. Then they fired off their guns and small-arms in celebration, and on that day, August 30, 1812, the place took the name which it has kept ever since, and became Fort Ross.

The Russians clung to that barren coast for some years, and gave other names. Few of them lasted. Upon a high flat-topped mountain they left an inscription and the name St. Helena, honoring perhaps both that favorite Russian saint and a princess. By memory that Russians had once been there, another place which they had called for a man, Tschernickh, came to be Russian Gulch.

The chief river along that coast was known to the Indians as Shabaikai. But the Russians, like everyone else, changed Indian names, tending to make them over into their own language. They twisted Shabaikai into Slavianka, "little Slav woman." This in turn became Slavyanskaya, "Slavic." The Americans finally called it Russian River.

After a few years the Russians went back to Alaska. All they left on that coast was a moldering stockade and some buildings. But, as always, a few names remembered them—Fort Ross, Mount Saint Helena, Russian River, and Russian Gulch. So the Russians from the north also left us a little of the heritage.

Chapter XXVII ❨ Of a new generation

AFTER the guns were cold at Yorktown, a new generation had begun to grow up of men who had never known what it was to live beneath a king. They were young when Mr. Jefferson bought Louisiana. They lived on through the times of Mr. Madison and Mr. Monroe. With graying hair they elected Andy Jackson and Mr. Van Buren. In those years they fought the British again by land and sea. They admired their first cotton gin, and heard the whistle of their first steamboat. The men of that generation wore tall beaver hats and trousers; no longer, wigs and small-clothes. In the giving of names, they generally kept the old customs which had come to them from the years following the Revolution, but they added a few.

Most notably, the men of this generation carried forward the tradition of using already established names for states and territories. In their years, eight new ones were organized, all with old names.

The former French province of Louisiana, like the Northwest Territory, was large enough for several states, and there was no reason why any one of them should bear the name which had applied to the whole. In 1804 Congress cut off the more thickly inhabited lower region and called it the Territory of Orleans from its chief town. The upper region with its seat of government at St. Louis was left as a vast, still-to-be-divided remainder called Louisiana.

The next territory was formed in 1805. Jefferson was President, and he perhaps remembered that he had once suggested the name

Michigania. Now, however, the classical ending was dropped, and the territory was merely called Michigan, after its lake.

Illinois still further set the pattern for the establishment of the local name. It had been known as a tribal name for nearly two centuries. Jolliet and Marquette had applied it to the river on which the tribe lived. The region gradually came to be known as the Illinois country. In 1778 Virginia formed it into Illinois County. Without dispute Congress made it Illinois Territory in 1809, and it later assumed statehood.

During these years, however, the Territory of Orleans did not rest easy. The Creoles wanted the old name again, and even the newly arrived Americans must have felt that Orleans was unsatisfactory. There was a continual inconvenience in distinguishing between Orleans, the territory, and New Orleans, the city. The Americans had no tradition of the city-state, and even resented the implication that any one city should dominate. Plymouth, Providence, and New Haven had once been colonies named for their first settlements, but all of these had disappeared from current use. Only in New York did state and chief city still bear the same name, and even there Albany had become the capital in 1797.

In 1811 a convention met to arrange for the admission of Orleans as a state. A movement arose to change the name to Jefferson. Since Jefferson had consummated the Purchase, there was a certain justice in the proposal, but its adoption would have constituted a startling break with tradition. Not even Washington had been so honored. Besides, Jefferson had many and bitter enemies. A certain Louis de Blanc de St. Denis, delegate from Attakapas, cried in excited Creole hyperbole that if such a proposition seemed to have any chance of success, he would take a barrel of gunpowder and blow up the Convention! In the end the old name Louisiana was readopted, and the state was thus admitted on March 3, 1812. Thereafter, for two months, the United States had both a state and a territory called Louisiana. On June 4th, however, after the precedent of Connecticut, Illinois and the other river-named states, an act of Congress was passed: "the territory heretofore called Louisiana shall hereafter be called Missouri."

The tradition of river-naming continued with the establishment of Alabama Territory in 1817. In the same year, however, an established name was first seriously threatened.

Mississippi Territory had been organized in 1798, and in 1817 a convention assembled to organize a new state. On July 17th, a delegate took the floor and proposed the name Washington. Most likely he pointed out that the other name pre-empted Mississippi for a small section, which included neither the river's source nor its mouth, and in fact only a small part of one bank. The other river-states might claim that geography and history justified their names, but Mississippi could not. The language, moreover, was actually foreign to the region—as well adopt Jefferson's old proposal of the Greek coinage Macropotamia, which had much the same meaning. Mississippi came from the far north, and was never heard among the Chickasaws and Choctaws until the French brought it. On the other hand, although many towns and counties had been called for Washington, no state had as yet honored him.

The arguments, both against Mississippi and for Washington, were strong, and the final vote was twenty-three to seventeen. Nevertheless, though threatened, the tradition of the established name won a six-vote majority, and Mississippi was added to the roll of states.

With the tradition of river-naming thus still again reinforced, the formation of Arkansaw Territory two years later was merely to be expected. The name, for tribe, river, and judicial district, had been well maintained ever since 1673. The French pronunciation, with the silent final *s,* was current. Spelling raised the only problem, and for some years the more phonetic Arkansaw had official standing.

Maine, cut off from Massachusetts in 1820, naturally kept its old name. Florida, on the other hand, might well have been thought too suggestive of foreign rule. The name had once been spread indefinitely over almost the whole continent. English encroachment—Virginia, Carolina and Georgia in turn—drove it back toward the peninsula, and French settlement at Mobile restricted it upon the west. Nevertheless, whether under Spanish or British rule, the province had never ceased to be Florida. When the United States acquired the peninsula in 1821 and organized it into a territory, the tradition of the name fortunately prevailed. Florida was thus saved from joining the ghostly ranks of Vineland, Norumbega, and Quivira.

The two territories established in the eighteen-thirties merely carried the tradition on. Chippewau and Huron were proposed for the region west of Lake Michigan, but in the end it merely took the Indian name of a river, and eventually became Wisconsin. Another tribal name, first recorded on the famous canoe voyage of 1673 and later applied to a river, yielded Iowa Territory in 1838.

By this time thirteen states had been added to the original thirteen, and three other territories had been formally organized. Not one of these sixteen names had been coined for the occasion. Eleven were of Indian origin, and all of these except Michigan were also borne by large rivers. Florida, Maine, and Louisiana dated back to early European exploration. Only Vermont and Indiana could in any sense be called new.

A List of Post-Offices in the United States first appeared as a separate volume in 1803. It was a pamphlet of thirty-eight pages, listing 1,285 offices. Although the Declaration of Independence was already twenty-seven years old, the names still remained predominatingly British, with only here and there one sprung from the country itself, Indian or otherwise.

The situation, however, was changing rapidly. As post-offices were established in smaller places, the informal names of these villages made their appearance. Moreover, when states were taking names of the land, towns began to adopt the new custom.

By 1815 the post-office list looked more American. A man might officially receive his mail at Narrows of Lackawaxen, Pennsylvania, or Mouth of Black River, Ohio, or Shoals of Ogechee, Georgia. Many offices bore the name Cross Roads, conveniently abbreviated as in Brown's ✕ Roads. The appended letters *c. h.* after a name indicated Court House. Some offices bore two names, so that whether you addressed your letter to Poplar Grove or M'Morrie's Store, it turned up at the same place, and fittingly passed through the hands of Jas. M'Morrie, Postmaster. A Georgian might post his letters at Cook's Law Office, and address a Virginian friend at Troublesome Iron Works. Many such names approached the grotesque, none more so perhaps than the New York office listed as Head of Cow Neck.

The more bizarre and cumbersome of these descriptive names gradually died out, but a few remained, such as Head of Grassy, Kentucky. The shorter and more natural descriptives remained upon towns by scores. The whole result was to unite country and names more closely. Big Stone Gap, Maple Grove, and Bear Creek were sound and honest as the hills and streams.

Many villages thus named during this generation grew into cities. About 1795 a Pennsylvania settlement took the name of its lake, and became Erie. In Massachusetts, Quequeteant, "place of falling water," was translated as Fall River. In Connecticut, the people of a little village, proud of having a new drawbridge, established themselves officially as Bridgeport.

Another town on Lake Erie took a well-rooted name. First of all, a Seneca Indian lived there, whose name, doubtless for good tribal reasons, meant Buffalo, and was so translated by the frontiersmen. The stream where he lived became Buffalo Creek. The town founded there was first called New Amsterdam because of some Dutch immigrants, but the Americans preferred Buffalo, and in the end established it officially, as one of the most colorful among the names of American cities.

Peoria, like so many other names, dated back to Jolliet and Marquette; it followed a common evolution—from Indian tribe to Indian village, to a lake, next to a French settlement, and finally to an incorporated town.

South Bend declared the town's location at the point where the St. Joseph River turned from a western to a northern course. Flint and Milwaukee took the names of their rivers, and Grand

Rapids more explicitly stated the location at the rapids of the Grand.

On August 4, 1830, the inhabitants of another undistinguished western village filed a town-plat. They had previously been known as Fort Dearborn; but Dearborn, the same for whom Lewis and Clark named a river, had merely been Secretary of War under Jefferson, and was no hero. Besides, military suggestion in the name of a town implied war rather than peaceful commerce. So, in accordance with the fashion of the time, the town-founders took the name of the river, and wrote Chicago upon their plat. It was a good example of a name adopted without knowledge of its meaning, for if the founders had known it to be Onion River, or allegedly Skunk, or Smelling River, they would very likely have kept Dearborn.

Far to the south, the same process was at work. Even before 1600 the Spaniards had listed Tampa as an Indian village. Since *itimpi* means merely "near it," the white men may have misunderstood that word to be the village when it really referred to something else, as happened with Texas and many other names. Later, Tampa became the name of a bay. A log fort built there in 1823 took the name of its commander, Colonel Brooke. But the settlers who gathered under its protection rejected the military name, and adopted Tampa Bay for their first post-office in 1831. They soon decided that Tampa alone was sufficient.

Also in the South, a settlement known as Ross's Landing was laid out as a town in 1838, and chartered in the next year. Its founders, deciding upon a change of name, took a Creek word meaning "rock-rising-to-a-point," probably applied to the near-by height known as Lookout Mountain. The town-founders spelled it Chattanooga.

On the farthest western frontier still another town was shaping. Some dozen citizens of Missouri banded together, and at a court sale on November 14, 1838, purchased 256 acres of land, including a ferry-landing on the Missouri just below the mouth of the Kaw. Shortly afterwards they met to choose a name. Their gathering place was a log-cabin on the river-bank where a lank and cadaverous "One-eyed Ellis" dispensed whiskey in tin cups.

The discussion, doubtless aided by the whiskey, was long and acrimonious. The favorite at the opening was Port Fonda, after one of the chief partners, but some of the others disliked Mr. Fonda. He violated the code of the frontier by boasting that he was not a workingman, and by signing himself "Abraham Fonda, Gentleman." A lesser stockholder, Henry Jobe, arose wrathfully, threatening direct action and shotgun-justice, if such a name should be foisted on the new town. Port Fonda was tactfully withdrawn, and the meeting was suddenly stalled.

Someone next produced a copy of that second Bible of the frontier, Noah Webster's spelling-book. At its back was a list of important rivers, mountains, and cities, both American and foreign. But not one of them struck the fancy of the assembly.

The inevitable humorist, a certain character known as "Squire Bowers," then suggested Rabbitville and Possum-trot. But no one had any real intention of ruining the investment for the sake of a bad joke.

The coinage Kawsmouth also met with no enthusiasm, but it pointed to the use of a local name. At last, after much disagreement, the vote went for the other designation of the Kaw, also familiar as the tribal name, and the half-dozen log cabins became Kansas. The site was platted as Town of Kansas in 1839, became City of Kansas in 1853, and in 1889 finished its evolution by becoming officially Kansas City.

Thus, in the period of a single generation thirteen towns destined to be cities took names which were already established. Seven of these—Erie, Peoria, Chicago, Tampa, Milwaukee, Chattanooga, and Kansas—were Indian. All the seven, however, having arisen by the process of transfer from some feature of the land, showed a tolerance for Indian names rather than a real liking for them.

The old ways of naming also continued, for in general no system of giving names, once established, ever died out entirely.

Across the Hudson from New York a town was laid out on the

Jersey shore. It took its name in 1820 by counterpart, and became the City of Jersey, and later, Jersey City.

In 1820 also the Legislature of Indiana took up a proposal to found a capital for their newly admitted state. There was much debate over a name. Rather strangely, some legislators wished to call the city for the old chief Tecumseh, even though he had fought against the Americans and been killed by them at the battle of Thames River, only seven years earlier. But the name finally adopted was coined in classical fashion. They took the semi-Greek name of the state, combined it with the Greek *-polis,* and made Indianapolis.

Someone with knowledge of Greek also christened an Ohio town. In the great era of water-transportation a canal was surveyed from Lake Erie to the Ohio River. At the highest point on this route a town was laid out in 1825. It might naturally have been called Summit, and the county there actually took that name. But probably wishing to escape triteness, the founders translated *summit* into Greek as Akron.

The old heroes of the Revolution still marched westward, and the new heroes joined their ranks. Each succeeding President and every political leader received his tribute of namesake towns. Many of them remained slovenly cross-roads villages, scarcely an honor to anyone. Columbus, so strangely resurrected from the past, maintained his popularity, and had better fortune; in 1812 the Ohio Legislature adopted his name for the new state capital.

One Revolutionary hero arrived late. Francis Marion, "the Swamp Fox," seems to have made little impression upon his contemporaries. Even his own South Carolina did not name a county or town for him until 1800. His popularity as a hero followed the publication in 1809 of his life by Parson Weems, that facile creator of legends who invented the story of Washington and the cherry tree. As late as 1817 there was only one post-office named Marion; within four years the number had jumped to six; there are now twenty-eight.

Similarly the popularity of Lafayette was delayed. In 1822 only four post-offices bore his name, most of them preferring the form

Fayette. In 1824, however, the old Marquis returned for a tri-
umphal tour. Four years later the number of his post-offices had
reached eighteen. Eventually the places named for him, in various spellings and combinations, reached a total of forty. To these
should also be added some of the score called La Grange, since
that was the name of Lafayette's country-seat and was thus first
popularized.

The popularity of Lafayette should remind all Americans that
the United States in its first years carried on a revolutionary enthusiasm such as was to be associated with Soviet Russia a century
later. Any man who raised the standard of revolt against royal
authority was likely to be hailed as a hero without further in-
quiry. Bolivar was naturally the most popular, but Kosciusko and
Kossuth had their towns and counties. Even the grotesque form
of Ypsilanti did not prevent the name of that Greek patriot being
given to a Michigan town, although its inhabitants have had to
suffer the ridicule of their neighbors ever since, and are regularly
abbreviated into Ypsy.

While most Americans thus loved revolutionaries, some succumbed to the spell of a glamorous tyrant. A wealthy landowner
in Maryland gave his plantations the names of Napoleon's greatest victories. But when he ran for office and was defeated, the
winner named *his* farm Waterloo. Martin Van Buren, later to be
President, was another admirer. When he heard that a village in
his own state of New York was to be called Waterloo, he was
indignant and contrived to have another place named Austerlitz,
exclaiming in victory: "There's an Austerlitz for your Waterloo!"

On the whole, however, even the splendor of the French Empire failed to fool many of the people very much of the time.
Though Waterloo was a British victory and we had just fought
the British, the list of 1822 showed five post-offices of the name.
In the most recent Postal Directory, Napoleon for all the glory
of his legend only breaks even with Bolivar.

The War of 1812 was neither popular nor very glorious, but it
produced a fair crop of heroes. The cynic might argue that the
phrase-makers had the better of it. Perry, who announced, "We

[234]

have met the enemy and they are ours," spread his name over many states. In Ohio, towns were soon called Perry, Perrysburg, Perrysville, and Perryton. MacDonough won an equally hard-fought and important victory, but failed to compose a good dispatch. Only two little towns bear his name.

Lawrence, who cried "Don't give up the ship!" was another hero, and the rough-and-ready Westerner William Henry Harrison, winner of victory on Thames River and the nickname "Old Tippecanoe." There was also Stephen Decatur who captured the *Macedonian,* and said "My country, right or wrong!" In 1820, after his death in a duel, President Monroe himself directed that a townsite in Alabama be named Decatur.

By all odds, however, the greatest new hero was that darling of the West, Andy Jackson. He bore a common name, and the six post-offices so called before 1813 may have been for other Jacksons. By 1831, however, there were forty Jacksons, including combinations like Jacksonboro. In that year Franklin, who had been the first postmaster-general, was the nearest rival among the hero-names, but there were only thirty Franklins. Washington stood at twenty-three; Lafayette, at nineteen; Jefferson, at eighteen; Wayne, at sixteen. In addition, every state west of the mountains and south of Virginia, with the exception of South Carolina, saw fit to establish a Jackson County. The popularity of Jackson was rather short-lived, however, and in the end he yielded before the more abiding qualities of other heroes.

Nevertheless, Jackson had the luck to win the unusual commemoration of a large city. Far in the south a settlement sprang up at a crossing of the St. John's River. The Indians had called the place Wacca Pilatka; the last part of this was pure Seminole for "crossing," but the first part was the Spanish *vaca,* "cow," taken over by the Seminoles, who had not seen cattle until the Spaniards brought them. The Spaniards themselves called it the Ferry of St. Nicholas, but the Americans translated the Seminole name as Cowford. When the town came to be founded in 1822, that name seemed hardly dignified. It might have been shifted to Oxford, a name which many villages had been proud to take over. But few of those Floridians had probably ever heard of a university. They all knew of Andy Jackson, however, and some of them had doubtless served with him when he slaughtered the Creeks, or took Pensacola, or "licked the British" at New Orleans. So their town became Jacksonville.

In this same generation the Americans moved across into Texas, and eventually established their own republic there. Since the Texans were really Americans, they gave the same names, and even kept the old heroes. The delegates who wrote the Texas Declaration of Independence sat at a town called Washington-on-the-Brazos. But the Texans also developed new heroes. At San Jacinto, on April 21, 1836, General Sam Houston waved his old campaign hat as a signal, and the Texans charged, shouting "Remember the Alamo!" Within a few months a town was laid out near the battlefield; its promoters combined patriotism with advertisement, and called it Houston.

In Massachusetts a town grew up at the falls of Merrimack River. It was something new in America. Thomas Jefferson would have liked the smoothly running machine-looms, and the hum of water-power. But otherwise he would have thought it an abomination, and all its cotton cloth far from cheap at the price of men and women living and dying in the drab streets of a company town, and working puppet-like at their machines from five in the morning to seven at night.

Nevertheless this town, for good and bad, looked to the future, and fittingly it took its name from the man who had done most to make it possible. He was a new kind of hero—not of the battlefield, or the senate chamber. But he knew the mysteries of cogs and pulleys, and how to make water power run shuttles. Like Fulton and Whitney, he was an inventor. He introduced cotton manufacturing to America, and silenced the good-wife's spinning-wheel, which had been humming since first there were firesides in Massachusetts. He and his fellows were to be heroes of the future, and it was only right that a great city should bear the name of one of them. Francis Cabot Lowell (he suggested the future also by having a middle name) died in 1817. His associates founded the Merrimack Manufacturing Company, and in 1826 named Lowell in his honor.

In that generation, as always, many old eastern names were put upon new western towns. Only one of these grew to be a great city, but its story is one which most Americans do not know, and might rather forget.

No one knows how long the tribes of the Creek Confederacy had held their lands in Alabama. They were there when De Soto fought them in 1540, living already in well-built palisaded towns. The Treaty of 1783 declared their lands to lie within the new United States, and after that, year by year, the land-hungry Americans jostled them. With patience worn thin, the Creeks let the British persuade them to war in 1813, and massacred the Americans at Fort Mims. Jackson led his Tennesseeans to a bloody revenge, and broke the Creeks in two battles. After that, it was a matter of time.

At last, in 1838, the Great Removal began, and the Creeks sorrowfully followed Choctaws, Chickasaws and Cherokees. They left their ancestral lands to pass into exile beyond the Mississippi. As their tradition remembers, the medicine-men took ashes from the old fires and carried them west for the founding of new towns. As they founded them, they used the old names almost as much as the men of Massachusetts had done long before. But just as Lexington differed from Laxton, the Indian towns in the old and new countries differed often in spelling. Thus arose the variance between Coosa and Cusa, Tallahassee and Tullahasse. Also from Tulsy "old town" the Creek medicine-men took ashes, and planting them far in the west called the new town by the old name. So it remained, like Boston or Hartford, the memorial of a people who brought old loyalties to new lands, and in the end it became a greater town than the older one, and was spelled Tulsa.

First of all, the colonists had named towns for towns of England. Next, the Americans had given the names of ancient Greece and Rome. From these customs, a third arose and mingled with them—to use any notable or fine-sounding foreign name, whether of city, province, or country, or even of a river or mountain.

Sometimes these sprang merely from admiration of a strange and marvelous name. More often they were given for advertising, to make immigrants or investors think that a place so-called must be of importance. Travelers, particularly the British, lavished their ridicule upon the log-cabin cross-roads labeled London or Paris.

Sometimes, however, such names had a nobler motive. The Americans had begun to feel that they were planting a new world of freedom. Though the beginnings might be humble, who could tell? Already Boston in Massachusetts had eclipsed Boston in Lincolnshire and men in every port of the world knew the Boston ships. So, often, the founders felt some counterpart between their new villages and the great cities of the old world. Odessa might hope to be a great wheat-shipping port, or Leipsic to rival its name-city as a market of furs.

Sometimes also the new names came with foreign immigrants. Vevay in Indiana marked a Swiss settlement, and Florence in Alabama was surveyed and christened by a far-wandering Tuscan. Dublin or Aberdeen often recorded nothing more pretentious than the homesickness of some Irishman or Scot.

Other motives also played their part. Warsaw, county-seat of Kosciusko County in Indiana, tied up with the love of revolutionaries, and so did Warsaw in Virginia. But in Georgia the name was probably from the Indian word which produced Wassau in Florida. Frankfort in Kentucky was at first Frank's Ford, called for a man killed there by Indians. In the South, where someone planted "China trees" for shade, the place might become China Grove, and then merely China. Even such a seemingly rootless name as Woosung, Illinois, apparently was so called because an old seaman lived there who had once made the voyage to China.

Some great names sprang from this new enthusiasm. Various imaginative people had not failed to compare the Mississippi with the Nile. Analogies were obvious enough. Both were great and muddy rivers, given to inundations, highways for travel. The hope was also expressed that a new and greater civilization, surpassing even that of ancient Egypt, might soon develop along this "Nile of America." Such analogies and hopes soon suggested the transplanting of Egyptian names. In 1818 a St. Louis merchant laid out a town at the junction of the Ohio and the Mississippi, and incorporated it as Cairo. The site was unhealthy and bad luck dogged the town. Charles Dickens in *Martin Chuzzlewit* pilloried it as the City of Eden. It never rivaled its prototype, but the influence of its name was great. Because of Cairo (pronounced Kay-ro) all Southern Illinois came to be known as the Land of Egypt, or merely Egypt, and its inhabitants are Egyptians even to this day.

Farther down the river also, another town was laid out, shortly after Cairo. Its founders too cherished hopes for its greatness, and were conscious of the Nile of America. They remembered the great city of ancient Egypt, and called their new venture Memphis.

A town was also springing into importance on the line of the new Erie Canal. The site was swampy, but there was a developing industry in the manufacture of salt from springs and underground deposits. The settlement had arisen in desultory fashion, and had been called at different times Bogardus Corners, Milan, Cossit's Corners, and Corinth. The citizens decided upon incorporation in 1825, and Mr. John Wilkinson, the postmaster, suggested a name. He had read a poem describing the ancient Greek city of Sicily which had grown up near a marsh and salt springs. The name therefore became Syracuse.

The new fashion left its strongest mark upon regions which developed rapidly in the years following 1800. Ohio was unusually hospitable to foreign names, and one often furnished the cue for another. Most of the European capitals, from Lisbon to Petersburg, had namesakes in Ohio before 1840. They even jostled one another in rivalry. Berlin was a town and three townships, besides Berlin Center, Berlinville, and New Berlin. Paris and Rome were almost as popular. East Liverpool remains an important town, although Liverpool itself has vanished from the list of Ohio post-offices. The state was also sprinkled with names of Asia, Africa, and South America.

The early Ohioans seemed to have a special liking for Italy and Spain. From the latter they soon adopted Barcelona, Cadiz, Iberia, Malaga, and Navarre. In 1833 a settlement called Port Lawrence combined with another called Vistula, and became Toledo. No certain reason is known for this particular choice, but it was in the fashion. One tradition attributes the nomination to a certain merchant who declared that it "is easy to pronounce, is pleasant in sound, and there is no other city of that name on the American continent." The tradition may be correct; certainly such a word as Toledo with its alternation of vowel and consonant has at other times appealed to Americans in search of a euphonious name.

The wholesale adoption of foreign cities and countries added another characteristic and colorful touch to the American map. A traveler recorded:

On a board in front of a stage-office in Buffalo, I once read, "Stages start from this house for China, Sardinia, Holland, Hamburg, Java, Sweden, Cuba, Havre, Italy, and Penn-Yan."

This last village recorded in its name a mingled settlement of Pennsylvanians and Yankees.

In colonial times the central authority, whether General Court or royal governor, had controlled the naming of towns, and duplications within a colony had been unknown. But with the Revolution every man was as good as another to give a name. Freedom ran wild, and under the banner of democracy arose an unfortunate repetition of the more popular names. In a period of rapid expansion towns and counties were being established every day, and each county must be split into a score of townships. The demand for names outran the supply, and the result was both monotony and confusion.

Congress attempted no regulation, and the Post Office Department could exercise little control. More than one office in a single state used the same spelling, and on the contrary, one office might have two official names.

In New York, however, the situation became bad enough to goad the Legislature into action. On April 6, 1808, a resolution was passed: "Whereas considerable inconvenience results from several of the towns in the state having the same name . . ." Thereupon the Legislature without further regard for local feelings changed the names of thirty-three places. As an indication of the fashion of the time, it may be noted that fourteen of these received foreign names, ranging geographically from Edinburgh to Bengal.

Township names were reduplicated even more, but these caused less confusion. Nevertheless in 1827 the Legislative Council of Michigan Territory decreed that no town or township should be allowed a name already in the post-office list or differing only by having *New, West,* or any other addition. The law was later copied by other states.

A perhaps unexpected result of all such regulatory laws was to increase the proportion of exotic names. If a place could not become Washington, it was more likely to become Pekin.

By 1840, however, the situation had vastly improved. The Post Office Department by continuous pressure had managed to get rid of the offices with two names and to remove almost all the duplications within a state. It had succeeded, however, only by forcing many towns to add some distinction such as *North, New,* or *Center.* Various regions thus began to show some resemblance to the cumbersome and poverty-stricken nomenclature of New England, although for a totally different reason. The process also gave rise to some charming grotesqueries such as Parisville, or even St. Paris.

Perhaps governmental insistence made men realize that at times they might even gain advantage from a change. More likely, such changes merely sprang from the instability of the rapidly growing frontier. Certainly, however, the contrast with earlier periods was striking. Before the Revolution the shifting of a town-name (except to remove the original Indian appellation) was very rare. But for several decades after 1800 change became commonplace. A single legislative session in its mere routine might accede to the requests of the owners of a site or the inhabitants already in possession, and permit the change of a half dozen or more town-names.

Since no one was likely to seek the worse end, the motive for changes of names was always a hope for something better. If lots had failed to sell at Madison, its promoters gave it a fresh start and hoped for better things by calling it Carthage. Other changes were less mercenary but equally obvious, as when a New Hampshire town called Adams in 1800 became Jackson in 1829.

Partly for commercial reasons and partly for desire to appear more civilized, the citizens of settlements with frontier names constantly made them more respectable—and less colorful. Places called Tavern, Fort, Bridge, Creek, or Swamp usually dropped that distinction when they incorporated. Anything suggestive of rustic origin or frontier danger was likely to disappear. Panther Creek softened into Long Falls Creek. Indian Village suffered metamorphosis into Romeo, and the magnificent Outlaws X Roads dropped into merely another Vienna. Fortunately, like all attempts at reform of names, this movement stopped short, and many frontier names survived.

In certain regions even fairly well-established towns were subject to change. A traveler recorded in 1830 the eighteen leading settlements of Arkansas. Of these, seven have been washed away by encroaching rivers, or have vanished for other reasons. Six bear wholly new names. Three use the original name in somewhat changed form. Only two of the eighteen preserve the exact spelling of 1830. At the present time there are some fifty thousand inhabited places in the United States. It is a good estimate that extinct names to the same number exist in the records, for if many places have never been re-named, many others have been altered three times, or oftener.

The changes of name, however, were by no means limited to the frontier. Boston itself had a Cow Lane until 1797, but then its inhabitants rebelled, and gained their request to have it called High Street.

A certain primness also had its effect. In New York City a new fashion, popularized by the newspapers, preferred Hurlgate to Hellgate. That jolly village on Staten Island once called Cuckold Town was known no more. A place in New Jersey had borne the good English name of Maidenhead, and had so incorporated in 1798, but in 1816 the citizens availed themselves of the chance to honor a hero of the late war, and became Lawrenceville.

Thus in one way and another the generation following 1800 saw the nomenclature become rapidly more American. As might be expected, some of the more reflective citizens began to look about them self-consciously at what was happening. They offered occasional comments, often without approval. Timothy Dwight, the conservative and rather narrow-minded president of Yale College, declared: "There is something singular, and I think ludicrous, in the names given to townships in different parts of this country." He listed examples from New York of classical, Indian, Dutch, and Irish names mingling with abstracts such as Frugality and Enterprise. He failed, however, to appreciate either the luxuriance of the heritage, or its historical backgrounds.

On December 13, 1816, the first scholarly paper on American place-names was read before a learned society. That body was the New York Historical Society, and the author was Egbert Benson, one of the city's grand old men of the Revolution. He exercised the prerogative of age by using the title *Memoir,* and by allowing himself some digressions, but he supplied much meaty information, especially as to the origin and transformation of Dutch names. He offered some general comments, not without humor:

Naming counties, towns, villages, streets, forts, and so forth after the heroes and other worthies of our land, by formal public authority, is a sort of legislative monument, which has this to recommend it to republican economy, that it comes cheap, so that if on a just estimate of the name and fame, at a future day, it should be found not to have been worth preserving, there will be little, if anything, to be regretted as having been thrown away.

FIRST, the owners of the land had it surveyed, and from the survey a plat was drawn up, showing the plan of the streets. Then the owners petitioned the Legislature for incorporation under a certain name, and filed the plat. Generally the streets formed a checkerboard after the model of Philadelphia, and there were seldom fewer than ten each direction, though they might exist only on the plan and still be unbroken forest or a muskrat swamp. Usually from the beginning, these streets bore names. Thus every new town—and there were hundreds of them—required some twenty new names for streets.

No one passed any laws about naming streets, or even wrote a book of advice. As often in democracy, however, the result of complete freedom was not complete chaos. The town-planners tended to repeat traditionally, with slight variation, what was already familiar. So arose the four basic patterns of American street-names, more or less associated with different great cities, which served as models.

First of all, there was the pattern which might be said by paradox to be no pattern. The streets running in both directions bore names, and these followed no system. Boston furnished the model in the farther north. Most of the New England towns copied the Boston names, so that the typical pattern included State Street, Federal Street, and Congress Street, and probably Summer, Winter, Spring, Pleasant, and Commercial.

The older South also named its streets in both directions, taking its chief model perhaps from Baltimore, which became the first large southern city. But, even more than New England, the South held to itself, state by state, and even county by county. So no special series of names ran through the new southern towns. Instead, they more often named their streets for local heroes or plantation-families.

The most truly American pattern, however, remained that of Philadelphia—to have streets designated by numbers in one direction and by names in the other. The Philadelphia pattern spread west into Ohio and Kentucky and beyond. It followed down the Mississippi through Memphis, and took over many of the American-founded towns of Louisiana. It had outposts in New England —Bangor, New Bedford, Pittsfield, and others. It encroached strongly upon Virginia and Tennessee. Even in the farther South it furnished the pattern for many towns, such as Charlotte and Macon.

Like all systems of naming, it offered some problems. Where, for instance, should First Street lie? With a town on a river or lake, the conventional solution was to put First Street along the waterfront. Even so, time might bring difficulties. Often the shallow water was filled in, and First Street was no longer the first. These new streets were conventionally called Water or Front, again the Philadelphia pattern. On the other hand, a town laid out on a riverbank might find First Street caving into the water. Sometimes the river took the whole town, but sometimes only a section, so that perhaps Fourth Street became the first street, as in St. Joseph.

If no body of water was available to give a natural starting-point, First Street was merely placed along one edge of the plat. Then, if the city grew across that line, that part of it had streets which were outside the pattern.

Penn used for his cross-streets the names of trees—"that spontaneously grow in the country." Many founders of towns blindly followed his lead, using Chestnut, Walnut, and Mulberry, without any thought as to whether those trees grew there naturally. The trees, however, gave no indication of the succession of streets, and no order ever became conventional. The followers of the Philadelphia system, in fact, never solved this difficulty. In certain regions of Ohio and the states north and west, many towns used the names of the first five Presidents in order. Any American might be expected to know that Monroe was the third street beyond Adams. The election of a second Adams, however, spoiled the system, and the intensification of party strife at the end of the Era of Good Feeling made some of the later Presidents too unpopular.

The planning and naming of the national capital offered a third model for new towns. The whole city was split by two main axes into four sections, designated by the half-points of the compass. East and west of one axis the streets began with First, and so continued. North and south of the other axis the streets began with A Street and continued through the alphabet. Broad diagonal thoroughfares, called avenues, bore the names of the states. The avenues and the alphabetically designated streets were the important innovations.

Although a plan of Washington was published in 1792, its building proceeded slowly and its influence was delayed. Richmond, Indiana, platted in 1816, followed it. In 1821 Alexander Ralston, who had helped with the laying-out of Washington, was appointed to survey the site of Indianapolis, also to be a capital city. He consciously imitated Washington, but in the end Indianapolis showed little of the name-pattern except for a few diagonal avenues named after states.

The Washington plan and name-pattern, both usually simplified, spread on to an occasional Illinois town, across the river to Iowa, and thence north and west. But it was nowhere dominant. The Americans simply did not like it.

One detail only of the Washington-pattern became popular. The French *avenue,* meaning usually the tree-bordered approach to a country-house, had been used in English for some time. It had even attained rhetorical usage, as when a Revolutionary orator cried out: "Oppression stalked at noon-day through every avenue of your cities!" But let oppression stalk where it might, no American had Avenue as his address until after the founding of

Washington. Even the later popularity of Avenue may be partially credited to New York.

In 1807 a Commission was appointed to lay out a plan for the as yet unbuilt parts of Manhattan Island—"The leading streets and great avenues." On April 1, 1811, the map was finished and filed. It presented the basic plan and name-pattern of midtown and uptown New York which by the prestige of the city have become familiar to the whole world. The cross-town streets were numbered, after the Philadelphia fashion. The broad north-south thoroughfares were called Avenues after the Washington fashion; but, again after the Philadelphia fashion, they were numbered successively from First along the East River. The bulge of the island below Twenty-third Street, however, lay east of First Avenue; the Commissioners accommodated this geographical difficulty by the Washington device of using the letters of the alphabet from Avenue A to Avenue D. All the elements of the New York pattern were thus borrowed from Philadelphia and Washington, but their combination was something essentially new. The device of having numbered avenues cross numbered streets avoided the lack of system in the Philadelphia cross-streets. Yet the pattern was simpler than that of Washington.

Americans had been familiar with the Philadelphia pattern for nearly a hundred and fifty years before the New York adaptation even got on paper, and many more years elapsed before the midtown section became important. By that time most of the towns east of the Mississippi had already named their streets. The New York pattern was to be of influence in a few newer eastern towns, and in the newer sections of older cities, and especially in the farther West.

In naming their streets, the Americans were obviously torn between two basic emotions. First, they were a practical people, and vastly admired themselves for being so. Numbered and lettered streets thus attracted them greatly. One writer declared that a good street plan was incomplete:

unless there exists an orderly and methodical system of suitable names, so arranged as to enable the resident and the stranger within its gates to ascertain for themselves and without needless trouble or delay the relative positions of the different highways through which they may be called to pass.

Boston and Baltimore failed entirely to meet this requirement, and were rejected. Washington raised undue complications, and tended to defeat its own object. New York was the ideal of practicality, with the result that of all great cities it remains (with the exception of its downtown district) the easiest for anyone, resident or stranger, to find his way around in. Philadelphia was a compromise.

Its strength lay in that very fact. For, besides being practical, the Americans were like all peoples in having a strong tinge of sentiment in association with names. Names may be poetry; they readily become symbols of patriotism, achievement, or love of home. Numbers and letters sometimes attain symbolic value, but less easily and often.

The Philadelphia pattern allowed sentiment along with practicality, and its success fell little short of an overwhelming triumph. More than half of all our towns, perhaps three-quarters of them, have a system of numbered streets. The numbered avenues, after the model of New York, fail to appear in more than about one in six. About one town in ten shows the Washington pattern of lettered streets. The New York device of Avenue A makes a negligible showing. The repetition of individual street names tells the same story. Chestnut Street is far commoner than Pearl, and Pennsylvania Avenue is hardly in the running.

The growth of the great cities with their geometrical plans making no allowance for the lay of the land had another result. Ever since the first European settlement the number of named hills and streams had been steadily increasing. When settlers moved in, they first got along with names for only the larger features, but more and more of the smaller features gradually became better known, and thus acquired individuality.

Many such names existed on Manhattan Island, most of them dating back to the Dutch. More than two hundred are actually known, and many more have doubtless been lost. As the city advanced northward, decade after decade, the workmen filled in swamps and scraped down knolls. They warmed themselves at bonfires of the old bridges, no longer needed since the *kill* had been diverted into a sewer. According to the new plan, the old roads were abandoned, and their names no longer used. Eastern Road ceased to exist, although Fourth Avenue roughly followed its route.

Of the thousands who pride themselves on knowing the city, how many will undertake to find Bayard's Mount, or Bestevaer's Cripplebush, or Inclenburg, or the Otterspoor? Murray Hill is still a name—but where is Pot-baker's Hill? The Wading-Place has gone. Look for it with Cowfoot Hill. New York, not yet sophisticated, had not only one Kissing Bridge, but four. There was also what the Dutch called Malle Smit's Bergh. The English made it Mad Smith's Hill, and then Crazy Smith's Hill. And after that what became of it?

In one or two details the new plan failed of fulfillment. North of First Street the Bowery and then the Bloomingdale Road curved northward along the length of the island following the course of the old Beaver Path. The plan had contemplated no diagonal streets, but the Bowery managed to maintain itself, and north of Union Square the Bloomingdale Road became upper Broadway. So it remains—clear to Harlem River and beyond—an Indian trail with a half-Dutch name, carelessly winding its way among the skyscrapers of America's great checkerboard city.

Chapter XXIX ⟨ Flavor of the New South

AFTER cotton-growing began, another South arose, having little in common with the old South of tobacco and rice. Once plantations had been named for English towns or estates, so that they were often the same as the names of Massachusetts, or else the names had a masculine ring, brusquely informal, as in all those places called Hope or Folly or Chance. But in the new South the plantation names were feminine—delicate, and fragile, and pretty, like fine porcelains. They brought to mind, not the master and the slaves, but the lady who sat in the high-ceilinged parlor with the shades drawn, reading an English novel, or walked in the garden, after the sun no longer threatened her complexion.

So she chose a name for the new home, where the cotton grew in the broad fields of Alabama or Mississippi. She loved the thought of English country-life, and often used Manor or Hall. If the house stood on rising ground (as it might, to escape floods and ague), she called it Canemount or Mount Repose, even though the height was little more than a knoll. She loved trees, and so came Ashwood, and The Cedars, Magnolia Grove, and Elmscourt, Summer Trees and Greenleaves. She loved flowers, and named Myrtle Hall, and Rosemont, where a boy called Jeff Davis once lived.

Indian names were too rough and bristling. She read neither Greek nor Latin, but she knew a little French and Italian from her singing-master and so named Bellevue and Della Rosa.

Here and there some bold bachelor called his home The Hermitage. Stony Lonesome too had man-flavor, and Rattle-and-Snap. But those were few.

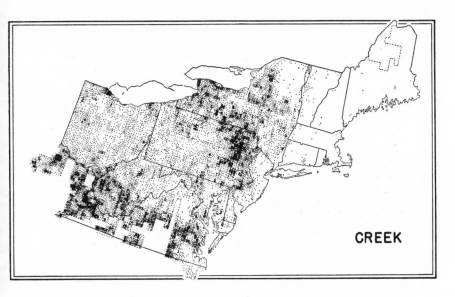

CREEK

NORTHEASTERN WATERCOURSE GENERICS

From Zelinsky (see p. 452). For discussion of these generics in the text, see Index. The maps show clearly the connection of *brook* with New England and the regions settled from it, e.g., northeastern Ohio. *Creek*

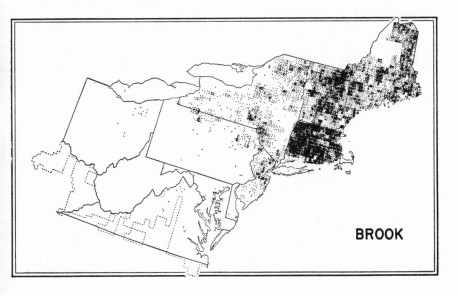

BROOK

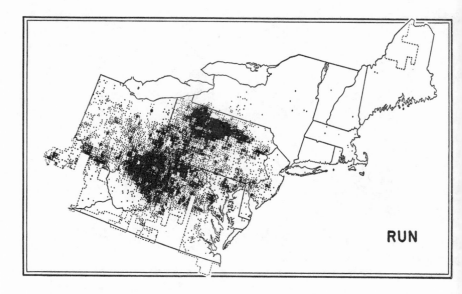

is common everywhere except in strong *brook* areas. *Stream* is definitely localized. *Run* coincides, north and south, with the North Midland dialect area; its greatest concentration is in the mountains. In southern West Virginia *branch* is used instead of *run*.

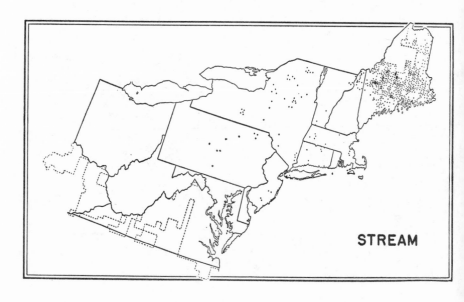

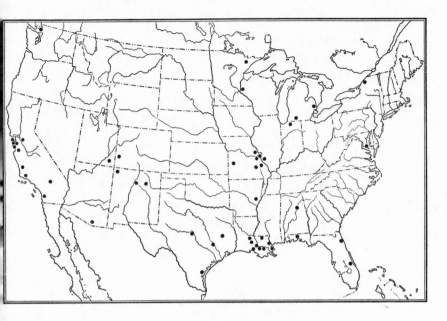

COUNTIES WITH SAINTS' NAMES

European scholars attempt to establish history by studying place-names. The present map represents how a scholar, five thousand years hence, might approach the study of our history by means of a chance-preserved map . . . Having put a dot to mark each county for which the name includes the separate prefixes St., Ste., San, or Santa, he would have established the chief areas of early Catholic influence. He would, however, be likely to make certain false deductions. For example, St. Clair County in certain states represents a family name and not a naming from a saint. Similarly, Sanpete County (Utah), Sanburn County (S.D.), and a few others might well confuse him. Such coincidences are a constant hazard in linguistic place-name study which lacks historical check-points. For these reasons a single map of this kind is of small value. If, however, it can be checked and confirmed by other similar mappings, the results become highly authoritative.

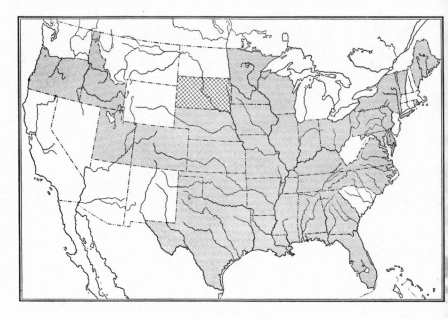

STATES WITH COUNTIES NAMED FOR WASHINGTON

Thirty-one states have Washington counties; in addition, South Dakota has one which, though established with boundaries, has never been organized with a government.

Six of the original thirteen colonies have no such county. They were all among the smaller ones, and had most of their counties named before 1775. West Virginia did not happen to contain the county named Washington at that time of its separation. In the central part of the country Michigan is the only dissenter, perhaps because its local Indian name Washtenaw (used for a county) was too similar. By the time the far-Western states were being organized the magic of Washington's name had somewhat faded, as the map shows graphically.

Nevertheless the tribute is impressive. Washington County in Maine is the most eastern in the country. Washington County in Oregon once touched the Pacific Ocean, but has since been restricted by a division.

She read the poets—not Chaucer or Pope, but Shakespeare and Scott and Campbell, at least. So the roll of plantations still makes lines of poetry spring to mind:

> In *Belmont* is a lady richly left ...
> On *Linden* when the sun was low ...
> And it's down by the banks of the *Airlie* ...
> If thou would'st view fair *Melrose* aright ...
> O, young *Lochinvar* is come out of the west.

More still, she read Scott's novels, and from them she named Woodstock, and Waverly, and Rotherwood and many others.

The years of the new South were few and quickly run. Sometimes the gentle lady who named the plantation lived to see a son brought home after Shiloh and to watch the columned house go up in fire. Her names lived longer.

One of them even won greatness beyond all her imaginings. For, more than once, it happened that the lady came to her plantation in winter when in the thickets the berries were red among the glossy leaves. And so she called the new home Hollywood.

There was another South too, of which that lady knew little. Of it was Captain Simon Suggs, who said, "It is good to be shiftly in a new country," a man's world of the Flush Times, of Natchez-under-the-Hill, and poor-white-trash. It read no poetry, and often could not read at all. It too left the flavor of its names.

In Kentucky the Harpes robbed and murdered until at last Captain John Leeper rode hot on their trail. He fired and brought down Big Harpe's horse. Lying pinned beneath the horse, Big Harpe begged for mercy, but Leeper shot him. He cut off the head, and placed it in a tree as a warning to others. So the place is still Harpe's Head Road.

In Alabama the itinerant preacher, Lorenzo Dow, held services and fiercely exhorted the people to reform. Many felt conviction of sin, and sought the mourner's bench. When they later asked the preacher what to name the settlement, he cried out, "Call it

Reform! Brethren, call it Reform!" So they did, and so it is still called.

In Mississippi two speculators founded towns separated only by a line. Tulahoma was the larger, but Pittsburg had the post-office, and a newspaper called *The Bowie Knife*. As rivals, they quarreled almost to bloodshed, but at last decided to unite. To symbolize this union, they held a wedding, taking a groom from Pittsburg and a bride from Tulahoma. In July, 1836, a preacher joined the two, and the towns also united. Discarding the old names, they became Grenada. Only Line Street remains to show that the one was once two.

Chapter XXX ❨ Melodrama in the Forties

THE eighteen-forties began with *Tippecanoe and Tyler too,* ran on through *Fifty-four-forty or fight,* and ended with *Old Rough and Ready!* That decade loved alliteration, and melodrama was its keynote.

The covered wagons reached "the Oregon country" in 1842; two years later they got through to California. The Americans had begun the most spectacular of their migrations.

All along those trails they strewed names. Emigrant Pass and Emigrant Lake still testify that their wagons passed that way, for they were always emigrants, never immigrants. Massacre Rocks and Battle Mountain tell their stories to him who knows the language—that where Indians killed whites, it was a massacre; but where whites killed Indians, it was a battle. Where someone died, and they piled stones on the grave to keep the wolves away, later comers might call it Grave Creek. Pilot Butte and Pilot Peak were their names for mountains standing high as landmarks.

From the emigrants, as from all travelers, came lost-and-found names. In carelessness or sudden alarm a man left something behind at a camping-place. Some other found it, and remembered the place by that name. Thus over the West spread the names of Knife Creek and Butcherknife, Pipe, Pistol, and Hat—such things as may be lost and found again. Even Horseshoe and Muleshoe may sometimes indicate, not a curve of the stream, but the finding of a cast shoe.

Also, like all travelers, the emigrants gave names only along a line. A stream usually took the name which the place of crossing brought to mind. If there was a rock there, that would be Rock Creek, even though there might be no other rock on the whole stream.

Travelers even earlier than the covered-wagon emigrants established a great name in that manner. Most of them followed the course of the Columbia River, and came to what were called the Cascades, where the river flowed through a range of high mountains. They called these "the mountains at the cascades" and later the Cascade Mountains, and the name spread north and south along the great range, just as the names given to hundreds of little streams at their crossings spread to cover the whole.

When more people arrived in Oregon, Amos Lovejoy and Francis Pettygrove laid out a little town, four streets each way, in 1845. Lovejoy was from Massachusetts and wanted it to be Boston, but Pettygrove was from Maine and wanted Portland. Being good Americans they flipped a coin. The name of a great city went spinning into the air. It fell for Portland.

The Mexican War was linked with the admission of Texas, a name much too well established to be changed. It was our first foreign war, except for some brief invasions of Canada and a little sea-fighting. The troops who crossed the Rio Grande and landed at Vera Cruz were the first expeditionary forces; they were also the first large body of American tourists. After the fighting was over, they spent their money freely, learned some Spanish, and got along very well with the señoritas. They came back, and spread a scattering of Spanish names all over the country.

They loved their victories most of all. Chapultepec was outlandish and hard to pronounce, but even so, it appeared. Monterey was unknown to the post-office lists before the War, but a few years later there were seventeen. Buena Vista, helped by its literal meaning, "fine view," soared from none to nineteen. A Palo Alto sprang up in seven states, and a Cerro Gordo in five. Resaca was transferred to Georgia, where ironically it was to become the name also of a battle in the Civil War.

In contrast to the early wars, the Mexican War was remembered less by its heroes. Scott and Taylor had names which were too common to be distinctive. In spite of its grotesquery, Taylor's nickname of Rough and Ready was drafted, and there were soon nine such post-offices. Minor heroes, such as Quitman and Ringgold, soon had their roll of towns and even of counties.

Two great cities bear what may be called Mexican War names, but they fall into the class of Cleveland and Rochester.

Few Americans can even identify George Mifflin Dallas. A well-born Philadelphian, he attended Princeton, and then began the career of gentleman in politics. He became senator, minister to Russia and to Great Britain, and vice-president under Polk. In 1846, the war-year, the administration was popular in Texas. That spring, the Legislature created and named counties for both the president and the vice-president, and Dallas was also established as a county-seat.

If he ever heard of his namesake, he was probably not greatly complimented. Conservative, cosmopolitan, and wealthy, Mr. Dallas would scarcely have appreciated the raw western village. He could not have known that only through it would his name be preserved in common speech. An unremembered vice-president, he is honored by a larger city than is any president except Washington.

The rival city of Dallas was much like it in naming. William Jenkins Worth as a young officer had fought bravely in the War of 1812, and almost died of a wound received in the desperate fight at Lundy's Lane. As a general he was the hero of Monterey, led the landing-operation at Vera Cruz, and fought magnificently in all the battles of the campaign against Mexico City. Off the battlefield he was narrow-minded and egotistic, and grew puffed up with his own heroism. He cabaled against his commander-in-chief and old friend, General Scott, and had to be placed in arrest. He was forgiven, however, and sent to be commander in Texas, where he died.

His body was laid at the crossing of Broadway and Fifth Avenue, but as the millions pass the column bearing the names of his victories, few remember who he was. On the Texas plains an army post was given his name. It still remains Fort Worth, the largest of our cities to bear a military title. Although Worth was only a minor and doubtful hero, good fighting generals are rare enough in our history, and any city bearing the name of one of the best of them may well be proud of it. (By one of the frequent ironies of history, Worth's great commander-in-chief is honored by the small town still called Fort Scott.)

The eighteen-forties witnessed melodrama also with the coming of the railroads. The earlier lines were built to link towns already named, but even so, most of the way-stations had to be established. Some of these were regularly named, but the railway-builders merely followed the customs of the times, except that they naturally called a great many stations for themselves, their brother-officials, and their larger stockholders. Many points were never formally named. Where plain Pat Flaherty was section-boss, the siding would soon be known as Flaherty's. If he escaped the perils of whiskey and rail-traffic for a few years, his name might become so well established that the succeeding post-office or town simply was Flaherty.

The Georgians were among the first to be enthusiastic about the new railroads. In 1836 the Legislature passed an act for the construction of the Western & Atlantic to connect northern Georgia with the Tennessee River. The Georgia end of the line was located vaguely until surveys could establish the most practical point. In the next year the appointment as chief engineer went to Stephen H. Long. (This was the same man who as Major of Engineers had conducted a western exploration in 1820, and from whom one of the most magnificent of our mountains was called Long's Peak. This same expedition had invented the term "Great American Desert.")

Long soon drove a stake at a point in northern Georgia which has ever since remained the hub of southern railroads. Since this was to be the terminus, it was with rare directness simply called Terminus. A dozen houses sprang up in expectation of the railroad.

In 1843 the ex-governor, Wilson Lumpkin, visited the locality. The villagers were honored by the presence of greatness. They had apparently come to feel that Terminus was only a makeshift name, and it might well have become Lumpkin, if that honor had not already been claimed by another Georgia town. The great man, however, was accompanied by his charming sixteen-year-old daughter Martha. Southern chivalry was evoked, and Terminus was officially chartered as Marthasville.

Certain ungallant railroad-men, however, looked upon Marthasville as a namby-pamby name for a place which was undoubtedly to become a great center. In particular, Mr. Richard Peters of the Georgia Railroad, now rapidly approaching from the east, disliked the idea of announcing that his road was ready to accept freight for delivery at its terminus of Marthasville. He wrote his superior, making known his qualms and asking him to suggest a better name.

This chief engineer, J. Edgar Thomson, was of the new school. He was a young man of engineering genius who had just been to Europe, not to look at cathedrals, but to study railroads. His Latin was small and his Greek less, but he was a man of native ability and decision. (He was destined to become one of America's first

railroad barons, consolidating the Pennsylvania Railroad and locating the famous Horseshoe Curve.)

In 1845 he acted with his usual decision, and overrode linguistic
barriers as in the years to come he was to override the Allegheny
Mountains. Mr. Peters later reported the words of his reply:
"Eureka!—Atlanta, the terminus of the Western & Atlantic Railroad. Atlantic, masculine; Atlanta, feminine—a coined word—
and if you think it will suit, adopt it."

Mr. Peters was delighted, and thus issued his circulars, ignoring that Marthasville was named by legislative act. The prestige
of the railroad was so great that the citizens acquiesced, and at its
next session the Legislature, agreeably yielding to local sentiment,
substituted the new name in the act of incorporation.

In this decade the frontier, aided by steamboat transportation,
advanced rapidly along the upper Mississippi. Whether because of
the prevailing spirit of melodrama or some other reason, all the
great names of that region arose by devious and unusual processes.

For many years explorers had been searching that somewhat
mythical point, "the source of the Mississippi." In 1832 the Rev.
William T. Boutwell and Mr. Henry R. Schoolcraft, the great
investigator of Indian lore, reached a small body of water called
by their guides Omushkos, "elk lake." The explorers decided that
this might be claimed as the origin, and set about replacing the
commonplace name. Mr. Boutwell crudely turned "true source"
into Latin as *veritas caput*. Thereupon Mr. Schoolcraft, joining the
tail of the first word and the head of the second, ingeniously produced Itasca.

From very early times the French had known a large tributary
of the Mississippi as the Saint Pierre. The Americans translated
this as the Saint Peter. Near its mouth, on the Mississippi, a few
settlers built log cabins, and in 1841 Father Lucian Galtier established a mission there. As he later wrote:

In the month of October, logs were prepared and a church erected,
so poor that it would well remind one of the stable at Bethlehem.

On November 1st, he consecrated the new log church, dedicating it to the apostle to the Gentiles, and at the same time expressing his hope that the little settlement might bear the same name.

I had previously to this time, fixed my residence at Saint Peter's, and as the name of PAUL is generally connected with that of PETER, and the gentiles being well represented in the new place in the persons of the Indians, I called it Saint Paul. . . . Thenceforth the place was known as "Saint Paul Landing," and, later on, as "Saint Paul."

Father Galtier also had other reasons than the purely religious; as he added, "The monosyllable is short, sounds well, and is understood by all denominations of Christians."

That whole region was as yet a part of Wisconsin Territory, but its eventual separation and statehood was certain. It was, however, lacking in a name, and for the first time in the history of the organization of territories the problem became pressing.

The region had a better right than any other to be called Mississippi, but that name was pre-empted. The inhabitants might naturally have turned to some other river, but their streams were singularly inappropriate. No American state could be named Saint Peter or Saint Croix, Cannon, Rum, or Crow Wing. It remained for some unknown genius (there are at least three candidates) to cut the knot like another Alexander. Or perhaps he might be compared to Peter the Great who, told that he had no north-east coast, replied, "Make one!" Having no suitably named river, this undaunted resident of that frontier region talked with the Indians, or more probably looked into some book, and discovered the Sioux name of the Saint Peter. It meant "cloudy water," since the river in flood was whitishly turbid. Travelers had recorded its spelling in various forms such as Menesotor, Menisothé, Minnay Sotor, and Menesota.

The name was dignified and sonorous, and represented the tradition of Indian river-names. It had the weakness of being extinct, and at the last moment a rival arose. For the first time the question of a name produced a skirmish on the floors of Congress.

Mr. Martin of Wisconsin introduced a bill to establish the Territorial Government of Minnesota. It was referred to the Committee on Territories, and reported back on February 17, 1847. But the originator must have been piqued to find that something had happened in Committee, so that his bill read to establish the Territorial Government of Itasca.

Mr. Martin was immediately on his feet with an amendment to strike out the word Itasca wherever occurring and insert in lieu thereof the word Minnesota.

Before anything further could be done, Mr. Fries of Ohio gained the floor and declared that he had recently been insulted by various members of the House because of his attitude on slavery. There followed for over an hour, while a great name hung in uncertainty, an acrimonious discussion. The remarks became more and more bitter, and were approaching the obscene when a rule upon limitation of debate brought the matter to a halt.

Mr. Martin's amendment was then just about to come to a vote, and the House suddenly became excited over names.

Mr. Winthrop declared that, if Minnesota failed, he would move to substitute Chippewa for Itasca.

Mr. Thompson expressed a dislike of "all these Indian names." He proposed that the new territory be Jackson, "as a proper tribute to that distinguished patriot."

Mr. Houston of Delaware promptly rose with the inevitable reply:

If one of the future States of this Union was to be named after any American citizen living or dead, he thought it would be decidedly better to call it after the Father of his Country.

After further discussion, the flurry subsided as quickly as it had arisen. "The question being put on Minnesota it was agreed to without count."

The actual organization of the new territory was defeated, and the question of name was unofficially referred back to local decision. In 1848 a Convention assembled at Stillwater, and on August 26th a Committee on Resolutions met during the noon recess in a storeroom. Among its members were the Rev. Mr. Boutwell, who argued for his own handiwork, Itasca. General Henry H. Sibley, on the contrary, argued for Minnesota, of which he may well have been the original begetter. Even at that date, however, he was forced to explain the source and application of the word. The Committee discussed spelling and pronunciation, and the Convention in adopting the report voted: "the orthography of Minnesota . . . shall be according to that used in this resolution."

The controversy over Minnesota was a critical point in the history of state-naming. The Indian-river tradition was still strong, but for the first time Congress had shown an inclination to take a hand. Moreover, the care about the spelling of the word indicated that the old easy-going period was coming to an end; very likely it was a recognition of the confusion arising from the Arkansas-Arkansaw controversy.

One step remained to complete the cycle. In 1852 the Territorial Legislature memorialized the President to discontinue the use of Saint Peter River, and substitute Minnesota River in official use. An act of Congress confirmed the alteration and popular usage soon followed. Such a deliberate change in the name of a large river was without precedent since the years when English, Dutch, Swedes, and French had squabbled over names as symbols of empire.

In those years men sought Heaven-on-Earth, and the names preserved the record of that search. At Phalanx in New Jersey the Fourierists planted their community. In Ohio some German separatists built themselves Zoar because Lot fled there from the wickedness of Sodom, and it is written: "The sun was risen upon the earth when Lot entered into Zoar." At Economy, Utopia, Harmony, and New Harmony others of the chosen few tried to build tight about themselves the walls of their own little worlds. But among those who became as brothers, the followers of Joseph Smith grew to be greater than all the rest together.

In Ontario County, New York, he saw visions. Near Manchester stood an ordinary hill, but young Joseph Smith knew it as the

Hill Cumorah. The angel Moroni told him to dig there, and find certain gold plates. The Eight Witnesses testified that the plates had "the appearance of gold . . . for we have seen and hefted." A century later, when the Saints were rich and powerful, they returned and bought that land, so that now the Hill Cumorah is as surely named a part of the United States as any Baldy or Round Top.

Then the Book of Mormon came into being, and many people followed its words. The Gentiles murdered Joseph Smith in an Illinois jail, but of the remaining faithful Brigham Young forged a strong people. Like Moses, he led them through the wilderness; standing on a mountainside he looked out at last, and said, "This is the place!"

They were Americans, and few of them were men of learning. Most often they gave simple American names in that new and desert land. Where they settled, the mountain men had already plainly named the Great Salt Lake. The Saints let it stand, but the stream which had been called Utah River, they renamed. Since they had come like Israelites to the Promised Land, they called it the Jordan.

Upon its banks they founded a city, four-square. Not when William Penn dreamed of Philadelphia or L'Enfant planned Washington was an American city set apart for a greater future. This was to be no mere earthly capital, but a sacred refuge. A great city should have a great name. That they did not call it Zion or Jerusalem seems strange. Perhaps they thought that such a name might help stir up hatred among the Gentiles, as had happened before at their towns called Adam-Ondi-Ahman and Nauvoo. In the end, like other Americans of the time, they took an established name of the country, not too short to lack dignity. First the quorum of the Twelve decided, and then the public assembly confirmed that it should be City of the Great Salt Lake.

The whole region had as yet no name. They often called it Zion, but that was by figure of speech, and for a name they borrowed from their own holy word. In the Book of Mormon, that part called the Book of Ether, you may read how Jared and his brother and their families migrated into the wilderness to a Promised Land, and in the Chapter 2, Verse 3:

And they did also carry with them Deseret, which, by interpretation, is a honey bee; and thus they did carry with them swarms of bees.

Deseret was not the name of a place, but in the story it brought to mind a far-off valley, "which is choice above all other lands." Also it was like the word *desert*. So they called their new country and their government, Deseret.

As they spread about in it and planted colonies, they gave mostly American names, but differed in two ways. Since they felt themselves a chosen and separate people, they spoke to one another as "Brother Joseph," or "Sister Sarah." So they naturally called their towns by baptismal names—Abraham, Heber, Hyrum, Brigham City. Even when they named a county for the President of the United States, they called it Millard, not Fillmore. Also they called themselves the Latter-day Saints, and the word *saint* was common among them. From this custom sprang several towns, such as St. John and St. George, named not for any beloved apostle or any dragon-slayer, but for John Rowberry and George A. Smith, good Mormon church officials.

The Mormons gave no more Biblical names than other people, but they had a treasure-store in the Book of Mormon. Joseph Smith had recorded many names, some the same as those of the Bible, others like them but a little different. So, besides Deseret, towns sprang up for Moroni the angel, Alma and Nephi the prophets, and Lehi the king, and many others.

The forties ended with the greatest melodrama of all. During two generations, the Spanish settlements in California had grown slowly stronger. The country filled in with little names in the usual ways, the only strange one being that sometimes they put out beef as bait for bears, and the place took its name in that way —La Panza, "the paunch"; La Paleta, "the shoulder-blade." The Californians also explored a little to the eastward and gave religious names to the two great rivers—San Joaquin for the saint who, tradition holds, was the father of the Virgin, and Sacramento for the Holy Sacrament. Beyond these rivers, they saw very high mountains, and called them La Sierra Nevada, "the range snowed-upon," which was such a common expression in Spanish that it was a description rather than a name.

After the annexation, the Americans had no hatred for the local people and customs, and they found the Spanish names easy to pronounce. Most of them remained in the proper spelling and more or less proper pronunciation. In fact, the Americans usually admired them greatly for their easily running sounds.

One of the places where the Americans first settled was at Yerba Buena, so called because of a mint-like plant growing there. This little adobe-built village stood on Yerba Buena Cove which offered a good anchorage near the inner tip of the peninsula between San Francisco Bay and the ocean. Near by were also the Mission and Presidio of San Francisco. The village, however, had the other name, was well contented, and might eventually have grown into a large city without changing it.

After the American occupation, however, a new spirit of enterprise sprang up in California, and some developers, among them the enterprising native Mariano Guadalupe Vallejo, planned a new town farther up the Bay. Vallejo's wife had been Francisca Benicia Carillo, and the new town was to be named in her honor (they said) San Francisco. But the more alert of the Americans of Yerba Buena suddenly saw through this subterfuge. Obviously these wily promoters were trying by means of a name to make the world think that their new town was the chief place on the Bay. A meeting of citizens was quickly called.

There was argument and opposition. The crusty editor of the recently founded newspaper threw his influence against the change. Nevertheless the motion carried.

On January 23, 1847, the Alcalde (as their mayor was still called) issued an explicit statement:

Whereas the local name of Yerba Buena as applied to the settlement or town of San Francisco, is unknown beyond the immediate district, and has been applied from the local name of the cove on which the town is built—therefore, to prevent confusion and mistakes in public documents, and that the town may have the advantage of the name given on published maps, it is hereby ordered that the name of San Francisco shall hereafter be used in all official communications.

The obdurate editor refused to change his masthead, and a week later declared stoutly:

Yerba Buena, the name of our town which means GOOD HERB is situated on San Francisco bay. . . . The town of Yerba Buena is called in some of the old maps of the country San Francisco—It is not known by that name here, however.

The editor maintained himself for seven weeks, and then, still repeating his preference for the old name, he capitulated, and published his first issue under the date-line San Francisco.

The disappointed promoters, thus forestalled, took another of Señora Vallejo's names, and founded Benicia, which (for lack of a good name or other reasons) never flourished.

Shortly afterwards the little village on the peninsula was again lucky. The namer in this case was John Charles Frémont, one of the most melodramatic figures of that melodramatic decade. Frémont had spent the last few years in wandering about the farther West, and in writing highly readable accounts of his adventures. In spite of his dramatic and egotistic qualities, he was singularly uninterested in naming. Most of the larger names in the territory were already well enough established, but even when he had a chance, Frémont often failed to rise to the occasion. He was the first American of record to see the beautiful sheet of water now famous as Lake Tahoe, but he recorded on his map the banal description Mountain Lake.

Nevertheless, his opportunities were great, and he left a far from negligible imprint. Doubtless from the analogy of Great Plains, he invented Great Basin—"a term which I apply to the intermediate region between the Rocky Mountains and the next range." He replaced the earlier names of a desert river, not too felicitously, by calling it after the German scientist Humboldt, who had never been near it. His writings also were so popular that they helped establish certain of his preferences and spellings. The frontiersmen regularly said California Mountains for the range which they crossed to arrive at the Spanish settlements, but Frémont preferred Sierra Nevada, and popularized it. He used the spelling Utah for the lake and river. He also sometimes wrote Nebraska River, but in the end was forced to use the well-established Platte.

Frémont made his best stroke in California. The Spaniards had neglected to supply a name to the passage connecting San Francisco Bay with the ocean. Although Frémont had never been to Constantinople, he fancied a resemblance between that ancient harbor and the western strait, and he felt also the coming commercial importance of San Francisco. He wrote accordingly: "I gave the name *Chrysopylae,* or GOLDEN GATE; for the same reasons that the harbor of Byzantium was called Chrysoceras, or GOLDEN HORN."

The name seemed a prophecy, for hardly had it been fixed before the Argonauts of '49 were pouring in through the Golden Gate, and hailing it as a good omen. These gold-seekers themselves were of all nations and all ways of life, and with their names they gave the final touch of melodrama to the decade.

The roster of their mining-camps was a list of nations—French Corral and Dutch Flat, Chinese Camp, Kanaka Bar, Sonora, Chili Gulch. It recorded where men of all kinds worked the gold or first discovered color—Soldier Creek and Sailor Creek, Mormon Bar, Nigger Hill. Every state and city sent its men; Michigan Bluff was close to Texas Hill, from which you might head for Illinoistown, Nashville, or Hoboken Creek.

They changed the language itself, making *diggings* into a common word. From some uncertain source, perhaps like *swamp* from English dialect, *gulch* sprang suddenly into use. They also put the final touch upon *slough.* Once it had meant a muddy place in a road, as when Chaucer's Host was afraid that the drunken cook would fall into the slough. When Pilgrim was mired in the Slough of Despond, the mire had grown deeper. In America the deepening continued, and water began to stand on top. By the time settlers had reached Illinois and Missouri any good-sized backwater was a slough. But the Californians went the whole way. All the great side-channels of the lower Sacramento became sloughs, though they were big and deep enough to give passage to large vessels, and one was even called Steamboat Slough.

In the actual names which they gave, the miners split into two directions. One kind was as strangely methodical as the other was wholly bizarre.

Method showed in the street-pattern of their second city, called Sacramento, from its river. The streets parallel to the waterfront were numbered, and those perpendicular were lettered, beginning with A Street on the north. There was no foolishness about such names. A stranger, an hour after landing from his steamboat, could find his way about the town as readily as the oldest inhabitant. Perhaps this was the reason such a pattern was established, for in that time everybody was a stranger, one might say, and there were no oldest inhabitants. Also, like everything else then, Sacramento was laid out in a roaring hurry, and no one may have had the time to decide upon names. Even I Street was allowed, in spite of people's constant tendency to mix it up with 1st Street. (In the end, it became such a nuisance that it was commonly written Eye Street.)

Like the naming of these Sacramento streets was the naming of streams in the mountains. The whole life of the Forty-niners was involved with rivers. They found rich diggings on the gravel-bars, and must have running water to work their cradles and rockers. In exploring the country, they kept close to the rivers, and since most of them landed at San Francisco and the gold-country was on the westward slope, they advanced into that country upstream, just as their ancestors had advanced into the Alleghenies. So they frequently came to a place where the river, to a man looking upstream, seemed to divide into two forks, almost equal. Naturally then they called them the North and South Forks. This was the more likely because everybody, as in laying out Sacramento, was in a great hurry, and they were all passing on to another place, never settling down. So even if some man named a stream, he might not stay there long enough to tell the next man what it was.

Thus the name-pattern of those streams became startlingly logical and systematic. Most of the rivers had a North, South and Middle Fork. Beyond that was the second degree in such names as The North Fork of the Middle Fork of the American River, which might be clipped to North-Middle American. Some streams went into the third degree as in The East Fork of the North Fork of the North Fork of the American, and the delightfully explicit West Fork of the South Fork of the North Fork of the San Joaquin.

Although these were the most cumbersome names ever given by Americans, they were also highly practical in an unmapped and scarcely explored country. If you told a stranger that the place he wanted was on Washington Street near Arch, you had told him nothing, but when in Sacramento you told him to go to J Street just beyond Fifth, he got there quickly by himself, as it was important he should when no one had time to guide him, and most people were strangers there themselves. So also, when you informed someone that a certain mining camp was on the South-Middle Yuba, you had really told him something.

As if to compensate for their naming rivers, the forty-niners lavished upon their creeks and mining-camps a whole treasury of fancy. How it got started is hard to determine. To be sure, the backwoods had a certain tradition of lusty humor in its naming. Many counties had somewhere a cross-roads with such a name as Pancake Hollow, Knock-'em-stiff, or Hell-fer-Sartain. Whiskey Creek hardly counted as one of them, for it was more a matter-of-fact memorandum that someone had once sold whiskey there, or run a still.

Possibly the California fashion began as a by-product of civic virtue. The miners of a certain camp squelched a crime wave by hanging three men on a convenient tree, and it thus became known in the early months of 1849 as Hangtown. From such precedent may have sprung Chicken Thief Flat, Cut Throat Bar, Murderers' Bar, Gouge Eye, Garrotte, and Second Garrotte.

Once the fashion had started, it spread quickly. Primarily it gave vent to the lusty high spirit which was the distinguishing mark of that amazing time. No censorship restrained it; society was of men only. Most of them looked upon their sojourn in California, particularly in the mining-camps, as a temporary and riotous adventure. Few would have wished to establish a permanent address at Mugfuzzle Flat or Stud-Horse Canyon, but as a passing fancy they enjoyed the amusement, and vied with each other in grotesquery. Doubtless the more sophisticated often invented the most outlandish terms; two Harvard men named Shirttail Canyon.

Drink and cards, favorite male vices, furnished many incidents which were enshrined and then forgotten. Euchre Bar, Poker Flat, Seven-Up Ravine, and Red Dog stood over against Whiskey Bar, Milk Punch, Port Wine, and Brandy Gulch. Perhaps with these last should be placed Delirium Tremens.

Many of the seemingly outlandish ones were merely commonplace frontier names, unusual only in being applied to places of residence—Dead Mule Canyon, Jackass Gulch, and Hardscrabble.

The English also had a tradition of giving humorous names to fields, especially of far-off places. Timbuctoo may thus have come to California with some Englishman. Lousy Level is to be found in Hertfordshire, as well as in the Sierra Nevada. (The gold-rush also acted in reverse, so that California soon became a field-name in various English counties.)

Some names involved profanity and other plain language. Guano Hill was perhaps not pronounced as spelled. Ladies' Canyon, according to tradition, once referred to an intimate part of the female person. Argument still continues as to whether Putah Creek was an Indian name or only a disguise of some Spanish-speaking pioneer's *Puta,* "whore."

On the other hand, a few places had religious names such as

Gospel Gulch and Christian Flat. The latter indeed may have been for a man so named, as was certainly true with Angel's Camp.

As in every region, some places received good advertising names—Gold Hill, and Rich Bar, and Ophir. As a miner wrote:

Somewhere in Genesis mention is made of a river in paradise running through the land of "Havilah, a country rich in gold." We were shy on the river, but the balance of the quotation seemed appropriate enough, so I christened the proposed town "Havilah."

The gold country, however, was unique in having a large number of definitely forbidding names—Hungry Camp, Humbug Canyon, Hoodoo Bar, Poverty Hill, Nary Red. Such a name was often given by opposites, where a rich strike had really been made, in the hope of keeping rival miners away.

Many of the names seem wholly grotesque, but many of these must have arisen by way of description, however fanciful, or from some trivial incident on which the namer fastened eagerly. Bogus Thunder suggests an incident; tradition holds that it was because the noise of a waterfall was taken for thunder—but this sounds like an obvious explanation which would later be invented. Finnegan's Lane may have involved an Irishman somewhere, but merely to take the obvious suggestion of such names is to go astray as often as to go right. Jim Crow Canyon may have been for a Negro, just as likely for a white man who "jumped Jim Crow," quite possibly for a crow seen there, or for any of several other reasons. One man's guess is as good as another's when it comes to Chucklehead Diggings, Churntown, Fly Away, Gomorrah, Hell-out-for-Noon City, Hen-Roost Camp, Slap-Jack Bar, Slumgullion, You Bet, Love Letter Camp, One Eye, Poodle Town, Quack Hill.

Most of these camps were short-lived, and never had post-offices. Nevertheless they were genuine; men, and sometimes women, lived there. The forty-niners were true sons of Captain Gabriel Archer. Their country offered the most unrestrained and flamboyant experiment in American naming.

Chapter XXXI ❰ "Ye say they all have passed away . . ."

THE frontier was not only of the land, but also in the minds of men. In all countries people had developed a love for the strange and wonderful and far-off. Mr. Pope's works stood higher on the shelves, and people read Wordsworth and Cooper and Scott. They enjoyed pastoral landscapes no longer, but looked admiringly at canvases of the Hudson River school—chasms and waterfalls and rough mountains veiled in mist. Gothic was the new style for churches, and when Bronson Alcott and Henry Thoreau built a summer-house for Mr. Emerson, it had pointed windows like a cathedral. As people's minds ran, so went the names.

The new fashion had made its first showings not long after the opening of the century. There was something of it in the borrowing of far-off Toledo and Memphis, and in the plantation-names of the cotton states with their memories of poems and novels.

One of the early names to be taken directly from a poem was chosen by a New York town-meeting in 1805. Someone had read Goldsmith's *Deserted Village,* and quoted the first line:

Sweet Auburn, loveliest village of the plain.

The meeting adopted it, and the name spread. It had everything that people of those years loved—mellifluous sounds, a vague poetic exhalation, even advertising value. Probably no one stopped to consider what its actual meaning was, and if anyone had, he would probably have been unable to make out that its proper American equivalent might be Eel Creek. Apparently also no one was deterred by the possibility of jokes about "the deserted village." As usual, the founders failed to consider location a matter of importance. Far from being villages "of the plain" some Auburns were in such hilly country that a tablecloth could cover all the available level space. One of the hilliest, in California, was named in 1849 by miners from Auburn, New York.

But there was no doubting the charm. Even conservative Maine, New Hampshire, and Massachusetts admitted the newcomer. Connecticut, as usual, disregarded fashion; but Ohio, child of Connecticut, with its love of the new and unusual, had two Auburns.

Far in Alabama some Georgians located lands, and then returned to bring their slaves. While at home, one of them mentioned the need of a name, and his sweetheart exclaimed, "Name it Auburn, sweet Auburn, loveliest village of the plain." This anecdote of 1836 has double significance. It showed the influence of reading, and also sounded the new feminine note.

Most of all, men and women, they read Scott. Waverly equaled Auburn in popularity, and Melrose was a close follower. Scott aided by Burns supplied a whole group of Scottish names.

In 1826 Cooper published *The Last of the Mohicans,* many of its scenes laid in the vicinity of Lake George. Cooper, however, did not care for that name, or for St. Sacrament, as the French had called it. He therefore had his Natty Bumppo declare the Indian name of the lake to be Horicon. This was a pure fiction; Cooper had seen that tribal name on some old Dutch maps, and put it into his character's mouth. Readers, however, took it to be genuine, and it nearly displaced the established one. Within three years, a semi-official *Atlas of the State of New York* referred to "the Horicon or Lake George." Cooper's usage survived for a town and stream.

In general, however, Americans either did not read much or were not much influenced by what they read. They borrowed more names from the Bible than from any other book, although its influence should be called religious rather than literary. But even if the Biblical names and those from the Book of Mormon

[271]

are added to the gatherings from Scott, Shakespeare and all the others, the proportion of "literary" names is small.

Just as -*ville,* however, spread the French influence more widely than the individual French names, so the romantic poets and novelists were most far-reaching through the name-elements which they supplied. From Scott came *glen,* a purely Celtic word, not English at all. He also popularized the Scottish and the northern English *dale. Vale,* a good rhyme for *dale,* soon joined the pair. About the middle of the century a town here or there was being named Oakdale, Ballard Vale, or Glen Wild. Since in Celtic the noun preceded the adjective, Scott's names were of the form Glencoe, or Glenartney, and the Americans usually kept the same order, as they had learned to do already with Mount and Lake.

Others quickly came into use. *Hurst, mere,* and *mead* were good old English words still preserved in place-names, but not used in common speech. They had failed originally to make the passage; their American equivalents were *thicket, pond,* and *meadow.* At last they were revived as names of towns and country-houses, often with their meaning only partially grasped, or neglected entirely. *Burn* was Scottish and older English for a small stream, but in the United States a place with such a name often stood on the bank of a river, creek, or run. *Brook* was traditional only in New England and regions settled by New Englanders, but it too was caught up in the new fashion for the antique. So was the French *mont.* Along with the rest -*side* sprang into new life from its frequent poetic use, especially by Scott:

> Spare not to spur, nor stint to ride,
> Until thou come to fair Tweedside.

Another revival was *wood.* Americans had always said *woods,* and so the word came to suggest any bit of second-growth forest, neither grandly primeval nor prettily park-like. But without its *s,* the word suggested the romantic outlaws of Sherwood, and any number of English country estates.

Glen, wood, and the others were a treasure-trove in the mid-century. One could be linked with another to make Glendale or Glenwood, Brookdale or Woodside. They went with common words—Hopedale or Broadmead. They were especially good with trees—Elmhurst or Maplewood or Oakmont.

One of their devotees was the developer laying out a district for summer homes or for one of the new suburbs which the railroads were making possible. Such names came to enclose New York City like a ring of outer fortifications—Oakwood, Hillside, Montclair, Englewood, Scarsdale, Larchmont, Glen Cove, Greenvale, Rosedale, Cedarhurst, Edgemere.

The charm of these names for that generation was manifold. They were "poetic." They brought to mind English country estates—and our more cultivated people, in spite of two wars, remained ardently Anglophile. The names were also snobbish and exclusive. Common Americans had post-office addresses ending in Creek, Gap, Bottom, and Bluff; but Dale, Hurst, and Mere were above the mob. Most of them also suggested beautiful landscapes, and thus expressed the very real love of natural scenery which that generation had developed.

Their exclusiveness and suggestion of beautiful scenery were perhaps responsible for their popularity as names for the new cemeteries which were beginning to replace the old church-yards. Even if a city-dweller could escape moving to the suburbs in his life, he was nevertheless very likely to end up finally in Oakmont or Woodland.

On the whole, however, that interest in scenery left less mark upon the map than might have been expected, because of certain inhibitions of the English language. A Frenchman could express his admiration of a view by Belle Rivière, and a Spaniard could say Buena Vista. But something prevented a speaker of English from giving such a name as Beautiful River, or Pretty View. The closest that the Americans could come to expressing that emotion in names was with Fair and Pleasant.

Fair went as far back as Fairfield in Connecticut. Its founders of 1646 may have been praising its beauty, but must also have been echoing, after the fashion of the time, the name of one of several English villages. Ironically, one Fairfield in England is known to have been really *forfield,* "hog-field," from a root still preserved in *farrow,* and very likely all of them first meant merely the field where some Saxon kept his swine. Fortunately, however, this meaning had been long forgotten, and *Fair* did good service. Its being archaic and poetic was only to its advantage, and it farrowed a numerous litter of Fairview, Fairburn, Fairdale, Fair Haven, and many others.

The older English equivalent of *pleasant* had been *merry,* as preserved in Meriden, "pleasant valley." *Pleasant* became thoroughly American, and was easily coupled with such endings as Gap, Creek, and Corners. Mount Pleasant appeared in colonial times, and was often repeated. While Fair and Pleasant thus multiplied, however, *Beautiful* kept out of the Post-Office Guide along with *Fine* and *Pretty,* as if they all were obscenities.

To express the idea of beauty more surely, the Americans took foreign words. Vue de l'eau in Massachusetts must have seemed more esthetic to its namers than Waterview. Belle was almost as popular as Pleasant in the mid-century, and produced not only Bellevue, but also Belleview, Belle Centre, and Belle Creek. Its masculine form never prospered; Belmont was preferred to Beaumont. To the American mind beauty was feminine only.

With this new interest in natural scenery and the improved transportation offered by the railroads, Americans began flocking to see Niagara and their other scenic wonders. They also began giving them new names. Many of the visitors were bridal couples, but even without this motivation the comparison of a high, windblown waterfall to a veil was obvious. Even if it had not been, Tennyson's line:

Slow-dropping veils of thinnest lawn

would have been enough. So Bridal Veil Falls became as hackneyed as Lover's Leap.

Many names thought to be unsuitable were changed. A lofty

point in the Highlands of the Hudson had been known as Butter
Hill, from its Dutch name Boter Berg. At the urging of the popular poet N. P. Willis, this became Storm King Mountain. An
elderly gentleman and some schoolboy companions visited a certain rock in Pennsylvania, ceremoniously read Bayard Taylor's
description of the Burns Festival at Moss Giel in Scotland, and
christened Moss Giel Rock.

The earliest English explorers, like the Spanish, had recorded
Indian names with respect; they were still hoping to discover another Mexico or Peru. The settlers soon came to look upon an
Indian as a treacherous savage, dirty, ignorant, poor, and heathen.
Indian names fell into the same disrepute. After the Revolution
the Indian menace was wholly removed from the sea-coast areas,
and at the same time the new doctrine of the noble savage was
growing popular. Indian names enjoyed a slight new popularity,
especially for counties, but the classical revival worked against
them. Men accustomed to the melodious Greek and Latin found
them harsh and barbarous. In 1794 David Humphreys wrote:

CONNECTICUT!
Thy name uncouth in song.

James Kirke Paulding composed a satiric passage of many lines
consisting entirely of Indian names:

Currituck, Cummashawo,
Chickamoggaw, Cussewago,
Cananwalohole, Karatunck,
Lastly Great Kathtippakakmunck.

He added in an ironic footnote that they were "highly sonorous,
and only to be paralleled by a catalogue of Russian generals."
Gradually, however, the prejudice lessened. First the states, and
more slowly the towns, began to take names from rivers and
mountains. Such uses as Chattanooga and Chicago, however,
showed no particular enthusiasm for things Indian; they were

merely names which happened to have been Indian originally, but had long since become familiar to American ears and tongues.

The admiration of Indian names as such began with the new love of the strange, mysterious, and primitive. An American reading *Marmion* might come upon the lines:

> Kentucky's wood-encumber'd brake,
> Or wild Ontario's boundless lake.

In a favorite poem he would thus see the possibilities of the native names, and might realize that his ancestors in wiping them out had not done so wisely as they had thought.

Seekonk, founded in 1812, was the first Massachusetts town to take an Indian name deliberately; Saugus soon followed in 1815. But these were premature, and there were no others until Chicopee in 1848. The forties indeed really saw the revival under way. New Englanders in the middle seventeenth century had been seeking an illusion of peaceful civilization by replacing Agawam with Ipswich; two hundred years later, their desires were reversed, and a new town was established as Agawam.

While the frontier regions went on disliking Indians and their names, the more settled regions thus began to use them. The revival of an ancient name for a particular place was only one method. The ordinary American, as opposed to the frontiersmen, considered tribal distinctions unimportant, and so he thought nothing strange in transferring an Iroquois name to Louisiana or a Cherokee name to Pennsylvania. Famous chiefs were admired as good warriors, or defenders of the liberty of their people. Powhatan, Tecumseh, Pontiac—like Kosciusko and Bolivar—became names of towns and counties. Even the grotesque Cornplanter appeared as a Pennsylvania town. Osceola, a Florida Seminole, gave his name to seventeen places, in far-scattered states.

Some names were actually coined. In 1816 Schoolcraft, the great authority on Indian lore, furnished Algonac for a Michigan town—"In this word the particle *ac* is taken from *ace*, land or earth; and its prefixed dissyllable *Algon*, from the word Algon-

[276]

quin." He added his opinion that by such procedure, "our geographical terminology might be greatly mended," and many agreed with him.

Most of the contemporary literary figures either by practice or direct advocacy favored Indian names. Washington Irving wrote a whole essay on the subject. The popular Lydia Sigourney took *Indian Names* as the title of her best-known poem:

> Ye say they all have pass'd away
> That noble race and brave;
> That their light canoes have vanish'd,
> From off the crested wave;
> That, mid the forests where they roam'd,
> There rings no hunter's shout;
> But their name is on your waters,
> Ye may not wash it out. . . .
>
> Old Massachusetts wears it
> Within her lordly crown,
> And broad Ohio bears it
> Amid his young renown.
> Connecticut hath wreath'd it
> Where her quiet foliage waves,
> And bold Kentucky breathes it hoarse
> Through all her ancient caves.

Whitman beat the drum loudly in his *American Primer:*

I was asking for something savage and luxuriant, and behold here are the aboriginal names. . . . What is the fitness—What the strange charm of aboriginal names? . . . They all fit. Mississippi!—the word winds with chutes—it rolls a stream three thousand miles long.

Longfellow in *Hiawatha* and other poems did much to establish a poetic vogue. In *Evangeline* Caroline Norton read the strange-sounding Atchafalaya, the river where the lovers failed in their meeting. She had it cut upon a seal, and later found that the King of the Belgians had been equally impressed by the same

word. Neither knew the meaning, but for once the romantic instinct was right; "long river" is no bad symbol of destiny.

Although the revival of Indian names rested basically upon a
genuine enthusiasm, it picked up much shoddiness and dishonesty.
As the religious mind has often been too ready to admit a pious
tale without questioning its actual truth, so the romantic mind
accepted a pleasing story and shaped facts to its own wishes. It
desired musical names, but the Indian words were harsh and un-
melodious. With an old-established name, therefore, the romantics
merely declared it to be beautiful anyway; they praised the melody
of Massachusetts and Connecticut, although one can hardly
imagine any words less musical. With other words they selected
the least ugly forms, and shifted consonants as they preferred. Ni-
bthaska became Nebraska.

Such procedure in itself had everything to recommend it. Noah
Webster gave it authority in the introduction to his *American
Spelling Book:*

Nor ought the harsh guttural sounds of the natives to be retained in
such words as Shawangunk, and many others.

The dishonesty, however, arose in the praising of Indian names
as melodious in contrast to English, when they had merely been
made so.

The romantics also desired names with a suggestion of poetry.
The simple primitive descriptives supplied almost nothing of this,
but such people generally know next to nothing of Indian languages, and so suffered little restraint. Mississippi, "big river," was
a simple Indian name, but a Frenchman's false translation "vieux
Père des Rivières," led to millions of American schoolchildren
being taught the falsehood that Mississippi meant "Father of
Waters." It was a falsehood not only about a single name, but
about Indians in general—for such a figure of speech would
hardly have been used for a river.

The closest American equivalent of Minnesota would probably
be "muddy river." That would never do! But *-sota,* the scholars

admitted, might mean "cloudy." Given an inch, the romantics took a mile. "Cloudy" suggested "sky," and "sky" suggested "blue." In the end Minnesota was said to mean "sky-blue water"!

The fanciful interpretation of two Florida names supplied perhaps the height of the romantic. Itchepuckesassa, "where there are tobacco blossoms," was probably only the Seminole's equivalent of "tobacco field," but it was rendered: "where the moon puts the colors of the rainbow into the earth and the sun draws them out in the flowers." Tsala Apopka was merely "trout-eating-place"; frontier Americans made it over into Charley Apopka. But the romantic translation declared it to be "Where the earth makes the island of the sun in the lake that rises out of the earth."

When such translations were circulated, it is no wonder that people believed Indian names to be sometimes remarkably descriptive, sometimes remarkably fanciful, poetic, and "full of meaning."

The great majority of our present Indian names of towns are thus not really indigenous. Far even from being old, they are likely to be recent. Ipswich is two hundred years older than near-by Agawam. Troy or Lafayette is likely to be an older name in most states than Powhatan or Hiawatha. The romantics of the mid-century and after applied such names, not the explorers and frontiersmen.

The revival of Indian names affected the country considerably, although not so much as its devotees would have wished. Their enthusiasm differed from earlier ones by being a kind of gospel, and attempting not only to give the new names, but also to replace the old. Irving, however, did not succeed in having the country become Alleghania or Appalachia, and Whitman was not able to displace Baltimore, which he especially disliked.

Indian names thus arose upon many new towns, railway-stations, and streets. They were placed upon mountains which no one had bothered to name before. But when the enthusiast wished to make wholesale replacements of older names, he committed the fallacy of emphasizing one phase of history at the expense of the rest, and broke himself against the granite of local pride. In traditions as in blood, the people of the United States were vastly less Indian than European. To have changed Virginia to Rappahannock, or Baltimore to Patapsco would have been a triumph of mere pedantry.

As with all human activities, personal squabbles were often of more weight than the testimony of history and language. In the forties an advocate proposed that the name of a certain territory should revert to a more pristine form. The attempt failed, for reasons described by a contemporary:

The Legislature solemnly decreed that the name should be spelled Wisconsin, and this probably more from opposition to the individual who attempted the restoration than from correct literary taste, or any regard for the original Indian name.

An incident of the far West mingled all the romantic naming-habits—the love of nature, of Indian names, of poetry—at the same time throwing the frontier into contrast.

In March, 1851, a battalion of California mounted militia was pursuing a band of hostile Indians into the Sierra Nevada. The horsemen followed a reluctant and half-treacherous guide, old chief Ten-ei-ya. Their commander was a colorful old reprobate, Major Savage, renowned for maintaining a harem of five squaws. The men were mostly of the frontier, with a large contingent of Texans. As usual in California, however, all classes of men were mingled, and along with the frontiersmen were a few whom the current phrase would have described as "gentlemen of culture and refinement."

Among these was Lafayette Houghton Bunnell. He had had medical training, and was addressed as "Doc," but his special duty was to act as interpreter if any Spanish-speaking Indians, renegades from the missions, should be captured. Besides having some knowledge of medicine and languages, Bunnell was a reader of poetry, fully imbued with the romantic love of nature.

Toward the close of a day the company came suddenly to the brink of a vast and unprecedented chasm—its immensity even magnified by the shadows and mists. "As I looked," wrote Bunnell, "a peculiar exalted sensation seemed to fill my whole being, and I found my eyes in tears with emotion."

They followed a steep Indian trail to the floor of the valley, and camped by the rushing river. Most of the men were more interested in entering a notable Indian hide-out than in having discovered one of the world's scenic wonders. A volunteer went off to find a ford, got a dousing in the water, and returned to stand shivering and steaming before a fire. Supper was finished; pipes were lighted; the free talk of the frontier passed back and forth. Bunnell and a few others felt the awe of their surroundings:

"The coarse jokes of the careless, and the indifference of the practical, sensibly jarred my more devout feelings."

To bring the talk into line with his thoughts, Bunnell addressed the man who stood drying his clothes:

"You are the first white man that ever received any form of baptism in this valley, and you should be considered the proper person to give a baptismal name to the valley itself."

"If whiskey can be provided for such a ceremony, I shall be happy to participate; but if it is to be another cold-water affair, I have no desire to take a hand."

The talk drifted off again, but the idea had been planted. In a lull someone remarked:

"I like Bunnell's suggestion of giving this valley a name, and tonight is a good time to do it."

"All right," cried another, "if you have got one, show your hand."

The matter became a sport. Different men cried out names—some of them romantic, some foreign. But Bunnell noted that many were Biblical; more than they would admit, he thought, the men had been stirred by what they had seen.

Bunnell himself said that he saw no need of borrowing from another country—"An American name would be the most appropriate." Being a man of that time, he naturally suggested, "it would be better to give it an Indian name." He mentioned the only one which could as yet be associated with the place, the name of the Indians whom the company had pursued there—Yo-sem-i-ty.

But the man who stood steaming replied gruffly, "Devil take the Indians and their names! Why should we honor these vagabond murderers by perpetuating their name?"

Another cried, "—— the Indians and their names . . . Let's call this Paradise Valley."

Then a rollicking Texan shouted out to the whole camp, and put the question:

"Hear ye! Hear ye! Hear ye! A vote will now be taken to decide what name shall be given to this valley."

The rough-clad men gathered from the other fires. Only the sentries kept their posts. The horses champed along the picket line. The fires leapt high in the darkness, and the unseen cliffs towered above.

As Bunnell later reported:

The question of giving it the name of Yo-sem-i-ty was then explained; and upon a *viva voce* vote being taken, it was almost unanimously adopted.

The name, as was later learned, meant Grizzly Bears, being applied to the tribe because of their ferocity. It had the usual vicissitudes. An army officer later established the spelling as Yosemite, perhaps under the belief that it was Spanish, but the name thus democratically voted by the assembled company resisted essential change.

The first visit lasted for only three days, but the battalion returned for a longer period. The naming of many canyons and waterfalls occurred during these two visits. Two forces were in conflict. The frontiersmen gave their own names, but Bunnell and a few others labored to prevent sacrilege.

The common imagination ran to such descriptions as Giant's Pillar, Sam Patch's Falls, and the Devil's Night-Cap. Bunnell found that he could displace these only if the new name was simple and apt enough for use in common speech. Now and then he had a bit of luck. One squad, hurrying back to camp to avoid a storm, saw clouds settle upon a mountain, and named it Cloud's Rest. Again, near a point where three similar peaks stood up sharply, five Indians were captured, three of whom were brothers. The coincidence led to the peaks being called the Three Brothers. Such names were suitable to both parties, but in spite of Bunnell's efforts a certain number of commonplace frontier names like Indian Creek were established.

Bunnell labored valiantly to learn and implant the aboriginal names. The guide Ten-ei-ya, having tried to escape, was kept tethered to a rope, and Bunnell thus had an unusual opportunity, though a limited vocabulary, to discuss nomenclature.

The Indian names, however, proved disappointing, and Bunnell was honest enough to admit that they were neither melodious nor poetic. Some of them were downright obscene, like the original name of the Three Brothers:

They were called by the Indians "Kom-po-pai-zes," from a fancied resemblance of the peaks to the heads of frogs when sitting up *ready to leap*. A fanciful interpretation has been given the Indian name as meaning "mountains playing leap-frog," but a literal translation is not desirable.

Such names as Py-we-ack and Yo-wy-we were merely ridiculous in sound, and the latter meant "wormy-water," because of its twisty course. Of another, Bunnell honestly declared:

It is derived from Too-leol and We-ack, and means ὁ πόταμος, ὁς διά πέτρας οὐρεῖ. This name has been published as if by authority to signify *"The Beautiful"*—how beautiful, the learned in Greek may judge.

Besides Yosemite, only Ahwahnee, Pohono, and a few others were found worthy of perpetuation. The name of the old chief remained as Tenaya Lake and Canyon.

Denied Indian support, Bunnell did his best with the vocabulary of romantic poetry. He named Vernal Fall because the spray gave the effect of spring showers, and he clinched his naming with a quotation from Byron. He replaced the undignified Yo-wy-we with Nevada Fall because it was closest to the Sierra Nevada. He himself avoided the worst clichés, but at the suggestion of a friend one of the falls became Bridal Veil. His knowledge of Spanish led him to translate an Indian word into El Capitan, rather than into the Captain, or Chief.

Bunnell had a certain talent at naming. He might easily have strewn the Valley with tinsel, or "Indian" names dishonestly prettified and mistranslated. But he was sincere, and when a statement was made that a certain name for a fall meant "a shower of sparkling crystals," Bunnell declared it only laughable.

Within a few years, so fast was the transition from Indian-fighting to tourist-travel, sightseers began to pour into Yosemite. Gushing females, and their masculine escorts, planted such romantic banalities as Cathedral Rocks and Inspiration Point.

During the whole middle of the century, the romantics seemed much stronger than they were, because they did a great deal of talking and writing. The opposite side was expressed by the Congressman who said he disliked "all these Indian names," and by the frontiersman whom Bunnell quoted: "—— the Indians and their names." Although such people did not write the books, they probably represented a greater number of solid and patriotic Americans than Irving and Whitman had readers. The weakness of the romantics even at their height was to be seen in the shift in the tradition of state-naming during the fifties.

THE Compromise of 1850 began the decade, and carried with it
two names. California, older than Virginia or Massachusetts, was
too well established to suggest change. The part annexed to the
United States had been Alta California, but even in Mexican
times its greater importance had led to its being known informally as California. The Americans merely dropped Alta
officially.

With the new territory the case was different. The Mormons
had recently organized it as Deseret. But Deseret came from the
Book of Mormon, a work regarded as infamous by the great majority of Americans. Politically also Brigham Young was suspected of wishing to establish an independent government, and
many objected to recognizing him, and the name which he had
presumptuously set up.

There was moreover an obvious substitute, which was in accordance with tradition. As early as 1720 the Spaniards had written down the name of a tribe as Yutta. The Americans spelled it
Ute, Uta, or Utah; Frémont in his reports had favored the last.
The name had been applied to a lake, and to its out-flowing
stream which the Mormons re-named the Jordan. A river bearing
a tribal name was thus available, and in addition Senator Benton,
Frémont's father-in-law, was largely concerned with western
affairs.

The Mormons, however, were strongly for Deseret, and for the
first time local sentiment clashed with Congress. The religious
question was kept politely out of public debate. Mr. Benton said

that he opposed Deseret because it suggested *desert,* and was repulsive. The Mormons, on the other hand, passed a resolution: "Do they object to the name of our state? It is good enough for us who have to wear it." Always before, Congress had accepted the local preference, but this situation was unique. There were objections also to Utah—the Indians of that name, some branches of them at least, were notoriously dirty, lice-infested, and grasshopper-eating. Nevertheless, a section of the great body of legislation known as the Compromise of 1850 established: "a temporary government by the name of the Territory of Utah."

The organization of the annexed region of Nuevo México followed later in the year with no more change than to establish the American form New Mexico.

Utah had broken the tradition of the acceptance of local preference, but had again used the Indian name of a local tribe and river. An even greater break soon occurred. The settlers in the northern part of Oregon Territory, which had been formed in 1848, became ambitious. Following good American precedent, they memorialized Congress in 1853:

that all that portion of Oregon Territory . . . should be organized as a separate Territory under the name and style of the "Territory of Columbia."

Except that it was not Indian, Columbia had all the usual requirements of a state name. It was taken from a great river of the region, was the local choice, and was popular, patriotic, and sonorous. A bill for its organization passed the Committee, and came to the floor of the House. Joseph Lane, Delegate to Congress from Oregon Territory, spoke in favor of it without referring to the name. Columbia seemed about to pass without debate, but suddenly Mr. Stanton of Kentucky gained the floor.

Mr. Stanton: I desire to move to amend the bill by striking out the word "Columbia" and inserting "Washington" in lieu thereof. We have already a Territory of Columbia. This District is called

Columbia; but we never have yet dignified a Territory with the name of Washington.

Mr. Lane: I shall never object to that name.

Mr. Stanton: I have nothing more to say, except that I desire to see, if I should live so long, at some future day, a sovereign State bearing the name of the Father of his country.

Another member concurred, as a quick wave of hero-worship swept the House:

Mr. Stanly: There has been but one Washington upon earth, and there is not likely to be another, and, as Providence has sent but one, for all time, let us have one State named after that one man.

He went on to point out the confusion to arise from another Columbia, in his enthusiasm forgetting the confusion to arise from another Washington.

Two days later, however, Mr. Evans of Maryland gained the floor. He had been absent, he said, from the other session. He favored retaining Columbia:

for the single reason that our geographical nomenclature has become such a mass of confusion that it is almost impossible when you hear the name of a town, to know in what part of the world it is, much less to know in what part of the United States it may be found.

He added the common-sense argument: "We have perhaps one hundred counties and towns of the name of Washington." Finally he pointed out that objections to Columbia did not necessitate Washington:

I think it far more proper to avoid the difficulties of geographical nomenclature by giving to this Territory some one of the beautiful Indian names which prevail in that part of the country.

There was pertinence in all that Mr. Evans said, except his assumption that the Indian names of the Northwest were beautiful. They were actually perhaps the worst in the whole country, pre-

senting such mouthfuls as Snohomish, Skagit, Cowlitz, Wahki-
akum, and Klickitat. But otherwise Mr. Evans showed excellent
good sense in all he said. Unfortunately, as he realized, his remarks came too late, and he was really addressing the Senate
from the floor of the House.

Some senators indeed made an attempt to prevent the duplication. Stephen A. Douglas proposed Washingtonia, and gained a
recommendation from the Committee on Territories. In the end,
however, he did not press for change.

Washington had been previously proposed as a state-name, and
the Mississippi convention had come close to adopting it. Probably, sooner or later, it was inevitable. Nevertheless, the duplication was one of the most unfortunate events of our naming-
history. In the course of time the expression District of Columbia
fell into comparative disuse, so that its duplication of a state-name
would have been of little importance. But the two Washingtons
(not to mention all the smaller ones) have grown steadily in
importance, necessitating an ever more frequent and tiresome
mention of "Washington state" or "Washington, D. C." The two
initials have become attached to the name of the national capital
like an ugly parasitic growth.

Utah and Washington broke tradition. Individual members of
Congress undoubtedly began to realize that things might be done
with names. In the organization of Kansas and Nebraska, however, the older tradition again held sway. Kansas took the well-
established name of tribe and river. Its neighbor followed the
route of Minnesota. The chief river was the Platte, an uninspiring
name. But Frémont had often used the older name Nebraska. As
early as 1844, the year of Frémont's return, the Secretary of War
reported upon the region:

The Platte, or Nebraska, being the central stream leading into or
from the great south pass, would very properly furnish a name to the
territory.

Nebraska, like Oregon, thus came to bear a name once applied to a river, although the rivers themselves were called Platte and Columbia.

Chapter XXXIII ❨ Of the cities of the Fifties

WELL before the mid-century *-ville* and *-burgh* had passed their peak. Too many towns had been hopefully platted and then lapsed into open fields, or an unpainted tavern at a muddy crossroads. When a town-planner scanned the census of 1850, he found that of the hundreds only Louisville, Nashville, and Pittsburgh had as yet amounted to much. A story of Missouri shows the depth to which *-ville* had fallen. The founder had first used the pet-name of his daughter Sarah and called it Sedville. A friend objected that the suffix "was decidedly objectionable . . . as it did not comport with the large flourishing city of his dreams." He suggested a classical-sounding termination, and the town became Sedalia.

In the mid-century, up-to-date founders used no suffix at all, or added City as a separate word. The active region of settlement, and therefore of naming, lay at that time in the rich farming lands of eastern Kansas and Nebraska. The cost of platting a site was small; the chance of profit to the speculator was good; plans for a metropolis cost little more than for a village. Hundreds were laid out, and each was called a city so regularly that the phrase "kiting a town" came into use to indicate that City had been attached like the tail of a kite. Sometimes the name took the even

[289]

more grandiloquent form, such as City of Plattsmouth. Horace Greeley commented:

It takes three log houses to make a city in Kansas, but they begin calling it a city so soon as they have staked out the lots.

On June 24, 1854, the Omaha Indians by treaty gave up some of their lands. The Council Bluffs and Nebraska Ferry Company immediately gained possession of a town-site, and had a plat prepared. By September an elaborate map had been printed, and Omaha City was launched.

Once the boom-period was ended, City became useless and an awkward nuisance. Successful ones like Omaha merely dropped it. If the place remained a village, City was ridiculous and ironic. Usually it remained only on towns for which it served as a good mark of distinction, as in setting off Kansas City from Kansas. It gave dignity to very short names like Sioux City or Mound City, or undistinguished names like Central City. Some towns preserved it officially, although seldom so called. On the other hand, New York City and Washington City had no official standing, but were still thus mentioned for distinction from the states.

The Greek equivalent of City was -polis, and it had been used occasionally ever since Jamestown, perhaps humorously, had been called Jacobopolis in 1607. As Annapolis it became a state capital, and this tradition passed on to Indianapolis and Arkopolis. The last, however, lost in a local squabble, yielded to the more native Little Rock.

The town-kiters of the fifties used -polis occasionally, but the magnificently platted Kansopolis fizzled out. By and large, that suffix with its suggestion of metropolis was a little too grandiose even for the city-dreamers.

In 1852 the citizens of a little settlement not far from St. Paul were in need of a name. As with many great inventions, partisans have hotly pressed the claims of two rivals, Mr. Hoag and Mr. Bowman. The supporters of the latter at least tell a more circumstantial story.

[290]

Mr. Bowman was editor of the local paper. As such, he became familiar with the many names suggested for the town, but he felt them all lacking in something. One day he set off on horseback to visit friends in a village some thirty miles distant. The way was long, the horse jogged steadily, the editor's mind was active. To pass the time, he began to conjure up names. He invented many, and rejected them. Still jogging along, he began to consider *-polis,* and to make combinations with it. At last he began to work upon a pleasing idea.

Near his town was a beautiful waterfall. In the language of the Sioux, a waterfall was *haha;* water itself was *minne.* White men by a misunderstanding had coupled the two words, and produced Minnehaha Falls, a name thus meaning "water-waterfalls-falls." By complete though natural misrendering of *haha,* the name had been romantically translated as Laughing Water.

Like Shakespeare and other vigorous makers of language, the frontier American had no prejudice against the marriage of Greek and barbarian. Mr. Bowman's active mind worked quickly through Minnehahapolis and produced Minnehapolis, which he thought appropriate and expressive enough, but lacking in euphony. He decided it would sound better, if the *h* should be silent. All this inspiration occurred to him near a place on the road called Halfway House.

On his return, Mr. Bowman and his friend Mr. Hoag advocated the name, and finally presented it at a meeting of citizens. The meeting, with excellent sense, decided that a silent *h* might as well be dropped completely, and so adopted the name with the spelling Minneapolis.

The flabby decade of the fifties produced no heroes, and the earlier heroes had already been fully used. Four cities, however, took their names from men whom most Americans would be unable to identify.

On the bank of a Pennsylvania river an Indian village was standing when white men first penetrated there. The frontiersmen called it Capouse, from the name of the chief. After the

Revolution, Connecticut men tried to establish a village to be named Unionville, but since it lay along the river among high hills, it was known usually by the common folk-name Deep Hollow. When the village failed to thrive, the neighbors sometimes called it in derision Skunk's Misery. Some settlers named Slocum operated a forge and a distillery, and in 1816 changed the name again, to Slocum Hollow. Still the village languished, and in 1840 consisted of only five battered houses. In that year the two Scranton brothers and their three partners moved in, and set to work on the problem of smelting iron-ore from the local anthracite coal. Being ingenious and persistent, they solved the difficulties, and hoping for better things at last, they re-named the place again, calling it Harrison in 1845, after the deceased President. But soon another shift seemed advisable, and for advertising purposes it became simply Lackawanna Iron Works. In 1847 a third Mr. Scranton arrived, bringing a new aid of capital and energy. With a single family now dominating, the name took the pseudo-classical form of Scrantonia in 1850, and within a year was simplified to Scranton. Like Lowell, the great city of anthracite preserved the name of that new type of American, the industrialist. It is notable also as a place which has borne eight recorded names, besides the epithet Skunk's Misery.

A full continent removed, the beginnings of another city also took the name of a man. About 1786 a baby had been born in the Suquamish tribe. They were no powerful nation, only a group of salmon-fishers living on the green shores of an intricate bay. As a child of six, the naked Indian boy may have seen his first white men, when Captain Vancouver came working up the Sound, mapping and naming as he went. Years later, when the Hudson's Bay fur-traders came, the boy had grown to manhood, and was a chief. He was a big fellow; the Canadians nick-named him "Le Gros." The head trader, who spelled the chief's name See-yat, did not like him. "This fellow is a scamp," he wrote, "a black heart ready to pick a quarrel." Again he entered in the journal, "Chief See-yat has murdered an Indian doctor . . . I wish they would determine on shooting the villain." Later on, See-yat settled down, and let a Catholic missionary baptize him as Noah Sealth. In the fifties, when Americans began coming, he was an old man. He got along well with them. They liked the chief so much, in fact, that when some of them laid out a town in 1853 they called it for him, using the spelling Seattle.

This naming, curiously, came to worry the chief considerably. In spite of his conversion, he stuck to a tribal belief—if anybody mentioned his name after he was dead, his spirit would be troubled. If so, he must be having a very restless time. But very possibly the current pronunciation of Seattle is so far removed from the original that it is not recognizable.

The last great city of Minnesota also followed the regional tradition of antiquarianism. In 1856 the owners of a townsite on Lake Superior came to the Rev. Mr. Joseph G. Wilson, a Presbyterian missionary of the vicinity, and promised him a gift of two lots if he would suggest a good name; they doubtless approached Mr. Wilson because Presbyterian ministers, in distinction from Methodists and some others, were well educated. Mr. Wilson conscientiously visited several of the more lettered local inhabitants, hunting for a book on early regional history. He at last found "an old English translation of the writings of the French Jesuits," and read in it of Daniel Greysolon Du Luth who had voyaged to Lake Superior in 1679. He may also have gathered that Du Luth was one of the best of the early French officers, although he could hardly have learned of the noble letter to Frontenac in which Du Luth, in the best code of the old regime, declared that he "feared not death, only cowardice or dishonor." Mr. Wilson was not so narrow-minded as many ministers of his time, and did not withhold his admiration from a Catholic. He presented his choice, along with other names, at a meeting of the proprietors. After discussion Du Luth was selected, and was recorded as Duluth.

Too many men throng to the gates of fame, and some must be forgotten, even though they too were of epic stuff. One such was born on a farm in Virginia in 1817. His life was a saga of the early United States. He went west as a young man, and worked as surveyor, schoolteacher, lawyer, and small-town editor. He developed into a man to command respect even on the turbulent frontier. He stood six-feet-two, broad of shoulder and powerful. Men knew him as tireless and determined, yet a good companion, mingling geniality and dignity. He raised a company of infantry, and as captain led it from Vera Cruz to Mexico City. Back from the war, he made the overland crossing to the gold-fields in 1850. California was full of energetic and talented men, but he more than held his own. He killed a man in a duel, and was elected to Congress in the same year. When guerrilla warfare raged in bleeding Kansas, President Buchanan picked him as a strong man to restore order. A ballad was composed in his honor:

> Now set your flags a-flying,
> And beat the ready drum,
> For joy to Southern Kansas,
> The Governor has come!
> He's cowed the Fort Scott ruffians,
> He's set the people free,
> And all the brave defenders
> He's treated clemently.

At that time the boundaries of Kansas Territory extended to the Rocky Mountains and included the new Pike's Peak gold-fields. A party of miners named their settlement Denver, after the governor.

James William Denver went on to become Commissioner of Indian Affairs, and a general in the Civil War. As with Dallas, Rochester, Cleveland and so many others, a city remains as his memorial, but few ever think of the man.

In contrast to the preceding period, only one city-name of the fifties sprang directly from an established name. In 1566, Menéndez, the Spanish founder of St. Augustine, had written of a lake called Maymi, and a few years later another Spaniard translated this as "very large." The name was transferred also to the river flowing from the lake, the spellings varying as much as Mayami and Aymai.

During the two and a half centuries before Florida became

part of the United States, the Americans spread across the mountains, and came to know a powerful tribe bearing some such native name as Omaumeg, "peninsula-people"; English-speaking tongues twisted this into Miami and also into Maumee, both Ohio rivers. When the Americans went into Florida, they apparently identified the southern and northern words. In the fifties, the name became that of a post-office and struggling settlement on that Florida river. Miami thus appears in Ohio and in Florida, although in the two places it originated from different languages and words of different meanings.

Innumerable towns and villages bear descriptive names such as Red Bank and Flat Rock; hundreds commemorate the native trees, alphabetically from Ash Grove to Willow Springs. But strangely few great cities were named descriptively, and only one for a native tree. As might be expected, it is in a region where trees were few, and men had learned to prize them.

Across the Bay from San Francisco was a stretch of flat land scattered with magnificent California live-oaks. In Mexican times it had been known as Encinal del Temescal, "oak-grove of the sweat-house." The Americans who planned a town there may not have known Spanish, but they could see the trees. In simple description they called it Oakland.

Chapter XXXIV ❨ How they fought again

THERE was the sound of guns once more, and the first firing was, by irony, at a place bearing the name of Thomas Sumter who in

the Revolution had fought the redcoats so bravely with his guerrilla band that men called him the Gamecock.

As they fought, naming went on, as it had in the Revolution.
In those years men talked much, as they still argue, as to whether
the War was to keep the Union or free the slaves. But to look at
the map, you would say it was for the Union.

The way of naming towns by abstracts was nothing new. It
went back to Hope-in-Faith, Concord, and Providence. But it was
like Bible-naming, and never became popular. The Union of
England and Scotland was in 1707, and Union Street in Boston
probably commemorated it. During the Revolution the union of
the colonies was a watchword, and Uniontown in Pennsylvania
thus took its name. Sometimes, however, the word recorded only
the joining of two villages or districts, or even of two streets. In
the new plan of New York, the Commissioners instructed the
surveyor to lay out a square where Bowery Road united with
Bloomingdale Road, and they called it Union Square. The Post-
office List of 1813 showed ten offices for Union, eight for Concord,
and seven for Liberty. Freedom made its appearance a few years
later.

In 1830 Daniel Webster cried, "Liberty and Union, now and
forever, one and inseparable!" The namers, however, put Union
first. By 1855 with disunion becoming daily a more imminent
peril, the number of post-offices, such as Union, Uniontown and
Unionville had soared to eighty-nine. A comparable count shows
that Liberty had risen to thirty-seven. Both of these were well
distributed north and south, but Freedom—now listed at thirteen
—was mainly northern.

In 1862 Union touched one hundred ten. Liberty had added
only seven; Freedom only one.

For what it may be worth, the evidence of the names indicates
that the American people have always held Union most dear.
Liberty has been a bad second; Freedom and Independence have
trailed far behind. Even if all three are joined, they fail to rival
Union.

Justice has made only a rare showing, but Fair Play has served as a popular equivalent, and in the Civil War period reached a total of eleven post-offices. Peace, like Justice, has been thought unsuitable, but Concord, Amity and Harmony have supplied the idea, in their total approaching Liberty. Among non-political ideas, Hope, the first thought of the builder and last refuge of the defeated, has often stood second only to Union. Honesty, though it may be the best policy, has never been thought an acceptable town-name.

As for the idea of making money, American namers have masked it decently in many ways, such as Richfield, Richland, and Richville, and occasionally Prosperity and Commerce. They have also shown a considerable trust in Providence, but no respect for Prudence.

Although Union was the rallying-cry, the new state then formed did not take that name. When the mountain counties of Virginia held with the North, the people elected delegates to a convention to establish the new government. The first suggestion was for New Virginia, but the more extreme delegates wished to reject Virginia, policy and name alike. They fell back upon the old tradition of a chief river bearing the name of an Indian tribe. A special committee reported for "the State of Kanawha." An amendment to substitute West Virginia was lost.

The people then elected delegates to a new convention to form a constitution for Kanawha, and thereupon these delegates, in spite of legal difficulties, took up the question of changing the name under which they had been elected. Argument grew hot.

Mr. Sinsel took high grounds, wishing to retain Virginia because it suggested the mother of the Savior, and the Virgin Queen.

Mr. Brown, delegate from Kanawha County, replied ungallantly that the vestal character of Queen Elizabeth was not so well attested as some other facts in English history.

Mr. Parker objected. There might well be "too much Kanawha." They had already a county, two rivers, and a Kanawha Court House. It might produce confusion in postal matters.

Mr. Lamb broke out in a tirade against Virginia. What had the western counties ever received but oppression and outrage? He wished to cut loose entirely.

Mr. Willey, disclaiming personal interest, stated that his constituents were sentimentally unwilling to have a new state at all, unless they could keep the old name.

Mr. Paxton raised the point of legal difficulties.

Mr. Van Winkle objected to anything having a "Virginia" in it.

Mr. Stuart reported that his constituents had voted for the new state with a protest about the name.

Mr. Batelle declared: "I, for one, want a new name—a fresh name—which if not symbolical of new ideas would at least be indicative of our deliverance from very old ones."

A strange omission from the arguments was any reference to the propaganda-value of the retention of Virginia, which would thus advertise to the world that part at least of the prestige of that oldest state was devoted to the preservation of the Union.

When the vote was finally taken, loyalty to the old name rolled up a clear majority. The count stood:

West Virginia	30
Kanawha	9
Western Virginia	2
Allegheny	2
Augusta	1

The people accepted the new constitution. Since the convention, however, may have acted beyond its authority, a strictly legalistic interpretation might still declare the *de jure* name to be Kanawha.

They fought, and the names of those battles were not strange names, hard to fit upon the tongue—of France, or Africa, or the far seas, north and south. But they were the names of little towns with familiar endings—Gettysburgh and Vicksburgh, Chancellorsville and Murfreesboro. Or they were those the Indians left, like Antietam and Chickamauga; or of the little country churches of the South—Shiloh, and Bethesda, and Big Bethel; or the simple names of hills and streams—Little Round Top, Lookout

Mountain, Stone River, and the Big Black. Or else they were names of plantations and taverns and crossroads—Five Forks, and Yellow Tavern, Fair Oaks, Glendale, and Seven Pines. Or again, they were names that the English had brought into the land—Winchester, Malvern Hill, and Cold Harbor. When they fought two bloody days at Fredericksburg, few remembered it was named for an English prince.

The names of those battles had the true flavor of the land—Wilson's Creek, and Bull Run, White Oak Swamp, and Ball's Bluff, Pea Ridge, the Wilderness, and Chickasaw Bayou.

There were many heroes of that war, and their names went upon counties and towns and squares. But the greatest, and he who became the second hero of the nation, was not a soldier.

Even while Abraham Lincoln was still only a Springfield lawyer, he had his first namesake town. In 1853 three men laying out a site in Illinois hired him to prepare some papers, and then called the place Lincoln. He advised them against it with his dry humor, remarking, "never knew anything named Lincoln that amounted to very much."

After he became a war-president, his name spread everywhere. Yet there was something true in his comment. Though one Lincoln became a state-capital, yet in general the many places named Lincoln did not amount to very much. The same may also be said of course for the many places called after Franklin, Jefferson, and some of the other great heroes. With Lincoln, the result had a certain poetic justice. He was the common man's hero, and in the United States the small town has always been the citadel of the common man.

In Missouri one county was divided against another at the beginning. In 1861 the men of Pike, who stood for the Union, prepared to invade Calloway, which held with the South. The fighting-men of Calloway had mostly gone to join the army, but the grandfathers and boys came out with squirrel-rifles and shotguns, and a Quaker cannon. They bluffed the Pike County men,

[299]

and made an agreement, neither to invade the other. So Calloway County ran its own affairs, and being independent, came to be known as "The Kingdom." A cross-roads settlement there is still Kingdom City.

In the western mining regions, Northerners and Southerners sank most of their differences in the common frenzy of gold-hunting. In one district there was a General Grant mine, along with a General Lee. Although the men were mostly northern, they allowed mines to be named the Jeff Davis, the Stonewall Jackson, the Confederate State, and the Bonnie Blue Flag.

Southerners tried to name another mining-town Varina, after the wife of Jefferson Davis. But when a northern judge was asked to head a legal document with that name, he boldly replied, "I'll see you damned first!" Then, with excellent tact, he wrote the name Virginia, to which no Southerner could object. (Thus arose the northern Virginia City, but the southern one, greatest of all the mining towns, took its name from a miner nicknamed Virginia.)

When another man was about to name his mine, he read in the newspaper an account, where the reporter had written vividly: "Grant encircled Lee like a giant anaconda." So the mine was named the Anaconda, and later the name was transferred to a town.

After the Confederate cruiser *Alabama* won fame, some southern miners used the name, and it was applied to a range of desert hills in California. But after the *Kearsarge* sank the *Alabama,* some Northerners in return gave that name to a great snow-capped mountain which has ever since towered high above the scrawny Alabama Hills.

The end of that war was at a place with an old name. Of May 26, 1607, Gabriel Archer had written, "We parted from Kind Woman's Care, and . . . went ashore at a place I call Queen Apumetec's Bower." John Smith wrote of "the pleasant river of Apamatuck." The Indians there were called the Apamatucks, and their river came to be spelled Appomattox. At last in 1845, when Indian names had come into fashion, a district toward the headwaters of the river became a county, and its seat of government, after the custom of the South, was known as Appomattox Court House. After April 9, 1865, it was a famous name.

Chapter XXXV ⟪ How Congress took over

IN THE Civil War period, nine names of states were established, but only West Virginia sprang in any way from the War itself.

In 1806 Captain Zebulon Pike had led an expedition into the southwestern part of the Louisiana Purchase. He was not a giver of names, and generally accepted those already established. His spellings showed how far a man might vary from the original even when he knew something of the language. Thus he wrote La Touche de la Côte Bucanieus, when his Frenchmen were apparently trying to tell him La Fourche de la Côte de Kansas. In November, Pike began to see ahead a dominating snow-covered mountain which he called Grand Peak. It became known through his reports, and before long the Americans called it Pike's Peak, although he had never so named it.

After the discovery of gold there in 1859, agitation began for the establishment of a new territory in "the Pike's Peak region." The commonly used name was definitely out. Pike had risen to be a general, and had been killed, valiantly fighting, at the battle of York in 1813. Some counties had been named for him, but he was no major hero. A state could not take his name, when Jefferson, Jackson, and many others were still unhonored.

In 1859 a bill presented to the House provided for Colona Territory. Probably this was formed from Colón, the Spanish form of Columbus, and was thus an equivalent of Columbia. The bill failed, but was only the first of many. Before long, the competition of names for the new territory became a derby with at least fifteen entrants in the running, and a dark horse finally nosing out a victory in the home stretch.

Within a few weeks, the Committee on Territories recommended the name Jefferson, but a Republican representative immediately moved to substitute Osage. Again the bill died. The inhabitants of the region liked Jefferson Territory, and a year later petitioned Congress for recognition under that name. Senator Green of Missouri, however, took over the sonorous Spanish name of a far-western river, and introduced a bill "to provide for a temporary government in the Territory of Colorado." This river was nowhere near the gold-mining region, and the name met little favor.

Suddenly an unprecedented rush of names sprang into competition. A newspaper reported:

The Senate Committee have before them the following names: "Yampa" interpreted Bear; "Idahoe" meaning Gem of the Mountains; "Nemara"; "Colorado"; "San Juan"; "Lula" interpreted Mountain Fairy; "Weapollao"; "Arapahoe," the name of the Indian tribe inhabiting the Pike's Peak region. The House seems to have hit upon the very appropriate name of "Tahosa" which means Dwellers on the Mountain Tops. This or "Idahoe" will probably be adopted. Among the anti-barbarian names suggested, I have heard those of Lafayette, Columbus, and Franklin, each entitled to the highest consideration.

Needless to say, most of these "translations" of the Indian names were highly romantic.

Idaho became the favorite. A local convention accepted it, and the Committee of Territories approved. In 1861 a bill was presented, and everything seemed settled.

Underground, however, some influence must have been at work. The Territorial delegate had apparently discovered that the name did not mean "Gem of the Mountains." Possibly he feared that like many other Indian names it meant something better not translated. The presentation of the bill occasioned a sudden reversal. A senator took the floor:

> *Mr. Wilson:* I move to amend the name of the Territory by striking out "Idaho" and inserting "Colorado." I do it at the request of the delegate from that Territory, who is very anxious about it, and came to see me today to have that change made. He said that the Colorado River arose in that Territory, and there was a sort of fitness in it; but this word "Idaho" meant nothing. There was nothing in it.
>
> *Mr. Green:* The name of Idaho was put in at the instance of the delegate from the Territory.
>
> *Mr. Wilson:* He has changed his opinion.

By this time there had been so many changes of name that one member was found to be laboring under the delusion that the Senate was changing the name of what was informally known as Arizona. After he had been set right, the new amendment was agreed to.

A final hitch occurred when a California senator objected to what he considered the unwarranted appropriation of Colorado:

> *Mr. Gwin:* I will vote to reconsider because I have been cheated out of the name. . . . I think it is the handsomest name that could be given any Territory or State . . . I want to give that name to the Territory of Arizona.

His objection was not sustained, and on February 28, 1861, the much be-named territory was at last organized as Colorado.

Only two days later, two more territories were established. Dakota took the name of an Indian tribe, and raised no difficulty. The other, however, like Utah and Colorado, had begun unacceptably. The region had commonly been known by the name of a tribe as Washoe. This lacked dignity, and the Committee on Territories fell back upon the old tradition of an established local name. The Committee selected the chief mountain range, Sierra Nevada, and shortened it to Nevada.

Washoe remained in use, and Nevada met much local opposition, which came to a head in 1864 when the territory was assuming statehood. In the Constitutional Convention the secretary began by reading: "We, the people of the State of Nevada ..." A delegate moved to substitute Washoe. The local people knew, as Congress probably did not, that the Sierra Nevada lay almost entirely within California, where a town and county already were called Nevada. They felt also that "snowed-upon" had too much Arctic suggestion, and was far from accurate, their sage-brush country being chiefly notable for lack of either rain or snow. Some delegates preferred Humboldt. Esmeralda, a local mining-camp, entered the running. Sierra Plata, "mountain-silver," was put forward, and then Oro Plata, "gold-silver." Perhaps by this time the matter was approaching the ludicrous. The suggestion that the state should be named Bullion can hardly have been serious.

In the end, Nevada was sustained, and again Congress had given, not accepted, a name.

In 1850 New Mexico had been established with boundaries extending from Texas to California. It was further enlarged by the Gadsden Purchase in 1853. Miners soon began to enter the Purchase, and a new territory was proposed. In 1854 the first memorial was presented to Congress, and three names were suggested. Gadsonia was a classical adaptation of the name of the negotiator of the purchase. Pimeria, from the Pima tribe, was a name by which the Spaniards had known part of the region. Arizona was derived from the old mining district; Father Ortega had written it down a century earlier and it had been used occasionally. At the same time the old name had another revival in the formation of the Arizona Mining & Trading Company.

Two years later, another convention gathered in Tucson. One of its leading members was Mr. N. P. Cook who was active also in the Company. Curiously enough, the convention approved Arizona, and later in the year Mr. Cook, as delegate-elect to Congress, was urging that name. Arizona thus repeated the story of Indiana in which the name of a commercial enterprise was involved with that of the state.

Arizona was first declared a territory in 1861—by the Confederate States of America! A battalion of California volunteers, however, soon occupied the region for the Union. Rather strangely, the use of the name by the Confederates did not react to its prejudice, and Arizona was finally established by Congress in 1863. Actually the "little spring" was not in the territory at all, but several miles south of the boundary, in Mexico.

Idaho had failed only by the narrowest of margins to be applied to Colorado. Unlike most defeated candidates, it gained a second chance.

The name itself may have had two origins. The Kiowa-Apache name for the Comanche was Idahi, and since both of these tribes ranged in the Pike's Peak region, the miners may have thus learned the name. But the Comanche were a branch of the great Shoshonean people who also lived in the Snake River country; in their language Ee-dah-how was a greeting roughly equivalent to the English "Good morning!" One meaning which it certainly did not have was that which was most commonly given. Primitive Indians had no conception of precious stones. "Gem of the Mountains" was merely another dishonest translation, but it exerted a powerful fascination.

In 1860, when gold was discovered in the Shoshone country, Idaho was being bandied about in the newspapers as the probable name of a new state. Any such name was sure to be picked up and used, just as Oregon was spread about during the period of the boundary-dispute, and California was fastened upon eastern towns after '49. One of the new mining-camps was called Idaho, just as likely because the miners had read about it in the newspapers as because they knew the Shoshone language. In 1862 an Idaho County was formed.

The Committee on Territories, however, had its own plans, and early in 1863 Mr. James M. Ashley of Ohio (a man who was to leave his mark on the map) introduced a bill "for the territory of Montana." The House passed it, but by this time the Senate also had learned the fun of playing with names, and Montana met opposition:

> Mr. Wilson: I move to strike out the name of the Territory, and insert "Idaho." Montana is no name at all.
> Mr. Doolittle: I hope not. I hope there will be no amendment at all. Montana sounds just as well as Idaho.
> Mr. Wilson: It has no meaning. The other has.
> Mr. Doolittle: It has a meaning. It refers to the mountainous character of the country.

Momentarily defeated, Mr. Wilson later returned to the attack. "Gem of the Mountains" was again cited as the meaning, and this time the Senate passed an amendment. As Idaho, not Montana, the territory was referred back to the House. Mr. Ashley was reported as angry, and he was a man whose anger was not to be taken lightly. He moved not to concur in the Senate amendment. But the sponsors were chiefly interested in some kind of territorial organization, not in any particular name. The House concurred in spite of Mr. Ashley, and he was left with Montana on his hands.

James M. Ashley deserves commemoration as a namer. He was born in 1822, brought up religiously, and designed for the ministry. At sixteen he ran away from home. In knocking about the western states, he maintained his basic Puritanisms except for acquiring the incongruous habit of vivid profanity. "However," it is recorded, "when speaking in churches he tried hard to restrain himself." He was a born extremist—fearless, violent, and implacable. After being editor, lawyer, and merchant, he ran for Congress in 1858. It was a rough-and-tumble campaign. Someone threw a live goose at him during a speech. He knocked out a heckler. In the end, his florid oratory served him well, and he was elected.

He was appointed to the Committee on Territories, and served on it for ten years. During that time it organized, and was largely concerned with naming seven territories from which eight states were formed.

This almost unparalleled opportunity may have aroused Ashley. More likely, he had merely that interest in names which a man may or may not have—like a musical ear, or a taste for the novels of Henry James. Having little education, he was not concerned with linguistic or historical proprieties. He liked a name to be high-sounding and oratorical, and he also wished it to be at least superficially appropriate.

Ashley's influence upon naming may have been greater than can be known. He was a man of strong opinions and stronger speech, and in committee probably expressed himself fully upon Colorado, Nevada, Dakota, and Arizona. He may well have determined the choice of some of these names. As his seniority in the House increased, he came to have more influence. He stood out almost alone for Montana as against Idaho, but was defeated. He was no man to accept defeat.

A few months later, Ashley introduced another bill to form the Territory of Montana. He had carried the Committee again. The proposal now was to use the name for a new territory to be formed out of that vast region of Idaho lying east of the summit of the Rocky Mountains.

Montana might have been derived from either a Latin or a Spanish adjective meaning "mountainous." Its advocates could cite Livy's *loca montana,* and the authority of other classical writers. In 1858 a group of miners had located a town-site in the Pike's Peak gold-diggings. One of them was Josiah Hinman, a college graduate. He named the place Montana, which some of his partners (although presumably not Mr. Hinman) took to be "the feminine of mountain." The Kansas Legislature granted incorporation, but the town languished and died—except its name.

Governor Denver, the same for whom the city was named, apparently remembered Montana. As he told later, he suggested it in conversation with Stephen A. Douglas as the name of a territory. Douglas said that he was going to introduce a bill to organize some new territories, and was wondering what to name them. Denver suggested "Colorado," but Douglas took a map from his desk:

Douglas: I have that name selected for one down here [pointing to the map], but I want a name for this territory up here [pointing] in the mountains.
Denver: Why not call it Montana?
Douglas: What does the word mean?
Denver: It is a Spanish word, and means a mountainous country.

Douglas stepped into the hall, and called to his wife, who was a good linguist. She came to the head of the stairs.

Douglas: My dear, do you know any such word as Montana?
Mrs. Douglas: Why, yes, it is a Spanish word and means a mountainous country.
Douglas: [returning to the library] Denver, that is all right. I will just call it Montana.

Mr. Douglas never sponsored a bill for a territory of Montana, but from him to the Committee on Territories, and so to Mr. Ashley, were easy steps. However he may have learned the name, Mr. Ashley made it his own, and led a vigorous fight for it, both in '63 and in '64.

On March 17, 1864, a memorial from the citizens of Idaho was read in the House, requesting that their eastern portion should be separated, and bear the name Jefferson Territory. The next day, the name Montana was debated at length:

Mr. Cox: Before the question is taken on the passage of the bill, I desire to say that I do not like the proposed name of this new Territory. I do not know whether it is Spanish, French or English.
Mr. Ashley: It is a Spanish word, meaning mountainous.
Mr. Cox: I know. But I ask the gentleman whether he cannot give it

a name that will be a little more significant. Cannot he give it an Indian name?

Mr. Washburn: I suggest that the gentleman from Ohio propose that it be called Abyssinia. [Laughter]

This last was to ridicule both Montana and Ashley, who as a radical Republican was considered too friendly to the Negroes.

Mr. Cox then declared that the people wished for Jefferson Territory. The Republicans, however, had no desire to honor the father of the Democratic Party, and Ashley merely replied, "Oh, well, we are opposed to that."

Mr. Cox next, with questionable taste, proposed facetiously that the territory be called Douglas. The vote, he thought, could be unanimous. The Democrats could take it as honoring their recent chief, and the Republicans could vote it because of Frederick Douglass, the famous Negro leader.

Ashley held his ground, and in the end the House accepted the name as approved by the Committee. Two weeks later in the Senate, debate blazed up. The learned senator from Massachusetts was a good friend of Ashley's but he nevertheless took the floor:

Mr. Sumner: The name of this new Territory—Montana—strikes me as very peculiar. I wish to ask the chairman of the committee what has suggested that name. It seems to me it must have been borrowed from some novel or other. I do not know how it originated.

Mr. Wade: I cannot tell anything about that. I do not know but that it may have been borrowed from a novel. I would rather borrow from the Indians, if I could find any proper Indian name.

Mr. Sumner: I was going to suggest that in giving a name to this Territory ... I would rather take the name from the soil, a good Indian name.

Mr. Wade: Suggest one and I will agree to it.

Mr. Sumner: I am not familiar enough with the country to do so.

Mr. Howard: I was equally puzzled when I saw the name in the bill. . . . I was obliged to turn to my old Latin dictionary. . . .

It is a very classical word, pure Latin. It means a mountainous region, a mountainous country.

Mr. Wade: Then the name is well adapted to the Territory.

Mr. Howard: You will find that it is used by Livy and some of the other Latin historians, which is no small praise.

Mr. Wade: I do not care anything about the name. If there was none in Latin or in Indian I suppose we have a right to make a name; certainly just as good a right to make it as anybody else. It is a good name enough.

Mr. Wade thus stood upon the authority of Congress, and the Senate approved. Some still pointed out that since the larger part of the area lay in the Great Plains, the names Idaho and Montana might well be reversed. But Mr. Ashley at least had had his way in getting Montana on the map somewhere.

The origin of another name, though not its final approval, occurred in 1866.

During the Civil War the Five Civilized Tribes had made the political error of allying themselves with the losing side. Their warriors had fought along with the Confederate troops in the West. Defeat brought retribution; a delegation of chiefs was summoned to Washington, and forced to cede some of the tribal lands to the federal government. Among the delegates was the Reverend Allen Wright, a well-educated man, chief of the Choctaws. Apparently he had been considering the question of a name.

When the draft of the new treaty was being prepared, the Commissioner of Indian Affairs asked the delegates, "What would you call your territory?"

Without hesitation, Mr. Wright replied: "Oklahoma."

The name which he had coined was a simple one in the Choctaw language——*okla,* "people," and *homa,* "red."

Among the mountains of northeastern Pennsylvania lay a beautiful valley. The Delaware Indians called it "at the big flats," a name which in its most extended form would have been Mecheweami-ing. The Indians themselves clipped and contracted this until it became something like M'chweaming. The white settlers reduced it to Wyoming.

In 1778 the name became one of bad omen when a band of Tories and Iroquois first defeated the settlers, and then massacred three hundred, including women and children. In 1809 Thomas Campbell published his romantic and sentimental poem of the incident, *Gertrude of Wyoming*. (Not knowing the proper pronunciation, he accented the word on the first syllable.) The poem became popular, and Wyoming prospered along with the other names from romantic poems and novels. It became the name of counties in Pennsylvania, New York, and West Virginia. By 1867 there were ten Wyoming post-offices, ranging from Rhode Island to Kansas and Nebraska. In 1868, when a new territory was to be organized, Mr. Ashley proposed Wyoming, and the Committee on Territories used that name in the bill.

In both House and Senate argument flared up. The connection with Pennsylvania and with Campbell's poem was well known. Though the Congressmen had usually no knowledge of Indian languages, they still could recognize the blatant incongruity of shifting a local eastern name to a far-western territory.

> *Mr. Schenck:* I ask my colleague why, in the name of common sense, this Territory is to be called Wyoming. What is the association or connection of that name with this particular district of country?
>
> *Mr. Ashley:* I will say ... that I selected that name because it designated better than any other name which I could find the character of the Territory, Wyoming, meaning in Indian language "large plains." I thought it more appropriate than Cheyenne, Shoshonee, or the name of any Indian tribe, mountain, or river within the limits of the Territory.

In the Senate the Committee on Territories recommended the change of Wyoming to Lincoln. Mr. Sumner, who had opposed the President in life, objected to that name, returning to the old tradition when he declared that the names of states should come from the region itself. Various Indian tribes were suggested—

Cheyenne, Shoshone, Pawnee, Sioux. Someone proposed Platte, from the river.

The senators were at much disadvantage, for most of them knew little about western geography. Cheyenne received most attention. Objection was raised that it meant "snakes." Another senator replied that the meaning was unimportant, and cited that Chicago was getting along well with a name "derived from an animal so odious as not to be named in the Senate Chamber, or scarcely anywhere else."

> *Mr. Morton:* It occurs to me that this word is not a very handsome
> one. There are some words in the language which are never
> dignified and cannot be made so . . . You cannot make a very
> handsome word of Chien.
> *Mr. Sherman:* "Cheyenne." [Pronouncing it as if spelled Shay-en.]

But Cheyenne was finally quashed when a senator pointed out its possible derivation from the French *chienne,* or at least its resemblance to that word, meaning, as he politely put it, "female dog."

The debate dragged out through the longest discussion of names ever to occur on the floor of Congress. The chief argument against Wyoming was its rootless artificiality. In its favor was its literal meaning, although the region was also largely mountainous. But no good substitute could be suggested, and at the same time the beauty of the name and its poetic associations appealed to many. Senator Cameron of Pennsylvania arose, and graciously said that his state would be happy to supply a name for a new one, where doubtless many Pennsylvanians had already settled. In the end, Mr. Ashley had his way again.

After 1868, Dakota was still to be divided, and Oklahoma to be fixed; New Mexico would still raise argument. Nevertheless, the process of state-naming may be said to end with the establishment of Wyoming Territory on July 25, 1868. It had begun with the naming of Florida by Ponce de León on April 2, 1513.

The United States is still a young country, and only a rash

prophet would venture to predict that the number of states, even within the continental limits, will remain perpetually at forty-eight. But sentimental attachment is such that no section of a state will probably be willing to surrender its name. The names thus serve as an important political balance-wheel.

The original colonies were named chiefly under royal and aristocratic influence. From the time of the Constitution for more than sixty years, the established and locally desired name was preferred. After Utah and Washington, Congress determined the names.

Yet, from beginning to end, much the same mental processes dominated the namers. The foundation of a colony or a state was a weighty business, and its naming was taken seriously. The senators and representatives of the Civil War period were much like other Americans, of that time and earlier. Whatever association first suggested a name, it must then meet certain tests. Was it dignified? Was it appropriate in meaning? And in application? More often than would be expected among a people still involved with the struggles of the frontier, yet another question was asked —was it beautiful? In the final discussion, that justification bolstered Wyoming:

Mr. Sumner: What suggested this name for this Territory?
Mr. Doolittle: It was suggested by General Ashley.
Mr. Sumner: But what suggested it to General Ashley?
Mr. Doolittle: Because it is a beautiful name.

The answer is significant. Like many other early Americans, the hard-swearing, hard-fisted representative from Ohio had also a sense of beauty, and loved the poetry of names.

Naturally, the conception of beauty changed with the times. A good royalist found it in the names of the royal family; a classicist admired those which resembled Greek or Latin; a romanticist saw beauty in the strange names of the Indians.

Even so, a certain similarity is again apparent. The names were either given or approved by men in public life, and such men were used to addressing a meeting. Even in a frontier convention, the delegates must have tried each name in their mouths to discover how well it would resound from the platform. As a Congressman stated of Wyoming:

It is not only euphonious, but a word adapted to the use we are able to make, in speaking the English language, of our vocal powers.

As orators, they liked long and rolling polysyllables. Although ordinary English delights in one-syllable words, Maine is the only such state. Six of the names are of two syllables. Twenty-four have three syllables, fifteen have four, and two have five. Twenty-eight of the names fit into the pattern most beloved of the orator—a long word accented on the next-to-last syllable, such as Montana or Minnesota.

Chapter XXXVI ❨ Of the last flourishing

By 1868 not only had all the states been named, but also all the important natural features, and nearly all the great cities. Nevertheless, in the next two decades, the settlement of the country proceeded more rapidly than ever, and probably more names were given than in any earlier period of equal length.

The chief regions of development were those of the Great Plains and Rocky Mountains which already had a thin scattering of names from the mountain men, the explorers, and the covered-wagon emigrants. After them followed the miners and cowboys. In the Southwest the newcomers lived in contact with the old

Spanish-speaking settlers, and took over many names. From the Mexican *tanque* they learned to say *tank* for a rock-pool where rain-water collected. *Arroyo* in Spain meant a running brook, but in the Southwest it was usually a dry bed for most of the year. They also took over *ciénaga,* "swamp," often changing it to *seneca.*

As in California, the Spanish names suffered little change. The sounds were easy, and most of the Americans picked up enough Spanish to keep the words straight. Cíbola, a Mexican name for the buffalo, shifted to Sea Willow in ordinary speech, but kept its original spelling upon the official maps of Texas. Such a name was almost certain to return to the Spanish pronunciation eventually, like Miguel Creek in California, which passed through a stage of being McGill. Among the very rare folk-etymologies from Spanish the most notable was not western at all, but originated from Cayo Hueso, "Bone Key," in the Gulf of Mexico; from this came Key West.

The most publicized folk-etymology in the country was originally Spanish, but passed through a French translation. In 1594 a band of Spaniards had pressed north on the ever-recurrent search for wealthy cities to be plundered. They quarreled among themselves; one leader killed another; the priest refused to go farther in such company. Some of them pressed on, and disappeared completely. Years later, their bones were found near a river. They had died unshriven, with blood on their hands. Their chances for salvation were considered very dim, and the place took the name El Río de las Animas Perdidas en Purgatorio, "River of the Souls Lost in Purgatory." French trappers rendered this as Purgatoire, and American cowboys made the French into Picketwire. Locally the stream may still be called either Las Animas, Purgatoire, or Picketwire.

Better than those left over from French and Spanish, certain often-repeated folk-names preserve the flavor of the early West. The common Lost River and Lost Lake arose in various ways. East or west, any stream which sank beneath the surface took that name. An isolated lake among mountains was sometimes reported, and then could not be found again. It became known as Lost

Lake, and even when discovered might keep the name. Another time, some people when themselves lost might stumble upon a lake and illogically give it that name, on the principle, "Indian not lost—wigwam lost." Occasionally perhaps some isolated valley or lake might be named fancifully, as if it were a lost sheep or a lost soul.

The Devil's western holdings became varied and numerous. However profane he might be in speech, the American did not apply the name of God to places. When he wished to give any idea of the supernatural, he resorted to the Devil. If the Sioux *wacan* indicated that a body of water was spirit-haunted, the American usually translated it as Devil's Lake. When he saw a mass of columnar basalt so gigantic as to suggest more than human power, it became The Devil's Postpile. More often, the idea of the torture of hell was involved, half-humorously. A dike of hard rock projecting from a mountainside often presented a regular curve suggesting a gigantic slide. But its jagged top also suggested an extremely painful process. So it became The Devil's Slide with the implication that his imps would put poor lost souls to sliding down it.

Such names had been fairly common in the East, but the more spectacular western scenery suggested them more frequently. Probably every mountain state has at least one Devil's Canyon. The usage survived into recent enough times to provide the Devil's Golf-Course. Hell was often used with much the same ideas as Devil. With the aid of alliteration, any bad stretch of trail or river became Hell's Half-Mile, and any particularly desolate area was Hell's Half-Acre.

Deadman Creek also became conventional, if the body of an unknown white man was found by a stream. If the remains were of an Indian, the name would be Indian or Dead Indian Creek, because, the frontiersman believed, "Injuns ain't people." If the man could be identified, the stream would more likely be known by his own name. If the death was of such ancient time as hardly to suggest a person, the name might be Skull Creek or Skeleton Creek. If the body was decently interred and the spot marked,

Grave Creek would probably result. If foul play was evident, it might be Murder Creek. But, by and large, when winter blizzard or unknown accident had done its work, Deadman Creek told the story.

In many regions, mines were extremely numerous. A directory for three Idaho counties in 1865 listed about 700, all named. A mine often took the name of its owner or its location, but many also were distinctive. Miners were notoriously sentimental, and scattered such names as Sweet Betsy, Little Maud, and Gentle Annie. In the Black Hills, however, a dozen claims are said to have been named Emma, for a popular prostitute. Sentiment also approved naming the claim for the old home-town or state. Among the most famous of later California mines were the Idaho-Maryland, and the Lone Star. Miners were also professionally optimistic and superstitious, and many of them had an eye for advertising. Any or all of these motives produced Sheba, Branch Mint, Golconda, Bonanza, Golden Reward, King of the West, Sultan, Empire, and King Solomon. Pure superstition figured in the Cloverleaf and the Horseshoe. Names like Hoodoo and White Elephant may have tried to placate the gods of chance by an unpropitious name. Any little incident of the discovery could be taken as a good omen. According to tradition, the famous Searchlight, still the name of a Nevada town, arose because the prospectors noticed the name on a box of matches.

A chance word might be enough. In 1878 the Schieffelin brothers, Ed and Al, set out to prospect in the Apache country. Someone advised Al not to go—"all you will find will be your tombstone." He named his mine The Tombstone, and it started one of the most famous of mining towns. When they were still prospecting, Ed left camp, and on his return, Al told him, "I've struck it rich this time." "You're a lucky cuss!" said Ed, and so came The Lucky Cuss Mine.

Another famous post-office in Arizona originated as a mine. The day of discovery was December 25th—"It was Christmas day in the morning; so we filled our stockings and named the place

[317]

Christmas in honor of the day." (Along with Santa Claus, Indiana, also named in the holiday season, the Arizona office does its principal business in December.)

The tradition of naming ranches went back to Spanish grants, which supplied saints' names for many California towns and villages, and in one case became the famous Santa Anita race-track. Americans, however, were often content to let the owner's name serve. The town of Goodnight in Texas, an amusing name to non-Texans, sprang merely from the ranch owned by Charles Goodnight. The brand, however, often became more famous than the owner, especially if ownership changed or one man owned two ranches. From brands arose a whole series of western towns— Ucross, Anchor, Twodot, Kaycee, Cee Vee, Circle Back. (Some letter-names also began with initials carved in trees, as with J.O. Pass in the Sierra Nevada.)

Mines and ranches took names by local process, without benefit of much tradition and without need of approval by central authority. Counties and incorporated towns followed the older fashions. The unparalleled rapidity of development had a bad effect upon names—there were simply not enough to go around. The difficulty showed up most of all in counties. The Civil War, indeed, had supplied a fine new crop of heroes, and most of the western states turned up with counties named Lincoln and Grant. Since the western men had fought mostly with the western armies, those corps-commanders were more often commemorated. Nebraska named no county after McClellan, Meade, Hancock, or Burnside, but chose Grant, Sherman, Sheridan, Hooker, Howard, Logan, McPherson, and Thomas. Such older heroes as Washington and Jefferson still remained popular. Even Knox and Wayne achieved Nebraska counties, but probably more because some immigrants had come from eastern counties of those names than because those Revolutionary generals were still active heroes.

Union veterans, rather than Confederate, settled the West, and so the heroes of the Lost Cause gained less recognition. Texas counties enshrined Jeff Davis, Stephens, Lee, Stonewall, and Hood, along with some less-known local commanders. Arkansas, either broad-minded or careless, maintained Lee and Cleburne along with Lincoln, Logan, and Grant, the last having Sheridan as its county-seat.

Unfortunately, a great many counties had to be formed. Contemporary presidents and national leaders took over some, but many came to bear the names of legislators, so undistinguished as hardly to be identified at all in later years. A popular couplet truly declared:

> Many a legislator's bid to fame
> Is a county born to bear his name.

Advertising was a commoner motive with town names—Garden City, Fairview, Centropolis, even Eden and Paradise. Hopes of bonanza farming inspired the often-repeated Wheatland. In general, however, advertising took a more subtle form.

Often it lay behind a transferred name. Pittsburgh had long since lost its connection with William Pitt, in the popular mind, and had assumed new connotations. Towns named Pittsburgh in western states were founded in the hope of becoming centers of steel-manufacturing or coal-mining. In Alabama the same process was at work at the establishment of Birmingham by a land-company in 1871; the founders had no sentimental attachment to an old English home, but wished to publicize their venture as a city of iron and coal.

The strength of the advertising spirit showed strikingly in the separation of the Dakotas. The name for the territory dated only from 1861, but a few years later the inhabitants already felt much sentimental attachment to it. Possibly of more weight, a certain amount of money had been spent in advertising Dakota lands to the world. When the admission of two states instead of one seemed likely, each section decided that it would be Dakota, and began recommending excellent names for the other. The southern area pre-empted the name in conventions of 1883 and

1885, but had to disgorge because of northern protests. The Committee on Territories reported:

The name Dakota is as dear to the people of North as of South Dakota. The residents of the northern section justly claim to have given that name to one of the principal productions of the Territory, and to have made "Dakota Wheat" famous throughout the world.

The name Lincoln went begging, and Senator Butler of South Carolina, ex-Confederate Major General, rose to cry his wonder:

Has it come to this, in a Territory claimed to be filled by loyal citizens, Union soldiers, that the name of Lincoln is distasteful to them? ... If I thought so, I should blush for shame.

A Solomon was needed for judgment, but none appeared. The final result was about as satisfactory as if the famous baby had been split in half between its two claimants. Neither division actually got the name, but each shared it with the other, disfigured forever by an awkward North or South.

Sentiment and advertising were in fact often allied. In early New England, an English rather than an Indian name inspired confidence, besides touching the heartstrings. The same was true all through the West, as the eastern names migrated. Actually, much of the migration of names was from west to east. California, earliest of the mining regions, was the mother of Nevada and the other mountain states, much as Virginia was the mother of Kentucky. Even Oregon has its Ukiah, Chico, Susanville, and Cloverdale, all immigrants across its southern border. Many western names went still farther east. Modoc in South Carolina was a back-wash of the Modoc War fought in the desolate lava-beds of northeastern California in '72 and '73.

Foreign names, especially German and Scandinavian, sometimes came with the immigrants, and sometimes were planted to inspire confidence and attract immigrants. Bismarck, honoring the Iron Chancellor, became a state capital.

The naming of a town for a person might be good advertising. Who could doubt the honesty of land-titles at Lincoln? In a period when business practices were shot through with fraud, Washington and Jefferson could do nothing to protect their good names. Living men, however, sometimes regarded such use with suspicion, and a type developed which might be termed "the reluctant hero." John Kirkpatrick helped found a Missouri town in 1878, but lost confidence: "It will never amount to anything, and I don't want it named for me." Being a wheat-town, it became Odessa, and gave the lie to Mr. Kirkpatrick by developing prosperously. In 1891 Mr. Shelby used even stronger language of the Montana site which had chosen to "honor" him: "That mudhole, God-forsaken place . . . will never amount to a damn!" Again the town belied the prophecy.

Generally, however, the perpetuation of a man's name in a county or town was received as a compliment. In 1887 a community of Quakers in California wished to honor Whittier. The old poet was much moved. Close to death, childless, he felt that he was acquiring a kind of posterity. He wrote a gracious poem, bequeathing his name:

> The Love I felt, the Good I meant,
> I leave thee with my Name.

The railroad-station and the post-office carried on with western naming. The mine and the ranch had been wholly local, but the railroad company and the Post-Office Department worked from the outside, and to some extent imposed their wills. The western railroads had a much greater influence upon naming for the reason that they were built across undeveloped country. Towns, even counties, took their names from railroad-stations.

The first transcontinental, finished in 1869, was built by the Union Pacific from the east and the Central Pacific from the west. Charles Crocker, one of the "Big Four," had immediate charge of the construction of the Central Pacific, and determined the names of stations. His preference was for the locally established names of the old emigrant trail, and the towns between

Sacramento and Ogden still ring solidly because of his good sense —as with Emigrant Gap, Battle Mountain, and Wells. Early in 1868 his rail-head came to Truckee Meadows, but he had already used Truckee for a station higher up on the river. The new station would obviously be important, for it was the junction point for the Comstock Lode silver mines. The name Argenta was suggested, but Crocker had no liking for flossy names. Some veterans of the Mexican War put forward one of their comrades, who had risen to be a general in the Civil War, and fallen at the battle of South Mountain. Crocker liked the idea, and called the station Reno.

General Grenville M. Dodge was probably responsible for most of the original Union Pacific stations. His line also preserved the older names—North Platte, Cheyenne, Laramie, Rock Springs, and Green River. Evanston, however, took its name from a railroad surveyor. With one name, Dodge paid a debt to friendship and patriotism. In 1867 he camped at a spring near the line of survey in company with General John A. Rawlins. During the war they had called Rawlins "Grant's conscience," and some men said that next to Lincoln himself he had helped save the Union. As he camped with Dodge, he was already coughing away his life with tuberculosis contracted in the hardships of four years' campaigning. With that touch of poetry which ran through his life, he happened to say that if anything were ever named for him, he wished it would be a spring. When the railroad was built, Rawlins was close to death. Dodge called for him the station nearest the spring. It became only a grimy little railroad town, but Rawlins was a charcoal-burner himself once, and perhaps would not mind.

Later railroad builders largely rejected the tradition of Crocker and Dodge, perhaps because their lines crossed country even more thinly supplied with local names. With most companies, some particular official attended to the naming, and some of these men added as many as a hundred names to the map. Some stations began merely as work-a-day railroad terms. Thus Helper in Utah, now a thriving town, was at first merely the place where an extra locomotive was added to help the train up a grade.

Whatever official was doing the naming naturally thought of his friends in the company, or perhaps complimented his superiors. Fargo, largest city in North Dakota, was called for a director of the Northern Pacific. Billings, third city of Montana, was for a president of the same road. A graceful compliment to a large stockholder sometimes seemed polite or politic. Williston, North Dakota, took its name from S. Willis James who held a large block in the Great Northern. Compliments to whole groups of stockholders had interesting results. Because many Englishmen had invested in the Great Northern, a string of stations along the line became Leeds, York, Rugby, Tunbridge, and Berwick. When the Santa Fe built southward across Oklahoma, Philadelphia capitalists had largely supplied the funds. As a result, seven Oklahoma stations echoed names on the Pennsylvania main-line west of Philadelphia—Wayne, Paoli, Wynnewood, Berwyn, Overbrook, Ardmore, and Marietta.

The official entrusted with naming tended to develop a kind of philosophy on the subject. One of these was H. R. Williams, vice-president of the Milwaukee. Any name, however first suggested, had to pass his severe scrutiny. As he wrote:

There are a great many things to be considered in the naming of a station. I will mention some of them as follows:

1. A name that is reasonably short.
2. A name easily spelled.
3. A name that in the Morse alphabet will not sound like any other name.
4. A name that when written in train orders will not look like that of any other station in that vicinity.
5. A name that will not sound like any other name when being called out in checking baggage or freight.
6. A name that will be satisfactory to the Post Office department . . .
7. A pleasant-sounding name.

Such a severe standard of rejection naturally led to the use of many unusual and bizarre names.

Mr. Williams named thirty-two stations in the state of Washington alone, and offered brief comments upon their strikingly different sources:

Boylston—after a Massachusetts town.
Beverly—after a Massachusetts town.
Smyrna—foreign.
Corfu—foreign.
Othello—after the play.
Warden—after a heavy stockholder.
Roxboro—after a Massachusetts town.
Ralston—after a health food.
Revere—after Paul Revere's ride.
Malden—after a Massachusetts town.
Kittitas—after the Kittitas Valley.
Marcellus—named after some person in the East. I cannot now recall who it was.
Marengo—after the Battle of Marengo.
Paxton—a chance selection.
Servia—after the foreign country.
Taunton—after a Massachusetts town.
Vassar—after the college.
Jericho—after the Palestine Jericho.
Tiflis—after the Trans-Caucasian town, some of the farmers having come from that country.
Cheviot—a chance selection.
Horlick—after the malted milk.
Laconia—on account of its location at the summit—was named after what I thought was Laconia in Switzerland located high up among the Alps, but in looking over the Swiss map this morning I am unable to find a place of that name there.
Lavender—a chance selection.
Renslow—a chance selection.
Rye—after Rye, New York.
Whittier—after the poet.
Kenova—a chance selection.
Lavista—for the fine view, it being located high among the rocks at the south end of Rock Lake.
Palisade—because it is located on a formation similar to the renowned Palisades of the Hudson.

Pandora—after Pandora's Box.
Pine City—a local name.
Seabury—after a Maine town.

The workings of such standards of rejection can be seen in many changes and alterations of station-names. A Dutch capitalist called DeGeoijen invested largely in the Kansas City Southern, and christened several places. He gave his own name to one of them, but this was soon simplified in spelling to De Queen. (Inevitably, this led to a town paper called *De Queen Bee*.) The railroad maintained the good Dutch names Amsterdam, De Ridder, Nederland, and a few others; but Wilhelmina was shortened to Mena.

Other shortenings were numerous. On the Southern Pacific, Dutch Corners became Ducor. An early Texas pioneer had given his name to Chappell Hill; the Houston & Texas Central shortened and familiarized it into another Chapel Hill.

Morrow on the Burlington in Kansas caused much confusion. When a traveler said "I want a ticket to Morrow," almost any agent was likely to reply, "Then, come back tomorrow!" At the expense of lengthening, Morrowville solved the difficulty.

Confusion of names could be serious also. On the "Katy" in Texas one station was Primm and the second down the line was Plum. After a while, the similarity caused a confusion of orders, and a very disastrous wreck. Primm promptly took the name of its postmaster, and became Kirtley.

Like the railroads, and for much the same reason, the Post-Office Department exercised a stronger influence in the West than in the East. Before 1800 post-offices were comparatively rare, and many well-established villages got along without one. Even throughout the next half-century, settlement tended to keep ahead of the post-office. Only after the Civil War did the actual naming of a post-office rather than of a settlement become common.

Argument might have been raised about whether certain western post-offices were really places. The office of Burnt Ranch,

Oregon, moved about following the homes of various postmasters over a range of several miles. The office of Wildman, Oklahoma, was in a kind of cook-wagon, and was hauled about through the Wichita Mountains at the convenience of the shifting population of the region.

Such examples may have led people to realize that a post-office was not exactly a town, and so might be differently named. Certainly, like the names of mining-camps, those given primarily to post-offices displayed more whim than those given to towns.

The position of the Post-Office Department was curious. As in any bureaucracy, there was a love of system and order, much of which could be practically justified. On the other hand, the Department itself was politically controlled in a notorious fashion. As a bureaucrat, a Department official might not like the requested name for a new office in Idaho or Kansas, but if he objected, the unknown applicant might turn out to be a local politician who would write to his congressman.

Doubtless any Assistant Postmaster General would have been glad to apply to post-offices most of Mr. Williams's seven criteria for stations. But the Department did not have such absolute control. Nevertheless it exercised a certain power of veto, and also managed to supply from Washington a fair number of names.

Upon one point the Department was adamant. Unutterable confusion had resulted in earlier times from the duplication of names within the same state, and such a condition must not occur again. Paragraph ♯ 17 in *Special Instructions to Postmasters* read:

Before approving applications for the establishment of new post-offices, postmasters should consult the Postal Guide and see that the name selected has not already been given to a post-office or county in the same or an adjoining state.

There was apparently no other unalterable rule. Doubtless the Department would not have approved a profane or obscene name, or one which in the heat of the Civil War would have been thought treasonable. When a choice was possible, the Department agreed with the railroads in preferring names which were short, simple, and euphonious.

Often, however, applications merely requested that the Department should supply a name. This was the more likely to occur when the first name or names had been vetoed because of duplication. When the local people thus threw in the sponge, some one of the higher clerks of the Department had his opportunity. One of these for many years was a certain Captain Tuley, a veteran of the Civil War. He made these selections, "sometimes honoring a fellow-clerk in the office . . ." He was also reported to have named post-offices "for practically all of the kids and babies in his immediate neighborhood." Being aware of the practical difficulties of the service, Captain Tuley and others doubtless preferred short names. In the newer states the large number of very short names of girls may preserve the memory of those "kids and babies." Oklahoma alone has Amy, Eva, May, Ora, Eda, Fay, Ida, Iva, Ola, and Ona.

An anecdote demonstrates the rootlessness of such names. A clerk who gave many of them was T. Martin Scranage. In the course of time another clerk complimented him by establishing the post-office of Scranage, Alabama. The name was rare, and Mr. Scranage had a niece interested in genealogy. She made a trip to Alabama to find what branch of the family had settled there. Naturally she found no answer until she went to Washington and consulted her uncle.

Seen from the local point of view, the naming of post-offices assumes a quality of folk-lore, in that the same type of story turns up in various regions.

The commonest is the tale of the accidental name. The scene is usually a country-store where the store-keeper with a crony or two sits cogitating over the application. He must select a name. He has never named anything in his life, and he is handicapped by a limited vocabulary. Every apt name which occurs to him, like Lincoln or Columbia, turns out to be already used "in the same or an adjoining state." He chews the pencil. Thereupon a name suddenly appears before him. His eye perhaps falls upon the stove.

He focuses upon its name in raised letters of cast-iron, and Clio (California) is born. Or he sees a can of sardines upon the shelf, and the name is Lamoine (Washington). Sardines may shift to baking-powder, and the result is Bebe (Texas). Or, again in Texas a woman comes in to ask for a yard of cloth, and the post-office becomes Yard. Texas offers still a third variant, when the name is supplied by a missent letter from Tennessee, and the result is another Memphis.

Of slightly differing type is the "Why Not . . ." story. A man eating peanuts remarks, "Why not call it Peanut?" And Peanut (California) it is. This story passes into the second degree. "Why not . . . ?" has been offered so many times that at last it becomes "Why not call it 'Why Not'?" There was once a Why Not in North Carolina, and is still a Wynot in Nebraska.

The story of the altered spelling seems peculiarly Texan. "We wanted Neches, but there was a Neches already; so we spelled it Weches." The same process, tradition holds, produced Voca from Avoca, and Tascosa from Atascosa.

Another might be called the tale of final desperation. Washington turned down our names four times; then someone said: "What is the matter with calling it 'Likely'? It is not likely there will be another town in the state of that name. Likely we will get it and likely not." So it is Likely (California). Texans, as usual, had trouble on account of the large number of offices in their state. When Greenville was rejected because there was another one too near, the inevitable someone remarked: "Send in Moscow; that is far enough away so there will be no objections."

There is also the story of "no significance whatever." In Texas, Art sprang neither from devotion to the creative life nor from any Arthur; it was chosen merely for brevity. When Mr. Otis Brown, a methodical Texan, was to select a name, he read through the railroad-guide and picked Irving, for the simple reason that he liked the name. Mr. Charles Mullan of Iowa leafed through the Post-Office Directory, and decided that Waterloo had "the right ring to it." A Missouri tale is of a newly appointed postmaster who turned to a map of South America, put his finger blindly upon it, and thus got Callao.

An ever-recurrent story is—The Post-Office Department named this place; we didn't want the name, but they made us take it. Though the Department flatly denies any such tyranny, the story flourishes. It arose probably when a name was rejected because of duplication and another name given by request. After a few years local tradition could easily shift. Or a local postmaster may have suggested or accepted a change of name; finding it unpopular, he would then blame it on Washington. The frequency of the story suggests, however, that now and then some clerk, humorous-minded or officious, may have perpetrated some petty tyranny never recognized by the Department.

The queer name of Difficult in Tennessee is said to have arisen because Washington rejected the first name as too difficult. Perhaps the letter read: "The name of your post-office is difficult . . ." and the local namers took it as a suggestion.

Stories of names arising from clerical errors, illegible penmanship, and bad spelling, are many and credible. Tolo (Oregon) attempted to reproduce Yolo (California). Darrington (Washington) was supposed to be Barrington. As usual Texas supplies a whole list—Bogata for Bogota, Algerita for Agarita, Divot for Pivot, Hillister for Hollister, and Plaska for Pulaski. The most interesting conclusion from these many "mistake names" is that people cared very little about a mere post-office. A similar mistake made with a town would have been almost certainly corrected at once.

In contrast to the oppressed Indian, the oppressed African left little mark upon the map. Pinder Town in South Carolina preserved the Kongo *mpinda,* "peanut," but white men probably did the naming after the word had become current in local speech. Doubtless many hundreds of small streams and swamps were named by Negroes, but their namings cannot be distinguished.

An occasional place preserves some memory of before the War.

Meeting Street in South Carolina is said to have been a spot where slaves from neighboring plantations made rendezvous on the occasions when they were allowed a few hours of freedom. The term *quarter,* as in Granny's Quarter Creek, may also be a relic of slavery.

After the War, the emancipated people commemorated their liberty in a few names like Lincolnville and Freedman's Village. Booker Tee in Oklahoma celebrated one of their leaders, who was also honored by Mt. Booker in the Cascades. Nicodemus in Kansas was named for a legendary slave and hero of songs. Iconium in Oklahoma originated when a colored preacher happened upon the name in his Bible—but many whites gave names in the same manner.

Unfortunately the rich imagination and verbal luxuriance of the race had free play only in the informal names of its own districts. Catfish Alley in Charleston became the most famous, but even the small city of Monroe, Louisiana, was enriched with Congo Street, Adam and Eve Alley, Solomon Alley, Elysian Fields, and Concrete Quarters.

Many Indian names are locally "explained" as being Negro dialect. Pocotaligo, originally a town of the Yamasee Indians, is thus said to be the advice for getting rid of a certain pest: "Poke 'e tail, 'e go!"

In the years following the Civil War a horrible malady called "good taste" began to rage throughout the United States. It was the disease of people who were basically unsure of themselves. Those suffering from it became artistically timid, insipid, and sterile.

In naming, which is a kind of art, the stricken people preferred conventional terms of pale elegance. They rejected the honest names of earlier times, and rejected also the vigorous names of the great industrial age in which they lived. Their namings tended to be effeminate, snobbish, Anglophile, and full of liquid sounds.

An earlier generation had at least been positive, and even creative, by introducing Dale and Glen. In the seventies and eighties such names were already stale, but they were more fashionable than ever.

Good taste feared most of all any suggestion of vulgarity. Under vulgarity could be included not only obscenity, but even any idea of earning a living, and at times almost any suggestion of reality. Many old names were therefore wiped out and replaced, so that people of good taste could live there. Long Island suffered particularly. Cow Neck disappeared along with Cow Harbor, Drown Meadow, Old Man's, Oysterponds, Rum Point, and Musketo Cove. Hungry Harbor became Brookfield.

The West was as bad as the East except that fewer people of good taste as yet inhabited it. Nevertheless a California balladist sang:

> The first place that I got into is now
> called Placerville,
> In them days it was Hangtown, but they thought
> that ungenteel.

In California also, someone shying at the sexuality of Bull named Man Cow Rock. In Illinois the Rev. J. L. Hawkins planted Bosky Dell:

Consulting my dictionary, one day, I met with the word *bosky,* designated as obsolete, a synonym for brushy. I was pleased with it, and not long afterward, in the course of a sermon . . . I used the words Bosky Dell. A gentleman and lady of literary taste and culture . . . called my attention to it, expressing themselves pleased with the description, and especially with the poetic beauty of the term Bosky Dell.

When a town was being laid soon afterward, the founder was persuaded to use the name.

Good taste might have gone much further than it did in displacing the old names, if it had not been inherently timid, and especially sensitive to laughter. In the vicinity of New York a kind of test-case arose at Dobbs Ferry. This old and genuine name would probably have yielded to some romantic inanity, except for a vigorous pen. Mr. William Allen Butler, being a successful New York lawyer, was one of the aristocracy and could afford to defy fashion; he was also a master of light satiric verse. Over Dobbs Ferry he lamented ironically:

> But ah! the deep disgrace is
> This loveliest of places
> A vulgar name should blight.

A lawyer himself, Mr. Butler recognized the economic motive:

> They say "Dobb's" aint melodious,
> It's "horrid," "vulgar," "odious" . . .
> But Dobb's especial vice is
> That he keeps down the prices. . . .
> A name so unattractive
> Makes villa-sites inactive.

Then he launched a telling salvo against

> all speculators
> And ancient-landmark traitors,
> Who all along this shore
> Are ever substitutin'
> The modern highfalutin'
> For the plain names of yore.

He called the roll of their crimes:

> They've wiped out Tubby Hook,
> That ancient promontory
> Renowned in song and story
> Which time nor tempest shook,
> Whose name for aye had been good,
> Stands newly christened "Inwood."

By the aid of such a champion Dobbs Ferry remained Dobbs Ferry.

One contribution of the period was a partial solution to the problem of the lack of system in the cross-streets of the Philadelphia pattern. When the new Back Bay district of Boston was laid out, the streets were given names in the fashionable aristocratic and Anglophile tradition, but the names were arranged in alphabetical order—Arlington, Berkeley, Clarendon, and so on to Hereford.

Some years later, in 1880, Alexander B. Hagner wrote elaborately, urging that the Washington lettered streets be changed and given patriotic names following the Back Bay system. Congress failed to act, but the device was used here and there in the outlying districts of various cities, especially in California.

The system had the definite attraction of combining practicality and sentiment. Its difficulties were that it could not be extended beyond twenty-six, and that *x* and *z* were hazards. San Diego avoided the first difficulty by repetition of the pattern—a great writers' section, a trees' section, and so forth. Xenophon and Zola proved useful in the first; the use of Upas among the trees suggests a quiet joke.

The seventies and eighties were notable for a growing self-conscious interest in the whole subject of names. Various magazine articles criticized the state of our nomenclature, their authors viewing with alarm more often than pointing with pride, as might be expected in an era of good taste.

The beginnings of a sound scholarship also appeared with two studies which may be termed classical. In 1870 Dr. J. Hammond Trumbull published his *Composition of Indian Geographical Names*. Only three years later appeared William H. Whitmore's *On the Origin of the Names of Towns in Massachusetts*. After seventy years, these two remain unimpeachable in method, and generally sound in conclusions.

The first whole book on American names, though a small one, appeared in 1888. Its title was the simple *Names and Places;* its author, the geologist, J. D. Whitney. His name itself was notable on the American map. In the sixties he had conducted a survey in

California, and two of his young men had named Mount Whitney, which later surveys determined to be the highest point in the United States. As a scholar of naming, Dr. Whitney was not so eminent; but his book, and his career as well, indicated the new importance which scientists were attaining. He himself attempted, with only partial success, to establish Cordilleran as a name for the whole system of western mountains.

In the same period, however, scientists solved one of our most ancient problems. The eastern mountains, once mapped, stood out as a unit from Georgia to New York, or even farther north. But the early settlers had come to know parts of them under many different names. By a slow process of elimination only two designations at last stood in rivalry for the whole system—Appalachian and Allegheny. In 1861 Professor Arnold Henry Guyot (his name also is on a California peak) was ready to publish an important geological study of the mountains. He apparently hesitated between the names. His map, prepared in advance, used Allegheny, but his final title was *On the Appalachian Mountain System*. The authority of his study apparently established scientific usage, which filtered down through school geographies and eventually became popular usage too.

Mountains, so long neglected by Indians, pioneers, and practical men, became the special field of scientific naming. Not only did scientists name mountains, but also mountains were named for scientists. The Humboldt is almost the only river bearing a scientist's name, but there are many mountains, east and west. The magnificent chain of the southern Sierra Nevada might be called the Scientists' Range as properly as a lesser row of eastern peaks is the Presidential.

Chapter XXXVII ❲ "Change the name of Arkansas–Never!"

Aᴍᴏɴɢ the forty-eight, Arkansas was the only name about which pronunciation and spelling ever rose to be a major issue.

After the Louisiana Purchase, the Americans took over the approximation of the French pronunciation, and often spelled the name accordingly. In 1819 an Act of Congress formally established the Territory of Arkansaw.

In that same year a plain and vigorous American citizen was making his way to the great West from his native Long Island. He was William Woodruff, a printer by trade, and a publisher by instinct. A man of little education, he had strong opinions, and in language was a purist. He even dared attack Noah Webster for including "lengthy" in his dictionary: "What are we coming to? If the word is permitted to stand, the next edition will authorize the word 'strengthy.'"

In the capital of the new territory Woodruff set up a press, and undertook to publish a newspaper. In the first issue he reprinted the act creating the Territory, which eight times used the spelling Arkansaw. Not impressed by a mere Act of Congress, Woodruff changed the spelling to Arkansas.

The population of the Territory was then about ten thousand, many of whom could not spell at all. Even if they could, they probably had no preference for one spelling over the other. The influence of the vigorous-minded editor could thus be tremendous. Apparently even Congress forgot about the original spelling, and later bills used Arkansas. Reprintings of the original act, even in

[335]

official documents, simply changed the spelling without comment, as if a mere clerical error were being corrected.

A strange situation next developed. Just what pronunciation Woodruff preferred is uncertain. As the years passed, however, the citizens of the state generally spelled Arkansas and pronounced Arkansaw. But throughout the United States a feeling existed that the printed form of any name was official and that pronunciation should conform. Many people began to say Arkánsas.

The new tendency also infected the residents. In the forties the two senators differed. Vice-President Dallas, as presiding officer, courteously solved the difficulty by always addressing the one as "the senator from Arkansaw" and the other as "the senator from Arkánsas."

Gazetteers of the mid-century showed the confusion. One allowed both forms. A second spelled Arkansas Territory and Arkansaw River. A third offered: "Arkánsas, formerly pronounced Arkansaw." A fourth merely put: "Arkánsas." The development of Kansas, although the resemblance was accidental, helped the new pronunciation. So also did the word Arkansan which almost demanded an accent on the second syllable. But the natives, firmly rooted among their bayous and hills, said Arkansaw.

After the War, immigrants brought the new pronunciation with them. It came to be common usage in Little Rock. By 1880 anyone might have decided that Arkansaw was a dying and backwoodsy manner of speech.

Any such judgment would have failed to reckon with the extraordinary power of local pride. Suddenly the natives got their backs up: "The books said it was Arkánsas, did they? But who made the books? Damn-Yankee books!" Like the inhabitants of weaker states generally, the Arkansans also managed to develop a sense of being persecuted by their stronger neighbors: "Maybe it was Missouri as much as the Yankees." An Arkansan wrote: "So far as Missouri could do it, she attempted to fasten on the people of Arkansas forever the spelling, Arkansaw."

The Legislature finally took action, and in 1880 appointed a learned committee. Under such circumstances a group of

Arkansans can hardly have been unprejudiced, and their findings might well have been foretold. They buckled to the work with enthusiasm, and called to their assistance, "history, tradition, philosophy." They were not above drawing aid and comfort from the Yankees, and elicited a letter from Longfellow: "I confess I prefer the sound Arkansaw as being more musical than Arkansas." In their final report all the cited authorities preferred the local pronunciation—so unanimously indeed as to arouse a suspicion that contrary opinions may not have been considered worth preserving. In 1881 the Legislature took action in a resolution officially establishing the local manner of speech, and declaring the other, "an innovation to be discouraged."

Local opinion having spoken, the whole tradition of American democracy came to its support. Illogical it might be, troublesome to schoolchildren, even ridiculous—but within a few decades all the world agreed to spell Arkansas, and pronounce Arkansaw.

No, not quite! The Arkansas River flowed for a long distance through Kansas. On its bank stood a town, and its inhabitants preferred it to be known as Arkánsas City. Dictionaries soon began to declare against them. Nevertheless, all the traditions which granted the state the right to fix its name may also be invoked for the town. If the citizens care to fight their battle through, they should win. Certainly every inhabitant of the state of Arkansas should grant the justice of their cause, and courteously say Arkánsas City.

Curiously enough, the years of the Arkansas crisis saw a similar controversy with a city name. A settlement which grew up at the falls of an Indian-named river was always pronounced by the inhabitants—Spokán. The editor of the first newspaper, reasonably, spelled the name in that manner. Perhaps he was personally disliked; for this spelling irritated a large body of citizens, and they founded a second newspaper devoted to the maintenance of a final, though illogical, letter. As with Arkansas, a quite unreasonable situation became tied up with local sentiment and patriotism. All good citizens religiously *write* Spokane, and just as carefully *say* Spokán.

From the legislative action of 1881 probably arose one of the great American folk-tales—the oration of Cassius M. Johnson on changing the name of Arkansas. Legend has it that the speech was delivered before the Legislature. The Hon. Mr. Johnson, however, seems to be wholly mythical. Many legislatures at the end of a session held informal mock meetings, in which they indulged in elaborate and riotous parodies of themselves. Some such session in Little Rock may have produced the oration. Just as likely it was first spoken in a bar-room, where it has since been most often delivered.

Its argument is simple: "Gentlemen, you may do anything else you like—but change the name of Arkansas, never!" As with other folk-tales, there are no established words. The procedure is that any blank-blank blank-of-a-blank that feels himself sufficiently blank-blank drunk can get on the blank-blank chair and deliver the blank speech with any blank-blank-blank variations he wants. Obviously no adequate published version can be offered.

The oration has been one of the humorous masterpieces of American nomenclature, but by no means the only one. Just as names have inspired poetry, they have also inspired comedy.

At some unknown date people along the Maine coast who did not want to be profane began to say "Go to Poodic!" Since this was an Indian name for a point of land, the expression was perhaps as much as to say, "Go jump in the bay!" In Connecticut a similar or perhaps the same word took the form Podunk. In 1846 a series of humorous magazine articles used the title *Letters from Podunk,* and the name became established as the joking equivalent of an insignificant, backward village. In time it sprouted a variant, Squeedunk.

Even before Podunk, humorists had seen the possibilities of American names, and the tradition continued. The period following the Civil War, that era of Mark Twain and the full flowering of native humor, saw a vigorous use of the names. Stage comedians softened their audiences by announcing themselves from Oshkosh or Punxsutawney. Stooges inquired: "What's Watts?"

and "What are Yonkers?" The letter *k* became essentially humorous, and supplied much merriment in Kokomo, Kankakee, Kalamazoo, Kaskaskia, and Keokuk. Any unusually named suburb took its ribbing—Hoboken, Weehawken, and Hamtramck.

A whole field of humor came to be the telling of stories to "explain" some strange Indian name. Sheboygan?—that was the disgusted remark of a chief when his squaw presented him with another daughter—"She boy 'gain!" Massabesic?—"Massa' be sick!" Loyalhanna produced the sentimental tale of an Indian girl named Hannah who loyally, with bow and arrow, supported the aging chieftain, her father.

Youghiogheny?—well, it came about this way: In the early days there was a settler went out in the woods, and he saw an Indian just the same time the Indian saw him. Each of them jumped back of a tree, and started figuring how to get a shot at the other. Pretty soon the settler put his hat on the end of his ramrod, and stuck it out from behind the tree. The Indian shot an arrow right through it, and he thought he'd killed the white man. He jumped out and yelled "Yough!" Then the white man shot *him,* and he jumped out and yelled "Yough-again-y!" So they called the river Youghiogheny.

In the actual process of naming, humor was rather unimportant, although a touch of it lay beneath many namings. Zephyr in Texas was christened by understatement because of a "blue norther." Deathball Creek in Oregon originated from the attempt of an amateur cook to make biscuits. Most humor of names, however, arose in retrospect.

Goodnight or Lovelady, when applied to a town, seemed funny to people who did not know that the name was taken from some man, who like any Smith or Johnson may have been a respectable and matter-of-fact person. Two not very notable names may become funny when they happen to be close together on the map—like Intercourse and Fertility in Pennsylvania. California possesses the amusing triad of Igo, Ono, and Peanut.

Folk-etymology may or may not be consciously humorous. But it has certainly produced a long list of delightful names such as

Ticklenaked, Smackover, Funny Louis, Cape Capon, Bone Venture, Laughing Gal, Pokamoonshine, and Zilly Boy, and probably Merrymeeting, Lazy Lady, Stop-the-Jade, and Stone Arabia.

Mere grotesquery, especially of Indian names, has been another source of humor. Such names can seem funny only if they are not too familiar. Massachusetts, Mississippi, Chicago, and Milwaukee are essentially just as grotesque strangers to the English language as are Paducah and Punxsutawney.

Americans cherish these funny names. Otherwise a laughable one would be changed. Talk to any average American about names, and he will be likely to say before long, with pride: "You know, we have a lot of very queer names down our way." Then he will prove his point by mentioning some.

If any competition could be held, the prize, however, would probably go to Arkansas. That at least is the only state-name which has managed, in spite of familiarity, to retain a touch of humor in itself. The point is illustrated by an often-told anecdote. There was, it seems, an Arkansawyer who went outside the state. Before long, someone asked him where he was from. "Well," said he, "I'm from Arkansas—now, *laugh!*"

Chapter XXXVIII ❰ Of rules and regulations

THAT growing self-conscious interest in names, which had marked the decade of the eighties, became more important in 1889, when a group of men drew together in Washington, D. C., to discuss certain problems. They represented various branches of the government—the Coast and Geodetic Survey, the Hydrographic Office, the Geological Survey, the Lighthouse Board, the Smithsonian Institution, the Departments of State and War, the Post-Office Department. Many of these divisions were busily making maps, and all of them were concerned with names. A map prepared by the War Department might bear different names from those on a map of the same region prepared by the Geological Survey. The experience of other countries showed that the delegation of power to a central authority might be the solution. After some conversations the group brought the matter to the attention of President Harrison, and on September 4, 1890, by Executive Order, he established the Board on Geographic Names.

Historians will recognize an aptness in the date; it is the year conventionally set for the closing of the frontier. The first attempt to regulate names on a national scale marked the ending of another kind of frontier period.

The Board consisted of ten members. Most of them were scientifically trained, especially in geology and geography, but they were government employees rather than theoretical scientists—practical men. They were thus well fitted to deal with naming in so far as it was a practical problem. They were not so well fitted to deal with its important phases which were illogical, traditional, and sentimental. The original Board rendered good service. It might have done better if its list had included a woman, a student of the English language, a journalist, a poet, and a hill-billy. Most of all they needed someone who had studied naming with relation to the history and traditions of the American people.

The primary duty of the Board was to render decisions upon disputed names and forms. Was a mountain near San Diego to be called Cuyamaca or Cloud Peak? The Board decided for Cuyamaca. A great majority of the problems involved only minor details of spelling. Probably no one in South Carolina or anywhere else cared whether a certain island was spelled Daufuskie or Dawfuskie, but such a variation of a letter could be a constant irritation until means were found for settling it. In its first year the Board rendered two thousand judgments.

The decisions were compulsory upon all government offices. The power thus exerted on the general public was immense, but not absolute, and in practice was sometimes wholly ineffective.

The Board, being practical, declined to attempt a re-survey of naming in general. With some millions of names in use, the magnitude of such work was enough to deter anyone. The Board also rejected the pedantic and impractical suggestion to restore the "original" names.

The Board soon found, however, that it must state some standards. Decisions rendered one by one, by whim or momentary preference, would soon produce hopeless inconsistencies. Along with its first report in 1891 the Board therefore briefly presented thirteen general principles. The first was by far the most important, and might stand as a kind of Magna Charta of our naming, a governmental recognition of the established custom of the country: "That spelling and pronunciation which is sanctioned by local usage should in general be adopted." The next three articles were corollaries to the first; their chief addition was that, when local usage was divided, and in doubt, preference should go to the name which was "most appropriate and euphonious." The last nine articles were specific recommendations, guardedly stated. Names should avoid the possessive forms, diacritic characters, and hyphens. They should drop *City* and *-town*, the *-h* of *-burgh,* the *-ugh* of *borough,* and the appended *C. H.* for *Court House. Center* should be used for *Centre.* Names consisting of two or more words should be written as one word.

These nine specific articles were practical in the sense that they made for uniformity and efficiency. They were impractical in that they could not be made to work.

The Board stated, rightly, that its recommendations were in harmony with the general evolution of American naming. What it failed apparently to realize was that any attempt at enforcing authority was likely to reverse the course of that evolution. Vermonter or Missourian alike might not care a penful of ink between *-borough* or *-boro.* In fact, as a practical man, he might even prefer *-boro.* But if anyone told him he *must* use *-boro,* he was likely to invoke all the shades of the Founding Fathers in asserting his inalienable right to -*borough*.

The Board got along very successfully with the names of the many minor natural features which were to be placed on maps. With towns and counties, it took the established form at the price of inconsistency. The spelling was Alleghany in Virginia, Allegany in New York, and Allegheny in Pennsylvania—and the Board recognized that these were chickens already hatched. The real trouble arose through the Post-Office Department.

Significantly, the first Report of the Board included some adverse criticism:

To a much greater extent, however, than the railroads has the Post-Office Department confused the nomenclature of the smaller towns and villages by attaching names to the post-offices not in accordance with those in local usage.

A representative of the Department was a member of the Board, and the suspicion arises that he may have had much to do with securing the nine specific recommendations, which really came into conflict with the basic acceptance of "local usage." The next step also suggests that the Department was merely waiting for the Board to strengthen its position.

In 1894 the Department began a wholesale standardization of post-office names according to the Board's recommendations. Most of the names affected were those of new offices, and the edict was accepted without question. When the town was old and established, however, the story was different.

The change from -*burgh* to -*burg* was one of the most striking; it seemed to Germanize the country overnight, as the old Scottish spelling was wiped out. In one instance, the reaction was quick. A small but old town in New York was Newburgh in 1894, found itself Newburg in the Post-Office list of 1895, but was back as Newburgh in 1896. Again officialdom had gone down before vigorous local sentiment.

The largest -*burgh* to be affected was the great city at the forks

of the Ohio. Ever since its naming by General Forbes it had remained a stronghold of the Scotch-Irish and the Presbyterian
Church. Its citizens had bothered little about the spelling of the
name. A charter of 1816 had used -*burg*. In 1890 some of the
newspapers used the *h*, and some did not; the post-office was officially Pittsburgh. The situation was obviously confused, but left to
itself it would probably soon have worked out a solution. The
First Report of the Board, however, had rendered a decision for
Pittsburg.

The Presbyterian Irish, unlike the other Irish, are not highly
race-conscious, and few of them were probably aware that the -*h*
was part of their birthright. They are, however, a notoriously stiff-
necked and democratic people; if told by self-styled higher authority to do anything, they are very likely to do the opposite.

Year after year, confusion in the name grew worse. Neither side
yielded. The Department changed the post-office in 1895, but it had
not the slightest power over the Pittsburgh *Gazette,* the Pittsburgh Stock Exchange, or the University of Pittsburgh. By a
touch of the ridiculous, a man received a summons to the Circuit
Court of Pittsburgh, but to all other courts without the -*h*. The
Post-Office Department, however, could point to a whole string
of towns from New Hampshire to California which had meekly
consented to be Pittsburg.

In the end, the Department and the Board fell victims to their
political weak spots. A senator took up the case. By that time the
stirring-up of the whole question had caused an investigation of
historical sources, which showed that the -*h* really had tradition
behind it. The usual group of "many prominent citizens" supported the senator, and the Board felt political pressure. Chairman Gannett wrote on May 27, 1911: "Senator Oliver is very
anxious . . . to have the name changed." On July 19th, the Board
reversed itself, and declared for Pittsburgh; the Department
followed.

Although many hundreds of post-office names were changed,
the attempt at standardization was a flat failure. It came closest to
success with the elimination of the possessive form. Most Ameri-

caus omitted the apostrophe through ignorance or carelessness anyway, and were glad to be justified. Nevertheless, you must still write Veterans' Home, California, and Lee's Summit, Missouri, and a few others. The tilde and the accent-marks were not native, and never had vitality for the simple reason that the ordinary newspaper had no type for them. Nevertheless, Canon City refused to become Canyon City. The apostrophe, as a diacritic mark, survived in L'Anse, and some Celtic names such as O'Brien, and an occasional whimsy like Point O' Woods. Several places maintained *Centre* and *-borough*. The hyphen remained fairly common. Even C. H. persisted. King and Queen, C. H. in Virginia could date itself from 1691, and its inhabitants were certainly not going to take orders from any up-country town named Washington. The people, however, spoke most strongly of all on Principle ♯11:

In the case of names consisting of more than one word, it is desirable to combine them into one word.

In spite of official pressure Newcastle and Lafayette have only managed to split the field about equally with New Castle and La Fayette. Many places submitted at first, and later asserted themselves. Every list of changes of post-office names still contains some returns to two words. The instinct is sound. Glenlyon and Deeprun are distinctly something else when run together. As a single word, Bigprairie is grotesque. Coscob is simply not Cos Cob. Even the Department did not attempt Newyork, or Rhodeisland.

The Board was wiser than the Department; and especially in its first years, it usually avoided stirring up the hornets of local pride and prejudice. Nevertheless it had to reverse Marthas Vineyard to Martha's Vineyard. In making a decision the Board collected information from local sources, and regularly adopted the established name in its most practical variant. The members were of course subject to the conventions and preconceptions of their time. Living in the era of good taste, they always preferred colorless Burford to picturesque Stinking Lake. Polecat Ridge had no chance against Coldwater. The Board suffered also from pedantry, and usually wiped out the vigorous folk-etymology in favor of the original and undistinguished name, if it could be determined, thus producing a less varied name-pattern.

The members served on the Board as an additional duty, without compensation. Yet they served with zest. The interest of the subject often led them even beyond the needs of duty. Their reports added comments upon the origin of names. Who can read even the bald decision on Beaver Brook without realizing that the gentlemen were enjoying a certain humor of the situation?—

> *Beaver:* brook, tributary from north to Souhegan River, Hillsboro County, N. H. (Not Quohquinapassakessamanagnog, Quohquinapassakessananagnog, Quohquinapassakessanannaquog, nor Quoh-quinna-passa-kessa-na-nag-nog.)

Several members became enthusiastic students of place-names. Henry Gannett, who served from the beginning until 1914, compiled a large volume, *The Origin of Certain Place-Names in the United States.* Unfortunately it was chiefly the work of subordinates, and notable mainly for its inaccuracies.

Chapter XXXIX (Flavor of California

THE distinctive quality of California's later naming-history was its self-consciousness. Even the first Legislature, after establishing the original twenty-seven counties, had appointed a special com-

mittee to report "the derivation and definition of the names."
When the committee reported, a senator gained the floor "to
record his objections to the definition of the County of Yuba."
The report on origins was ordered to be printed, two thousand
copies in English, one thousand in Spanish. All this unparalleled
interest in the actual history of names was in 1850, during the
confusion of the gold-rush.

The naming of several cities indicated the continuing self-
consciousness. In 1864 a group of gentlemen chose a site for a
college. As trustees they purchased forty acres, but were unable to
agree upon what to call the town. On November 15th, they appointed a committee to consider the subject. The committee members took their work seriously. A month later they asked for an
extension of time. In January they again asked more time. In
February they submitted an inconclusive report, and continued at
work. All the trustees joined in the search. As one of them wrote:
"Young parents never pondered so long over the name of their
first baby."

A year passed, and like poets the trustees still sought a *mot juste.*
Mr. Olmsted, their landscape architect, wrote a long letter on the
subject, which is of interest not only for the town in question, but
also for contemporary thoughts about names in general. Like
many others, he was devoted to "the old English terminations of
localities"; he suggested *-burne, -lea, -mead, -croft* and many
others. One of these, he thought, might well be combined with
the name of one of the trustees. How about Bushnellwood or
Billingsley? Since the site was sheltered beneath high hills, he
suggested Leecombe, Leeley, Hurstlee, Shelterdene, Havenhurst,
and several more. Next he passed to Spanish. He liked *villa,* and
thought it superior to "the unfortunate French 'ville.' " Why not
Villa Hermosa? He made many other Spanish suggestions, and
finally remembered that the first owner of the property had been
Peralta: "It would be natural and proper to take it, and it is not
bad."

In May, 1866, after a year and a half of deliberation, the com-

[347]

mittee recommended Peralta, along with a pattern for street-names combining New York and Back Bay: "There should be scientific streets and literary ways—the streets to run north and south, the ways east and west; that the streets be called in alphabetical order after the names of American men of science, and the ways in like order after American men of letters." They submitted scientists from Audubon to Mitchell, and writers from Allston to Motley.

Peralta was an excellent name—historic, practical, and euphonious. In addition it would have supplied a good Latin motto for a university: *Per Alta,* "through the high things." Nevertheless, the trustees still sought perfection, and tabled the report.

A few days later the trustees assembled again, informally, at their still un-named town-site, where streets were staked out, and a house or two already built. They walked across the campus of their envisioned college, and tradition has preserved enough record to permit a moderately trustworthy narrative of events.

They came to a large outcropping of volcanic rock, and halted there, standing about, or sitting upon the ledges. Looking westward, they saw the magnificence of San Francisco Bay and the Golden Gate, beneath a high sun on a clear spring day. Some ships were outward-bound. Again they thought of the name. Mr. Billings was one of the group, and in conjunction with Golden Gate, someone facetiously suggested Billingsgate. But someone else, looking at the out-going ships, quoted, "Westward the course of empire takes its way." At that moment Mr. Billings experienced what he later called "a sort of inspiration." He cried out, "Eureka!—Berkeley said that! And that saying fits this location; so, Berkeley would be a good name!"

On May 24th the trustees adopted Berkeley. They thus brought to an end what was probably the longest self-conscious search for an American name, in the course of which more suggestions were made than in any other. The end was more fortunate than might have been expected, for they honored an eminent philosopher and an early supporter of American education, although they honored him in neither of those capacities but merely for a single famous

line which he happened to write. In spite of all their care, however, in the end they adopted "birch-glade," a name which literally at least was wholly inappropriate.

In the seventies, a colony from Indiana migrated to southern
California. They laid out a town upon a high slope at the base of
mountains, a site much like that of Berkeley. With Hoosier forth-
rightness they called it Indiana Colony. In 1875 they needed a
name for a post-office, and Colony seemed inappropriate. Various
citizens, as always, hurried forward with suggestions, all eager to
say in future years, "I named it!" A lover of Irving offered New
Granada. Indianola came from a Hoosier; Muscat, from a grape-
grower. A student of the classics proposed a Greek form. The
Indian vogue, however, was still strong, and someone wrote to an
ancient Mr. Smith, who had once been a missionary to the Chippewas. That tribe, it was true, had never lived within two thousand miles of the new town, but to the romantic mind anything
in the "Indian language" was indigenous and appropriate. The
suggestion was that Mr. Smith should translate into Chippewa the
words Key of the Valley, or Crown of the Valley. This was not
so simple, for among the primitive Chippewas had been neither
locked doors nor regal symbols. Mr. Smith, however, did his best
and returned four long names, such as Tá-pe-ká-e-gun Pâ-sâ-de-ná.
His correspondent ignored the first part of the names, and selected
the latter half, which was the same in all four. He struck out its
hyphens and accents, and proposed it at a meeting. Although half
of the name had been eliminated it was apparently presented as
still meaning "Crown of the Valley." The supposed significance
was pleasing; Indian derivation was fashionable; alternation of
vowel and consonant was euphonious. By a vote of seventeen to
four, the town became Pasadena.

The name proved serviceable, was much admired, was reproduced in several other states, and was given to a cruiser. It fur-
nishes good proof that a name, like a person, may rise above
questionable birth.

Advertising names are necessarily self-conscious, and California has been noted for advertising. The period of its development, however, particularly in the southern half, fell within a time when laudatory names were common everywhere, and California towns on the whole do not seem to have expressed greater pride in themselves than towns in many other states. One larger city, however, came to bear an advertising name, though a simple one.

In 1881 Mr. W. E. Willmore subdivided an oceanside barley-field south of Los Angeles, and followed fashion by calling it Willmore City. Like many other so-called cities it languished, and by 1888 went bankrupt. Someone decided it would be a good thing to lighten ship by casting out the Jonah of an unsuccessful name. At that time the Santa Fe had just consolidated a direct line from Chicago to Los Angeles, and the tourist business was looking up. The inhabitants of stagnating Willmore City looked out upon eight miles of curving beach with the blue Pacific rollers lazily tumbling into creamy foam. They decided to announce themselves to the world as a seaside resort, and took the name Long Beach.

In 1887 Mr. and Mrs. H. H. Wilcox laid out another California town. The taste of Mrs. Wilcox's parents in naming is shown by her own baptism as Daeida. She herself was more conventional. As always with the small and poorly recorded beginnings of great names, legend has been busy. The site of the town again resembled those of Berkeley and Pasadena, and on the near-by hills was some growth of native toyon, in those days often called California holly. A very unlikely story narrates that at just the proper moment a boy came along selling bunches of the berries, and so suggested the name. Even more dubious is the tale inspired by the undoubted piety and extreme puritanism of the Wilcoxes, that the place was really to have been Holywood.

But the name was not unique, or even uncommon. Already it was borne by plantations, villages, and post-offices. The most likely of the various stories is that Mrs. Wilcox met a southern woman on a train, and in talking with her found that her country home was Hollywood. The sight of some red-berried clumps of toyon near the new town may have made the southern name seem appropriate.

The strong tradition of Spanish names probably did much to save California from the advertisers. A lover of system might be glad to know that these Spanish names fall clearly into the conventional three periods. Deepest of strata lie the genuine names of the Spanish and Mexican settlement. The second period began with the American occupation, and continued through more than half a century. In those years Spanish names were often applied with more enthusiasm than prudence—Spanish words to an English tune. "River-view" was a good idea—so you asked some Mexican the words for *river* and *view,* or looked in a dictionary, and arrived obviously at Rio Vista. Any speaker of Spanish would have said Vista del Río, and would have shuddered at Rio Vista, and its numerous brothers and sisters, like Mar Vista and Sierra Vista.

The third period began about 1915 when the study of Spanish was introduced into many high schools, and proved very popular. Before long, a realtor trying to put Pinehurst into Spanish as Pino Monte might be informed by a bright son or daughter that Bosque de los Pinos would be more Castilian. Thus in the third period the pendulum swung toward an almost pedantic correctness. The developers of one large and expensive subdivision even made advertising capital out of hiring an expert to pass on the names, and also to make certain that the Spanish names of their streets did not duplicate those used anywhere else.

The height of California self-consciousness sprang from this new interest in correct Spanish. Los Angeles was one of the few Spanish names which the Americans found difficult to pronounce even approximately. Both meaning and spelling suggested the English *angels;* before long the *n* and the *g* took those sounds, and the whole pronunciation was really Americanized. This procedure was only to be expected, and was all to be desired. The new pronunciation indeed might have been called ideal—it was well suited to American tongues, it followed the spelling, it was euphonious.

The revival of Spanish, however, threw the whole field open to pedantry and linguistic snobbery. The newspapers ran articles, and letters came flooding in to the correspondence column. A few advocated a full return to the Spanish, although this would have introduced some quite un-American combinations of sound, and was, humanly speaking, merely impossible. Many compromised for a hard *g,* as if there were some virtue in connecting the city with *angles* rather than *angels.* The *o,* the second *e,* the first *s,* the second *s*—all became centers of controversy. The permutations of all possibilities theoretically allowed at least five hundred different pronunciations to enter the running.

Fortunately this antiquarian mania did not spread. San Francisco did not attempt to become Sahn Frahnceesco, or Detroit to seek its French womb as Daytrwáh.

Not even yet has Los Angeles become a safe word to pronounce. Self-righteousness still mouths the Spanish vowels with more than Spanish unction, and old ladies cling to their hard *g* as to hope of heaven. In despair or disgust a great number of people have merely taken to saying L. A., or Los.

Strangely, this degeneration of the name was allowed to occur during years when the Chamber of Commerce and other civic organizations were otherwise extremely active and amazingly successful in developing the city. That they realized the importance of the name is shown in various ways. Fulminations against L. A. and Los were frequent. Moreover, rumor has it that in those years a press-association reporter would find it not unprofitable to write "Los Angeles Harbor," instead of the more accurate San Pedro Harbor.

Another question thus arises. Perhaps the advertisers of the city worked upon the established principle of publicity—"It's better to have people talk about you, no matter what they say." They may have thought that the controversy led people at least to *pronounce* the name, no matter *how* they pronounced it.

[352]

Chapter XL ❨ Of modern methods

AFTER 1890, with the frontier no longer in existence, naming changed by becoming more official. From the very beginning indeed there had been a distinction between naming by official act and by folk-process. In general, anything existing by act of God was named informally. Some explorer or unknown settler might place a name upon a stream. It would become established in common speech, and written upon maps. Already fixed, it would eventually attain official status by being mentioned in land-grants, or as the boundary of a colony or county. Towns, counties, and other artificial establishments, however, were named at the time of formation by the official act creating them.

The distinction between the two kinds of naming, however, was somewhat vague. Lewis and Clark, though individuals, were also accredited officers of the government, so that their namings had a kind of official status. On the other hand, although Vermont, Kentucky and all the later territories and states came into existence by Act of Congress and not by act of God, yet the names for many of the districts had been already well established by folk-process.

Before 1890 neither the federal government nor the states had paid much attention to the naming of natural features. They were left to the people, and new names arose much as new words arose. The explorer, the surveyor, the settler, all got there first; Congress and the Legislatures accepted what was already established.

Toward 1900 the balance tipped. Among any people, naming is primarily a practical matter, like language in general, and a

[353]

stream needs a name only if it is important enough to make a name a convenience. Among inhospitable mountains, where men rarely penetrate, the smaller streams need not be named. So, by the end of the century when almost all the habitable parts of the country had been settled, further naming of natural features would have fallen off, if the federal government had not continued it, partly in the routine work of scientific mapping, partly for such immediately practical ends as forest-fire control.

As a symbol of change, the Board on Geographic Names was granted an extension of power in 1906. It no longer merely decided upon disputed cases, but was also entrusted with approving new names. The chief name-givers were no longer to be the wandering frontiersmen, but the members of the United States Geological Survey, the Forest Service, and the National Park Service. In mapping or exploring new areas, they noted such names as occurred, and added others. If old names were too often repeated, were obscene, or seemed otherwise unsuitable, they suggested changes. The tentative maps were referred to the Geographic Board.* In that office names were checked. Changes might be made, and the map sent back to its original bureau. In revised form the map went again to the Geographic Board; eventually approved, it went on to publication.

Legally the Board had no shadow of authority to enforce its names upon anyone except government employees in line of duty, but since most of the regions involved were thinly inhabited, little opposition could arise. In the course of time a general state of mind developed that the government had the "right" to decree names. Only now and then did outraged local people rise up in indignation and force the Board to reverse its decision and restore an old name. Somewhat more often they merely continued to say what they had always said, without caring what was printed on the map.

Power is a dangerous intoxicant; the Board, usually function-

---

* Although dedicated to the stability of names, the Board itself has, ironically, suffered from change. It has been successively the Board on Geographic Names, the Geographic Board, and Board on Geographical Names. (Physician, heal thyself!)

ing through its paid secretary, sometimes indulged in tyranny. One geologist put on a mountain the name of an old-timer, because the scattered settlers of the region called it that. The Board changed it to one of its own liking. The geologist changed it back, with an explanation. The Board changed it again. The geologist, a stubborn and conscientious fellow, put his original name on the map for the third time. The Board changed it, and sent a letter pointing out that any Civil-Service employee refusing to accept its decrees could be dismissed. The geologist, who was taking another job anyway, defiantly inserted the original name for the fourth time, and resigned. His map was published with the Board's choice. Local opposition developed, however, and to the geologist's glee, the later reprintings of the map were forced also to use the original name in parentheses.

Whether or not the Board always judged wisely, the whole process of naming was profoundly affected. Once a man merely named a mountain, and hoped that the name would stick. In 1871 Emerson had visited Yosemite Valley, and spent most of his time with John Muir. Later Muir wrote, "I have named a grand *wide-winged* mountain ... Mt. Emerson." Muir had no authority for the naming; he was not even the discoverer of the mountain; in later years his act would have seemed presumptuous. But the name survived. People sometimes had performed symbolic acts in the attempt to make their namings impressive and therefore permanent. A homesteader, standing beside a stream, made a formal statement in the presence of witnesses; a lady broke a bottle of spring water against the summit of a mountain. After 1906 the procedure was different. A society or civic body, wishing to honor some pioneer or poet, wrote to the Board; probably they also wrote to their congressman. If the peak was unnamed or if its name was not very fitting and well established (and especially if the congressman expressed his concurrence), the Board might graciously assent, and order the insertion or change upon future maps. Times had altered since the breezy old days of the frontier when one man's name was as good as another's.

Nearly always, however, the Board was passive, not active. It

merely accepted what was presented, so that the real naming
passed into the hands of the field-workers. Some of these accepted
it merely as a routine chore, but many felt the fascination and became enthusiastic namers. Some of these men individually added
hundreds of names to the map, although their own names may
never be remembered. Let Mr. A. H. Sylvester of the Forest
Service stand as their representative.

Sylvester worked first with the Geological Survey. In 1908 he
transferred to the Forest Service:

finding that in Fire Protection work it was very desirable, even impera-
tive, that natural features capable of being named should have them as
an aid in locating fires and sending in crews to combat them, I began
place-naming more diligently . . . New place names were submitted
with each map revision. I seldom went on a field trip without coming
back with some new names to add to the map. . . . Each succeeding
map revision showed more names until finally there are few features
unchristened.

In the tradition of John Smith, Sylvester named mostly by description, by incident, and in memory of his friends.

On one trip he had with him a ranger named Canby. They first
named two lakes after Canby's sisters, Mary and Margaret. This
started them on a series. As they stumbled upon more unnamed
lakes they called them Florence, Alice, Flora, Edna, Augusta,
Ida, and finally, "Victoria, for England's Queen." The Wenatchee
National Forest proved to be full of unvisited lakes, and the
naming-habit continued in later years.

The numbers of ladies' lakes grew until practically all the rangers'
and other Forest Service men's wives, sisters, sweethearts, mothers, and
daughters had lakes named for them.

Toward the end, a joker found still another and called it Brigham
—"and now Brigham is on the map surrounded by his harem."

Like most later namers, Sylvester had a respect for the work of
his predecessors and kept their names when possible, whether

Indian or English. He himself knew a little of the local language and something more of the Chinook jargon. *Klone* in Chinook means "three," and after paying three dollars for a dog, Sylvester named him Klone:

His full name was Klone pesitkim, three and a half, for I hadn't had him long until he killed a chicken for which I had to pay half a dollar.

Klone Peak, therefore, does not mean a triple-pointed mountain, but like many another American stream or hill commemorates a good dog, even though he may have begun as a chicken-killing pup.

Sheepherders are traditionally foul-mouthed, and many of their names were "unusable." Sylvester made one of them into Asel, and Cultus Hole preserved his adaptation by means of the Chinook word for "filthy."

To dispose of troublesome repetitions Sylvester developed his own system. There were too many Cougar Creeks. So he substituted Lion, Panther, Puma, Painter, and even the Chinook term Puss-Puss.

From the nicknames of two Scotch sheepherders he made a new formation:

I spelled two *Tu* and added the "mac" to it for Tumac which makes as fine a looking Indian name as I will ask you to find anywhere. My guess is that it takes humor as well as whimsy to name names.

Sylvester was an enthusiastic namer—conscientious, systematic, and imaginative. He once estimated that he had planted three thousand names. Add to his work that of a hundred of his fellows, and the rapid filling-in of the map under modern conditions becomes understandable.

During the generation succeeding 1890 the history of the country was less reflected in the names. Very few new counties were being formed, and not so many towns. Fewer new lines of railway were being built.

The War with Spain produced a certain number of places called for Dewey, Schley, Shafter and other war-heroes. At the time of the Russo-Japanese War the American sympathy for the "plucky little Japs" ran up the post-offices named Tokio to six, and Togo was also popular.

But obviously the later heroes had less chance. Washington had been commemorated in thirty-two counties; Jefferson, in twenty-four; Lincoln, in twenty-three. But Grant, father of victory and twice President, only equaled Nathanael Greene with fourteen. Garfield, the martyr-president, had five; McKinley, martyred a generation later, only one. Custer died on the Little Big Horn in 1876; glamorous in life and death, he was remembered with six counties, but he was the last of the military heroes to leave much mark on the map. Dewey gained only two. Theodore Roosevelt, in spite of all his popularity, was remembered with only two counties, though Van Buren had had four, and Polk, twelve.

Although the period saw great growth of cities, only one new name appeared among them. Developed by the United States Steel Corporation in the early years of the century, it took a name from the president of the company, and became Gary.

The last flurry over a state name occurred with New Mexico. Local sentiment was always strongly for the ancient name, but objections were raised elsewhere that the words suggested a part of Mexico rather than of the United States. Lincoln was urged at various times. Others advocated the romantic Montezuma. Senator Beveridge presented Hamilton. Acoma, from the ancient pueblo, was suggested for the shoddy reason that it would displace Alabama, and let the new state head the alphabetical list. But territorial representatives let it be known that any change of name might even lead the people to reject the proffered statehood.

Oklahoma, also having escaped some attempts at political tampering, had been admitted in 1907. Arizona, admitted five weeks after New Mexico, established the roll of the states on February 14, 1912.

Unspectacular details of common life may, however, affect naming more than wars or migrations. The development of Rural

Free Delivery in the early years of the century permitted the elimination of about forty thousand small post-offices, and their names vanished from the list. This was the greatest fatality of names ever to occur in our history, but in comparison with the whole number the loss of forty thousand was insignificant. Many of them, also, survived as community and cross-roads names. In the end their loss actually increased the total number of names, for in compensation, to aid delivery in rural districts, the custom arose in many states of naming country roads. The loss of one name thus often meant the gain of twenty others.

During the hurried advance of the frontier the demand for names had often outrun the supply, and driven people of systematic minds to take refuge in numbers. The device was commonest with a series of lakes, or something similar, seeming like beads on a string. The New Englanders were perhaps a little fonder of the system than were the other Americans. It was used with a chain of frontier posts in Massachusetts, and one of these, Number Four, was the scene of a famous fight; plantations in Maine bore numbers east and west of Machias, and some are still so designated. After 1800 the islands in the Mississippi were thus labeled all the way from Number 1, just below the mouth of the Ohio, to Number 124 near Baton Rouge. A decisive gunboat battle of the Civil War occurred at Island Number 10.

Other number-names arose from different origins. A famous southern colonial post was Ninety-Six, so called because it stood at that mileage from the beginning of the trail. Among post-offices, Eighty-four in Pennsylvania was established in 1884, and Fifty-six in Arkansas took over the number of a school-district.

Numbers and letters sometimes attained a strong hold on people's affections. Fifth Avenue became a word of glamour all over the United States, and C Street was poetry itself as long as the memory of the bonanza-days of Virginia City lingered among western miners. In general, however, numbers had less sentimental appeal than names. Even from the practical point of view numbers were not altogether preferable, because any extended system was likely to break down with time. When islands in the Mississippi washed away and new ones were formed, the numbers became merely misleading.

Most Americans acted on the firm conviction that a place, even a vague and unimportant one, deserved a name, rather than a number. In the process of settlement all states found need for some kind of sub-division of counties, which the Census Bureau came to list under Minor Civil Divisions. These small units were most commonly called townships, but also might be known as towns, hundreds, plantations, districts, or precincts, and by other terms. They came to number around fifty thousand. In the western states, the minor divisions at first bore only numbers, in accordance with the Land Office survey. Under the county system of government they exercised negligible functions, and aroused scarcely any sentimental attachment. Yet, year by year, more and more of them were named, until the merely numbered township began to vanish with the antelope and mountain-sheep.

The early use of numbers and letters, however, left curious traces. The first Oklahoma counties were originally designated by numbers, but in the first general elections the people adopted names. Later counties were provisionally organized under letters of the alphabet and names chosen at a later election—but K County merely became Kay. The railroad station Camphora in California was Camp Four on the line, and took its later name from the pronunciation of Mexican workmen.

One reversal of the ordinary trend is notable. In the early days of the automobile, enthusiasm for good roads led to the laying out, chiefly on paper, of many "highways." These were largely advertising devices. They had their distinctive colors and symbols, to be painted on telegraph-poles, and fixed to fence-posts; they had their slogans, such as "Follow the goat to the top of the world!" Each had a carefully chosen name, usually patriotic. The Lincoln Highway was the most famous, but there were dozens of others. As it happened, an edition of the *Encyclopaedia Britannica* appeared at the height of this development, and its editors were impressed. The more important "highways" were discussed in separate articles, with maps. Shortly afterwards, the system of Federal roads was inaugurated, and the old advertising names were replaced with a system of numbers. Most of the older names quickly passed out of use, so that anyone browsing through the *Encyclopaedia* comes upon the articles as a remnant of a past age. Like Fifth Avenue and C Street, however, some of the new numbered highways have attained poetic value; both U. S. 1 and U. S. 40 have figured in recent imaginative writing.

For streets, houses upon streets, and highways, obvious practicality has made numbers acceptable. With everything else the American people might be said by the early twentieth century to have established as an unwritten article of the Constitution: "A place shall be named, not numbered."

The end of the nineteenth century and the beginning of the twentieth witnessed a great development of American manufacturing. Factories took in raw materials, fabricated or recombined them, and turned out a new product. In the same way, the chief contribution of the period to naming was the development and popularization of the new names fabricated from the raw materials.

A few such were very old. Saybrook dated from 1636, and Connecticut had always shown a certain partiality for ingenious manufactures, whether of nutmeg-graters or of names.

In 1866 a town in Georgia took a name coined from Atlantic Transportation Company, and became Atco. The rarity of the process at that time, however, was shown by the later attempt of a historian to prove its Indian origin.

The methods of manufacture, though at first thought they might seem very numerous, were actually very few. Sometimes the mere union of two words produced something essentially new. Most people would regard Elrio as a name in itself, but it was formed from the Spanish *el río,* "the river." Clemscot suggests a British original like Kelmscott, but was named for "Clem" Scott.

Arock, Burntranch, Nowood, and Tomball are similar. One of the most delightful is Leaday in Texas for which a twice-bereaved widow joined the names of her two deceased husbands.

Actual fabrication from individual letters of the alphabet was rare. One practitioner of this esoteric art was J. B. Calhoun, land-commissioner of the Illinois Central in its early days. "By placing the vowel *o* three times, thus o-o-o, and filling in with the consonants t-l-n," he produced Tolono in Illinois. He similarly created Panola.

Backward spellings of familiar names gave rise to an appreciable number of others which were certainly original, not to say fantastic—Lebam, Seloc, Maharg, Rolyat. Texas by itself produced Reklaw, Notla, Sacul, and Tesnus. Enola Hill in Oregon was descriptive for the initiated. Wabasso in Florida was the reversal of a local Indian name, although also the exact spelling of the White Rabbit in *Hiawatha*. Romley in Colorado arose from Morley by reversal of the first three letters.

Some wholly new words arose by variation of spelling. Colstrip in Montana indicated the place of some strip coal mines. Somerange in Oregon was Summer Range. In Texas they were naming a place Ponte because of a bridge there, but someone sensibly remarked that no American would ever pronounce that word in two syllables; so they made a new word by spelling it Ponta. With these may be grouped such whimsies as Wifani Cottage and Atlasta Ranch.

The great majority of name-coiners have sought, not wholly to conceal the originals, but rather to suggest them, as by allegory. Such coiners took component parts of two or more names. Their favorite unit was the syllable. In Texas, as the old song goes, "There was a man who had two sons." Their names were Bickham and Jerome. So he put the names together and called the place Birome. There was another in Oregon who had two daughters, and they were Eleanor and Monica; so he made it Elmonica. The combination might spring from almost any coupling—the nicknames of two friends, a partnership, the first and last name of one man. Combinations of more than two names offered no difficulty. Emida in Idaho was for the families—East, Miller, and Dawson. Multorpor Butte in Oregon combined Multnomah, Oregon, and Portland, but the name proved a mouthful, and local people soon developed a tendency to call it Multiple Butte instead. Michillinda in California united the abbreviations of three states, and added an *a* to give the whole a Spanish look. Coalinga in the same state was a coaling station disguised by the addition of one letter.

The coiners also favored initials. Itmann in West Virginia was for I. T. Mann, president of a coal company. Alicel in Oregon was rather obviously Alice L. In the same state Pawn was for Poole, Akerly, Worthington, and Nolen. The founding of a Texas town led to a squabble over a name, which (tradition has it) was solved when a local Solomon discovered that the initials of the men—Owsley, Pruitt, Norman, Reiger, Welch, Turner, and Ezell—could be arranged into Newport.

Frequently part of a name was forced into service as a suffix. Oklahoma gave rise to Centrahoma and Indianhoma. A higher-located suburb of Pasadena became Altadena.

The ingenuity of the namers sometimes combined two methods. Ardenwald in Oregon was for Arden M. Rockwood, the last syllable translated into German. Ti in Oklahoma, in spite of its brevity, was formed by the complicated process of taking the initials of Indian Territory and reversing them.

The manufactured name appealed greatly to the founders of company-towns. Perhaps they felt that a town springing from an artificially created corporation should have an artificial name. The W. E. Steward Land Company yielded Weslaco; Louisiana-Texas Orchards, Latexo; Aluminum Company of America, Alcoa; Gallup American Coal Company, Gamerco. All over the country the ending *-co* came to have the value of a suffix, to indicate a company town.

Boundary names also came to form a special American group. About 1870 a steamboat plying the Red River and thus serving territory in three states was named the *Texarkana*. The word was also used for some locally manufactured bitters. Someone wrote the name in large black letters upon a pine board, and nailed it to a stump at a location on the projected line of a railroad. Texarkana survived for a town there, partly in Texas, partly in Arkansas, and close to Louisiana. Kenova in West Virginia, founded in 1889, recorded its location on the borders of Kentucky and Ohio.

The boundary name never became popular in the East and Middle West, but about sixty came to mark the lines between various southern and far-western states. The three chief railroads cross the Nevada-California line at Calneva, Calvada, and Calada. The state also has Calor, Calzona, and Calexico. Many boundary names also record a location on the line between two counties, or near the junction of three.

A name manufactured on the boundary-principle finally supplied, after three hundred years, an old need. The peninsula between the Chesapeake and Delaware Bays was explored by John Smith in 1608, and before many years English, Swedes, and Dutch colonized it. The region, although a geographical unit, was divided politically among Delaware, Maryland, and Virginia, and attained a name only when someone coined Delmarva Peninsula.

Chapter XLI ❮ Cause célèbre

ON MAY 8, 1792, Captain Vancouver had named a mountain for his friend Rear Admiral Rainier. By that period, international custom had ruled that a name used by the first responsible and scientific explorer should have standing. All nations accepted Vancouver's reports as authentic, and Mount Rainier appeared upon scores of charts and maps.

Wilkes explored Puget Sound for the United States in 1841. He gave nearly three hundred minor names, but respected those already placed by Vancouver. During the excitement of the Oregon controversy some Americans strove to turn the Cascades into the Presidents' Range. Mount Adams and Mount Jefferson were fruits of this planting, but the older Saint Helens, Olympus, and Rainier survived the patriotic attempt to make them Washington, Van Buren, and Harrison.

In the fifties, Theodore Winthrop, scion of a famous New England family, went wandering through the Puget Sound region, and gathered material for his much admired book, *The Canoe and the Saddle*. Using an incorrect spelling, he wrote:

Mount Regnier Christians have dubbed it, in stupid nomenclature perpetuating the name of somebody or nobody. More melodiously the Siwashes call it Tacoma—a generic term also applied to all snow peaks.

Winthrop was killed in an early battle of the Civil War. Half a century later his words were to be quoted like a text of Holy Writ, interpreted this way or that according to faction.

In 1868 Morton M. McCarver, a kind of professional town-planner, located a site on Commencement Bay in full view of the magnificent peak. Before a name was fixed, an admirer of Winthrop's book happened to arrive, and was eloquent in advocating Tacoma. He converted McCarver and his family so thoroughly that, as family tradition later declared, they stayed up all night talking over the new name.

The town thus became Tacoma, and the mountain remained Rainier. The people of Tacoma continued so to call it for fifteen years.

In 1883, however, a powerful director of the Northern Pacific Railroad was also president of the Tacoma Land Company. Wishing to publicize the town, he hit upon a bold device. Its announcement came in an official publication of the Railroad:

The Indian name Tacoma will hereafter be used in the guide books and other publications of the Northern Pacific Railroad and Oregon Railway & Navigation Co., instead of Rainier.

Railroad influence, tremendous in a still undeveloped region, officially began to work for Mount Tacoma.

The citizens of Tacoma took over the new name of the mountain enthusiastically. In 1884, the admission of the territory as a state seemed likely, and the difficulties of the name Washington had already become plain. The Tacomans therefore modestly put forward Tacoma for the new state, but in a period of intense rivalry among towns such a proposal aroused heated and effective opposition.

Soon after its organization the Board on Geographic Names took up the case. The evidence was roughly the town against the rest of the world. A name of excellent ancestry by geographers' standards and more than a century old was matched against one of dubious origin and very recent use. Mount Tacoma could be found in a few local newspapers and in railroad publicity; Mount Rainier, upon official maps and charts, and in atlases and gazetteers from all over the world. The Board naturally rendered a unanimous decision for Mount Rainier.

About the same time the influence of that particular director waned, and the Northern Pacific began to favor Seattle as a terminus. Its officials abandoned what one of them later called "the farce," and began to use Mount Rainier. Seattle leaped ahead in population and wealth; Tacoma, like a cast-off mistress, was left to brood by her deserted wharfs, and stubbornly to say Mount Tacoma, as a symbol of her former high place.

In 1893, a meeting was held of citizens of Tacoma to the number of 120, including Indians not taxed. The Indians were important, for they were local tribesmen and obligingly gave testimony which could be interpreted as favoring Mount Tacoma. Judge Wickersham read a paper in which he inquired:

What are the facts? What do honesty, euphony, simplicity, poetry, tradition, history and patriotism require of us?

He of course decided that all these high abstractions required everyone in the world to support the name promulgated by the Northern Pacific ten years before. The paper and the report of the meeting were immediately published as *Proceedings of the Tacoma Academy of Science.* No other publication of this "Academy" is extant, but the number of the libraries listing copies of this single one indicates that it was well distributed. The world, however, went about its business uninterested.

In 1899 came another blow. In setting off the region around the peak, Congress called it Mount Rainier National Park. Tacomans could see in this only the diabolical machinations of Seattle. Against all odds they continued to say Mount Tacoma, but the future looked dark.

The people of Tacoma, however, came of a race which had faced dark times before. Things had been bad during King Philip's War, and at Valley Forge, and after Chancellorsville. Joined to the old Americans were the recent Scandinavian immigrants, than whom no more stubborn people walk the earth. The odds might be heavy, but nevertheless as the new century ran on through the first decade Tacoma babies learned "papa" and "mama," and then soon were taught to lisp "Mount Tacoma."

The origins were shoddy; the conduct of the fight was often dishonest; the whole attempt was presumptuous, even preposterous. Nevertheless, it was magnificent! Not every day or every year do the people of a small city array themselves in battle against the world.

About 1910 Tacoma began to take the offensive. To say, as many outsiders did, that it was all a scheme to advertise the city is certainly wrong. That early western Chamber-of-Commerce spirit, at once cynical and sinister, was undoubtedly one chief driving force. You can almost hear them saying: "Well, we can't lose! If we win, O.K.—and if we lose, why, we've made everybody in the U. S. know the name Tacoma, and talk about it!" But there was something deeper. A generation of children had been born and grown to maturity hearing "Mount Tacoma," and being told the local traditions, which inevitably became more and more prejudiced. What may have been half a joke to the first settlers became desperate earnest to their children and the stuff of a crusade to their grandchildren. As if they were nature-worshipers, they declared that the mountain itself had been wronged! A book used the title *The Mountain that was "God."* Some of the propaganda bore the imprint, *Justice to the Mountain Committee.*

Among other publications was a poem by an Indian named Thomas G. Bishop. His simplicity in meter and grammar was perhaps considered evidence also of a naive honesty:

> Redmen called it Ta-co-bet, others pronounced
> it Tacoma or Rainier,
> Its true meaning is God's Mountain, which they
> worshipped most sincere.

A copious stream of "literature" thus poured out, and much of it was widely distributed, *gratis*. Its writers doubtless believed in what they advocated, but they used the only too common methods of propaganda. Half-truths were presented as whole truths; conclusions were stated vigorously, not proved; opposing evidence was omitted; the flag was draped around the cause; flow of emotion substituted for lack of logic. With such methods the crusaders put up a persuasive argument. "Tacoma is the Indian name of the mountain and therefore the original and rightful name. We all love Indians, don't we?—especially their names! It's very beautiful and very poetic—means 'great white breast', or 'mountain that was God'. Well, you know, something like that! Rainier was a nobody. And besides, he was British—Boston Massacre, Lexington, War of 1812, Ireland, India!"

There was no counter-propaganda. The rest of the state used Mount Rainier, but did not feel enough at stake to spend money defending what the Board had already approved. The Tacoma argument was convincing to anyone who knew nothing about the other side. Patriotic societies began to pass resolutions favoring Mount Tacoma. Learned societies, without investigating, proved gullible. The time ripened.

In 1917 the Tacoma influence was strong enough to pass through the Washington Legislature a resolution memorializing the Board to change the name to whatever it might think most appropriate.

The Board set a date for a hearing. The citizens of Tacoma made ready to present their case. They had been making excellent progress, and felt that at last the victory was close.

Two non-Tacomans, however, also appeared before the Board, and brought with them not only a collection of nasty facts but also some very fair native gift for sarcasm. The case for Tacoma was overwhelmed with its own inaccuracies, inconsistencies, and absurdities. Evidence showed that the Indians also called the mountain Puskehouse, Tiswauk, and Tuahku—why did not Tacoma advocate one of those names? If it felt so strongly about British names, why not object to Puget Sound or even to Mount Vernon? The Indian name for the site of their city was Chebaulip—why not change Tacoma to Chebaulip?

Moreover, the members of the Board, unfortunately for Tacoma, knew a great deal about the history of the name. They could hardly have been ignorant, for Tacoma had been plaguing them ever since 1890. The members also saw the matter from a national or international point of view. They saw the geographers of the United States ridiculous before the world. They saw nomenclature becoming a political football. Why should not the next step be that local advocates should demand that Puget Sound be changed to Seattle Sound? Even if Tacoma had had a good historical argument, mere practicality would have prevented the Board from reversing its decision of 1890.

The eminent naturalist C. Hart Merriam, as Chairman of the Board, delivered a statement. It had much the weight and dignity of a Supreme Court decision. The Board declined to reverse its previous ruling.

At that point the story should have ended. Tacoma had fought valiantly, and had lost. Her case, once put to the test, had proved ridiculously weak. Her citizens could, with dignity, have accepted the decision of the Board to which they had appealed. Instead, they were seized with a kind of infatuation. Before 1917 the Tacoma propaganda might be termed moderately dishonest; between 1917 and 1924 it was scurrilous and despicable. In Tacoma, people circulated and believed stories of the kind which are invented and accepted only in times of witch-hunts and spy-scares. Even as propaganda these stories were ridiculous, because they could so easily be proved false.

One line of attack was against Rainier himself. Actually he had served as a faithful, if not brilliant, naval officer. During the Revolution he gallantly engaged the American privateer *Polly,* and captured her after a hard fight in which he himself was badly wounded. He rose to be Admiral of the Blue, and after his retirement served in Parliament. He gave evidence of unusual civic virtue by leaving a portion of his estate to help defray the national debt.

But Tacoma set out to besmirch him as a cruel Briton who had ravaged our coasts. Although Rainier in a naval warship had fought the American privateer, the situation came to be reversed. Rainier himself was called the privateer, and from hostile privateer to pirate the step was easy.

Another attack would have been merely fantastic, except for serious consequences. The mountain, so a new story ran, had been named to advertise Rainier Beer; even more, in 1890 the brewing company had shipped to Washington a whole carload of its popular product, and presented this carload to the Board during the original consideration of the case; naturally the members became a little befuddled, and in a mixture of gratitude and befuddlement had voted for Rainier!

The picture of those bewhiskered gentlemen on their gigantic beer-bust is delightful. It is rendered unlikely, however, from the character of the men themselves, and also because the manufacture of Rainier Beer was not begun until some years after the decision had been rendered.

Tacoma believed, however, and acted hysterically. Under the eyes of their teachers, schoolchildren wrote thousands of letters protesting that their beautiful mountain should thus have been named to publicize a vile alcoholic beverage. One congressman stated that he had received 2,500 of them. His opinion was unaffected. But did the children themselves remain unaffected by being made the implements of the mass propagation of a lie?

In 1924 a Washington senator introduced a resolution to change the name by Act of Congress. He himself was so ignorant of the whole matter that he referred to Rainier as a general. The measure passed the Senate with little discussion, went to the House, and was referred to the Committee on Public Lands. The Committee appointed a public hearing for January 9, 1925.

There could obviously be no new arguments, and the question became purely political. This time, the whole state of Washington was aroused. Clubs, civic bodies, and individuals poured letters and telegrams in upon their congressmen, most of them strongly opposing Tacoma.

The old discussion, like a wounded snake, dragged its weary length through the hearing. The testimony is chiefly interesting as a demonstration of the degree of importance which the American people can attach to what is sometimes termed, "a mere name." A Tacoma advocate cried with all the ardor of a Patrick Henry: "She believes she is right. She believes she has been cruelly wronged. She has all the enthusiasm, the devotion, and the fervor of the martyr." On the other hand, an opponent stated baldly: "If you pass this resolution, it will be the main feature of our campaigns out there for several years to come." He went on to say that the next main issue would be the name—not the administration, the tariff, immigration, or the League of Nations.

Dr. Merriam, shifted from judge's bench to witness-stand, appeared for the Board, and testified vigorously in polysyllables:

Insidious way . . . not only untruthful but scurrilous . . . persistent and notorious propaganda . . . a death blow to the stability of international geographic nomenclature.

Representative John F. Miller led the attack on Tacoma, in even more precise language: "pure local selfishness." Of the sponsor of the resolution he remarked: "Now, I am not criticizing Senator Dill, but he simply did not know what he was talking about." Mr. James M. Ashton, a Tacoma lawyer, appeared for his city. He made much of a typographical error in Vancouver's report, his legalistic mind apparently hoping that the question of an S or an N might invalidate the whole document. But he also made the best summing-up of the controversy when he stated: "This whole situation is full of rabbit trails." It was—and many of the trails were littered with small pellets!

Congress failed to take action, and after 1925 the dispute quieted. It was no longer even a good lost cause. The proposition had been discussed too long, and ignominiously defeated too often. It had become a laughing-mattor and a bore. An occasional die-hard old-timer continued saying Mount Tacoma.

Chapter XLII ◖ Unfinished business

As LONG as a civilization remains vigorous, the process of naming and re-naming never ceases entirely. Yet the history of the last quarter-century indicates that in the United States the great creative period has ended. Naming has arrived at a stage of development when new and important issues seldom arise, when the minor shiftings and re-shiftings may be called a mere attempt to settle unfinished business.

In 1917 and 1918 a world war left less effect upon the map than the average presidential election of a hundred years earlier. Most of the few changes were with names containing the elements German, Kaiser, and Berlin. Others were scattering. Potsdam in Missouri became Pershing; Brandenburg in Texas, Old Glory; Kiel in Oklahoma, Loyal. Thalheim in California was translated to Valley Home. But numerous places called by such thoroughly German names as Leipsic, Hamburg, and Frankfort remained unchanged. Although Bismarck was widely publicized as the founder of German imperialism, the capital of North Dakota kept his name.

Thus what had happened during the Revolution was repeated. There was plenty of hatred and hysteria, but the attitude seemed to be: "It's *our* name now!" Moreover, two hundred years of German immigration had planted thousands of names; an unlettered American could not distinguish German from Iroquoian, and might himself be of German origin. When Germantown in Texas made the change, the citizens honored a local boy killed in France, not realizing or not caring that Schroeder was a thoroughly German name.

After the war some of the towns even reverted. Lens in Georgia became Berlin again, and Meekin in Illinois went back to German Valley.

Neither the names of battles, as in the Mexican War, nor the names of generals, as in the Civil War, became popular. Pershing commanded and led to victory more Americans than Grant ever saw or Washington imagined. His name stands on half a dozen villages, a county in Nevada, and a few streets and squares. The smashing of the Meuse salient was a brilliant victory, but not a single town is named St. Mihiel. Perhaps that one was too hard to pronounce, but only three villages are called Argonne, and their total population is about four hundred.

The reason was partly of course that the map was already well filled. Even so, the absence of such names was out of proportion. It was another evidence that the veterans remembered gas and French mud more than any glamour of war.

Far from celebrating military glory the most frequently given names were probably the simple ones by which the men of the

Forest Service commemorated former comrades, dead overseas. In English Mountain and French Mountain, both of Oregon, they commemorated also their allies.

In 1920 an Arizona copper-camp took the name Clemenceau. The old statesman apparently was moved, and in his will bequeathed a vase:

designed by Chaplet in a light lilac color, which will be found on the shelf above the mirror in my study. The vase will be placed in a suitable case in the high school of the town.

With French prudence he stipulated that, if the town was abandoned, the vase should be returned. As it sometimes happens with copper-camps, the town *was* abandoned—and the vase was returned to France. The Premier's original letter was framed, and still hangs on the wall of the office of the superintendent of schools for the district. Clemenceau survives as a post-office.

One unsettled problem is: Who determines the names of natural features? Fundamentally, names are a part of language, and the eventual power rests with the people. In an old country even a tyrannical government would hesitate to change the name of a river or mountain; such a decree would probably be as futile as a law that *cat* should henceforth mean *cow*.

The names of English natural features were fixed long before the establishment of a legal system. Blackstone did not even recognize the problem. Nevertheless, colonial governments sometimes assumed the right. State legislatures under a democratic system might reasonably enough believe that in naming as in other matters they represented the will of the people. But such attempts were few and sporadic.

Many of them sprang from the whim of some individual to which the Legislature obligingly yielded. Thus a law of 1889 ordered that:

the name of Bully Creek in Malheur county, Oregon, be and the same hereby is changed to Alder Creek.

Many such changes were ineffective, because the representatives misjudged the people's will. The California Legislature once honored a governor by calling Lake Tahoe for him. The governor was notoriously convivial, and the act produced little except the witticism that a large lake was not aptly named for a man who so seldom drank water. The law still stands, but not even the official road-signs of the state Highway Commission point to Lake Bigler. The Dakota Legislature, for purposes of publicity, once established that the James River should henceforth be the Dakota River. But everybody, including probably the legislators, continued calling it the James, or more familiarly, Jim River.

An improvement upon nature often produces a new feature, and by custom he who pays the piper calls the tune. One of our largest artificial lakes was named Almanor for Alice, Martha, and Elinore, daughters of the president of the power company. Congress appropriated money in 1900 for an improvement of New York harbor, and at the same time enacted that it should be known as Ambrose Channel.

The application of an old name may produce legal questions. For such reasons in 1889 the Tennessee Legislature resolved:

Whereas, Divers opinions exist as to the true source of the Tennessee River, thereby causing confusion in statutes, deeds, and other instruments . . . That the Tennessee extends from its junction with the Ohio River, at Paducah, in the state of Kentucky . . . to the junction of the north fork of the Holston River with the Holston.

Actually this law had no possible validity in the three other states through which the river flowed.

Large rivers and mountain ranges are generally inter-state, and so their delimitation has been a concern of the Board on Geographic Names. As if political- rather than geographic-minded, the Board has sometimes based decisions upon artificial boundaries. It laid off the Rocky Mountains according to state lines, so that with many ranges the one end lies officially in the Rockies and the other end in something else.

In the fifties Congress had re-established the old name Minnesota River, but an act of 1921 was still more radical. The name Colorado River, dating to 1604, was one of the oldest in the country. Applied first to a tributary, it worked down to the main stream and then along it in both directions. Somewhat upstream, however, lay one of the most inaccessible regions in the country. No one ever ascended the Colorado, and so its upper branches were independently named. It thus became, like the Ohio, a river which was "formed" by the union of two others.

The situation was common enough, and no one worried about it. The territory took its name from the river. When surveys were completed, the Colorado was found to flow nowhere within the boundaries of the state. Again no one was concerned. The ordinary man, if he had ever thought of the matter, would have held it unimportant, and would not have seen that anything could be done about it anyway.

Finally some eccentric genius worked out a solution, and the state became interested; for once, the proverb about Mohammed and the mountain could be reversed. The Grand River, eastern branch of the Colorado, arose in the mountains west of Denver. The Legislature therefore passed an act: "The name of the Grand River in Colorado is hereby changed to the Colorado River."

The validity of the act was uncertain, however, especially since the river maintained its old name unchallenged throughout its eighty-mile course in Utah.

The Board was in a doubtful position. Grand River had been scattered all over the West by French trappers. It was much too common, and the Board had a stated policy against such repetitions. But the Board also had declared that a longer branch should be considered the main one, and Green River was a much longer branch of the Colorado than was Grand River. Moreover, the name was long-established and hitherto unchallenged; if the Board eliminated it, the door swung ajar for Mount Tacoma and everything else. The Board, in the end, merely declined to take action, thus giving a milk-toast approval to the old name. Colorado took the case to Congress; Utah raised no objections. In both houses the question was debated as to authority, but the resolutions passed without real opposition.

The prestige of the Board was shaken. Fortunately, by 1921, the names of most natural features were fixed beyond the desire of anyone to tamper with them. From its official source at Lulu Pass the Colorado now flows to the sea. But one may safely guess that the old-timers will say Grand River for years to come, and in the end their tenacity may well bring a reversal.

Congress certainly acted without clear authority. As one member remarked, such an act could be nothing more than an advice to the people to say Colorado River. If the test should be made, the Supreme Court might uphold the power of Congress under one of the more general clauses of the Constitution—or it might rule that such an act constituted an infringement of our liberties.

In spite, however, of all actions of boards and legislative bodies many thousands of names still maintain themselves on a purely informal basis. Many new ones are constantly being invented, and many old ones die out yearly. The number of such names, and indeed of all place-names, may be said to stand in some proportional relation to human activity in any area. A muddy and polluted creek can be left almost nameless, but along a much-frequented trout-stream fishermen will give many names, because they find it convenient to be able to report: "I caught that big fellow up in Flat-Rock Pool." So also, thousands of cars may pass over a long stretch of desert highway without anyone feeling a need for names. But where U. S. 40 crosses the Sierra Nevada, every winter sees a battle to keep the highway clear of snow. In those few miles the snow-plow men have placed their own names thickly, so that in the fury of the storm they can quickly pass information as to conditions at Turnout, the Horseshoe, Big-Shot, or Tin Garage.

The boom-period of the twenties was highly conscious of advertising values, and a certain number of towns continued to change unpleasant-sounding or merely grotesque names of the frontier days. Mosquito shifted to Troutdale; Zigzag, to Rhododendron; Screamerville, to Chancellor. During the Florida boom the realtors changed, among many others, Crooked Lake to Babson Park, Hobe Sound to Olympia, Oldsmer to Tampashores, Ross to Sun City. Their Coral Gables, for sheer flamboyance, equaled any of Gabriel Archer's flights of fancy.

During these same vigorous twenties, however, Americans began to cultivate a more robust vernacular in both writing and speech. Through a century, under the influence of Good Taste, names had become more namby-pamby and insipid. At last the current was stemmed, or even reversed.

Bluff and *bottom* had developed as a fine pair of American words; later, both developed additional meanings, and some people became sensitive. Sometimes the new connotation was not without charm of imagery, as in Muses Bottom. Not unaccountably, however, the inhabitants of Indian Bottom chose to change that name to Blackey. But the great majority of places called Bluff and Bottom remained.

The revival of this more sturdy manner of speech can be seen in a few actual reversals. A California mining camp was once called Fiddletown, for the charming reason, it is said, that "the people over there are always fiddling." It later officially adopted the dubious Oleta. People still used the old name, and in the postwar period it was re-adopted officially.

In a California city a street was called Tunnel Road for the sufficient reason that at one end it became a country road and passed through a tunnel. It grew fashionable, and some of its residents who had not advanced from the mentality of the nineties wished a more elegant name. They agreed upon the banal and stale Woodmere. Appearing before the Council without opposition, they were successful. But the majority of the property-holders revolted against the displacement of their well-established name. The new street-signs were mysteriously torn down at night. Before long, the Council reversed itself.

Even a touch of the old free language of the frontier managed here and there to maintain itself. Will Barnes, in his excellent dictionary of Arizona names, records of one of them:

A rather vulgar origin. At a distance the peak resembles the edifice in the rear of most country dwellings. Early miners so called it for this resemblance.

On a General Land Office map of 1921 the name was allowed officially to stand as S. H. Mountain.

The appearance of many names expressive of modern ideas continued to show the American imagination was not decadent. Post-offices were called Xray, Phoneton, Electron, Radium, Gasoline and Radio. Van Dyke, Michigan, gave its streets such names as Ford, Packard, Dodge, and Cadillac. A Kansas town, dubiously called Bee Pee, became Chevrolet.

The heroes of popular literature, radio, and screen gained their memorials. There is a Gene Autry in Oklahoma, and a Tarzan in Texas. When Nevada ranchers fell into a dispute over a name, the squabble reminded someone of the quarrels in a comic-strip, and the place became Jiggs. Lum and Abner in their program made famous the mythical hill-billy settlement called Pine Ridge, but used the actual atmosphere of Waters, Arkansas. The people of Waters tuned in. Far from taking offense, they laughed and approved. In the end, they changed the name of Waters to Pine Ridge.

The Depression passed without much influence on naming. Even on the crowded map, however, a new Roosevelt appeared here and there, and Norvelt in Pennsylvania, by the application of modern methods, honored the most colorful First Lady.

As the shadow of war moved westward, Germania in Washington became Wellpinit, and Swastika in Arizona became Brilliant. But at that point the process stopped. During two years of actual warfare not a single German-named post-office was shifted. On December 7, 1941, there were four post-offices called Tokio. There are still four. The state of mind seems to be more strongly than ever that the names now belong to us—to alter them would be repudiation of our own history, weakness rather than strength.

As Mrs. Ara Green, Assistant Postmaster of one Tokio (population: 20), put the matter:

> I think those who think of changing the name of Tokio, Texas, have never thought seriously. Our aim in this War—we have started out to change the other Tokyo instead of this one.

In contrast to the independent spirit of the small town, the sensitivity of some intellectuals may be noted. On the campus of a leading university an axial road had been called Axis Drive for some years. After a gossip columnist had made a few jokes, it was meekly changed to University Drive.

With the defense of Bataan, General MacArthur sprang suddenly into hero's stature. A single West Virginia village took his name, and a certain number of streets.

In 1942 the Nazis erased from the earth the town of Lidice in Czechoslovakia, and declared the name abolished. An immediate reply was to plant the name upon a Federal Housing Project in Illinois. The gesture was typically American. No other people had so often borrowed names from other civilizations and so fully developed the habit of using them to express ideals.

Late in 1944 a Committee for the Rebirth of Distomo became active, after the destruction of that Greek village by the Nazis. Its aim was to change the names of the many places called Berlin, and to have them adopt Distomo. Although well sponsored, the attempt fell flat. Stubborn local attachment to the established name again triumphed.

The names also served other purposes. On Labor Day, 1942, the Office of War Information arranged a broadcast. Moscow in Vermont sent a message to the older Moscow. Corresponding messages went from Athens, Pennsylvania; Amsterdam, New York; Warsaw, North Carolina; Oslo, Minnesota; Berlin, Pennsylvania, and other counterpart towns.

The War also saw a new recognition of the military importance of names. The Army and the Navy both began to set up bureaus, but fortunately the work was co-ordinated under the Board on Geographical Names. With its staff suddenly expanded from two to one hundred fifty the Board set about to see to it that an officer ordered to hold the line of Beaver Creek heroically to the last man would not be forced lamely to inquire, *"Which* Beaver Creek?"* But fortunately the Board was offensive-minded, and most of its new energies were directed to transliterating and co-ordinating many thousands of names in far-distant parts of the world.

Chapter XLIII ⟨ Heritage

W<small>HAT</small> is the heritage?—First of all, it is a practical achievement. Nearly every place distinct and important enough to call for frequent location has received a fixed and usable name. Our ancestors might have done better than to leave us saddled with United States of America, and the duplication of the Washingtons. But generally speaking, the job has been done, and done efficiently.

A second feature of American naming is its variety. Such a statement must be maintained in the face of many pronouncements to the contrary. The Board on Geographical Names has deplored the repetition, and the monotony of our names has been a frequent comment of our own and foreign writers. Such critics, however, have not really examined the whole situation.

Repetition is commonest with the names of smaller natural features. Minnesota alone contains more than one hundred bodies of water bearing the uninspiring name Mud Lake. But this is exceptional, and even so, when the total number of our place-names runs into the millions, a great deal of repetition must be expected.

It exists to an even greater degree in other countries. England, smaller than Illinois in area, has five rivers named Stour.

Variety rather than repetition is certainly noteworthy of our towns. Nearly half of our post-offices bear names not used by any other. If to Washington are added all combinations like Washington Heights and Port Washington, the number is 121, but among unvaried names, Franklin appears to be the leader, with a total of only thirty-three. Again to offer comparison, within the narrow limits of England twenty-three places are called Charlton, and thirty more are so called with some distinction such as Charlton Abbots.

The variety of our names, however, arose naturally, more than from any conscious virtue of our people. The period of active naming extended over four centuries, during which time customs and fashions had a chance to change. The work was shared among all classes from border ruffian to Boston Brahmin. It drew upon various languages and races. Finally, it was largely accomplished under the influence of a strong patriotism which by hero-names and other devices produced, often consciously, a national and regional flavor.

Variety also sprang from democracy—that stubborn local pride in the local name, and the feeling that I have just as much right to give and keep a name as you have. Various movements to standardize naming were therefore never more than partially successful, and each added to the variety by planting a special kind of name, but never effacing a large proportion of the old ones.

Actually, the repetition of names is in itself of much interest. Such echoings display the migration of people and ideas, and are links between eras and regions. When the aircraft carrier *Princeton* is launched, the wife of the President of Princeton University is the sponsor, but interest in the ship is shared by the inhabitants of Princeton in twenty-four states, many of them named from the university or its town.

A third feature of the name-pattern is its close connection with both geography and history. In some curious way, indeed, the idea has at times arisen that our names, in comparison with those of Europe, are superficial and unhistorical. Any such belief can rest only upon a mere antiquarianism which feels that the emotions and ideals of 1066 or 1415 are more "historical" than those of 1840 or 1911. Even the much-belabored classical names are eloquent of our history—of enthusiasm for classical literature and post-Revolutionary admiration for the Roman republic.

Historically, the most interesting feature of our names is that they can so often be definitely linked with actual men and events. Washington, for a town in England, is of little more than etymological interest, because no one knows anything about its original Wassa. Our towns named Washington make the connection with a known man, and through him with an era, and an ideal.

A final value of our names is their poetic quality. Such an opinion must be maintained in the face of the indisputable fact that most of the actual American names, like most of the actual American people, are commonplace. Anything else would be both unthinkable and unbearable, just as the basis of a steady diet can be bread and cheese, but not ortolans and caviar. With names the tradition of John Smith is better than that of Gabriel Archer.

Our names, however, probably seem to us more commonplace than the names of foreign countries, because we are familiar with them and know what many of them mean. Comparison again may be to the point. Much, for instance, has been written in praise of the poetic feeling for nature displayed by Celtic place-names. A little study of Ireland or the Scottish Highlands soon dissipates the illusion. Ballymoney is only "big townland" and there are eight of them in Ireland. Benmore shows that the Celt's nature-naming was no different from other people's; it means "big mountain."

The real test for the poetic quality of the names of a country is whether they have appealed to its poets. When we put this test for American names, we find the same result as for so much else. The earlier poets had little feeling for our names, just as they had also little feeling for our scenery, or birds. Then for a while they were chiefly interested in Indian names. Bryant's use of Oregon may even have had something to do with its survival. Whitman also was devoted to Indian names, but he was not a pedantic linguist and frequently sounded the general roll of the states with great enthusiasm. The more modern writers have constantly used the names for poetic ends—Moody, Lindsay, Sandburg, Mac-Leish, Benét. To the list should be added Wolfe, Hemingway, and Steinbeck.

The poetry of a name may spring from three sources. There is the romantic appeal of sonorous sound and sensuous connotation, evoked by the strange and unknown. People who cherish a name chiefly for such reasons do not usually like to have it explained or translated. For them, the poetry is not enhanced, but vanishes, when they learn that Atchafalaya means "long river."

A second source of poetry is in the historical association of the places which lie close to men's hearts—in names like Virginia, Plymouth, and Concord, the shrines on our long pilgrimage. But again we must not err in thinking history something of the far past. The poetic suggestion of a name may be of recent growth—the glitter of Hollywood, the grim power of Chicago.

A third source of poetry is largely the opposite of the first. It is the poetic suggestion which springs from the inherent meaning, even though the actual event of the naming may be unknown. The United States seems particularly rich in such names—Sweetwater, Marked Tree, Lone Pine, Gunsight Hills. In this lies the charm of Cape Fear, Cape Flattery, Cape Disappointment, and Cape Foulweather; of Broken Sword, Broken Straw, and Broken Bow. These are the names which seem to have stories of life and death behind them—Roaring Run, Deadman Creek, Massacre Lake, Rabbit Hole Spring.

Many single names combine more than one source of poetry. Chickamauga is both romantic and historical. So is Mississippi, a name which evokes history and yet is itself a serpentine and uncouth hiss, like brown water eating at a levee bank. Golden Gate might be called at once romantic, historical, and meaningful.

Through the names, great and little, history and geography and poetry press in daily upon us. As the train announcer calls out the stations for a Philadelphia local, half the past of the nation unfolds. It is a rich and poetic heritage—even though its chief guardians are such prosaic books as the Reports of the Board on Geographic Names, the Post-Office Guide, and the Railway Guide, and the brown-lined U.S.G.S. maps.

Yet even beyond these is stored in folk-memory a rich heritage of informal names. Many such places have no strict limits. Who can bound the Middle West? What Mason and Dixon ever ran the line between the South and the Deep South?

There are plenty of other regional names. He is a good student of his country who can place them all—the Western Reserve and the High Desert; the Dixies (there are two of them); the Fire-lands and the Purchase; the Piedmont; Down East; the Panhandle; the Cherokee Strip; the Eastern Shore and the Eastern Slope; No Man's Land; the Cross Timbers. Not all are old; most people can remember the time before there was any region called the Dust Bowl.

Our cities have similar names. No one holds legal title to a lot in Hell's Kitchen, but the place exists, nevertheless. So do others—the Gas House District, the Golden Triangle, the Loop, the Back Bay, the Potrero, Algiers, the Neck.

Even the small towns offer the same richness. You can find it everywhere—Frog Hollow and Jugtown, Butchertown and Little Germany. The country districts are perhaps richest of all—Seldom Seen, Possum Glory, Chicken Bristle, Hog Eye, and Bug Tussel. Some might call these merely nicknames, but they can hardly be distinguished from other names except on a purely legalistic basis.

All such names are in fact strangely permanent. They cannot be stricken from the map by official decree, because they are not on the map. Fulmination against them merely gives them the lure of the forbidden. They can be removed only by depopulation of a region or by some other catastrophe great enough to open a gap in the folk-memory.

The land has been named, and the names are rooted deep. Lake Mead may fill with silt, and Lake Michigan again spill south to the Gulf—but the names may still remain. Let the conqueror come, or the revolution rage; many of our names have survived both already, and may again. Though the books should be burned and the people themselves be cut off, still from the names—as from arrowheads and potsherds—the patient scholar may piece together some record of what we were.

So after an age has passed, man (that curious mammal) may come again, piecing out the altered syllables, reading the names. By -ville and -burg he will know that here the Americans once passed. By Delmar and Texarkana he will trace forgotten boundaries. By Atco and Alcoa he will plot long-vanished industries. Lexington, Missouri, Fort Wayne—here, he will say, lived Americans, red men with scalp-locks, farmers with muskets firing from behind stone walls. Washington, Jefferson City, Lincoln—in some changed form he will read the names, and ask, "Were they men or gods?" Yes, here passed the Americans—tall men in coon-skin caps selling beaver-pelts, fat men in horn-rimmed glasses selling sub-divisions—Ten Mile Creek, Little Round Top, Mount Pleasant, and Richland. After all else has passed, the names may yet remain.

' [AUTHOR'S NOTE: Here ends the book as originally written; the supplemental material follows.]

Chapter XLIV ❨ Alaska

THE first bestowal of a name in the subcontinent now known as Alaska occurred on July 20, 1741, from the Russian ship *St. Peter* lying off the coast. Its captain was the Danish-born Vitus

Bering, but he was ill and confined to his cabin. His quarrelsome and inefficient Russian mates were in charge of operations; also on board was the highly critical German naturalist, Georg Wilhelm Steller.

What should have been a joyous occasion thus seems to have been a lugubrious one; at least, we would so gather from Steller's report:

> We came to anchor among numerous islands. The outermost of these had to be named Cape St. Elias, because we dropped anchor under its lee on St. Elias's day. For the officers were determined to have a Cape on their chart, although it was plainly pointed out to them [doubtless by Steller himself] that an island cannot be called a cape, but that only a noticeable projection of land into the ocean in a certain direction can be so called, the same meaning being conveyed by the Russian word *nos* [nose]. But in the present instant, the island would represent nothing but a detached head or a detached nose.

Nevertheless Cape St. Elias it was, and so it remains. Actually, the mates rather than the pedantic naturalist would seem to have the better case. Their cape is the most outstanding headland along more than a hundred miles of coast. As for the end of an island not properly being called a cape, that would seem to be something in Steller's imagination, for in spite of his confident statements there are numerous examples to the contrary.

The voyagers realized that what they had discovered was a part of the American continent, and so they gave no general name to the country. On the whole, moreover, the voyage was not prolific of names. Nine only were bestowed, all but one by the unimaginative system that had outraged Steller, that is, by tagging the landfall with the name of the saint whose day it happened to be in the Russian calendar. The only one of the later names to be preserved on the modern map is, however, the only one not named for a saint—the Shumagin Islands, which commemorate a seaman who died there. Cherikov in the *St. Paul*, who had become separated from Bering, also made some landfalls, but seems to have given no names at all.

The paucity of names, their monotony, and their low survival rate, are not surprising in view of the conditions. The weather was stormy, and the landfalls were generally mere glimpses of some surf-pounded, fog-shrouded headland which could not be accurately charted. In addition, the commander was continuously ill, and the voyagers suffered—in Steller's words—from "cold, dampness, nakedness, vermin, fright, and terror." These were not good conditions for the successful giving of names.

After Bering's voyage the Russian fur-traders began to make advances into the Aleutians, but little was done to establish geographical knowledge.

These fur-traders subdued the islanders with great brutality, but also associated with them on terms of intimacy. As evidence, one may point out that all the way from Attu to Unimak the islands, with few exceptions, bear native names. Also such a commonly repeated name as Chiniak is Aleutian, and has a significance in which early seafarers would have to be interested. It is, in fact, a signpost name, indicating a place where the sea was dangerous with rocks or otherwise impassable. The Russians also bestowed some names in their own language, but like fur-traders generally they were not interested in exploration and accurate mapping.

So, in the whole generation following Bering, only a single important new name was recorded. Even before Bering had sailed, the Russians in Siberia had heard from the Chukchi tribesmen of a "great land" lying to the eastward, across the ocean. What actual words the Chukchi used we cannot know, but the Russians translated them as *bolshaya zemblya*. Probably this never came to be used as a real name, and when the Russians reached this country they considered it merely to be a part of America, as it certainly was. The only present importance of *bolshaya zemblya* is that it has supplied the popular belief that Alaska means "great land."

That name itself began to appear shortly after 1760, in various spellings, as Alaeksu, Alachschak, Alaschka, and Alaxa. It was mentioned vaguely as an island close to the mainland but not the mainland; again, as a large island lying north of Kodiak. Since the only islands lying in that direction are a good deal smaller than Kodiak itself, such a description indicates that Alaeksu must be taken to be some part of the continent itself, presumably the peninsula to which the name Alaska has always been especially attached. This is the more likely since the word itself in Aleut can be translated as "mainland." In addition, a map based on voyages of the seventeen-sixties shows Alaxa as an island northeast of Unimak, which would actually have to be the tip of the present Alaska Peninsula. Whatever its original application, the name was destined for a long and devious but extremely successful future.

Only with the voyage of the great Captain James Cook in 1778 did the naming of the mainland coast really begin. This voyage is, in fact, almost a complete contrast to Bering's. The one is good reading for anyone who wishes to believe that Russians are natural bunglers; the latter is equally pleasant for an Anglophile.

By Cook's time, voyages of discovery had been in vogue for almost four centuries, and what we may call a code for the giving of names had been fairly well established. His namings therefore are of interest not only because he established the basic pattern, but also because the later explorers did as much as he did. First, if you were what we may call an "ethical" explorer, you respected the names already given. If the natives were friendly and if you could talk with them, you recorded their names—as Cook, indeed, had just done for most of the Hawaiian Islands. Along the American coast, however, he established little communication with the natives. On the other hand, he was meticulous in recording the few names, Russian and native, that he found on the Russian charts which he had with him. Actually, he went farther than he needed to do. Not only did he preserve Bering's name Cape St. Elias, but also he put it on the great mountain which Bering had seen but not named. He is also responsible for the first use of the term Bering Strait.

As for the large island Alaschka, which appeared on one of his charts, Cook hunted around for this, but was unable to find it—naturally, because it was not there. Justifiably a little irritated, he finally declared it to be imaginary, a sound conclusion, as far as an island was concerned. With its larger application Cook was also concerned, and he wrote:

The American continent is here called, by the Russians, as well as by the islanders, Alaschka; which name though it properly belong only to the country adjoining Oonemak, is used by them in speaking of the American continent in general, which they know perfectly well to be a great land.

In employing "great land," Cook was probably echoing earlier usage. What was of more importance was his testimony that Alaschka might indicate the continent. Cook himself obviously disapproved of this usage. Ironically, he was to be quoted as the chief authority for it, and because of his great prestige his testimony was to be of important or even decisive influence in finally establishing the name.

Cook's first landfall, on May 2, was a prominent mountain which a Spanish voyager had already called San Jacinto. Ignorant of this, Cook called it Mount Edgcumbe. He gave no reason for the naming, and it may have had a double origin. Mount Edgcumbe that overlooks Plymouth harbor, from which Cook had sailed, must have been one of the last bits of England that he had seen, and perhaps this far-off mountain reminded him of it in some way. But also, and certainly, Lord Edgcumbe was an admiral and the Treasurer of the Royal Household.

On this same day Cook came to a bay with some islands near its entrance, "for which reason I named it the *Bay of Islands.*" This name, though a commonplace descriptive, should remind us that by 1778 Cook was such an old hand at exploring that he was repeating himself. He had already used Bay of Islands for an inlet on the coast of New Zealand.

Late in the day Cook encountered "a fine gale," and then "clear weather." In the morning this unclouded atmosphere let him see "a very high peaked mountain, which obtained the name of *Mount Fair Weather.*" In addition, this was a counterpart echo of Cape Foulweather, which he had already bestowed upon a point far to the south.

At the same time he named Cross Sound, "as being first seen on that day so marked in our calendar," that is, Holy Cross Day.

These first four names illustrate his methods. First, he commemorated friends, brother officers in the Navy (especially those of high rank), other royal officers, and members of the royal family. Among the commemoratives we note Cape Douglas, "in honour of my very good friend, Dr. Douglas, canon of Windsor"; King's Island (now King Island) for one of the lieutenants; Bristol Bay, "in honour of the admiral Earl of Bristol"; Norton Sound, "in honour of Sir Fletcher Norton, Speaker of the House of Commons"; Cape Elizabeth, with the additional reason that it was discovered on the princess's birthday; Prince William Sound; Cape Prince of Wales.

Second, he gave descriptive names, many of them, for obvious reasons—Green Islands, Round Island. Of Snug Corner Bay he commented, "and a very snug place it is." Bald Head perhaps involved a touch of humor. Shoal Ness is of interest as marking an unsuccessful attempt to plant the archaic term for headland on a coast where the similar Russian word *nos* was already established.

Third, as with Mount Fair Weather, he named for incidents; as is to be expected, these names were more interesting. Point Possession recorded the taking possession of the country in the king's name, although Great Britain never pressed this claim. Sledge Island was thus called because of a Russian or Eskimo sled which the explorers found there. The River Turnagain marked the farthest point to which the ships penetrated in a long inlet; here also Cook repeated himself, since he had charted a Cape Turnagain in New Zealand.

Finally, Cook named by the calendar—not only Cross Sound, but also Mount St. Augustine, and Cape Bede. Such religious commemoratives suggest a Spaniard rather than an Englishman; the officers of the Royal Navy have not often been celebrated for their piety. Cook was apparently something of an exception, and we can note that he also commemorated several clerical friends. Perhaps, however, as his repetitions suggest, he was merely running out of names by this time and resorted in desperation to what the editor is careful to call "our calendar," lest anyone should think a good Englishman had turned Catholic. Actually the distinction is only theoretical, for in the Roman calendar also Augustine of Canterbury and the Venerable Bede are honored on May 26 and 27.

Cook not only thus charted the whole coast from its extreme south to Icy Point north of Bering Strait, but also he firmly implanted the most important names. Only in one instance did he fail to give a name where one was needed, and this was for an obvious reason. The code among explorers had never quite decided whether a man was justified in naming something for himself. Yet there was an obvious injustice in honoring the subordinate officers and not the commander. Cook handled the matter more tactfully than some other voyagers had done, and would do, by simply failing to give a name to the finest of all the inlets which he discovered. He referred to it merely as the "great river." When the expedition returned to England after his death, the matter was settled in a way described by the editor's note, "Captain Cook having here left a blank which he had not filled up with any particular name, Lord Sandwich directed, with the greatest propriety, that it should be called *Cook's River*." Altered to Cook's Inlet, it remains as a noble body of water and a fitting memorial to one of the most notable of explorers.

Cook had done his work so well as to inspire an epigram that he left his successors little to do except to admire. The chief interest associated with later explorers along the Northwest Coast lies in the diversity of their nationalities and languages, which has resulted in a pleasing variety of coastal nomenclature.

Even before the time of Cook the Spanish had sent one expedition into southern Alaskan waters, and in the next few years several others sailed north from San Francisco Bay. Few of their namings have survived, but here and there we meet with such a name as Arboles (trees) Island; Quemado (burned) Cape; and Bucareli Bay, commemorating a viceroy of Mexico. Some of the Spanish namings, taken literally, are colorful. Abreojo Rocks, sometimes translated as "Eye-opener," means more precisely, "Open the eye!" and is as much as to say, "Look out here for trouble!" Alargate Rocks represents the adaptation of a pilot's phrase, "Give this a wide berth." Quita Sueno Rock is "Quit dreaming!" or "Keep awake!"

Not one of the names here listed has a religious signification. At the end of the eighteenth century, the period of the Enlightenment, the influence of the Church had declined even in Spain. Except on one voyage, when they had a priest along, these Spanish naval officers seemed to consider themselves primarily European gentlemen rather than Catholics, and they rarely gave religious names.

In 1786 the French sent an expedition under La Pérouse. A few of his namings survived. One of these is Cenotaph Island, where he erected a monument to some of his men who had been drowned. Port Necker he named for the famous French Minister of Finance; Mount Crillon, for the current Minister of Marine.

There was even one Italian voyager, though he sailed under the Spanish flag. This was Malaspina, whose name is preserved on a large glacier, though it was not so called by him, but by the Americans many years later. In any case, it may be called an Italian name.

In all this voyaging the Russians counted for very little. Their only important exploration was that of Otto von Kotzebue in 1816. Kotzebue was a patriotic Russian, but of a German family. His chief contribution was the exploration of a deep inlet north of Bering Strait, which Cook had passed by. Capes Krusenstern and Espenberg, the guardian points of the inlet, commemorate two of Kotzebue's friends, who like him were of German origin, but served in the Russian navy—another instance of the internationality of the period. Goodhope Bay preserves, in translation, the explorer's momentary encouragement—Kotzebue was a great optimist—that he "might really hope to make a very remarkable discovery here." On the other hand, Cape Deceit (again, as so often in Alaska, the name has been translated) records a disappointment, and was so called for a "double reason," because he had erroneously expected to find a bay behind the cape, and because some of the local "Americans" had been inclined to cheat in their bartering.

How he named the inlet itself, and at the same time solved one of the problems of a voyager, may be told in his own words: "In compliance with the general wish of my companions, I called this newly-discovered sound by my own name, Kotzebue's Sound." We may guess that the commander did not require much urging and that the mates and scientific gentlemen knew what was expected of them.

Even after the time of Cook, however, the more important voyagers along the coast were the English; of these the most to be noted is Captain George Vancouver, who had sailed with Cook in '78, explored Puget Sound with his own expedition in '92, and finally returned to the Northwest Coast in '93 and '94. He charted with meticulous care, and necessarily had to bestow names by the dozen. He seems to be the one responsible for two characteristic usages of this coast. He commonly used *arm* for an inlet, and thus what Cook had called Turnagain River became Turnagain Arm. Vancouver also seems to have brought into use *canal* in place of *channel*. He himself, indeed, used *channel,* but he took over the word *canal* from Spanish charts and used it in an English context.

In his actual namings Vancouver showed little originality. He commemorated notables (Point Ramsden, "after Mr. Ramsden, the optician"), or his companions ("this island I named Detton's Island, after our wounded shipmate"). He was scrupulous about paying debts of international gratitude. Point Higgins was for the president of Chile; Behm's Channel (or Canal) for a Russian major who had aided Cook's expedition in 1779; Revillagigedo Island after the viceroy of Mexico, as a gesture of thanks for Spanish co-operation.

Like all explorers Vancouver gave a few descriptives, such as

Slate Island. Only a few of his names sprang from incidents. Two of these are Escape Point and the close-by Traitors Cove, where one of his boats was fortunate enough to escape from what was considered a treacherous attack of the natives. (Traitors was transformed into Traders for a while, but in the end returned to its original form.)

Because Vancouver's namings were recorded in well-published books and on good charts, most of them survived. He had no success, however, with his attempts to provide names for large sections. His New Cornwall, New Hanover, and New Norfolk have vanished.

To British explorers of the early nineteenth century goes the honor of exploring the northern coast. Three expeditions were necessary to outline it fully.

In 1826 Captain Frederick William Beechey attempted to exceed Cook's mark, but found himself blocked by ice at about the same point. He managed, however, to send one of his boats ahead. It rounded a bleak far-northern spit of land, and on its return Beechey called this Point Barrow, thus honoring John Barrow, traveler, writer, and geographer, second secretary of the Admiralty, and a chief promoter of Arctic exploration. By calling it a point and not a cape, Beechey gave an indication that he failed to recognize its significance. If he himself had been there, he might well have given the more honorific name.

In the same year—the expeditions hoped to meet—Captain John Franklin advanced westward along the coast from the mouth of the Mackenzie River. He named the British Mountains because they were on British territory, though actually they extend across the border. Point Demarcation was for him the "boundary between the British and Russian Dominions." Once on Russian territory, he graciously named the Romanzof Mountains for the former chancellor of Russia, who had been the patron of Kotzebue's expedition. Most of Franklin's complimentary namings were of the usual kind, but his Flaxman Island is a pleasing exception in favor of the arts, being named for John Flaxman, a then much-honored British sculptor. The season was an unfavorable one of storms, ice, and fog. Point Anxiety, named only two days before the expedition turned backward, reflected a growing sense of strain and hazard. Return Reef marked the point at which Franklin turned back.

In 1837 two Hudson's Bay men, Peter Warren Dease and Thomas Simpson, closed the final gap. They were highly uninspired namers, calling nearly everything after Company men. The only exception was Boat Extreme, which recorded the point where they left their boats and began to travel overland. Their chief discovery was a large stream: "We called it Colville River, as a mark of respect for Andrew C. Colville, Esquire, of the Hudson's Bay Co."

Long before the British had completed their coastal explorations, the Russians had begun to make settlements. Their chief foundation, one of the coastal islands, they called Fort Archangel Gabriel. In 1802 the local Indians massacred the garrison, but two years later the Russians reoccupied the site. Apparently deciding that Gabriel had failed them, they shifted allegiance to his more military colleague, and called it Fort Archangel Michael. The town that then grew up was called merely New Archangel, thus being distinguished from the older Archangel on the White Sea, and making no distinction between Gabriel and Michael. In common speech, however, the town came to be called by the Indian name Sitka. Its meaning, as with so many of the aboriginal names, seems to have been lost, but it was probably that of the local tribe associated with a village on the opposite side of the island from the present town.

During their near-century of occupation, the Russians made little penetration of the interior, but they gave many coastal names. As far north as the mouth of the Yukon, these Russian names interestingly supplement the English ones. The "big names" are English, since Cook and his successors were only concerned with the larger features. In between, the Russian fur-traders placed the little names. Most of these, as is to be expected, were simple descriptives. Frequently repeated were such adjectives as *bolshoi,* "big"; *dolgoi,* "long"; *zelonoi,* "green"; *viesokoi,* "high"; *kamenoi,* "rocky"; *krugloi,* "round"; *liesnoi,* "woody"; *tolstoi,* "broad." Of some special interest is *kekur,* which survives on Kekurnoi Cape and elsewhere. It means "pinnacle," but is not Slavic, being a word which the Russians had picked up from some tribe along the north coast of Europe or Asia.

Naturally the native animals and birds left their trace in the names. The Morzhovoi Peninsula is for the walrus; the Nerpichi Islands, near Sitka, for the seal. Govorushka Lake on St. George Island is for a kind of gull, though it means literally "chatterbox."

On the whole, however, the most remarkable thing about the Russian names in Alaska in their unimportance. First, the British named the larger features. Second, the Russians adopted many native names. Third, the Americans translated many names into English.

In the end, the important Russian names came to be those commemorating individuals, such as the Pribilof Islands, for the pilot who discovered them in 1786. Here too can go Baranof Island, called for the great Russian governor. Bering Strait actually owes its name to the Englishman Cook. Similarly, the Alexander Archipelago was named after the Czar, but by the Americans.

One important Alaskan name is of Russian origin but so disguised as to seem Indian. The Russians called one of the rivers Mednorechka, "copper," because of the metal found along its course. After the Russians had left, this name was passed on to the Americans, probably through the Indians, as Mednoviska, Midnooski, and finally as Matanuska. With the colonization of the valley in the nineteen-thirties it became widely known.

During their whole period of occupation the Russians clung to the seacoast, and their only important penetration of the interior was along the great stream that flowed into Bearing Sea through many mouths. The Russians adopted the Eskimo name Kwikpak, "river-big." This name was accepted by the geographers, and got on maps all over the world. Then, in 1846, Mr. J. Bell of the Hudson's Bay Company entered the country—as we might say—through the back door; advancing from the east he came to a very large stream, which the local Indians told him was called Yukon-na, "big river." Still further to complicate the situation, other Hudson's Bay men came to the chief Canadian branch of this stream still higher up and called it Lewes River.

Everything thus seemed set for a highly complicated naming-system. In later years, however—partly, no doubt, because Kwik-pak is a silly-sounding name to most people—the Indian name displaced the Eskimo one, except that the latter remained to designate one of the branches of the river in the delta. Finally, well on in the twentieth century, Lewes also was superseded. Yukon, having sloughed off the -na, meaning "river," thus ended a highly successful career by becoming the undisputed name of one of the world's great rivers, and of a Canadian territory as well.

In 1867, as any textbook of history tells us, "the United States purchased Alaska." Actually, this is a far from accurate statement. What was really purchased was Russian America.

Immediately a problem arose. By the very fact of the acquisition, the territory ceased to be Russian America. A new name, therefore, was necessary. Senator Charles Sumner, in a famous speech on the cession, put the situation well, in words which both expressed the general attitude of the time toward names and suggested a new one.

As these extensive possessions . . . pass from the imperial government of Russia, they will naturally receive a new name. They will be no longer Russian America. How shall they be called? Clearly, any name borrowed from classical antiquity or from individual invention will be little better than misnomer or nickname unworthy of the historic occasion. Even if taken from our own annals, it will be of doubtful taste. The name should come from the country itself. It should be indigenous, aboriginal, one of the autochthons of the soil. Happily such a name exists, as proper in sound as in origin. It appears from the report of Cook, . . . that the euphonious designation now applied to the peninsula . . . was the sole word used originally by the native islanders, "when speaking of the American continent in gen-

eral, which they knew perfectly well to be a great land." It only remains, that, following these natives, whose places are now ours, we,
too, should call this "great land" Alaska.

This passage introduces Sumner as the original sponsor of the
name Alaska. But there are other claimants. One of these is General H. W. ("Old Brains") Halleck, who suggested Alaska in a
letter to the War Department. Secretary Seward, who had ne-
gotiated the treaty, is put forward by his son-biographer as having
made the decision about the name. In reality, Alaska seems to
have been established by a kind of folk-process. At the time, no
territory was officially established, and so the question of a name
did not come before Congress. As usual, various names were suggested—Sitka, Yukon, Aliaska, Oonalaska, Aleutia. One newspaper even mentioned the name Alexander, in honor of the Czar,
who was highly popular because of his support of the United
States during the Civil War. The humorous coinage Walrussia
frequently appeared in the newspapers but need not be taken as a
serious contender. Curiously enough, there seems to have been
no suggestion of using the name Lincoln, another good indication that the martyred president failed to obtain heroic status in
the years immediately following his death.

On the whole, however, Alaska took the lead early; by mid-
1867 it was in general use. In the process of its establishment,
Sumner certainly had a hand; so did Halleck; so, quite possibly,
did Seward. But so, in all likelihood, did a lot of other people.
The *New York Times,* for instance, was using Alaska three weeks
before Halleck wrote his letter, or before Sumner's speech was
made available to the public.

Once Russian America had become inapplicable, numerous
people—journalists and others—must have looked at their maps
to see what other names were available. Anyone thus looking
would have seen *Alaska* in a prominent position. It seemed to
suit excellently—an aboriginal term, somewhat vaguely applied,
not confined within precise limits, readily expandable to cover
the whole area.

Some historical analogies may be offered. A peninsula—and so the name Alaska was applied before 1867—is not perfectly delineated as is an island, and there is often a tendency for the name to be extended more widely around its base. Thus, Italy was at first applied only to the "heel." So also Florida and California have exceeded their peninsular limits. Alaska offers another striking example.

During many years after 1867, the Americans paid little attention to the interior of Alaska, and the chief naming-agents were the chart-makers of the Coast and Geodetic Survey. Their important contribution was, in historical perspective, a surprising one.

In the past, when the Americans had taken over a region already supplied with names by former occupants, whether Dutch, French, or Spanish, they had accepted most of them. In Alaska, however, the chart-makers set out to replace the Russian names in a wholesale manner, usually by translating them into English. Thus Bolshoi became Big; Sievernoi, North; Zelonoi, Green; Toporkof, Puffin. This was probably not done out of any anti-Russian feeling, for at the time the two countries enjoyed friendly relations. This is borne out by the fact that features named after individual Russians generally kept their names. Even Tolstoi, "broad," was usually preserved, doubtless because it was thought to represent the family name. Neither can it be maintained that the nature of the Russian language—difficult and grotesque-seeming to speakers of English—was a deciding factor, for the same period saw the adoption of many Eskimo jaw-breakers such as Kuyuyukak, Kwikloaklok, Kwigillingok, and Pikmiktalik. Compared with these, such simple Russian words as *leesy,* "fox," and *dolgoi,* "long," offered no problems. Most likely, the feeling behind the translation was that the country was now American, and that the new maps would therefore be more useful with English names. On the whole, the result was good—chiefly because it failed to be completely successful, like most such movements. Thus Krutoi, "steep," once was preserved and once was translated. Sometimes, also, the translation by being made intelligible became more colorful. Slava Rossie, a cape on St. Matthew Island, was much more vivid when translated as Glory of Russia.

This last had been originally the name of a ship, and should serve to remind us of the prevailing habit among seamen of all nations of calling places after their ships. The coasts of Alaska are rich in such names, many of them colorful and seemingly inexplicable. Thus is to be explained Zenobia Rock, where a Russian ship of that name struck in 1855. Thus also comes that other classical name, Iphigenia Bay, named by George Davidson of the Coast Survey in a moment of historical reminiscence for a ship which had touched there in 1788. From other ships, we have the Vixen Islands, Saranac Peak, and City of Topeka Rock.

This George Davidson was an enthusiastic namer, and also a student of naming. To him we owe the explanation of one of the most curious of Alaskan names. Cape Nome first appeared on the British charts about the middle of the nineteenth century, but no one could find it to be a word either in English or Russian or Eskimo. Finally, in 1901, Davidson stimulated the Admiralty to an investigation, and received a letter which not only solved the mystery, but also told a highly curious story.

When the MS chart of this region was being constructed on board H.M.S. *Herald,* attention was drawn to the fact that this point had no name, and a mark (? name) was placed against it.

In the hurry of dispatching this chart from the ship this ? appears to have been inked in by a rough draftsman and appeared as Cape Name, but the stroke of the "a" being very indistinct, it was interpreted by our draftsman here as C. Nome, and has appeared with this name ever since.

This information is from an officer who was on board the *Herald* when the chart was being constructed.

Nome is therefore an authenticated example of the workings of mere error. This dubious ancestry has not interfered with its prosperity, and it now designates not only the original cape, but also several other natural features and a famous town.

American exploration of the interior had actually been begun while the country was still Russian. These expeditions sent out in the eighteen-sixties by the Western Union Telegraph Company were attempting to link America and Europe by an overland wire. When the enterprise was abandoned, the reports and maps were left unpublished, and so there was no appreciable influence upon naming. This is a good example of the fact that mere exploration does not necessarily result in names.

Far different was the first important official exploration of the interior. In 1885 an army expedition commanded by Lieutenant Henry T. Allen, Second Cavalry, left the south coast at the mouth of Copper River. Allen, a Kentucky-born West Pointer, was twenty-six years old; his "troops" consisted of Sergeant Robertson and Private Fickett. Also with the expedition were two civilians, prospectors, Johnson and Bremner. These names are mentioned since all of them except one were destined to be prominent on the map of Alaska.

The young lieutenant conducted what may be considered a model expedition, in nothing more admirable than in its careful naming. When possible, he recorded native names, even such a one as Lake Mentanontlekakat, which he ironically recorded as "euphoneous [sic]." He gave his own names when he was out of contact with the natives, and also when he had to identify some feature which the Indians had not even bothered to name. Their habits in this respect bothered Allen, and he once noted his puzzlement about a mere cut-bank of clay. "Why this should receive a name when prominent mountain peaks did not I could not ascertain." In such a comment, he merely displayed a common misapprehension. A "place" is named when it is of importance to the people concerned. The cut-bank doubtless noted a certain point on the stream or trail, whereas the mountain was too large and vague to be of any use to the Indians.

The expedition ascended along Copper River, crossed to the

Tanana, and descended that stream in canoes; finally Allen explored the Koyukuk basin on foot, accompanied only by Private Fickett and some Indians. In all this large region Allen established the basic name-pattern. Most commonly, if he could not discover a native name, he gave one honoring some individual—one of his companions, a superior officer, a scientist, a member of his family, or a friend. Occasionally he fell back upon conventional descriptives—as with Cathedral Bluffs and Mount Cone.

Along the Tanana, Allen named the chief bluffs, rapids, and tributaries. The great glacial stream known as Robertson River preserves the name of his sergeant. The equally notable Johnson River was called from one of his prospectors.

Allen found that the river itself was known to the natives throughout most of its course as the Nebesna. That it would have some name other than Tanana might have been inferred from the meaning of Tananata-na, "mountain-people-river," most likely to be given by people who are on the outside looking at the mountains. Because of Allen's more definite establishment of the clipped form Tanana, the name of Nebesna is now applied only to an inconsiderable part of the river's headwaters.

The lieutenant's greatest moment must have occurred on a May morning when he looked out at one of the continent's finest assemblages of mountain peaks. He named one of them Mount Blackburn, "in honor of Hon. J. C. S. Blackburn, of Kentucky." The second he was pleased to call Mount Tillman, "in honor of Prof. S. E. Tillman, of the United States Military Academy." The third he called Mount Drum, "in honor of the Adjutant-General of the Army." The fourth he merely noted "has been called Mount Sanford." In this last naming, Allen—good southerner that he was—was honoring his own family, more particularly Reuben Sanford, his great-grandfather. In thus bestowing a name, Allen may have set a new precedent. Mountains, lakes, and streams had frequently been named for fathers and mothers, for brothers and sisters, for wives and sweethearts—but never previously, perhaps, for a great-grandfather!

Three of these names still remain upon the great mountains

which dominate the Richardson and Glenn Highways. Mount Tillman, however, proved to be a ghost. One peak in the region, or perhaps the group of peaks taken together, as seen from a great distance, had already been named Mount Wrangell by Americans who thus honored the Russian governor. Although Allen knew of this peak and its name, he was apparently confused from his particular point of view, so that what he called Mount Tillman was really Mount Wrangell, or else he considered Wrangell to be a general name for the whole range.

A pair of Allen's namings suffered a later confusion. In descending the Tanana he had named one tributary the Goodpaster, after a Kentucky family; the next one, the Volkmar, after one of his superior officers. By some later confusion, perhaps the mere carelessness of a map-maker, the names were reversed, and they so stand today.

In naming Waite's Island, Allen took care to note, "Called in honor of Miss Waite, of Washington City, who has evinced a marked interest in the development of Alaska." Whether this interest of Miss W.'s centered upon a young lieutenant, we can only guess. (Two years later, Allen married a Miss Johnston.) Baker's *Geographic Dictionary of Alaska,* curiously ignoring this note, records with what seems a bit of primness, "So named by Allen, 1885, after Chief Justice Morrison Remick Waite."

That perennial problem of the explorer, how to give a name for himself without taking leave of his own modesty, Allen solved with considerable ingenuity. When traveling with the Indians along the Koyukuk, he found that they called most of the tributaries by some name ending in *-kakat,* meaning "mouth of." (This is, in fact, a common primitive practice, since streams are recognized by the nature of their outlet into the main river.) One of the largest of these tributaries Allen simply recorded, without comment, as the Allenkákat! The name, however, eventually reverted to the Indian term Alatna. Later explorers quite properly took care of Allen's memory by placing his name upon a high peak near the Canadian border and some miles south of the Alaska Highway.

Of the explorers, only Private Fickett failed to become an eponym. This was not Allen's fault, for he named a large stream the Fickett River, and so recorded it on his map. During the gold rush, however, some prospectors entered the Koyukuk basin. Apparently they were not able to identify the tributaries surely, and so they shifted Fickett to a small stream, from which it was eventually lost. The large stream they called the John River. Curiously, the man honored was no other than John Bremner, one of the prospectors who had accompanied Allen on the Tanana expedition and whose name already stood on a good-sized tributary of Copper River. Thus, in the north, he ousted his former comrade.

Henry T. Allen was destined for a notable career. He organized and commanded the Philippine Constabulary, and as a major-general in World War I commanded first a division, then a corps, and finally the American Forces in Germany. One may doubt, however, that he ever experienced a greater moment than when he looked out and named his four peaks.

The two prospectors who accompanied Allen may be taken as an omen of what was to come. Toward the end of the century gold-seekers began to wander more widely. Though they uncovered no rich strikes for a while, they explored much country, and one of them supplied an outstanding name. In the early times, various Russians, looking northward from the waters of Cook's Inlet, had seen snow-covered masses toward the north, and vaguely referred to them as "the big mountain." In 1794 Captain Vancouver, blessed with a clear day, looked north from his ship, and saw some "distant stupendous mountains covered with snow." Being a seaman and concerned with coastal features that could be surely charted, he paid little attention to the inland summits, and gave no name. Almost a hundred years later, in 1889, a prospector called Frank Densmore traversed the country north of Cook's Inlet and returned with the tale of a very great peak. Among the prospectors it came to be known vaguely as Densmore's Mountain, but in a country with almost a superfluity of magnificent mountains, no one was concerned about this one or put it on a map.

At last came 1896, a "presidential year," and others happened to go that way. One of them was W. A. Dickey, who, rather strangely, happened to be a Princeton graduate as well as a prospector. He and his partner, working through the region of this peak, fell in with two other prospectors who turned out to be rabid Democrats. These two so filled the atmosphere with arguments for free silver that Dickey became completely bored. In retaliation, he named the peak after William McKinley, Republican candidate, champion of the gold standard.

Probably he did not realize that he had thus named the highest mountain of the continent. Within a few years, however, other explorers discovered the truth. By this time McKinley had become President, and the name of the mountain began to seem appropriate—at least to Republicans. In 1901, McKinley became one of the "martyred presidents," and the name seemed still more appropriate. In this way, from a beginning that was almost a joke, the train of events established what seemed to be a suitable name.

In the years following 1897 the great wave of prospectors flooded into Alaska. They sought their fortunes along the smaller streams, and for the proper establishment of claims a fixed name was necessary. Even to the present time the parts of Alaska where the miners worked can easily be picked out on the map because of the marked density of names.

By the time of the strikes in Alaska, the Americans had been rushing off after the precious metals, in one direction or another, for close to half a century. There was even a tradition of names. Looking at the map of Alaska, a student of gold rushes begins to feel nostalgic. Oro Fino, "fine gold," in the country where no one spoke Spanish, has been picked up and transported right from California. El Dorado and Bonanza are now so well established in English as hardly to be considered Spanish any longer. There is California Creek, and also Montana Creek, and Idaho Creek—in fact, all the gold-mining states, and most of the other states too, have their streams once or oftener. Famous mines and mining districts reappear as creeks—King Solomon, North Star, Eureka, Homestake, Deadwood, Cripple Creek, and Ballarat from far Australia. As elsewhere, the optimism of Ready Bullion, Nugget, and Good Luck is set off against the pessimism of Poverty, Hungry, and Humbug. Grubstake suggests mere subsistence mining. But does Too Good Creek indicate something really rich, or something deceptive—"too good to be true"? And how about Big Hurrah? It is balanced by Little Hurrah, and so the "big" and "little" may refer to the size of the stream rather than to the loudness of the shout. But who knows now? Perhaps not so colorful, but equally eloquent, are the simple names, such as Coffee Creek, Potato Creek, and Tomato Creek. Did someone upset the coffee, or find a potato dropped by someone else, or open a far-packed can of tomatoes to celebrate a strike? There must be an underlayer of adventure; otherwise, no one would give such commonplace names.

Along with the unofficial penetration of the prospectors, governmental mapping continued—and naming, as a necessary part of the work. One distinctive feature of this process in Alaska has been the retention of a very large proportion of aboriginal names. This is probably to be connected with the increased respect for primitive peoples which was developing with the study of anthropology. In addition, much of the territory remained, as it still remains, an undeveloped region with few white settlers.

The work of adapting the native names was by no means always easy. Not only did the sounds give trouble when anyone attempted to reduce them to the English alphabet, but also the mere question of what was named bothered others besides Allen. Alfred H. Brooks, whose own name stands upon the great mountain range of northern Alaska, once complained, "the Alaskan Indian has no fixed geographic nomenclature for the larger geographic features. A river will have half a dozen names, depending on the direction from which it is approached."

Nevertheless, so many native names have been preserved that

the areas occupied by the different racial groups can be outlined on the basis of river names alone. The "panhandle" was the home of the Tlingits, and their -heni, "river," can often be distinguished. Athapascan-speaking tribes held the south coast and the interior as far north as the Arctic watershed; their -na is preserved in dozens of stream-names, and the Yukon itself was once the Yukon-na. The Eskimo word for river varied somewhat because of dialects, but is sprinkled along the western and northern coastal strips as -kwik, -kauk, and -ku.

When the meaning can be made out at all, the native Alaskan names are most commonly simple descriptives. Like other primitive peoples, also, the various tribes labored under no sense of obscenity. Thus Anaktuvuk Pass on the Arctic watershed is a narrow gap which forces the migrating herds of caribou to concentrate thickly. The name means something to the effect of "dung-all-around-everywhere."

The Arctic wastes of North America remained unknown to such a late date that they offered a field for explorers representing private patrons, who backed expeditions as they might back race horses. The most interesting of such enterprises were probably those financed by Felix Booth, the English distiller, who was thus enabled to have his named fixed on the Boothia Peninsula, the northernmost point of Canada and of the continent.

In 1890 an expedition entered Alaska under the patronage of *Frank Leslie's Illustrated Newspaper,* its objective not only to explore but also to fill columns. Once in the interior the explorers split into smaller groups. E. J. Glave, who descended the Alsek River, developed a philosophy of giving no English names at all:

The Indian names of mountains, lakes, and rivers are natural landmarks for the traveler, whoever he may be; to destroy these by substituting words of a foreign tongue is to destroy the natural guides.

So he refrained from giving names, largely in the interests of safety, but also because he thought the primitive names to be picturesque and to be a valuable record of tradition and language. If other explorers had agreed with him the name-pattern of Alaska, and of the world, would be vastly different.

On the other hand, E. H. Wells of the same expedition had a liking for flamboyant or even for "cute" names. He explored Forty Mile Creek, and on its headwaters called the basin Cobra's Head. Probably some meandering of stream, seen from a hill, resembled the well-known markings of that serpent. He also was responsible for Razor-back Divide, and for Kris Kringle's Mountains—as he put it, archly, "to properly recognize that old-timer of Alaska, whose unvisited haunts are quite likely to be in this mysterious range." As so often has happened, however, such names were over-fanciful, and all of them have disappeared. Kris Kringle's Mountains now stand, perhaps even too tritely, as the Alaska Range. Mansfield Lake, tamely commemorating a naval officer, is almost the only one of Wells's namings to survive. (Also of some interest is his folk-etymology, perhaps humorous, in turning Tok River into Tokio River.)

The most elaborate of the private enterprises, the Harriman Alaska Expedition, was of 1899; its patron, the railroad magnate, E. H. Harriman. He chartered a whole steamer and loaded it with eminent scientists, artists, and writers, besides his own family, including his young son Averell. The explorers were even organized into an elaborate system of committees, including one on Geography and Geographic Names. The chairman of this last was no other than Henry Gannett of the Board on Geographic Names. Thus traveling in a luxury scarcely known to explorers before or since, the party investigated the same coast that the hard-pressed Bering had discovered.

They came late; others had already done the basic work, both of exploring and of naming. Penetrating into one unexplored inlet, however, they saw unnamed country ahead. At one narrow passage the shipmaster hesitated. "Go ahead, Captain," said Mr. Harriman, "I will take the risk." (After all, the steamer was not worth more than a mere million or so, and Mr. Harriman would not be subject to court-martial if he lost it.)

Thus, in the upper waters of Prince William Sound, these late explorers enthusiastically let loose with a whole volley of not highly inspired names. Introducing the previously unused generic *fiord,* they (naturally) named Harriman Fiord, as well as Harriman Glacier (the largest in the vicinity). College Fiord was secondarily derived, after the bigger glaciers around it had been called Harvard, Yale, and Amherst, and the more dainty ones Radcliffe, Smith, Bryn Mawr, Vassar, and Wellesley. (Radcliffe Glacier was a tributary of Harvard.) In addition, there were a few obvious descriptives, such as Wedge, Crescent, and Serpentine Glaciers. One would have expected better results from the combined literary talents of John Burroughs, John Muir, and Charles Keeler, assisted by leading scientists, a member of the U.S.G.B. and a financial mogul. One thing at least can be said for the work of the expedition—its names remained. They had been clearly placed on good maps, and all these data were later published in fourteen magnificent and richly illustrated volumes.

With the twentieth century came the establishment of towns. Nome merely took the name of an established feature. Anchorage may be considered obvious. Almost equally obvious is Seward, commemorating the Secretary of State who arranged the purchase. Juneau is from Joe Juneau who first prospected in the area. Cordoba and Valdez, orginally named as harbors by voyagers of 1790, preserve two of the rare Spanish namings along the south coast. Valdez commemorates a Minister of Marine, Antonio Valdés y Bazan. Cordoba honors a brilliant captain-general of the Spanish navy, Luis de Córdoba y Córdoba. Wholly American is Fairbanks, named after a senator from Indiana, Charles Warren Fairbanks, afterwards vice-president.

With the advance of the twentieth century and the end of the gold-rush era, many names in Alaska became obsolete and even disappeared entirely. On the other hand, the government map-makers constantly entered new territory, recording many native names, and giving others of their own. In spite of this, the most striking characteristic of Alaskan nomenclature remains its sparsity. Marcus Baker in the second edition of his *Geographic Dictionary of Alaska,* compiled in 1906, listed about ten thousand names in current use. But this works out as only about one name for every sixty square miles.

Since 1906 the names of many mining camps have vanished, but many other names have been recorded or bestowed. Nevertheless, names remain extremely few, and their greatest concentration is along the coast. In the interior probably ninety-nine lakes out of a hundred remain anonymous. In the Arctic Quadrangle of the U.S.G.S. map, published in 1951 and covering more than five thousand square miles, only twenty-eight local names are recorded. In the northwestern quarter of the quadrangle there stands no local name at all. Alaska thus remains an open field for the bestowal of commemoratives. While this chapter was in writing, newspapers recorded the naming of Mount Pillsbury, a 5,710-foot peak, after the recently deceased Brigadier General George B. Pillsbury.

In restrospect, the greatest interest in Alaskan nomenclature lies in the complexity and variety of its stratification. Upon the basic layer of aboriginal names were imposed, along the coasts, the namings by the voyagers—Russian, English, Spanish, and French. The Russian fur-traders named many places along the coast, and many of these, though not all, were in turn translated by the Americans. Finally, since 1867, the namers have been Americans—fur-traders, prospectors, exploring army officers, chart-makers of the Coast Survey, geologists and map-makers of the Geological Survey.

Inevitably, and properly, the modern Alaskan has assimilated the motley names to his own speech habits so that he can live in comfort with them. He pronounces "Val-déez" unashamedly, preserving the Spanish accentuation, but abandoning the vowel qualities. With Eskimo and Indian names, also, he is likely to preserve the accentuation, and then merely let the spelling be his guide.

The modern Alaskans, like their fellow Americans elsewhere,

have not neglected the possibilities of humor. The comparatively warm weather of their southeastern "panhandle" has resulted in its common appellation, "the Banana Belt." This is in the tradition and quite up to the standard of the United States.

Chapter XLV ❰ Hawaii

In contrast to vast, continental, and arctic Alaska, the Hawaiian Islands are tiny, oceanic, and tropical. Instead of having been thinly inhabited by diverse tribes of nomadic hunters, the archipelago was anciently the home of a numerous race, speakers of the same language, civilized in their own fashion, organized into a complex feudalism based on agriculture. Since place-names always reflect the totality of a people and its country, the contrast between the subcontinent and the islands extends also to the name-pattern. In Alaska we note the sparsity of names and their stratification, those given by speakers of one language superimposed upon those given by speakers of another. In the islands, the names are very numerous and almost all of them appear to be of the Polynesian language.

As so often, however, what seems simplicity may actually be a reflection of ignorance. According to a legend—accepted by some scholars and scouted by others—a people called Menehune inhabited the islands at the time of the arrival of the Hawaiians. Tradition has remembered them in a few names. Thus, on Kauai, we find the Menehune Ditch, an ancient construction, and Ke-alapii-a-ka-Menehune, "the trails of the Menehune."

Certainly, if the Menehune existed at all, they gave names, like other people, and in all probability some of these would have been passed on. The assumption of a stratum of names from a language differing at least in some degree from that of the later immigrants would help to explain why certain of the names are either unintelligible in Hawaiian or else yield what seem to be unsuitable meanings when a translation is ventured.

Notable as examples of such names are those of several of the islands themselves. This is what a place-name scholar, suspecting an earlier stratum, would expect; the individual islands, being of outstanding importance, would have been named by the first inhabitants, and these much-used names would have been the most likely ones to be passed on to later immigrants, even though these spoke a different language. Hawaiian legend, indeed, is full of "explanations," but the stories are highly fantastic, telling of what parents and under what circumstances each island was "born," and thus merely substituting the problem of a personal name for that of a place-name without elucidating anything. Attempts by modern scholars to work out meanings in Hawaiian are scarcely more successful. Molokai, for instance, can be connected with a word meaning "turn back," and is generally rendered as "untwisted temple ceremony"—scarcely an interpretation that inspires confidence. Molokini is linked with the same word, and comes out as "numerous untwistings."

At this point, then, we might venture to apply a principle so nearly universal that it has even been called a law, that is, that unintelligible but repeated elements in names are to be referred back to some generic term in an earlier language. So, in the present state of knowledge, we can at least suspect that Molokai and Molokini display a common element, the significance of which would most likely be "island."

Almost equally unsatisfactory is the translation of Kahoolawe, for which we are offered the option, either "the taking away," or "the red dust blowing." So also it is with Niihau, when it can only be translated as "bound with hau bark." Lanai is given two meanings, both of which make some sense. "Swelling up" might describe the island as seen by a voyager from some particular direction; "day of contention" could preserve the memory of some ancient conflict. Unfortunately, each explanation saps the authority of the other, and again the real meaning may have to be sought in some deeper stratum, or else in some earlier phase of the Hawaiian language.

With three islands there seems to be some agreement upon a reasonable rendering. Maui preserves the appellation of a prankish demi-god of the Polynesian mythology, though why he should have become the eponym of this particular spot must remain unexplained. Oahu, as a central island, might well have been a "gathering place" at some time in the ancient history of the Hawaiian people, just as it is now the site of the capital city. Kauai—roughly, "drying-place"—might have been used for such purpose before it was regularly colonized.

As for Hawaii, it seems certainly to be Polynesian, but of such ancient origin as to defy attempts at translation. Elsewhere in the islands of the Pacific it appears in varying forms as Havaii, Hawaiki, and Savaii. Hawaiian legend has made it the name of the first discoverer, but its occurrence elsewhere argues otherwise and makes us rather set this explanation down as only another example of that world-wide human practice of inventing some heroic ancestor to explain an unintelligible place-name. Some scholars have thought that Hawaii echoes the name of an ancient homeland, perhaps even on the Asian continent. Another possibility is that it was once conceived as a mythical land of the future, or beyond the doors of death. In any case, it was apparently brought with the Hawaiians and was fittingly bestowed upon the largest island of this newly discovered group, as it had been bestowed upon such others elsewhere.

Once arrived in their new home, the islanders necessarily began to give names. They did so in ways similar to those followed by people all over the world. Of much greater interest, however, are the names arising from the nature of the environment itself or from the special qualities of Hawaiian culture.

Along with the other Polynesians, they were the most thoroughly oceanic of all peoples. One might almost say that they were, like the seal and the whale, mammals that had returned to the water. As a result, "places" at sea, such as the passages between islands, seem to have had as much reality to them as the islands themselves. In most parts of the world the various divisions of the sea are called after some land or land-feature that they border—the English Channel, the Strait of Gibraltar, the Gulf of Mexico, Long Island Sound. Exceptions occur, but the general practice is that the water is named from the land. Among these islands, however, the passages bear their own names, with the exception of Kauai Channel. Even for that one an old name is preserved—Kaieiewaho, "the arrogant outside," vivid enough for the longest of all the open-sea runs. As with the names for islands, these for the channels between them are undoubtedly of ancient application, and are therefore difficult to render. Alalakeiki is given as "the crying of children," and could preserve the memory of some incident, though one would suspect that it is some ancient term of which the meaning has been forgotten. Auau is rendered as "bathing," but may possibly be taken in the sense of "drenching," since this is likely to be a "wet passage." Alenuihaha and Pailolo, however, both seem to be descriptive, in Hawaiian, of the kind of water likely to be encountered —"great waves pursuing," and "rolling waves."

Most interesting of all names of the sea-passages is Kealaikahiki, "the way to Tahiti." This seems to hark back to the distant past when the Hawaiians still made voyages to the other archipelagoes.

Noteworthy also is the channel between Molokai and Lanai. This bears what seems to be an ancient name, Kaiwi, which is dubiously translated as "the bone." But it is also Kai o Kalohi, "sea of lingering." Not only is this latter clearly translatable, but also it is referrable to a historical event—that King Kamehameha IV, who ruled from 1855 to 1863, was once becalmed there for more than a week. Thus a recent name is superimposed upon an ancient one.

To dwellers on small mountainous islands, swept by the trade winds, such designations as north and south become secondary. Thus arose Koolau and Kona, which in origin probably meant "windward" and "leeward," and on most of the islands are used to designate the northeast or wet side as opposed to the southwest or dry side. From being mere geographical distinctions these names came eventually to specify legally constituted districts, and as such are still preserved on some of the islands. Also much more useful than mere north and south were Mauka and Makai, "toward the mountains," and "toward the sea." Abbreviated as Uka and Kai, these occur in many place-names.

Also noteworthy, as might be expected on islands, is a predominance of seacoast names. *Hono,* an old word meaning harbor, is often repeated, and yields Honolulu, "calm harbor," or as it is sometimes more archaically rendered, "fair haven." Beaches also had their individuality, and the most famous of these is Waikiki, "spurting water," doubtless named because some rock-formation caused the surf to shoot upward.

The chief mountains, also, give evidence that they were named by seafarers, that is, as landmarks. The volcanic Kilauea is simply "rising smoke-cloud." So also, descriptively, we have Mauna Lua, "twin mountain," Mauna Loa, "long mountain," and Mauna Kea, "white mountain." This last is most likely so called because of its occasional snow-cap. Some legends, however, make it "mountain of the whites," and tell that it was the home of certain fair-skinned people, whom some have tried to identify with shipwrecked European explorers.

Mauna itself is an interesting generic, being used not only for a mountain but also for the inland regions of each island generally, the equation being the natural result of geographical conditions in the islands, though it would have no relevance for dwellers on a continent or on a low-lying atoll.

Advancing inland, the islanders gave names to natural features much as any people must do. Commonly they coupled a generic term with a specific one. Thus many names of places begin with *wai,* "water," used to indicate a stream, pond, or spring. So we have Wainapanapa for a pond on Maui, "sparkling water," and Wailau in various locations, meaning literally, "four hundred streams," but doubtless applied to any well-watered place. Most often the name is descriptive, as in Waiwa, "bitter water," and sometimes fancifully so, as with Waiaka, "laughing water." The name may preserve that of some person associated with it, as in Waiokamilo, "Kamilo's water," and sometimes this person is a god, as in "Waikane." Sometimes the name preserves the memory of some incident, such as a battle—Waikoko, "bloody water," and Wailuku, "water of slaughter." In similar fashion, names were formed from *puu,* "hill," *pali,* "cliff," and other terms.

The islanders, in fact, seem to have been more prone than most people to give names. John Wesley Coulter, compiler of *A Gazetteer of the Territory of Hawaii,* comments that they even named "unimportant features," and "trivial landmarks." One must, however, take some exception to the use of such adjectives. The landmarks and features were presumably neither "unimportant" nor "trivial" to the people who named them.

The most interesting feature of Hawaiian naming, however, involves not natural features, but the artificial divisions which they imposed upon the land. Nowhere can be found a better illustration of the way in which the culture of a people is reflected in the name-pattern of the country.

In spite of their attachment to the sea the Hawaiians were primarily an agricultural people. Their arable land was scanty and thickly inhabited; their social structure, a highly developed feudalism. The largest geographical or political unit in which they thought was the whole island. Each of the larger islands was in turn divided into a small number of districts, each of them named. These were again subdivided, and then at a third stage of sub-division appeared the *ahupuaa.* This has been termed the basic unit, and on each of the larger islands these were numbered by hundreds, each with its own name. They were, moreover, still further subdivided into *ili,* which were correspondingly more numerous. In the single ahupuaa of Honolulu there were thirty-three, all named. The number of ilis must certainly have run into many thousands.

But with the ilis, we have scarcely reached the halfway point.

They in turn were divided into *moo-aina,* these into *pauku-aina,* and these finally into *kihapai.* The last can have been nothing more than little garden patches, a few yards square, such as a man might work with a hoe. Yet in all probability each bore a name, for in a primitive society lacking maps, identity can scarcely be maintained without naming. If such minute subdivision was carried out consistently, the total number of names must have risen into the hundreds of thousands.

This is not impossible, though it may seem so to inhabitants of the United States, which displays a remarkable sparsity of place-names. If we look at other parts of the world, we see that these high densities in the islands are not unprecedented. In certain parts of Sweden actual compilation shows the place-name density to be about 150 to the square mile. This figure may have been equalled or even exceeded in the cultivated areas of the islands before the imposition of modern methods of farming. By contrast, estimates for the continental United States yield a figure of only a little over one name to the square mile.

With the rapid decline of the native population and the development of large-scale agriculture, the smaller names—nowhere written down—must simply have perished by thousands. Fortunately, many of the ahupuaa names are still preserved and in use, to designate the curiously shaped districts of the islands, which generally begin on the beach and run back to the watershed, some of them being five miles in length and not more than a few hundred feet wide. In addition, many other names are preserved in the famous *Book of the Mahela* of 1848. Nevertheless, the disaster which overtook the nomenclature of the islands is comparable to the accompanying disaster which overtook the native population and way of life. One of the most interesting place-name patterns of the world must remain known to us only by description and inference, not by full record.

In 1778 Cook's topsails broke the horizon, and the old way of life came to an end. Not only was Cook a great explorer but he was also a highly ethical one. He therefore did not attempt to give names to the individual islands, but recorded those in use by the natives. With allowance for vagaries of spelling, these turn out to be the same as those by which they are now known.

With respect to the whole archipelago, the situation was different. Since names are of use to distinguish one thing from a like thing, and since the islanders knew no other archipelago, they had no need for a general name. Accordingly, considering the field free, Cook named the group after one of his superior officers, as explorers have done since explorers began. The one he chose was the First Lord of the Admiralty, the Earl of Sandwich.

This title, derived from one of the ancient Cinque Ports on the English Channel, means literally "sand-place," and would have been descriptive enough of any of the island beaches. The fourth earl himself was at this time a gentleman of sixty, in the corrupt government of George III a well-known but not exemplary figure. From a line in *The Beggar's Opera,* he was known to his contemporaries, not complimentarily, as Jimmy Twitcher. To posterity his title was destined to be notable because he put a slice of meat between two pieces of bread and thus invented a new way of eating and almost a new way of life. The United States also owes him a debt of gratitude in that his administration of the Navy during the Revolutionary War was unique for its corruption and incapacity.

Yet there was no denying that he was First Lord of the Admiralty, and that Cook was a mere captain. So the deed was done—as Cook, honest man that he was, would probably have said, "for better or for worse." Actually, it was one of the few of his namings which was not destined to stick.

It at least made a good try. With the announcement of the discovery the name was accepted by the civilized world, and was scarcely challenged for fifty years. It carried, however, a fatal flaw in its strong British suggestion. If it had been Midway Islands, or Volcano Islands, or something else neutral, Cook's christening might well have survived. Or, if the British had extended their sovereignty to the central Pacific, we should still have the Sandwich Islands.

But the course of history was to be different. Some years after Cook's departure, Kamehameha the Great established himself as ruler of Hawaii and finally was recognized as monarch over the other islands. The largest of the archipelago thus became also the seat of power, and its name could naturally be extended over the whole group. By this time, moreover, the natives knew that other lands existed, and so they had some reason to distinguish their own. Also, the islanders preferred Hawaiian to Sandwich, which latter was composed largely of sounds unknown in their own language. Kamehameha himself preferred the native name and is said to have objected to the use of the English one when conversing with Captain Vancouver in 1793.

In written documents, Hawaiian is recorded as of 1829, but it must have been in spoken use before that time. Nevertheless, Sandwich remained the common international designation throughout most of the nineteenth century. It was never official for the Hawaiian government, but under foreign influence it occasionally appeared, as if negligently, in treaties.

American influence in the islands was at first exerted through the two diverse agencies, whalers and missionaries. The two had little in common, except that they both came from New England. The whalers seem to be responsible for the two important names Pearl Harbor and Diamond Head. The former commemorates real pearls, although the fishery was never very important. The latter commemorates fake diamonds—actually, the quartz crystals which were found there. Thus it lost its old name Leahi, "crest of the ahi-fish," which it resembles, as seen from the east.

The missionaries, in recent times, have often been censured for the zeal with which they destroyed not only the native religion, but also the culture that went with it. An exception, however, must be noted in their remarkable preservation of the nomenclature. If they had been Catholic missionaries, we might now be faced with an array of saints' names. On the contrary, the Protestants not only did not replace the names, but also did much to preserve them by transliterating them into the roman alphabet and recording them. No important name seems to have originated under missionary influence. This is perhaps unique in history, when we consider the enormous prestige which the missionaries enjoyed. It is also a tribute to the tenacity of the native culture, even though that culture was fast disintegrating throughout the nineteenth century.

The modern development of the islands for sugar- and pine-apple-growing has left its marks—scars, we might even say, since by their very rarity the English-language names stand out the more incongruously. Most blatant of all, perhaps, is Spreckels-ville, echoing a name eminent in sugar circles. Watertown repeats a folk-tale—"It was named because there was no water there!" This seems more nearly correct than most such stories, since the place originally lacked water and was supplied by a pipeline. A few names may be termed hybrids. Thus Kurtistown was named for Curtis, a sugarman, but a *K* was substituted since the Hawaiian alphabet does not include *C*. Kamuela on Hawaii preserves the native pronunciation of Samuel, and commemorates Samuel Parker.

Kamuela had borne the old native name Waimea, "reddish water," but this replacement sprang from what anyone may consider good motives. After the annexation by the United States in 1898, the postal service was extended to the islands. In accordance with long-established and commendable practice, names of post-offices could not be repeated in the same state or territory. Waimea was retained on Kauai, and therefore changed on Hawaii.

On the whole, however, the annexation made much less difference than one would have expected. In addition to the Post-Office Department, there was loosed on the islands a whole host of governmental agencies—the Army, the Navy, the Coast and Geodetic Survey, the Geological Survey, the Board on Geographic Names. Though these agencies had their own practices of naming, they adapted themselves surprisingly to the established situation. The Board on Geographic Names rendered numerous decisions, but most of these concerned the spelling and application of old names, not the establishment of new ones. Interestingly, even at this late date, a decision was thought necessary that the islands should be called Hawaiian, not Sandwich.

The chief effect of governmental naming was in the establishment of the English-language generics. This may be considered inevitable, since the generic is rather a common noun than a proper one, and thus must always tend to conform to the prevailing language, which by this time had come to be English. Moreover, Hawaiian usage had often amalgamated the generic with the specific, so that *wai,* for instance, seemed to be part of the name itself. The islands thus came to be studded with the common American generics—bay, cape, gulch, gap, valley, ridge, and others. The only ones of special interest are loch and stream. The former may be put down as a fanciful or learned affectation. The latter may possibly go back to the missionary period for its origins, since the missionaries came chiefly from New England and since the use of stream as a generic is characteristic of the northern part of that area. In this debacle a few of the native generics managed to survive, thus really becoming words in the local English speech. Most notable of these are *pali,* "cliff," and *puu,* "hill," which are still common.

Although the islands have been notable as a mixing-pot of races, the number of Chinese, Japanese, and Portuguese names is negligible. Indeed, the last seem to be lacking altogether, unless we admit the doubtful and now obsolete Inez, which appears on an old map of Maui. Oriental names are usually those of camp-bosses, such as Yung-hee Camp on Maui, and Hyashi on the same island, which was originally Hayashi.

Since the language is now predominantly English, recent developments have inevitably established names in that language, especially for new housing sub-divisions and for streets and roads. But such innovations run contrary to a strong and even organized sentiment in favor of native names as representing the established and colorful tradition of the islands. Another Spreckelsville is probably impossible. In Honolulu the City-Planning Commission has even eliminated some of the English names and substituted Hawaiian ones.

Hawaii will become the only state in which both the important names and nearly all the small names also are of native origin. The latter distinction is also held by Alaska, but there the names of the important coastal features and of most of the towns and mountains are not native. Other interesting features of the island nomenclature are its oceanic quality, the survival of some of the native generics, and the density. The island of Oahu, for instance, even though the native names have largely vanished before the inroads of modern agriculture, still possesses a density which is probably three times that of the United States as a whole.

Chapter XLVI ❲ Current affairs — 1944–1958

To use the formula of the old-time novelist, our reader surely cannot have forgotten that the narrative of our original edition came to an end in the year 1944. At that time World War II was raging, though it was—as we were happily to discover—approaching its end. Little, therefore, needs to be added as to the effect, or the lack of effect, of that great struggle upon our nomenclature. Berlin in Alabama, bearing the name of Adolph Hitler's

capital, changed it to that of the capital of King Croesus by becoming Sardis. Your author commends this as a prudent selection, scarcely subject to political vicissitudes. The United States
is unlikely ever to become involved in a war with Lydia, especially since that once potent kingdom disappeared from the list
of independent nations in the sixth century B.C.

Neither has there been much effect of the Cold War. The
citizen of the United States has generally been able to distinguish
between the Russia of the Czar, which was respectable even if
not democratic, and—on the other hand—"them Bolsheviks."
If places named St. Petersburg did not become Leningrad, neither
did places named Moscow change to something else. At times
a certain agitation has arisen in California about the Russian
River, but the re-naming of a stream is a much more troublesome problem than the re-naming of a town, and nothing has
happened.

The Atomic Age, also, has left little imprint as yet. We may,
indeed, hail Atomic City (Idaho) as prophetic of a new era.
But no Fissionville or Plutonium City as yet has appeared in
the Post-Office Guide, though Uravan (Colorado) marks its
site as a spot where the associated metals uranium and vanadium
are mined. We should not expect, indeed, that the recent feverish
search should spot the map with Uranium Creek and Uranium
Hill as the search of a century earlier spawned Gold Creek and
Gold Hill. These modern prospectors hunted, with jeep and
Geiger counter, through a country which was moderately well
mapped and named. At most, they could do no more than fill
in here and there.

In this general filling-in process we can trace some tendencies
and find some indications of the working of the American mind
in the mid-twentieth century.

A still active field of naming concerns those artificial creations, such as highways, dams and the lakes behind them, bridges,
and such other constructions as may or may not be considered
"places" in the stricter sense of the word. Most of these are named
commemoratively for people—military or political figures, or

someone who sponsored or promoted the work in question. Sometimes the name is drawn, rather obviously, from an associated geographical feature. Neither type of naming adds much color to the map or is of great interest to the connoisseur.

As has always happened, popular usage now and then makes an official name over as it wishes. Thus, the great wartime highway to the north is officially the Alaska Highway, but is almost universally mentioned as the Alcan, from the fusion of Alaska and Canada effected during the days of its construction. Similarly the official New Jersey Turnpike seems always to be called the Jersey Turnpike. If this highway is at some time superseded, will the more recent road be popularly known as the New Jersey Turnpike and be officially the New New Jersey Turnpike?

A similar popular rechristening occurred with a large building on the outskirts of San Francisco. Constructed partially for the purpose of livestock exhibitions, it was so luxurious that it was ironically dubbed "the Cow Palace." This name is now universally in use and appears on the official highway signs, another evidence of that flair for naming which seems to be a kind of California heritage.

The filling-in also continues as more and more of the country is officially mapped. Again, the naming seems to be chiefly commemorative—for individuals or for pioneer families who were more or less definitely associated with the region. In the National Forests the names are often those of Forest-Service officials. In the mountain country, east and west, those honored are frequently people associated with some "outdoor" organization— a hiking or mountaineering society, the Boy Scouts, or a group of "conservationists." Although no one can strongly object to honors thus bestowed on worthy citizens, this type of naming again runs to the repetitious and commonplace, since necessarily a large proportion of these people bear common family names. Thus, California already has four mountains named Smith. If it wishes in the future to honor someone of the same name it will have to be by means of a John Smith or Robert Smith mountain. The use of the commoner surnames has already gone so far that we may even need to make use of the middle initial. Your author speaks with some personal application. There is already a Mount George Stewart in California, and he can expect nothing better than Mount George R. Stewart, unless indeed his name should sometime be thought more suitable for a swamp, mud flat, or dry lake, features of landscape about which the competition is not so keen.

Occasional commemorative namings are more colorful. Trojan Peak is for the University of Southern California, or perhaps its football team, generally known by that sobriquet. Goethe Peak in California and Rex Beach Lake in Florida both honor writers, though scarcely of equal world-wide fame. Of particular interest to those concerned with the study of names is Tam McArthur Rim in Oregon, perpetuating the nickname of L. A. McArthur. Although this gentleman labored variously, his consuming passion for thirty years was the study of Oregon place-names, and it is fitting that after his death he should become one of them.

Among recent namings only a few seem to be descriptive. Here may be noted Midget Lake in Michigan and Andesite Mountain in California, the latter presumably named from the kind of rock found there.

The Board on Geographic Names also continues to make decisions as to spelling. "Correctness" seems to be the general criterion, but now and then an established popular form manages to survive. Thus we find the recently authorized Prestile Stream in Maine, though the origin is actually Presque Isle. In the same state, Saint Croix has been allowed to stand, instead of the correct Sainte Croix.

Changes of name in the Post-Office Guide also supply an index for the times. Many of these are minor shifts and constitute further evidence of that restless oscillation which has been evident ever since 1894, when the Post-Office Department attempted to enforce the principles (see page 343) laid down by the Geographic Board. As always, popular revolt against Principle #11 accounts for most of the changes, and towns and villages

are still, in the main, objecting to being one and are establishing
themselves as two. From Sandlake (New York) to Willowranch
(California) and from Fivepoints (Alabama) to Mountainview
(Wyoming) it has gone, so that we now have Sand Lake, Willow
Ranch, Five Points, and Mountain View. On the other hand, a
comparative few have gone in the other direction; Kennebunk
Port (Maine) and Fair Mount (Georgia) have become Kenne-
bunkport and Fairmount. Sometimes the changes are minute, as
when La Fayette (Georgia) becomes LaFayette, thus maintaining the tradition of difficulty associated with that favorite name.

This rage for divorce has especially affected all words which
utilize, or seem to utilize, the French article. We now have La
Bolt and La Plant, both in South Dakota, and both at least partially justified, since they commemorate people of French ancestry. More curious is Laana (Pennsylvania), which has become
La Anna. Even more amusing is La Pine (Oregon). This was
originally Lapine, and was named in pseudo-French because of
the pine trees there, though it actually means female rabbit. With
such a craze under way, we can wonder that Lemongrove (California) chose to become Lemon Grove instead of Le Mongrove.

As other evidence of the continuing revolt against the principles,
we may note Dlo (Mississippi) becoming D'lo, Centerville (Alabama) shifting to Centreville, and Okean (Arkansas) reverting
to a more intelligible O'Kean. Even in such a well-stabilized state
as New York old controversies continue as Plattsburg returns to
historical Plattsburgh, and Ardsley on Hudson joins with two
similarly named towns to resume its hyphens and be Ardsley-on-
Hudson.

Some of the more minute changes seem to be motivated by a
kind of schoolmarm love of correctness. Traveller's Rest (South
Carolina) becomes Traveler's Rest; Dos Cabezos (Arizona) re-
sumes its correct Spanish spelling as Dos Cabezas; Corona Del Mar
(California) goes to the trouble of officially becoming Corona del
Mar.

Also noticeable is the still continuing "flight from the frontier."
Grave Creek (Oregon) renounces its heritage and now is Sunny

Valley; Skull Creek (Colorado) is etherealized in Blue Mountain; Hobo Hot Springs (California) loses all of its color by becoming Miracle Hot Springs. As a slight evidence of a reverse movement, the academically suggestive Yale (Washington) has now become Cougar.

Of somewhat similar nature are the shifts involving the elimination of a name which may be construed as having vaguely unpleasant or primitive suggestions. Smith's Turn Out (South Carolina), mentioned as a fine example of an early name (see page 122), has chosen to seek refuge in the complete banality of Smith. Lemturner (Florida) shifts to Garden City; Grubbs (Delaware) goes romantic as Arden; Fry (Texas) smugly announces itself as Thrifty. Add also the shifts of Tipple (West Virginia) to McGraws, and of Strool (South Dakota) to Prairie City.

A double shift occurred within the last few years for the post-office of a minute hamlet in Georgia. It was Dewyrose, became Dewey Rose, and rests now (though can we think permanently?) as Dewy Rose. A letter from O. W. Adams, the postmaster, explains the history:

Dewyrose got its name from dew on the roses out in the yard, and was about three miles from its present location; then there was a railroad built a depot here, and not thinking about how the place was spelled put a sign on it Dewey Rose [for the admiral?]. So the postoffice was Dewyrose one word, and the depot or railroad was Dewey Rose up to about eight years ago. The postmaster at that time died, and a young man was appointed; he thought that both should be spelled the same, and it was changed to Dewey Rose; some of the older people did not like it so well but did nothing about it until the railroad tore down the depot and all signs; during this time the postmaster resigned to be a preacher and I was appointed as postmaster; no one was doing anything about the name. So one of the old ladies of the community wanted it changed back to its old name, but wanted it spelled Dewy Rose two words.

The most famous alteration of recent years is that of a town in New Mexico where the citizens, with some reason, became tired of their commonplace designation Hot Springs, and borrowing from a radio program became Truth or Consequences. This name, however, violated what seems to be an unwritten law against excessive length. It is usually abbreviated in speech to T. or C., and the official road signs show it as Truth or C.

Doubtless a mere love of fun was involved in this naming, and one is glad to be able to report, from further evidence also, that humor has not altogether died. Its stronghold now seems to be in Kentucky and West Virginia, as even a brief listing from that region may indicate:

> Fed > Hihat
> Hot Spot > Premium
> Omarsville >Kaliopi
> Red Dragon > Blue Pennant
> Pippapass > Pippa Passes

The prize, however, may well go to the West Virginia community which has made Mountain out of Mole Hill.

The postwar years have seen the founding of some towns, but the typical new creations have been sub-divisions. The names of these latter are generally commonplace, tried-and-true, and safe. They are usually duplex, and for the elements they depend largely upon those popularized during the middle of the nineteenth century, as described in Chapter XXXI. Thus we have such names at Parkside, Fairhills, Crestmont, Brookmont, Woodside Hills. The repetitious use of *hill, highlands, height,* and *ridge* indicates the extent to which Americans are lured by the hope of a view, or else—as the cynic might suggest—by the snobbish prospect of looking down on others. A traditional dendrolatry may account for the common employment of *wood, oaks,* and other tree names. Vague suggestions of Old-World grandeur—and snobbery again—propagate *manor, park,* and *estates.* The architecture in these sub-divisions is often modernistic, experimental, and even bizarre; the names are of the mid-nineteenth century.

Many of them are not even apt. Rollingwood, near San Francisco, was succinctly described by one of its residents: "Flat country; no trees!"

The motto of the age is apparently "Play it safe!" There is even evidence of timidity. Middlesex in one of our suburbs seemed to be excellent (that is, safe), carrying connotations of English exclusiveness, and yet not being fancifully foreign. But when the newspapers happened to run some stories about a shift from female to male by means of a surgical operation, Middlesex became Windsor. The name was adopted although there were six streets already so named in the different towns of the same suburban area—still another indication of the snob-appeal associated with certain British names, especially those connected with royalty.

This was in California, where many names are not deeply rooted. In the older states such attempts at change may stir up a hornets' nest of opposition. Even more than a hint of a middle sex does not avail, and the Board on Geographic Names declares officially that a hamlet in Maine is not Todd's Corners, but Sodom.

In Longmeadow, Massachusetts, there was and had been since time immemorial a small stream known as Grassy Gutter. It thus preserved an ancient and very rare generic term. From it had come Grassy Gutter Road, and some of its citizens wished, so to speak, to get out of the gutter. In February, 1954, the citizens met in full panoply of town meeting to discuss whether it should become Remy Road or Wilkin Road. It was argued that Gutter was "nasty," and that its legal recognition was disgraceful. But a local lawyer rose to make an eloquent and impassioned plea, not only for the retention of Gutter, but for a halt in the trend toward wiping out the names which had decked the New England scene since the time of the Pilgrim forefathers. Gutter was saved!

In contrast to general mid-century colorlessness, perhaps a natural reaction from it, was a consuming interest in the contemplation of "queer names," regarded as a legacy of the past and from more primitive times. My correspondence file from people who have read the original edition contains more letters upon this topic than upon any other. The subject is a popular one for magazine articles; *Life* once printed a list of several hundred such names. Even newspaper stories, apropos of nothing, not infrequently offer information on queer names in some part of the country. So great is the interest, indeed, that out of deference to it I considered devoting a whole chapter of this supplement to its consideration. I decided, however, in the negative—partly because on re-reading Chapter XXXVII, I decided that I had said in summary about all that I wanted to say, and partly out of what might be considered mere cussedness. The fact is, I do not like to admit that any name is queer, or perhaps I consider all names to be equally so.

What is really strange, and often so strange as aptly to be considered "queer," is the way in which a name happens to be placed upon a particular spot. Thus, the name itself may be commonplace, its story, interesting.

For instance, Punxsutawney in Pennsylvania is always placed high on the list of oddities. But there is nothing inexplicable about the literal meaning of the name, which is of Algonquian origin, and signifies "punkie-town." As for *punkie,* it is a word actually taken over by the settlers and still current in some parts of the northeastern states, meaning the pest that would elsewhere be called a sand-fly or midge or no-see-'em. If we could carry the story farther back, we might then, indeed, arrive at something really interesting. Was the place merely named because the insects were particularly numerous in a swamp there? Or did the name spring from an incident in which some early travelers suffered from the punkies, as related by the missionary John Ettwein under the date of July 19, 1772, in his journal? Or, as a hint in the journal suggests, did it really spring from an Indian myth?

Thus, with Punxsutawney, the name is superficially strange because of unusual spelling, and possibly because of association of its sounds with certain meanings in English. Once translated, however, it is simple, and any real strangeness must be sought rather in what lies behind it.

Certainly, each to his taste! If anyone wishes to collect what he thinks to be queer names, I wish him luck. My trouble is that when I look through one of these lists, I am immediately struck by the fact that a large number of the examples are quite matter-of-fact. The compiler has merely thought them unusual because he was rather ignorant of languages and of the processes of name-giving.

An occasional project of the kind catches my fancy. For instance, one gentleman has gone through the records and compiled a list of places which have only two letters. He records Ai in Ohio, Ti in Oklahoma, Ed and Uz and O.K. in Kentucky, and T.B. in Maryland. This is a kind of sheer intellectual whimsey which is too little cultivated in the modern world.

Naturally, I try to go on and discover the origin of these names. T.B., according to a note of the compiler, is not derived from a sanitarium, but from the initials of one Thomas Brooke, a seventeenth-century Marylander. O.K. is fairly obvious, and so is Ed, which is doubtless only a shortening of Edward. Ti, as it happens, has been already explained on page 363. Ai and Uz are Biblical—the first, the scene of one of Joshua's victories; the second, the land where Job lived.

But with these two-letter names we are not yet at the ultimate. Is there not—oh, searchers after the unusual!—within these boundaries, some name consisting of only *one* letter? Some genuine name, I mean, not merely something on the pattern of C Street and Avenue A. Thumb your lists, scan your maps, do not forget past times! I await your findings.

Let me also say that I have entered into one contest of this sort, though outside our boundaries, and I make a claim to be winner. This concerns the number of successive dots that may stand above a name, and was started with Fiji, which has three. Later, Ajijic in Mexico, with four, took the lead. Recently, however, I located in the Mexican state of Chiapas, the town of Pijijiapam.

I shall end this excursion into the rational-irrational by only expressing my wonder that the great master of such things, James Thurber, has never seriously entered the field of names.

For full consideration of postwar developments, a few words should be offered about the advance of scholarship. On the whole it is less than anyone might have hoped and predicted in 1944. Nevertheless, two extensive works on individual states have appeared—Gudde's on California and Kenny's on West Virginia. Parts of the great Missouri collection have appeared, but the death of that veteran and devoted scholar Robert L. Ramsay has caused an interruption in the work.

Perhaps the most important development has been the establishment of the American Name Society, with membership open to all interested people. Since 1953 it has sponsored the publication of the quarterly journal *Names.* Thus for the first time the name-scholars of America have begun to attain the position that their European counterparts have occupied for a century. Although organized and incorporated in Illinois, the Society has had by far its largest membership, as might almost have been predicted, in California.

The question of who controls our names, already discussed in Chapters XL and XLII, still continues to produce interesting cases.

In 1945 the California legislature solemnly took action on Lake Bigler (see page 375), even though no one had actually so called Lake Tahoe in many years. That this ancient dead-letter act should be dug from the files for the express purpose of being repealed is surprising. I should like to think, but do not know, that the discussion of the matter included in this book had some influence upon legislation.

The same page of the original edition also offers a comment on the anomalous definition accorded the Rocky Mountains by the Board on Geographic Names. The politically-based definition has been replaced by a geographical one, and the mountains are now defined as being the eastern belt of the North American cordillera, extending from New Mexico to the Liard River valley in Canada.

The Board has also taken action to solve an impasse in California. The interesting system of river-fork naming has been described in Chapter XXX. In this nomenclatural exuberance the designation North Fork of the North Fork of the Yuba River had been applied to two streams. The Board got rid of this duplication by designating one stream the Downie River, thus giving further currency to the name of "Major" William Downie, who was already remembered by Downieville. The Board also eliminated some fork names by designating that certain streams were to be known merely as the North, Middle, and South Yuba. This had been, indeed, the common practice of local speech for many years.

When official enactment thus coincides with popular usage, everything can go merrily. Otherwise the result is curiously unpredictable. When writing in 1944 I ventured a very guarded word of caution as to what the tenacity of old-timers might accomplish with respect to the case of the re-naming of the Grand River to be the Colorado. Actually, as far as I can tell, this decision is now fully accepted.

On Manhattan Island, however, we have a contrary instance. In "early times" there had been on that island a country way known as West Road. In the general re-mapping and re-naming of the city, this became Sixth Avenue in 1811. In the later years of the century the elevated railroad was built, and Sixth Avenue became an unlovely street, with property values far below those of Fifth Avenue. But shortly before World War II the elevated was removed, and rehabilitation seemed possible. Some felt that the name itself was a handicap, and thus originated Avenue of the Americas.

It was a gesture more grandiloquent than practical. Though it made use of "Americas," one might even call it un-American, in so far at least as it ran counter to the habits of the people of the United States. American it might be in the sense of Latin-American. It had, indeed, a definite Latin turn to it, as if coined—La Guardia was mayor—by one of the many thousands of New Yorkers of Italian ancestry.

In the face of a considerable opposition, the council and mayor approved the change, and it became legal in October, 1945. The result has been much confusion and a general continued use of Sixth Avenue. A bill was proposed as early as 1947 to revert officially to the old name, but it was shelved somewhere. Nevertheless the people themselves have given a sufficient veto.

In 1955, on the ten-year anniversary of Avenue of the Americas, a newspaper conducted a poll. By better than eight to one, people preferred Sixth Avenue, and ordinarily used it, ignoring the official name. Among those interviewed was the Executive Director of the Avenue of the Americas Association, which had always supported the change. He was quoted: "There's a great deal more acceptance of the name." If so, this makes one wonder how little acceptance there must have been previously.

Those interviewed, as quoted by the *New York Times,* give a cross-section of American criteria on nomenclature, though in the curiously formal kind of speech which that great journal thinks fit for its columns, however unlikely it may be on the lips of actual New Yorkers.

Let us take first those supporting the change. The comments in parentheses are my own.

Baker (reacting by mere emotional response): "I've used it since its inception. I like it."

Accountant (reacting by snob-appeal): "It has elegance."

Electrical contractor (with an eye to property value): "It builds up the avenue."

A sampling of the more numerous opposition displays equally interesting results:

Salesman (presenting the practical difficulties of change): "You tell someone anything but Sixth Avenue and he'll get lost."

Lawyer (also moved by practicality and tradition): "It's easier, shorter. Just a habit, I guess."

Delicatessen owner (echoing the well-established American and

English-language antipathy to long and highfalutin names): "It would be very incongruous to call ourselves—let's see—the Avenue of the Americas delicatessen."

Cab driver (a son of John Smith and not of Gabriel Archer): "I'd lose my upper plate if I had to pronounce that other name."

The case rests in utter confusion. Mail is delivered to either address. Buses and subway stations are still marked as they were before 1945. Most people speak in the old fashion; some, in the new. The whole affair should be a sermon and an object-lesson to anyone contemplating the change of a well-established name. It is also a demonstration that New Yorkers, when it comes to changing one of their names, can be as stubborn and as set in their ways as the citizens of any Vermont village.

Yet you can never tell. In New Amsterdam there was a burgher who signed himself Isaacq Bedloo. After the English took over, he held various offices and was a man of some importance—his name spelled Bedlow or Bedloe. Shortly before 1670 he became the owner of a scrap of land in New York harbor. At that time it was called Love Island, probably from a curious provision that persons on it were free from warrants of arrest. It came to be known, however, after its new owner.

Within a few years Isaac Bedloe died, but his name clung tenaciously. It did not, indeed, remain unchallenged. Like many small and unimportant places, the island was variously known at different times. Its Indian name is recorded as Minisais. It had once been Love Island, and it is later recorded now and then as Kennedy Island, Corporation Island, Great Oyster Island, and Fort Wood. The Board on Geographic Names ruled that it should be Bedloe Island. Thus the name had endured for more than two and a half centuries—an almost infinite length of time in these United States. It had kept the name even after the Statue of Liberty had been erected upon it. Then at last, in 1956, Congress took action, and President Eisenhower signed the bill, that it should be Liberty Island.

Although the new naming can scarcely be claimed as highly

inspired or original, it nevertheless represents a fine tradition and is a name to which, in itself, objection can hardly be taken. Anyone can argue, also, that the island had actually had various names, and that Isaac Bedloe is no person of heroic stature in the nation's history. Moreover, for many years people had ordinarily said, "I am going to see the Statue of Liberty," and not, "I am going to Bedloe Island." Perhaps for all these reasons, in contrast to the furor about Sixth Avenue, almost no voice of protest was raised.

Still, the matter has serious theoretical aspects. How far is this sort of thing going to go? In comparison with a name which is far older than the nation itself, any particular Congress is ephemeral. Representatives and senators, elected to serve for a few years —by what right do they assume the prerogative of tinkering and tampering with an ancient heritage of the people?

Possibly we may yet have to organize an Association for the Preservation of Historic Names.

Sometimes, however, the people themselves speak, and this is particularly true in that very literal sense of "speaking," that is, in questions of pronunciation. To date, Congress does not seem to have passed decrees about pronunciation, and the Board on Geographic Names does not ordinarily consider it.

The problem of Los Angeles has already been discussed in Chapter XXXIX, but more is to be added. Investigating for his study of California place-names, Professor E. G. Gudde used the objective technique of questioning numbers of University of California students from different parts of the state as to this name. He found that they universally employed the anglicized pronunciation. Youth thus having solidified its ranks, the future could scarcely be in doubt. Moreover, L. A. and Los still continued to make inroads, and—perhaps even more sinister—was the tendency, especially among the young, merely to compress a name into "Los-ann-lus." Finally—if such a word may be used—Mayor Bowron appointed a "jury," consisting of members of pioneer families, professors of Spanish, radio announcers, and newspapermen. After a deadlock of several weeks, the group came to its verdict on September 12, 1952, announcing that the pronunciation should be "Los An-juh-less." Whether city officers would be fined or disciplined if they should subversively use any other than the decreed pronunciation has not been brought to my attention. The mayor himself, a member of the Hard-G Party, lamented: "This means breaking a habit of most of my lifetime." Then, accepting the decision, he added, "I'll go along."

The most precedent-shattering action of recent years involved Cape Canaveral. This name, as noted in Chapter III, was one of the oldest and most firmly established in the country, going back to the Spanish voyagers of the early sixteenth century. By Act of Congress it became Cape Kennedy, shortly after the assassination of the President in 1963. Under the emotional involvements of the time the action occurred with negligible objection. It raises, however, the question of commemorative, and even political, shifting of names, a practice which has been more typical of Europe, especially of the Soviet Union, than of the United States.

So, for a third time, nearly a quarter-century after the first time, I come to the end, and can only declare the business unfinished still—at ten-seventeen on the morning of the nineteenth of January, in the year 1967, A.D.—as good a time as any other at which to halt.

Author's Postscript

Under the circumstances, I hope that no one will be too much outraged at the omission of some favorite name. There are millions of names in the United States, and only a small fraction of them could be included. The purpose of the book is to present the process of naming, not to make it a place-name dictionary. A "standard of admission" has, however, been kept clearly in mind. Names have been discussed (1) because they were of "national" significance, that is, were presumably of interest to all Americans, e.g., names of states and large cities, (2) because they illustrated the habits or fashions of place-naming, e.g., Troy, Texarkana, (3) because they fell into line in connection with the work of some particular namer, e.g., Smith, Vancouver, (4) because their manner of origin seemed of unusual interest, e.g., Smackover, Berkeley.

Many incorrect stories about the origins of names have been considered and rejected. Failure to refer to them does not necessarily mean that I was ignorant of them. Continual refutation of worthless theories and traditions would merely have been tedious.

Further to satisfy an interest in place-names, the reader will find a number of books. The United States, however, is as yet far from covered by adequate place-name dictionaries, and it is to be hoped that some survey upon a national scale may be one of the post-war undertakings of American scholarship. Anything like adequate coverage is now available for only five states, viz., Arizona (Barnes), Minnesota (Upham), Oregon (McArthur), South Dakota (W. P. A., ed. Ehrensperger), Washington (Meany). Good, but less comprehensive, studies have been published for

Nebraska (Fitzpatrick, Link), Oklahoma (Gould), and Pennsylvania (Espenshade). Several other important state surveys, e.g., California (Gudde), and Missouri (Ramsay), are approaching completion. A large number of excellent special studies are available, but these are all too frequently out of print, or are buried in the file of some scholarly journal.

I am highly grateful for all these works, and have used them whenever possible. On account of the spotty coverage, however, I have had to gather a large part of the information from original sources, and to interpret it according to my own lights. Constant recourse to these sources was also necessary because *Names on the Land* deals primarily with processes, whereas nearly all previous studies have dealt with results. For the same reason, there has been no model available for the general plan of the book.

Somewhat reluctantly I have refrained from including a full bibliography and citations. A bibliography on place-name studies for the United States is being prepared by Dr. Harold W. Bentley of Columbia University. In most instances, also, the source from which the material is drawn has been made obvious in the text.

Since readers may be interested in the way in which materials for the book have been gathered, I offer a brief classification of source-materials. (1) Scholarly studies of place-names, such as the dictionaries mentioned above and the more specialized studies, e.g., those of Eckstrom, Farquhar, McJimsey, William A. Read, Allen Walker Read, Wagner, and many others. (2) The original narratives (or, if the original has been lost, the closest to it available) of expeditions on which names were given, e.g., Ponce de León, Lewis and Clark. (3) Local histories, including the W. P. A. state guides; I went through all of these, and in particular drew my conclusions as to street-name patterns from study of the city plans. (4) Maps, gazetteers, postal guides, railway guides, etc.; I have frequently found it helpful to spend an hour or so over the topographical maps of some critical region, such as Tidewater Virginia, eastern Massachusetts, Delaware, central New York, or the Kentucky mountains. (5) Government documents, such as colonial records, the Congressional Record, and the journals of legislatures. (6) Conversation or correspondence with people who have given names, e.g., A. H. Sylvester, J. Martin Scranage, and A. F. Buddington. (7) Conversation with, or "pumping of," people familiar with the place-name pattern of a special region, such as R. P. Blackmur and Carlos Baker for Maine.

I shall be happy to receive further information about place-names, and would welcome particularly any letters from people who themselves have given names or who have been closely connected with such people.

In the research preliminary to the writing, and in the writing itself, I have incurred debts to many people, and to all of them I wish to return sincere thanks. I cannot, however, refrain from mentioning in particular a few from whom I have received special courtesies—Harold W. Bentley, Saxe Commins, Christian Gauss, Francis P. Farquhar, Robert Hitchman, S. Griswold Morley, Robert L. Ramsay, Allen Walker Read, and the late A. H. Sylvester. Much of the work was done during the academic year 1942–3, while I was Resident Fellow in Creative Writing at Princeton University, and enjoyed excellent working conditions under the terms of that appointment.

G. R. S.

University of California,
Berkeley, California

Notes and References

In 1944, when publication of the original edition was being planned, wartime restrictions on paper precluded any extensive appendix of bibliography and citations. As now presented, references and citations are given when the source of information is not clear from the text and when it is to be found in some out-of-the-way document, or when a debatable question is involved. To have given all references would have resulted in an unwieldy and generally useless compilation. Any scholar wishing to check the information will naturally turn to documents and histories dealing with the place in question; to give, here, exact references to the many hundreds of sources would facilitate such a scholar's work, but would not be essential to it; such inclusiveness would, at the same time, increase the bulk of the present volume and thus render it less generally available and useful, without increasing its own accuracy.

The spelling within quotations has been modernized. Most of the translated quotations are my own renderings.

The compilation of the references has been much facilitated by the existence of the Sealock-Seely bibliography (see below), together with its supplement. Another supplement, for 1949–52, is promised for the near future. Since no serious work on American place-names is likely to be undertaken without access to these bibliographies, I have referred to works appearing in them merely by the author's name (with additional information when necessary) and by the indication SS or SS–S, thus avoiding the necessity of giving lengthy references. In addition four important general works not included in these bibliographies are listed below.

Notes and References

The following works are noted by the shortened form here indicated:

Gudde   Erwin G. Gudde, *California Place Names* (1949).

Hodge   *Handbook of American Indians North of Mexico,* F. W. Hodge, ed. (1907–1910).

Mathews   Mitford M. Mathews, *A Dictionary of Americanisms* (1951).

OED   *Oxford English Dictionary*

SS   R. B. Sealock and P. A. Seely, *Bibliography of Place Name Literature: United States, Canada, Alaska and Newfoundland* (1948).

SS–S   P. A. Seely and R. B. Sealock, "Place Name Literature, United States and Canada, 1952–1954," *Names,* iii, 102–16.

In the interests of simplicity the various state guidebooks of the WPA series, issued under slightly different titles, are all indicated by the same formula, viz., WPA *Alabama Guide.*

The method of handling the notes is not a makeshift device necessitated by the use of the old plates but is one that I have used in several previous books and found advantageous. In my opinion the text of a book should be written and presented for continuous reading. Calling the reader's attention to footnotes merely distracts him. If he wishes to check up on the author or acquire additional information, he should do so at the end of the chapter by turning to the notes then. I have therefore constructed text and notes on what might be called parallel tracks, identifying the place of each note by means of the page reference and some significant words. In the case of quotations, I have given the first words in quotation marks.

Many references are to works published since the time of the original edition and obviously not used in its preparation. At the present these are the most authoritative accounts and the most convenient for reference. I have therefore included them in the notes, and have sometimes omitted the pre-1945 sources which I actually used.

In addition to references, the notes supply some additional material, especially on controversial points. I have, however, generally restrained myself from opening up new topics, since the book was never intended to present its subject exhaustively—and, indeed, even a whole library could hardly be sufficient for exhaustive treatment of the place-names of the United States.

Page

3 "numbered by millions." No authoritative investigation of the number of our place-names is available. A well-qualified scholar, A. W. Read, in a paper read before the American Dialect Society in 1941, offered a preliminary figure of "well over a million." My own tentative estimates by means of extrapolation from state and county compilations put the number much higher— say, three million, with another million of obsolete names. This would mean only about one current name per square mile—very low, by European standards. Naturally, a good deal depends upon what one considers a place-name. For instance, some would count street-names and others exclude them.

4 Onomatologists, highly concerned with an overpowering number of individual names, have given little attention to the general problems discussed in this chapter, e.g., the psychology and processes of naming. In this connection I may refer to two of my own articles, "What is Named" (SS), and "A Classification of Place-Names" (SS–S). A valuable contribution is J. B. McMillan, "Observations on American Place-Name Grammar," *American Speech*, xxiv, 4. This led to my "Further Observations on Place-Name Grammar," *ibid.*, xxv, 3, and his reply, "A Further Note on Place-Name Grammar," *ibid.*, xxvii, 3.

6 Quilby, etc.: On Quilby, see Read, *Louisiana Place-Names of Indian Origin* (SS); Callemongue: Harrington (SS, p. 147); Uktena: James Mooney, "Myths of the Cherokee," *Bur. of Amer. Ethnology, Ann. Rep.* (1900), *Pt. I;* Glooscap: Ekstrom (SS); Allegheny: Heckwelder (SS, p. 101).

7 Rapidity of change: This is a sweeping statement, and may be challenged. I believe, however, that it can be defended, and that it results partly from the fact that the ordinary place-name, consisting of specific-generic, is twice as long as the ordinary word, and thus becomes subject to the special processes affecting long

:vords in most languages. When a name consists of a whole phrase these processes are further exaggerated. To give a single and simple example, a stream called Whitbeck would have been obviously "white brook" to a fourteenth-century Englishman. To a present-day Englishman, however, Whitbeck is incomprehensible since the *i* has shortened because of its position before two consonants and since *-beck* has become obsolete in ordinary language. Perhaps the original statement may be more fully worded: "Not only are names subject to the special developments associated with long words, but also, by preserving obsolete words and forms as 'fossils,' they tend to become unintelligible to later speakers of the same language." I think also that other factors, such as those mentioned in the text, may be of importance.

8 "some few hundreds of names . . . " G. L. Trager in a review (*Int. Jour. of Amer. Linguistics,* xii, 109) comments on this sentence, "This, of course, is the old chestnut about the 200-word vocabulary of the unlettered peasant." I cannot see the pertinence of the comment. To maintain that a person's whole vocabulary is 200 words is different from maintaining that a very small part of a person's vocabulary is several hundred words.

8 "placed their names thickly . . . " Trager, *op. cit., supra,* again raises an objection: " . . . nor is there any reason to suppose that the settled Pueblos 'placed their names thickly' by contrast with the nomadic Pawnee." In reply, I would only venture to suggest that Dr. Trager should not fall into the undergraduate's booby-trap of stating a universal negative. At least, he might have written, "I know of no reason." That, however, might suggest some lack of reviewer's omniscience. My authority for the statement is Harrington, *Ethnogeography of the Tewa Indians* (SS) pp. 94, 97–98. As one of the most detailed and authoritative of all studies of Indian place-names, it might well be studied by anyone setting up a scientific standard for onomastics and wishing to commit a universal negative. Harrington's work certainly supplies a reason—and I should say, a good reason—for the statements about the Tewa, undoubtedly a pueblo tribe, and the nomadic tribes. As his example of the latter Harrington

uses the Omaha; I substitute Pawnee, as a tribe of similar habits, but more likely to be generally known.

11 Florida: Antonio de Herrera y Tordesillas, *Historia General* (1601), Dec. I, lib. ix, cap. x, xi. Herrera was obviously interested in names and name-giving, more so, I think, than any of the other early Spanish historians and chroniclers. Those interested in nomenclatural history must be often in debt to him. On pronunciation of Florida, *v.i.*, note to p. 20. The record does not make absolutely certain that the name was bestowed before the landing was made, but the probability seems very strong that this was the case.

12 "Arrived there . . . " "Instrucción dada por el Rey á Pedrarias Dávila" in *Coll. de los Viages,* M. Fernandez de Navarrete, ed., iii, 344; "First you must name . . . ": "Real cédula dando facultad á Francisco de Garay, *ibid.,* iii, 162.

12 "It was the custom . . . " Herrera, *op. cit.,* Dec. II, lib. 10, cap. 6.

13 Tortugas: Herrera, *loc. cit.,* in note to Florida, *supra.*

13 "The Spaniards never . . . " I am endebted to S. G. Morley and Erasmo Buceta for aid in translating this bit of tricky Spanish, which reads in the original, "los Castellanos nunca repararon en corromper poco los vocablos." See Herrera, *op. cit.,* Dec. III, lib. viii, cap. viii.

13 Symbolic rites of naming: See H. R. Wagner "Creation of Rights of Sovereignty through Symbolic Acts." *Pac. Hist. Rev.,* Dec., 1938. The most elaborate rites of which I have encountered the records are those of Oñate upon entering New Mexico (see p. 24 and Wagner, *op. cit.*) For baptism, see p. 156. See also A. S. Keller, O. J. Lissitzyn, and F. J. Mann, *Creation of Rights of Sovereignty through Symbolic Acts* (1938); these authors, however, minimize the importance of the name-giving.

15 California: Gudde in his *California Place-Names* (1949) and in "The Name California" (SS–S) has differed to some extent with my theory of the development of this name. I have replied in "More on the Name California" (SS–S), maintaining the position here taken, which I preserve unchanged. Bibliography on the name may be found in the works cited above.

17 Cabrillo: For a discussion of the voyage with bibliography and good notes on place-names, see H. R. Wagner, *Cartography of the Northwest Coast of America . . .* (SS).

17 Jordan: Herrera, *op. cit.,* Dec. III, lib. vii, cap. viii.

18 Appalachian: early mentions under various spellings make this a tribe, a town, or a province. Actually it could probably have been properly considered any or all of these. This is only another example of applying European preconceptions to Indian actualities. Explorers seem constantly to have been looking for names to indicate small units (towns or districts), larger units (provinces) and still larger units (kingdoms). The more primitive Indians, however, thought and named only in terms of small units, and did not consider that a district would have any other name than that of the tribe living there. The conception of a people taking its name from a previously established name of the country (as the Icelanders are called from Iceland and the Canadians from Canada) was probably quite unknown, although a tribe itself might receive a name by description from the place it lived, e.g., Quapaw, "down-stream people," or from a natural feature, e.g., Seneca, "people of the standing stone."

When the people moved, their "country" thus moved with them (see under Illinois, pp. 85–87). In early American usage we thus naturally get the use of such expressions as "the Illinois country," and the large number of states bearing tribal names is thus made easier to explain, though generally the progression seems to have been tribe-river-state.

18 "because at the entry . . . " See, in Hakluyt's *Voyages,* "The True and Last Discovery of Florida."

20 Florida, pronunciation: A shift of accent from middle to first syllable would be peculiar, and does not occur with other words similarly accented in Spanish. Even the Florida Mountains in New Mexico are locally pronounced with the accent on the middle syllable. (At least, they were so pronounced when I inquired in 1942; but the informant said he supposed they ought to be pronounced the other way, and perhaps by now the analogical adjustment has occurred.) The reason for Flórida is,

I think, that it has the same spelling and is so pronounced in Latin. In the sixteenth century many books and maps were printed in Latin, and many more Englishmen were familiar with that language than with Spanish. By this theory the name would always have been pronounced in English as Flórida. I have tried to find the name in verse, to check the accentuation, but have not been able to locate an occurrence earlier than ca. 1611; in this the present accentuation is used. (See *Narratives of Early Virginia,* L. G. Tyler, ed. [1907], p. 203.)

22 Roanoke: Tooker (SS, p. 197). I insert a *perhaps* here, and unfortunately nearly all translations of Algonquian names must be received with similar caution. Steady advance in the study of Algonquian has been made in the last few years, but I do not believe that there has yet been an equal advance in the study of Algonquian names.

25 El Paso: Since *paso* can refer to a mountain-pass as well as to a stream-crossing, and since the English *pass* also has this meaning, there has been a tendency to think that El Paso refers to the mountain-pass through which the river flows just to the north of the present city. The context of the original use of the name renders this interpretation very unlikely.

26 Santa Fe: There is doubt as to whether Oñate or his successor actually founded Santa Fe.

27 Martha's Vineyard: The publication of this book gave rise to an editorial "The Naming of Our Island" in the *Vineyard Gazette,* June 22, 1945, which was sent me, along with a letter of the same date, by Henry B. Hough, President of the Dukes County Hist. Soc. Since Mr. Hough is also editor of the paper, I presume that he wrote the editorial too. In both he throws doubt upon the idea advanced by Fulmer Mood (SS) that Gosnold had a daughter named Martha. He seems also to favor Brereton rather than Archer as the name-giver, though I cannot see much strength in the argument. He congratulates me, however, on "the spirit in which you wrote," and I wish to congratulate him similarly. I have let the text remain unchanged, having already protected myself by a "probably." Un-

less new records are found, there is no hope of settling the matter absolutely.

33 Information on Smith, including the quotations, is from *Travels and Works of John Smith,* Edward Arber, ed. (1884). The use of the third person in one of the quotations arises from the fact that this section was written by Walter Russell and Anas Todkill, two of Smith's companions.

33 Potomac, Susquehanna: Smith, *op. cit.,* p. 346, generalizes, "The most of these rivers are inhabited by several nations, or rather families, of the name of the rivers." The language suggests that Smith considered the tribes to take their names from the streams, but his ability to communicate with the Indians was so slight that we cannot take his opinion as being of much weight. Kenny, *West Virginia Place-Names* (SS) has assembled the evidence on Potomac; Donehoo, *Hist. of the Indian Villages,* etc. (SS), on Susquehanna. Neither commits himself. I myself have a good deal that I might offer on these names—too much to present here in a footnote. Even so, I think that the final word cannot as yet be written, and that the sentence in the text is still about as much as can be surely stated. Popular theories as to Susquehanna range from making it "long crooked river" to "straight river." Take your choice!

34 Dudley Carleton's letter: Alexander Brown, *Genesis of the U.S.* (1897), pp. 113f.

38 Massachusetts: Trumbull (SS, p. 108). Though dating from 1867, this study by the redoubtable name-scholar J. H. Trumbull still serves as evidence that a good piece of scholarship is not easily superseded.

40 Kennebec, Penobscot: Eckstrom (SS). This work is excellent, not only on these particular names, but also on the general Indian system of river-naming.

40 Nahumkieck: Cotton Mather, *Magnalia Christi* (ed. 1820), i, 63. Mather had in mind the word forming the name of the prophet Nahum, usually connected with a root *comfort,* and a root which ordinarily means *bosom* but which by some extension of meaning might be taken as *haven.*

42 Maine: For "the Maine" in Virginia, see Alexander Brown, *The First Republic in America* (1898), p. 308. I now believe even more strongly than at the time of first writing this passage that the name in New England arose in contrast to the islands, and should therefore be taken in the sense of "mainland." The analogies of Epirus and Alaska (Chap. XLIV) are of weight in this connection. See also Matthews (SS, p. 98) for an excellent article, arriving at the same conclusion. Quite possibly an important factor in establishing the name was James Rosier, *True Relation* (1605), the first important account in English of the exploration of what is now the Maine coast. In this short narrative the expression "the maine," usually so spelled, occurs no less than eighteen times! It always refers to this part of the mainland. As used by Rosier it is a common noun, though he twice capitalizes it. Later comers, however, could easily have taken it from him and used it as a place-name.

44 Maryland: J. T. Scharf, *Hist. of Maryland* (1879), i, 51–52, presents this account, based upon the Ayscough MSS and Sloane MSS in the British Museum, which I have not examined personally.

46 There is, of course, nothing unusual in colonists transferring names from the "old country." Ancient Greek colonies, e.g., Megara in Sicily, sometimes bore such names. The Spaniards also, well before the settling of New England, had transferred such names as Cartagena, which was so named by Columbus himself. In New England, however, the practice seems to have been more fully codified into a system than in any other region of the world.

47 "Why they . . . " Whitmore (SS).

48 "for as there are . . ." Cotton Mather, *op. cit.* (p. 40, n.), i, 83.

49 "Up westward . . . " William Wood, *New England's Prospect* (1634). I have not been able to find a Roxbury in England.

50 "the governor . . . " *Winthrop's Journal,* Hosmer, ed. (1908), p. 94.

50 "Old Boston . . ." Cotton Mather, *op. cit.* (p. 40, n.), i, 87.

51 Connecticut. My statement that the second *c* has never been pronounced is, of course, beyond proof. The examples of the name in Hodge, however, seem to show the earlier spellings lacking a consonant at this point, with a *c* or sometimes a *gh* intruding later. As with so many other points, this should be investigated by a competent Algonquinist.

52 Saybrook: On this and on Connecticut towns in general see the excellent study by Dexter (SS).

52 Norwalk: Trumbull, *Composition of Indian Geographical Names* (SS).

53 "having in a sense . . . " *Rhode Island Rec.,* I, 22.

56 Charles River controversy: Wm. Bradford, *Hist. of Plymouth Plantation; Mass. Rec.,* I, 237.

56 "called by the name . . . " *Mass. Rec.,* iv, 124.

56 "Now your . . . " *Prov. Papers, New Hampshire,* i, 208.

57 Virginia names: With counties there is little difference between the methods of Virginia and of New England. Still, the counties bearing Indian names and those named from local settlements may be said to be of local origin.

58 Flower dieu Hundred: This appears in many different spellings, some of them even suggesting that it might have been a variant of Florida. It was, however, the family name of the wife of the patentee, which survives as Flowerday and in other spellings. (See Paul Wilstach, *Tidewater Virginia,* 1929).

58 Newport News: My account is chiefly based upon Alexander Brown, *First Republic in America* (1898), p. 459. Work appearing since 1944 throws doubt upon this explanation. See C. W. Evans, "Newport News: What's in a Name?" in *Newport News' 325 years,* A. C. Brown, ed. (1946), and P. B. Rogers (SS-S). Both these writers end in doubt, and Rogers concludes: "It is now time for all to admit freely that . . . nobody today really knows how the city got its name." I certainly agree, as far as absolute knowledge is concerned. I cannot see, however, that these later writers have wholly negated Brown, especially since in his statements that the last word is spelled Newce, Newse, and Nuce he seems to be using documents to which

they have not had access. Moreover, their argument that the name cannot be connected with Thomas Newce because he arrived in Virginia only a few days before its first recorded appearance seems to me reversible. May not this almost simultaneous appearance actually indicate a connection with the Newces? In fact, if it was known that they were to make a settlement there, the place might have been named for them even before their arrival.

58   "no place . . . " *Narr. of Early Virginia,* L. G. Tyler, ed., p. 195.
59   "to change . . . " *ibid.,* p. 259
59   "the Isle of Hogs" *ibid.,* p. 174.
60   The idea of a "true source" haunts American exploration, and has a continuing effect on naming. See, e.g., p. 257.
61   On these generics see Mathews, McJimsey (SS), Wilbur Zelinsky, "Some problems in the Distribution of Generic Terms . . . " in *Annals of the Assn. of Amer. Geographers,* xlv., 319–49. Marsh is common as a descriptive term, rare as a place-name. The history of swamp is remarkably obscure. Mathews comments, "The earliest examples . . . occur with reference to Virginia, but the term had no doubt existed earlier in local use in Great Britain." Etymologically the word is connected with *sump. Neck* for *narrow passage* is an obvious metaphor; *neck of the woods* is given by OED as an Americanism. Change with time, e.g., deforestation, may make this name inapplicable. Thus, at present, there is no obvious reason why Dutch Neck and Penn's Neck, both in New Jersey, should record that generic. Teaneck (N.J.) is derived, according to Pennington (SS), from the Dutch family name Ten Eyck. See also p. 63.
62   Chippokes: Tyler, *op. cit., supra,* p. 83, and note. For Chipoak, which I have written as Chip Oak, see U.S.G.B., *Sixth Rep.,* under Upper Chippokes.
63   *kepan:* Eckstrom (SS), pp. 123–24, 174; Trumbull (SS, p. 27).
64   "called in . . . " *Mass. Rec.,* i, 97.
65   "the beavers . . . " *Winthrop's Journal,* J. K. Hosmer, ed., i, 73
65   Butterfield Meadow: *ibid.,* i, 192.
65   Sachem's Head: *ibid.,* i, 226.

65 Bloody Point: *provincial Papers,* New Hampshire (1867), i, 64–65.

65 "because we . . . " Whitmore (SS).

65 Moskitu-auke, etc.: Trumbull (SS, p. 27).

68 Manhattan: The complicated question of the Hudson voyage cannot be discussed here, but I believe that historians should give it more consideration with respect to place-names. The interpretation which is presented here seems to me still, after more study and thought and after the passage of some years, to be sound. Meteren states that Hudson had maps from "a certain Captain Smith." One of these maps must have been, I believe, a prototype of that reproduced by Alexander Brown (*Genesis of the U.S.,* i, 456). In connection with names the most interesting thing about this map is that it has Manahata on the west bank of the river and Manahatin on the east bank with no indication that there is any island corresponding to the modern Manhattan. By assuming that Hudson had a map related to this one, showing perhaps only the mouth of the river along with the names on both sides of it, we account for a great deal: (1) for Hudson's failure to give a name to the river, since he could not consider himself the discoverer; (2) for Juet's spelling Manna-hata, which is very close to that of the map; (3) for Juet's wording, "that side of the River that is called Manna-hata," which strongly suggests that he was using an already established name; (4) for the ship's grounding on the Manna-hata side when driven by an east-northeast wind.

Since Manhattan was a tribal name at the coming of the Europeans, I should maintain that they took the name of the island from that of the tribe. This was early Dutch opinion (see De Laet, Chap. 9). In prehistoric times the tribe may have taken its name from that of the island, and in that case a toponymic significance should be sought for it. This is a problem for Algonquinists, but to take the meaning as "hilly island," as some incline to do, seems to me to raise topographical difficulties. Manhattan has some hills, but to be specified as hilly it should be notably hillier than near-by islands. Is it hillier than Staten Island or than the western end of Long Island? Moreover, would Manhattan be specified as an island by primitive people? It is so large and so nearly a part of the mainland that its insular quality is not striking.

71 Whore-kill: For further discussion see C. A. Weslager, "An Early American Name Puzzle," *Names*, ii, pp. 255–62; and A. R. Dunlap, *op. cit., infra* in note to p. 76; SS, p. 145. Weslager agrees with the explanation here offered. Dunlap remains uncertain. Either may be consulted for the references. I am somewhat surprised that the name, which does not seem to me a very remarkable one, should have caused such an expenditure of ink.

72 Dutch controversy with New Haven: *New Haven Col. Rec.*, i, 265.

73 Rhode Island: The particular interpretation here given is my own. See also Kohl (SS) and "The Name Rhode Island" (SS). The anonymous author of the latter quotes Roger Williams as using the name "Rode Island" unofficially in 1637. This suggests a Dutch influence or else "Road Island" for a harbor, and seems to me to strengthen rather than weaken the argument in the text.

74 Camel Creek, etc.: The whole question of place-names from the names of exotic and even mythical animals is a fascinating one, though the explanation is usually simple enough when it can be discovered at all. California has Camel's Hump, an obvious description, and Elephant's Back, which is obvious when one sees the shape and color of the mountain in question. In the same state, the repeated Kangaroo (see Gudde) is probably from the native kangaroo rat; Caribou, which occurs several times in California, is apparently a miners' name, echoing the Cariboo district of British Columbia (see my "Caribou as a Place-Name in California," *Calif. Folklore Quarterly*, v, 393). Tiger in the Gulf states may be for a stray jaguar (*tigre* in Mexican Spanish), but the panther (puma) was commonly called *tiger* in the southern colonies. *Lion* also generally refers to this animal (*león*

[454]

in Mexican Spanish, *mountain lion* in most of the western states, and sometimes *lion* in colonial documents).

74 "which sufficiently shows . . . " I have quoted this from Israel Acrelius, *New Sweden,* p. 64, who is quoting from Adrian van der Donck's *Representation of New Netherland.* In the translation of van der Donck in *Narratives of New Netherland,* J. F. Jamesson, ed. (1909), p. 314, the wording is considerably different. Incidentally, van der Donck elsewhere argues from place-name evidence.

75 Swedish names: My original chief source was Amandus Johnson, *Swedish Settlements on the Delaware* (1911). A valuable recent work is A. R. Dunlap, *Dutch and Swedish Place-Names in Delaware* (1956). For possible Finnish names, see Dunlap and Moyne (SS–S).

76 New Amsterdam streets: The deductions are my own; the source of the basic information is that great storehouse of facts compiled by I. N. Phelps Stokes, *The Iconography of Manhattan Island* (1915–28); Benson (SS) also is useful.

81 New York: The material on names in this chapter is based on the publications of the English Place-Name Society. On Philippa and her inspection, see B. C. Hardy, *Philippa of Hainault* (1910) for references. There is some question whether there were actually two embassies or whether the two accounts make it only appear so.

82 Ivan H. Walton, "Origin of Names on the Great Lakes," *Names,* iii, 239, offers a fuller discussion of the number of the names presented in this chapter; many of the authorities cited are secondary. He does not refer to this chapter, but I cannot see that he supersedes any of its conclusions.

82 Ontario: H. E. Hale, *Iroquois Book of Rites* (1883), p. 176, gives it as from the Huron *ontare,* "lake" and the ending *-io,* which he thinks originally meant "great," and was so used in this name. Later, he believes, *-io* assumed the meaning "good," or "beautiful." The French usually understood it in the last-mentioned sense. Perhaps it was of somewhat generalized meaning, like our modern English "fine." It occurs also in Ohio.

83 "Lake Superior . . . " Jonathan Carver, *Travels Through the Interior Parts of North America* (1778), p. 132.

83 Niagara: The meaning is thus given in Hodge, together with references.

84 Erie: *Jesuit Relations,* R. G. Thwaites, ed., xlii, pp. 176–83.

85 "To say 'Illinois' . . . " These are Marquette's words; see Section 6 of the journal of his 1673 voyage in Thwaites, *op. cit.,* lix.

86 Michigan: As with Manhattan and other names the question as to whether the derivation is from a natural feature or from a tribe which took its name from that natural feature can perhaps never be finally settled, and probably is of little interest to most people. For the literal meaning, see Hodge.

86 Ohio: See note to p. 148.

86 Milwaukee: The meaning is disputed, but I have again followed Hodge.

86 Chicago: The quotation is from Henri Joutel; see Pierre Margry, *Mém. et Doc.* (1879–88), iii, 485. For articles treating the name, see SS, p. 75, and Hodge.

87 "the great river . . . " Chapter XII of the journal of Father Claude Allouez, Thwaites, *op. cit.,* li.

88 The great Mississippi voyage of Jolliet and Marquette is to be found in Thwaites, *op. cit.,* lix, and elsewhere.

88 Wisconsin: F. G. Cassidy of the University of Wisconsin, whose *Place-Names of Dane County, Wisconsin* (1947) is widely recognized as the most notable intensive study of our names to date, writes me (Sept. 21, 1956) that the source of Wisconsin must still be considered uncertain. He believes that it is Algonquian; the only origin he suggests is that given in the text. This still seems to me to be the origin. The writing of the initial *M* might even be nothing more than a mistake; on the other hand, the mistake might be in the later substitution of *W,* which the early French generally rendered with a complicated symbol. I would like to see some investigation at the chirographical level.

89 Missouri: Here as elsewhere I have tried to keep from getting involved in controversies (unnecessary for place-name study)

about the meaning of tribal names. Many such names are extremely old, and unless the meaning is obvious, there is generally little possibility of settling upon a sure derivation. This can be seen by the situation in other parts of the world. In spite of immense work and magnificent scholarship, controversy still rages about such names as German, and no one has even a vague idea of what Hellene may mean, and by what process it shifted from a small tribe to a whole people. Moreover, folk-etymology has an excellent chance to work with such ancient names. Thus even if it should be proved linguistically that Missouri should mean "big canoes," this would not prove that the tribe used big canoes but might only indicate that an ancient name of quite different meaning had gradually assumed this form. The whole field of ethnic names, not only in this country but all over the world, calls for much more study.

89 Omaha: See note to p. 137.

89 Kansas: See *Spanish Exploration in the Southwest,* H. E. Bolton, ed., p. 257n.; "The name 'Kansas'" (SS–S) lists 68 different spellings, without giving sources, including Akansea and perhaps some others which are not referable to Kansas.

90 Iowa: The derivation is my own, and is perhaps a bold one. It seems to me, however, to be tenable. Hodge gives many forms, some of which differ from Iowa as much as Ouaouia does. An approximation of the modern spelling seems to begin with the Lewis and Clark expedition. The location of the Ouaouiatonon is proper for the Iowas, and this geographical evidence is weighty. Anyone studying the spellings assumed by Indian names, as I have been forced to do, cannot but be struck with the great variety and wide range. The form of a name, it would seem, depends much more upon the nationality, education, etc., of the transcriber than upon what the Indian said, as it would now be transcribed by a trained phonemist. To date, linguists have studied with great intensity the sound-shifts within a language and its dialects, but have paid little attention to what happens when a word (which is most often a name) is transferred from one language to another. For a quick appraisal of

the problem one can look at the various forms recorded in Hodge for Iowa, Milwaukee, Seneca, and other such names.

90 Although here mentioned only casually, the question of how the tradition of a name has been maintained is often of the utmost importance. Even apparently strong linguistic evidence is of little weight if some possibility of a tradition cannot be established.

93 Mississippi: A résumé of names for the river is to be found in W. A. Read, *Louisiana Place-Names of Indian Origin* (1927). See also, T. L. Thompson, *Pub. Louisiana Hist. Soc.,* ix, 92ff.

97 Texas: Hodge; see also "The De Leon-Massanet expeditions" in *Spanish Exploration in the Southwest,* H. E. Bolton, ed., and "Exped. of Don Domingo Terán," in *Prelim. Studies of the Tex. Cath. Hist. Soc.,* ii, 1, which contains the list of instructions.

98 "which said . . . " *N.J. Colonial Docs.,* i, 9.

99 Delaware: A. R. Dunlap, "Names for Delaware," *Names,* iii, 230, presents a full discussion; the 1665 reference to Delaware as a district is from *N.Y. Colonial Docs.,* iii, 9.

100 "inhabitants of New Hampshire." Charles Deane, "Indenture of David Thomson," *Mass. Hist. Soc. Proc.,* xiv, 375.

101 "ye towns . . . " *Prov. Papers of New Hampshire,* p. 374.

104 Pennsylvania: For Penn's letter about the name, see *Pa. Hist. Soc. Mem.,* i, 201, and later printings.

104 "And thou, Philadelphia . . ." Espenshade (SS) p. 31.

105 "the things . . . " Penn's "Further Acct. of Pennsylvania" in *Narr. of Early Pennsylvania,* A. C. Myers, ed., p. 260.

105 "a large . . . " Myers, *op. cit.,* p. 243.

106 "Octorockon . . . " Myers, *op. cit.,* p. 230.

107 "Philadelphia . . . " Myers, *op. cit.,* p. 304.

108 Transfer of names: If the language is a written one, more especially since the advent of printing, the transfer of a name from one language to another by means of the written or printed form is also possible, and indeed may be very common. (See note on Florida, p. 12.)

110 Tenafly: This is a name about which people get singularly

wrought up. I have had several letters, giving such various derivations as Willow Meadow, Little Valley, and Along-the-swamp. I took *thyne-vly* from the WPA *New Jersey Guide,* which seems to be using an archaic spelling for the modern *tuin,* "garden." To derive Tenafly from *tuin-vly* seems to me possible; an interconsonantal vowel sound would tend to develop because of the difficult *-nvl-* group of consonants. The meaning "garden valley" seems good enough.

111   Harlem: Even to maintain that Harlem suffered a change of spelling is perhaps going too far, since seventeenth-century orthography was dubious in Dutch as well as in English. I have found the name as Haerlem and Haarlem, and further search might uncover it as Harlem, even in a Dutch context.

111   Dutch place-names: Study of these names is still in an unsatisfactory condition, and many contradictory derivations will be discovered. For authorities, see SS, p. 280. Omitted from this list is one which I have found useful, *viz.,* W. H. Carpenter, "Dutch contrib. to English in America," *Mod. Philology,* June, 1908.

111   Barnegat: See van der Donck's map of 1656.

112   Swedish names: Amandus Johnson, *op. cit.* (see note to p. 75).

115   "I have followed . . . " *N.J. Col. Docs.,* I, 117.

116   The fact that very common plants are unsuitable for identification and therefore are rare as place-names has not been widely grasped. Thus Gould (SS), p. 42, states: "Queerly enough, the jack oak or black oak, the most abundant tree in Oklahoma has but one creek named for it." Similarly, McArthur (SS), p. 129, comments: "Considering the enormous quantity of firs in Oregon, it is quite remarkable that there are not more geographic names with 'fir' in them." We may consider that both these writers are arguing in the wrong direction. The very abundance of the trees is what keeps them from being common in place-names. A similar but not quite identical argument applies to animals (see pp. 116ff, 133f).

118   True Love Creek: *Palmetto Place-Names* (SS), p. 144.

118   Mattapony: William Byrd in his *Progress to the Mines* (1732)

mentions the Po as one of the four branches of the Mattapony; so this name at least must be older than that date.

120   Milford: My colleague Ronald Walpole suggests a Welsh origin, because Milford Haven is the most important of the British Milfords. Dexter (SS) also suggests Milford Haven, but without direct evidence. The WPA *Connecticut Guide* states, "named for the town in Pembroke, England [!]" But there are at least twelve Milfords in England; since the town was founded early (1639), I see no reason to suspect Welsh influence.

122   Trenton: J. O. Raum, *Hist. of the City of Trenton,* tells a delightful legend that the place was first named Littleworth, which may be derogatory but is also both a common English village-name, and a good parody of English village-names.

122   The planned town was not universal in New England, but it was certainly typical of the region.

123   Folly, Hope, Adventure: These three names may sometimes have been used in more prosaic fashion than their modern meanings would suggest. The OED gives *folly* as a "clump of fir-trees on the crest of a hill" in English dialect, but the earliest citation is of 1880; the use of this word as a topographic term is being investigated by Meredith F. Burrell, Chief of the U.S.G.B. *Hope* can have meant a small bay and had other topographical meanings, which are preserved in English and Scottish place-names. *Adventure* commonly meant merely enterprise or project. These usages may have helped give rise to the humorous or satirical usage. Nearly every small town has at least one house, overambitious or architecturally ludicrous, which is called so-and-so's Folly. This is also a British usage, dated from 1654 in OED. See also OED for the suggestion that the name may sometimes have been used in an endearing sense, as "delight" or "favorite abode."

124   Boston streets: In addition to authorities mentioned, see A. H. Thwing, *The Crooked and Narrow Streets of Boston* (1920).

129   Lover's Leap: The name occurs in the British Isles, but I find no discussion of it in works on British place-names. This is the natural result of what may be considered the general policy

among European onomatologists to ignore recent nomenclature. Few of them are really students of place-names. Instead, they are learned linguists, specializing in the etymology of names, but ignorant of the ways in which human beings actually give names, and not really interested in the matter. I consider this unfortunate. Here, for instance, it prevents us from determining authoritatively whether Lover's Leap existed in England before Byrd's time, and therefore might have been learned by him during his long residence in England. *The Imperial Gazetteer of England and Wales* (1860) connects the name in Derbyshire with an attempted suicide of 1760, well after Byrd's time.

130   "We laid . . . " William Byrd, *A Journey to the Land of Eden* (1733).

133   On the question of the generic-specific word-order see McMillan and Stewart, *op. cit.* in note to p. 4.

133   Drybeck, Drybrook, and Dryburn occur rarely in England.

135   Alabama: Read (SS, p. 42).

135   New Orleans: Pierre Margry, *Mem. et Doc.* (1879–88), v, 599ff, shows that the name was established before the city.

136   Arizona: W. C. Barnes (SS), though uncritical in approach, gives the necessary references.

136   Rocky Mountains: This theory of the origin of the name was, I believe, first advanced here; it has not been challenged, and it now seems even stronger to me than it did in the beginning.

137   Ozark: The French preposition-article is to be found also in Ausable, N.Y., and probably in Omaha, i.e., *aux Mahas,* since the tribal name seems originally to have been Maha, and to have picked up the extra syllable with Lewis and Clark.

137   "A deadwater . . ." Read, *Louisiana Place-Names of Indian Origin* (SS), p. xii, quoting Pénicaut. Pénicaut is very valuable on names, supplying also the origin of English Turn and others.

138   "The kings . . . " Father Bobé, whom I quote from Parkman's *Half-Century of Conflict;* I have also used this book and his *Montcalm and Wolfe* for other information on pp. 138–39.

139 Horse Meadow: WPA *New Hampshire Guide.*

139 Wheeling: Since 1945, this name has been discussed at length by Kenny (SS), who ends by being "inclined to favor the Indian origin." From his presentation of the evidence I am even more fully convinced of the conclusion as here stated, although there is no possibility of checking the accuracy of the story.

139 Tug Fork: Lewis Collins, *Historical Sketches of Kentucky* (1847); James Mooney, "Glossary of Cherokee Words," *Bur. Amer. Ethnology, Ann. Rep.* (1900), *Pt. I.*

140 Duncan Campbell: His story is told in Sir Thomas Dick Lauder, *Legendary Tales of the Highlands* (1849); also, Francis Parkman, *Montcalm and Wolfe* (1884), ii, 449–51. Readers of poetry will remember it from R. L. Stevenson's *Ticonderoga.*

147 Tennessee: In a Spanish context this name is probably recorded as Tanasqui in 1567. See Woodbury Lowery, *The Spanish Settlements* (1911), p. 295. If so, Tennessee is, I believe, the fourth state name to be recorded as a place-name in America. The earlier ones are Florida (1513), California (1524 or slightly later), New Mexico (1563).

148 "The Ohio . . . " C. F. Post, "Two Journals of Western Tours," in *Early Western Travels,* R. G. Thwaites, ed. (1904), i, 245n. This note may have been written, not by Post, but by his companion and the original editor of the journals, Charles Thompson. The information, however, may well have been supplied by Post, and Thompson himself can rank as a contemporary authority. Until the Algonquinists agree upon some other explanation, I rest my case on this quotation, which is, like that for Chicago (p. 86), early and authoritative. It has been missed by most scholars who have considered the name, except for that old master, Trumbull, in his "Composition of Ind. Geographical Names" (SS). For general discussion, see Kenny (SS), Donehoo (SS).

150 Curry He: Fink (SS, p. 186).

151 Kentucky: Hewitt (SS, p. 93); J. M. Brown, *Political Beginnings*

of Kentucky (1889), p. 10, note; letter from Arthur C. Parker, Oct. 22, 1942.

151 Lulbegrud: Haber (SS); John Bakeless, *Daniel Boone* (1939).

152 Barrens: Mathews presents citations going back to New England in 1651, but the common use of the word is certainly trans-Appalachian. "From there . . . " Henning's *Virginia Statutes at Large,* ix, 563. On the other generics, see Mathews.

153 Lamoille: See Zadock Thompson, *Hist. of Vermont* (1841), iii, 100. For other "mistake names" see under Nome, and p. 329. J. P. Clement, former director of the *Hist. Rec. Survey of Vermont* writes me (April 9, 1956) that, in spite of search, he has been unable to find any map actually inscribed *la mouette.* In my opinion this failure is of little importance; the mistake might have occurred on the occasion of transcription from MS map to printed map, or might have occurred at the first writing of the name on the original MS map. Mr. Clement also doubts that a river would have been named after a gull, but I fail to see why. In suggesting other possible origins he seems to me to jump from frying-pan into fire by bringing forward an idea of his friend Pierre de C. la Rose that "Mouelle is a diminutive of Moue [mouth], whether the dictionary carries it or not," and that the name therefore "could refer to the actual mouth of the river; or it might be that some Indian lass of the vicinity had a pretty little mouth." Probably he does not mean to be taken seriously in this last, but I do not believe that we should start manufacturing words that are not in the French dictionaries just to explain place-names—especially when there is a plausible (even if not confirmed in print) story of origin already available. Nevertheless I appreciate Mr. Clement's letter, and I wish that others had gone to as much trouble in trying to check other names for which the explanation is still uncertain.

155 Oregon: See my article "The source of the name 'Oregon'" (SS, p. 174). Bracher (SS) from further examination of maps decides

that the probability of the theory is increased. Since I first put the idea forward, there has been no attempt at refutation, and the explanation seems to have been rather widely accepted. On the other hand, the slow spread of knowledge is discouraging. Thus George Stimpson's *Book about American History* (1950), a volume in many places offering good information on place-names, offers no comment for or against the theory, an indication probably that the author had not heard of it. The same is also true of the so-called "revised" (3rd) edition of McArthur's *Oregon Geographic Names* (1952), although McArthur himself had written me before his death, expressing interest in my article.

155 Wilkes-Barre: Espenshade (SS); he states that he has found the name spelled in seventeen different ways.

157 "Sir, is there . . . " Translated from Palou's life of Serra; elsewhere the chapter is mainly based on the diaries of Crespi and Portolá, for which see Gudde.

163 Lexington, Ky.: R. H. Collins, *Hist. of Kentucky* (1877), and W. R. Jillson, *Pioneer Kentucky* (1934).

164 The summation of places named for Washington is to be found in the publications of the George Washington Bicentenary Celebration (see under Lawrence Martin in SS).

165 Bunker Hill: The authors of *Place-Names of Hertfordshire* (Eng. Place-Name Soc., 1938) believe that the American Bunker Hill must have been "named in the first place after one of the English places." This seems altogether unlikely in view of the known existence of John Bunker (see *Mass. Rec.* I, 212, and elsewhere). Besides, natural features were rarely named after natural features in England. The Hertfordshire volume also states that most examples of the name in England are probably derived from that in America. The authors of the Middlesex volume (Eng. Place-Name Soc., 1942) state: "Bunker's-hill is a common field and farm name in this county and elsewhere. . . . It may occasionally contain the recorded name *Bunker* but the frequency of the combination *bunker* and *hill* suggests that

the name of the . . . battle must for some reason have become popular as a place-nickname." In this passage I would question only why the learned gentlemen suddenly use the strange term "place-nickname." I myself would venture to suggest that the word *bunker* (recorded in the OED as of 1805, meaning an earthen seat or bank in the fields) may also have had an influence in England.

166 Vermont: A good deal remains to be explained about the origin of the name. Benson (SS) attributes it to Young's *Conquest of Quebec,* but I have read Thomas Young's poem of that title without finding anything. See also Clement (SS).

167 The interpretation of Lemon Fair as a folk-etymology is my own.

170 U.S.A.: SS gives a considerable bibliography; I have found Burnett the most useful. An idea that has recently become somewhat popular is that Thomas Paine coined the name, but I find nothing to substantiate this view which I cannot trace farther back than an "it is claimed," on p. 179 of M. A. Best, *Thomas Paine* (1927). I cannot discover that Paine used U.S.A. before *Crisis II* (Jan., 1777). It is curious that he has been credited with the coinage, for he actually seems to have avoided the name, using it but rarely and preferring America. Perhaps as a master propagandist he thought U.S.A. to be cumbersome and legalistic, and considered America to be more emotionally evocative.

173 Fredonia: See SS under S. L. Mitchill.

173 Washington Irving: His "National Nomenclature" (1839) in *Wolfert's Roost.*

175 Juan de Fuca: See H. R. Wagner (SS, p. 28), i, 159; ii, 393; Walbran (SS); Meany, *Origin of Wash. Geographic Names* (SS).

177 "The strongest . . . " John Meares, *Voyages,* i, 250.

179 Vancouver: My characterization of him is doubtless too severe; in Alaska he showed off to better advantage than in connection with his failure to discover the Columbia.

179   Gray: McArthur (SS) under the entry *Columbia,* and the references there given.

183   Tiber: W. B. Bryan, *Hist. of the National Capital* (1914–16), i, 53.

185   Seneca: This is a most interesting name for its wide variety of forms and its various modes of transmission. It should certainly be studied, if only in Hodge, by anyone wanting to see how the recorded spelling of an Indian name can vary as the result of the language of the person transcribing it.

185   "classical belt": This group of names is probably of more interest to more people (to judge from my correspondence) than any other in the country. Various legends circulate. Articles and newspaper stories will be found in SS. I have followed Palsits (SS) for the factual background, but have drawn my own deductions.

186   Cincinnati: Hume (SS) and Lotspeich (SS).

187   Styx: WPA *Alabama Guide,* p. 386.

189   "Strange is . . . " Kenny, *West Virginia Place-Names* (SS).

189   Saratoga, etc.: The text may be conveniently found in *The Complete Jefferson,* Saul K. Padover, ed. (1943), pp. 236–38. This makes moderately clear how the names were derived and the region to which each refers.

191   Tennessee: P. M. Hamer, *Tennessee; A History* (1933), p. 172.

193   Luzerne: Espenshade (SS); it commemorates Anne César, Chevalier de Luzerne, first Minister of France to the United States.

193   *Burg, ville,* etc.: A valuable recent contribution is Wilbur Zelinsky, "Some problems in the distribution of generic terms . . . , " *Annals of the Assn. of Amer. Geographers,* xlv, pp. 319–49. I do not believe that anything here stated is negated by this detailed study, and I happily note that I even spotted the concentration of *-ville* in southeastern Pennsylvania which shows up strikingly on Zelinsky's map.

196   Matthew Arnold: See his *Civilization in the United States* (1888).

198   For a good recent study of migration of a name, see Kramer

(SS–S) who uses Andover as his example.

199 A correspondent and a reviewer have taken me to task for writing that Fort Wayne was "near the battlefield." The distance is eighty or ninety miles. Looking at the situation from the distant viewpoint of California, I still see the two points as comparatively near to each other.

200 "The mania . . . " *Writings of Thomas Jefferson,* vol. IV, H. A. Washintgon, ed. (1854), p. 335. The quotation is from a letter to Doctor Rush, Sept. 23, 1800.

201 Youngstown: WPA *Ohio Guide;* a letter (Aug. 3, 1945) from Lewis A. McArthur, eminent scholar of Oregon place-names, now unfortunately deceased, informs me in good-humored fashion that John Young was his great-great-grandfather, and not as anonymous a character as I had supposed.

202 Rochester: *Rochester Hist. Soc., Pub. Fund Series,* iii, pp. 305–14.

203 Change of street names: For both quotations see I. N. Phelps Stokes, *Iconography of Manhattan Island,* under dates Feb. 11 and Apr. 19, 1794.

205 Harrisburg: Espenshade (SS).

205 "I am not sure . . . " Letter cited *supra,* note for p. 200.

206 Intervale: Zadock Thompson, *Hist. of Vermont* (1842), i, 6, note; Mathews offers a good list of early occurrences. My presentation of this term has brought me two friendly and learned letters, raising certain objections to Thompson's etymology, from a homonym of the Old Pretender, *viz.,* Henry James, of New York, who supports a derivation from *intervallum,* i.e., land "between walls." In so far as *intervale* is from *interval,* it is derived eventually from *intervallum.* But in the topographical use the association with *vale* seems essential. On the other hand, Thompson's Latin is certainly not of the best. *Inter* can scarcely mean *within,* which should be *intra.* I should therefore offer some apology for my own words, "with rare exactitude."

206 Gore: As a common noun meaning a wedge-shaped piece of land, the word dates back to King Alfred (see OED), but its

place-name usage seems to be limited to New England. Mathews does not include it, but DAE gives Attleborough Gore as of 1749.

207 "named at a . . . " R. W. Emerson, *English Traits* (1848, 1856).

209 Canton: *Orig. of Mass. Place-Names* (U. S. Writers' Program); WPA, *Illinois Guide.*

209 French names: See the items indexed in SS, p. 284. Valuable for general reference is J. F. McDermott, "Glossary of Mississippi Valley French," in *Washington Univ. Studies, n.s., Language and Literature,* No. 12 (1941).

213 *Portage, rapids,* and other generics: The best general source on the development of these words is Mathews. I am complimented that *Names on the Land* is there cited as an authority on the use of *sny.*

213 "the Virginians first took the names over . . . " This is perhaps an overstatement. Yet it may certainly be argued, to explain the comparative disappearance of *pond* in the Middle West. The whole Ohio Valley was claimed by Virginia and organized into counties. The earliest penetration of the region by speakers of English was from Virginia, or at least from Virginia and the middle colonies, certainly not from New England.

214 This chapter is primarily based upon the journals of the Lewis and Clark expedition.

215 Milk River: Streams flowing from beneath a glacier are often so called, e.g., there are two Milk Creeks in Oregon.

215 *Cabri:* In standard French this means "roebuck," but in the American West it was translated as "goat."

219 This chapter is largely based upon direct study of maps.

219 "The most of . . . " John Smith, *A True Relation* (1608).

220 Great American Desert: See W. Barrows, "The Great American Desert," *Mag. of Western Hist.,* ii, 2. The term is generally considered to have originated from the S. W. Long expedition of 1819–20, as narrated by Edwin James. In that account both the deserted nature of the region and its dryness are emphasized, so that one may consider that *desert* is there used in either or both senses.

220 *Wash,* etc.: Mathews can be profitably consulted for most of these. The history of some of them is highly complicated, e.g., *peak* (not in Mathews). In England this term applies to a district, and may have no etymological connection with the later use of the same sounds and spelling to mean mountain. The Spanish (and Portuguese) word is *pico,* and this was particularly applied to Teneriffe, which became well known to English sailors in the sixteenth century. *Peak* (from *pico*) thus came to have some limited circulation in English from that time. Its common usage in the United States, however, seems to me to have originated as I have stated in the text, granting that in the Southwest *pico* was also an influence. The Spanish *paso* must be allowed a similar influence on *pass.* In early American usage *pass* sometimes, rather confusingly, occurs in place-names. As far as I have discovered, however, *pass,* as thus appearing, refers to some such passageway as a toll-gate. As a common noun *pass* has meant *passage* in English since 1300 (see OED), and the application could be topographical. But this does not seem to have developed into a place-name usage until much later. I think, therefore, that the Western U.S. use of *pass* developed on the spot under French (and Spanish) influence.

222 Cedar: To the botanist the western "cedar" commonly is a juniper, but the West was not named by botanists. The term *juniper,* however, has become known in more recent years, and is now rather widely applied as a place-name—partly to break the monotonous repetition of *cedar.*

223 Siskiyou: Gudde gives a good discussion, ending: "Neither version has been substantiated by documentary evidence, and the real origin may forever be shrouded in obscurity." The Chinook origin still seems to me better attested and linguistically simpler, but this does not constitute proof, and I commend Gudde's statement.

224 "familiar proper ... " G. F. Ruxton, *Life in the Far West* (1848).

224 Scott's Bluff: The story is told in Edwin Bryant, *What I Saw in California* (1848), and in Washington Irving's *Adventures of Captain Bonneville* (1837).

225   Russian names: Gudde, under heading *Russian,* etc. I am indebted to the late Professor Alexander Kaun for translations of the Russian. Gudde merely gives Shabaikai without suggesting that Slavianka might be connected with it. I am, however, the more ready to make the connection because I cannot see what reason other than folk-etymology would have caused the Russians to give such a highly unusual name as Slavianka. There were certainly no little Slav women around; also, I do not believe that that "slav" would have been what they would have said. Why not "little Russian woman"?

226   Louisiana: Ficklen (SS); Alcée Fortier, *Hist. of Louisiana,* iii, 79.

230   Buffalo: Fillmore (SS), and William Ketchum (SS). There has been argument as to whether the name may have originated directly from the animal. The buffalo must always have been very rare in this region, but that in itself is no reason against a naming for the animal (see p. 116 and note). An interesting letter in Ketchum from Hon-non-de-uh (N. T. Strong), a Seneca Indian, makes the case very good for the origin of the name as given in the text.

234   "There's an Austerlitz . . . " WPA, *New York Guide.*

235   Decatur: WPA, *Alabama Guide.*

238   Woosung: Ackerman (SS).

241   St. Paris: There is actually a St. Paris in the canon, but this Ohio town was first named Paris, and I think that the present name is used for differentiation, not to honor the saint.

241   Interesting legislation on naming is to be found also in an Illinois *Act to provide for townships,* Apr. 1, 1851: "Towns [townships] shall be named in accordance with the express wish of the inhabitants . . . and if there shall not be a degree of unanimity . . . the commissioners may designate the name." The act also provided that no two towns should have the same name. Similar legislation of somewhat later date appears in a Territory of Dakota law of Mar. 9, 1883.

242   Eighteen Arkansas towns: Allsopp (SS) i, 65, quoting Timothy Flint.

243 "There is . . . " Timothy Dwight, *Travels in New England and New York* (1822), iv, 36.

243 "Naming counties . . . " Benson (SS).

244 This chapter is chiefly based upon the direct study of street-name plans in the older sections of our cities.

247 "unless there exists . . . " Hagner (SS).

249 Names on Manhattan Island: I. N. Phelps Stokes, *Iconography of Manhattan Island* (1915–28).

251 Harpe's Head: WPA, *Kentucky Guide*.

251 Reform: WPA, *Alabama Guide*.

252 Grenada: WPA, *Mississippi Guide*.

253 Lost-and-found names: I have collected a number of these, especially from McArthur (SS) *viz.,* Butcherknife, Gumboot, Jackknife, Pistol, Sardine (the last is for a tin of sardines). McArthur was a very careful worker, and all these stories were told him by identified individuals, who generally stated that they themselves were involved with the naming. There is no reason to doubt the probability of this last, for McArthur was working on his book early enough ("many years" before 1927) to have talked with these pioneers who actually gave the names. There is no reason to think such names especially common in Oregon; other states have merely lacked such an assiduous early worker. I think, therefore, that onomatologists should accept lost-and-found names as a minor category of incident names.

253 Cascade Mountains: McArthur (SS) presents a full discussion.

253 Portland: McArthur (SS), as usual, gives full details, including the coin-tossing story.

254 Monterey: The approved Spanish spelling *Monterrey* never established itself in the United States.

255 Railway sidings: Sage (SS) is worth quoting: "There are now towns, which in my boyhood were merely railway sidings named for the section bosses who lived there and whose names are preserved in the communities that gradually grew up there."

260 Minnesota: Upham (SS): *Congressional Globe,* Feb. 17, 1847.

262 La Panza, La Paleta: I accepted this origin, perhaps rashly, from

Sanchez (SS). Gudde is silent about this origin for La Paleta, and questions it for La Panza. The internationally named Nellie Van De Grift Sanchez was not a very careful worker, but she was connected with an old Spanish-California family and was in touch with that tradition. She picked up the idea somewhere, and it may be right.

264 Great Basin: J. C. Frémont, *Rep. of the Exploring Expedition,* etc. (1845), p. 175.

265 Golden Gate: Gudde gives the source of the quotation and further data.

265 Gulch: Mathews considers the origin of the topographical use of *gulch* to be uncertain; his first citation is from Newfoundland for 1835.

269 Mining towns: The California State Library has kindly supplied me with a list of 151 "unusual" names of mining towns in the state, including most of the names here mentioned. I sometimes doubt whether all these places actually existed. May not some of them merely have been dreamed up by fun-makers, any time between 1849 and the present? Yet certainly the great majority of them can be definitely located.

269 "Somewhere in . . . " Asbury Harpending, *The Great Diamond Hoax* (1913), pp. 102–3.

271 "Name it . . . " WPA, *Alabama Guide.*

271 Horicon: David H. Barr, *Atlas of the State of New York* (1829); J. F. Cooper, preface, in later editions of *The Last of the Mohicans.* Horicon also exists as a name in Wisconsin, probably a transfer from New York. The preferred modern spelling seems to be Horicon, though Cooper used Horican.

273 Scarsdale: A letter from G. H. Danzberger (June 9, 1945) lets me know that this name dates from 1701, and echoes Scarsdale in England.

274 Belmont: My friend Clifford H. Bissell, than whom no one knows more about French grammar, points out to me that Belmont is also masculine; I think, however, that it appeals to the unsophisticated American mind (mine, for instance) as being feminine.

275 Moss Giel: MacReynolds (SS) has treated the names of Bucks County, Pa., in detail which has been equaled only by a few other American studies.

275 "CONNECTICUT . . . " David Humphreys, *A Poem on the Industry of the United States* (1794).

275 "Currituck . . . " J. K. Paulding, *The Lay of the Scottish Fiddle* (1813). Another such poem is G. B. Wallis's *Lovely Rivers and Lakes of Maine.*

276 "In this . . . " H. R. Schoolcraft, *Personal Memoirs* (1851), p. 550.

277 Atchafalaya: T. W. Higginson, *Henry Wadsworth Longfellow* (1902), p. 195.

278 "Father of Waters": W. A. Read, *Louisiana Place-Names of Indian Origin* (SS) p. 39; Le Page Dupratz, *Hist. de la Louisiane* (1758), p. 141.

279 Itchepuckesassa: For this and some other fanciful renderings, see Drew (SS); more careful translations may be found in W. A. Read, *Florida Place-Names of Indian Origin* (SS).

280 "The Legislature . . . " Brunson (SS).

284 Yosemite names: L. H. Bunnell, *Discovery of the Yosemite* (1880); also, Bunnell (SS). M. S. Beeler, "Yosemite and Tamalpais," *Names*, iii, pp. 185–88, believes the literal meaning of Yosemite to be "the killers," though admitting the possibility of its connection with "bear."

284 El Capitan: Dr. Lynn White, President of Mills College, writes me (June 7, 1945) that there is a prominent landmark in western Texas called El Capitan and looking much like that of Yosemite. He suggests that through the Texans in Bunnell's company the name was transferred to California. This is possible, but the priority of the names would have to be established. A name in Texas is not necessarily older than a name in California. One could argue that some of these Texans, returning home, carried the name with them. Besides, Bunnell's own statement about the name cannot be ignored.

284 Inspiration Point, etc.: Our national parks, notable for spectacular and even grotesque scenery, have attracted many names

of the same sort. The most notable collection is offered by the Grand Canyon with its Vishnu's Temple, Vulcan's Throne, etc.; Clarence E. Dutton began the practice in the 1880's. See Wallace Stegner, *Beyond the Hundredth Meridian* (1954), pp. 191–98.

288 Washington: *Cong. Globe,* Feb. 8, Feb. 10, Mar. 2, 1853; Meany, *Origin of Wash. Geographic Names* (SS).

288 "The Platte . . . " *Exec. Doc. 28th Cong., 2 Sess.,* v. 1, No. 2.

289 Sedalia: S. B. Harding, *Life of George R. Smith* (1904).

290 "It takes . . ." Horace Greeley, *An Overland Journey* (1860), p. 39.

291 Minneapolis: Henry A. Castle, *Minnesota* (1915), iii, p. 1583.

294 Denver: "Place-Names in Colorado," *Colorado Mag.,* v. 17, pp. 192–93; J. C. Smiley, *Hist. of Denver,* pp. 187–223.

294 Miami: The case of the two Miamis seems to be about as good an instance of coincidence as we can find. Yet, even so, there is the possibility that the form and pronunciation of one or the other might have been influenced by that of the other near the final stage of development.

297 West Virginia: G. D. Hall, *The Rending of Virginia* (1902), pp. 397–404; Kenny (SS).

299 "never knew . . . " WPA, *Illinois Guide,* p. 592.

300 Kingdom City: WPA, *Missouri Guide.*

301 Pike: In addition, the general has gained the rare distinction (through Pike County, Mo.) of having his name become a common noun—first as the nineteenth century *pike,* and then as the twentieth-century *piker.* At least two other of our counties have enriched the language, i.e., Bourbon (Ky.) and Buncombe (N.C.). I think that Tulare (Calif.) can also be added, since *tularemia* is probably to be considered as derived from the county rather than from another source.

301 Côte: In the plains country this word seems to have been used by the French to indicate, in particular, the line of bluffs occurring where the general level of the land breaks off at the edge of a river valley, such as that of the middle course of the Platte. By mis-translation to *coast* and by a retained use of the old name

of the river, we have The Coast of [the] Nebraska. This was later misunderstood and romanticized as having originated because the plains resembled the sea. Mis-translation, after such fashion, is a factor not infrequently occurring, e.g., in Lake Superior, p. 83. A striking example is the rendering of Llano Estacado as Staked Plains. Many stories have been told to explain this name. The explanation is that the equivalent should be Palisaded Plains, with reference to the rampart-like cliffs at the top of which lies the region in question. See H. E. Bolton, *Coronado* (1949), p. 243. Compare the use of the name Palisades along the Hudson River.

303 Colorado: L. R. Hafen, "Steps to Statehood in Colorado," *Colorado Mag.*, iii, pp. 97–110, and the discussions in Congress there noted.

304 Nevada: H. H. Bancroft, *Hist. of Nevada* (1890), p. 150, and the documents there noted.

305 Arizona: H. H. Bancroft, *Hist. of Arizona* (1889), pp. 508–21; *Cong. Globe*, Apr. 3, 1860; *Alta California* (San Francisco), Oct. 28, 1856; *Sacramento Union*, Oct. 17, 30, 1856; Barnes (SS).

306 Idaho: *Cong. Globe*, Dec. 22, 1862; Feb. 12, 13, Mar. 3, 1863; Sanders (SS).

312 Wyoming: *Cong. Globe*, June 3, July 22, 1868; H. H. Bancroft, *Hist. of Wyoming* (1890), pp. 739–40, and documents there noted.

312 Ashley: See *Names*, iv, 176–77, for a letter by Ashley about his activities as a namer. Written long after the events and probably without consultation of documents, it is doubtful or wrong on some points, but adds certain details of interest.

314 "It is . . ." *Cong. Globe*, June 3, 1868.

314 Five-syllable names: I count the two Carolinas as the only state names to be fully five-syllabled. Pennsylvania, etc., as commonly pronounced, fuse the *-ia* into one syllable.

315 *Tank:* Mathews favors a direct development from the English use of the word. Since *tanque* is Mexican-Spanish and since the use of the word in English is confined, as far as I know, to the Southwest, I think that the statement in the text is a fair one. I myself see no objection to believing that the usage may

have sprung from both Spanish and English, but most etymologists seem to follow biological analogies and to think that such a double origin is the equivalent of a man's having two fathers.

315 On Picketwire, see McHendrie (SS): Albert Matthews, "The Purgatory River of Colorado," *Colonial Soc. of Mass. Pub.*, vi, 307–16. Historically there are some obscurities in the story, but the linguistic relations seem to be well established.

316 Devil: In contrast to the use of Devil, the name God rarely appears as a place-name in the U.S., probably out of Protestant respect for the Third Commandment. We may contrast the frequent use in Spanish America of such names as Nombre de Dios. A certain number of such names, given under Spanish influence, survive in the U.S., e.g., Corpus Christi. A thoroughly English-language example (letter from F. L. Wells, Dec. 12, 1945) is God's Buttocks, a name for a hill in New Hampshire, perhaps no longer current. This is doubly unusual in that it couples the divine name with a mild obscenity. Probably some such names circulate orally without getting into print on the maps, but they must be very rare. McArthur (SS) gives no example for Oregon, and I do not think that he would have omitted it if he had found one.

317 Because of the necessity of filing claims with precise identification, many thousands of mine-names are recorded in the early directories, which were doubtless issued largely for this very purpose. The one cited is George Owen's *General Directory and Business Guide* (1865).

317 Christmas, Tombstone: Barnes (SS). Although double or even multiple causes for the origin of a particular name must occur with some frequency, namers rarely record more than one reason. The Christmas mine is a good example. The language shows that the discoverer was thinking not only of the actual date, but also of the idea of a Christmas present.

319 On Dakota, see *Cong. Rec.*, v. 19, pt. 3, p. 2805; *ibid.*, v. 19, pt. 4, pp. 3139–40; *ibid.*, v. 20, pt. 1, p. 812; also Ehrensperger (SS), from which the couplet is quoted.

321   Whittier: I let the passage stand as first published, though I now realize the situation to be curious and dubious. The whole eight-line poem appears in B. F. Arnold and A. D. Clark, *Hist. of Whittier* (1933), with a heading in *Contents*, "Gift of Name." Since Whittier was still writing at the time of the town's foundation, I naturally assumed things to be as I have stated them. Later, E. G. Gudde discovered that the lines are the last eight (with change of two words) of "A Name," written by Whittier in 1880 and addressed to his namesake grandnephew! By substituting "town" for "boy" excellent sense has been made. If Whittier himself made the adaptation and sent the poem, what is stated here in the text is substantially correct; this seems quite possible. But the change may have been made by someone in the town of Whittier. The curious situation is thus more illustrative of the vagaries of human conduct than of the processes of naming.

322   Rawlins: J. H. Wilson, *Life of John A. Rawlins* (1916).

323   English names along the Great Northern: WPA, *North Dakota Guide,* under Leeds; for Pennsylvania names in Oklahoma, see Gould (SS).

323   The quotations from Mr. Williams are from a letter written by him to Victor J. Farrar, May 25, 1916, a copy of which was kindly supplied to me by Robert Hitchman; it was originally written to supply information to E. S. Meany when he was collecting material on Washington place-names.

325   For the many stories about the origins of town-names, I have relied chiefly upon the WPA Guides, Massengill (SS), and the various state place-name books. I personally talked with Mr. Scranage, and I also have a letter from him (May 19, 1942) giving information about Captain Tuley; on this character, see also Gould (SS). The origins of such names as Scranage, Ala., and of the Dutch names noted on p. 325 show the fallacy, at least in the U.S., of attempting to study place-names wholly by intensive concentration on a small area. The broad view is often necessary.

328   Whynot: This name appears on recent maps of North Carolina,

and so must have maintained some kind of continuous existence as a crossroads settlement, though I was unable to find it as of 1944. These rural community names, which are neither post-offices or incorporated towns, have a word-of-mouth rather than an "official" existence. Thus I have been informed that there is a Whynot in Mississippi, and have no doubt that there is, but I have not been able to locate it in print.

329   *Palmetto Place-Names* (SS) p. 183, yields the information here presented about Negro namings in South Carolina, including the anecdote on Pocotaligo.

331   The ballad is to be found in John A. Stone, *Pacific Song Book* (1861).

331   Bosky Dell: Ackerman (SS).

333   In addition to their use for street-names, alphabetical patterns have been occasionally employed for railroad stations. A letter from Miss Irene Neu, Research Assistant for the Burlington Lines (Nov. 19, 1945), comments on the stations between Lincoln and Kearney, Nebraska: "Chief Engineer Thomas Doane's Yankee worship for order evidently prompted him to arrange them alphabetically." This arrangement may still be followed from Crete to Lowell, but it is broken because of earlier and later established stations. In the desert country of California the Santa Fe named stations from Amboy to Goffs, and at one time apparently extended the system through Homer and Ibex to Klinefelter (Gudde).

334   Appalachian: See Whitney (SS) p. 7ff.

335   On the Arkansas controversy, see J. H. Shinn: *Pioneers and Makers of Arkansas* (1908), pp. 20–22; F. W. Allsopp, *Folklore of Romantic Arkansas* (1931), pp. 87–90; *U.S. Statutes at Large,* Aug. 2, 1813, Mar. 2, 1819, Apr. 21, 1820. Secretary of State (U.S.), *Biennial Rep.,* 1924.

337   Spokane: See Meany; Nelson W. Durham, *Hist. of the City of Spokane* (1912), pp. 337, 341. I have also a letter from the Rev. W. L. Davis, S.J., of Gonzaga University (October 4, 1945) giving confirmatory information based upon an un-

published thesis, *Early History of the Spokane Press* (Gonzaga) by W. E. Mulligan.

338 Podunk: For an early occurrence (as Podank) see *Connecticut Colonial Rec.,* i, 8; Eckstrom (SS) pp. 166–67; articles indexed under *Podunk* in SS.

340 On the development of the U.S.G.B., see the introductory sections to the larger reports of the Board itself. Gannett's letter (p. 344) is in the files of the Board.

352 Gudde offers a full bibliography on these California names. See also Chap. XLVI, and Stein (SS–S).

355 U.S.G.B.: See the reports of the Board; Burrill (SS).

355 Christening a mountain, etc.: Meany, *Orig. of Washington Geographic Names* (SS), under Mt. Spokane and Lincoln Creek.

357 Sylvester's namings: From a letter written me by Mr. Sylvester, January 9, 1943; this appeared, in substantially the same form, in *American Speech;* see Sylvester (SS).

358 New Mexico: L. Bradford Prince, *New Mexico's Struggle for Statehood* (1910), pp. 60–64.

362 "By placing . . ." Ackerman (SS).

362 Enola, Pa., according to Espenshade (SS), although it spells Alone backward, was named from a girl so called, who in turn was named from a character in a novel. One would suspect that the novelist had coined the name from Alone, thus symbolically representing a lonely character.

364 The complicated bibliography of the Rainier controversy may be found in SS. My own belief, from the evidence, is that the Tacoma Academy of Sciences was organized to publish this one paper and had no other existence. The action has imprinted itself on the scholarly world; this "Academy" is listed among the learned societies, and its single publication in the bibliographies of their contributions to learning.

373 World War I changes: A small town in Indiana has managed to get stuck in a straddle. Civically it remains East Germantown, but has a post-office called Pershing.

374 Clemenceau: Barnes (SS); a letter (April 12, 1943) from R. A. Taylor, Supt. of Schools, Cottonwood, Ariz.

374 "the name of Bully Creek . . ." McArthur (SS) and the Oregon law there noted.

375 "Whereas, Divers . . ." *Acts of Tennessee,* Apr. 6, 1889.

376 Colorado River: See action of Colorado State Legislature of Mar. 24, 1921; of U.S. Cong., July 25, 1921; of U.S.G.B., Nov. 2, 1921. The town of Grand Junction, named because of its location and at the junction of the Gunnison with the Grand, maintained its name and still does. Grand Valley and some other places also remain in this, so to speak, orphaned condition.

378 Coral Gables: The name actually dates back to pre-boom days, but received most of its publicity in the 1920's.

380 "I think . . . " Letter to me from Mrs. Green, Feb. 20, 1944.

380 Axis Drive: Far be it from me to reveal the name of the university thus allowing itself to be bullied.

385 Panhandle: H. L. Carter has pointed out in a review that at least eight states have "panhandles." The term also has local usage as, for instance, in San Francisco.

386 Alaska: A bibliography is in SS. Baker (SS) is excellent, supplying references for almost all the source-books on Alaskan nomenclature down to 1906. Also outstanding is Wagner (SS).

386 Bering: See the voyages as edited by F. A. Golder (1922, 1925).

388 Alaska: See my "The Name Alaska," *Names,* iv, pp. 193–204.

389 Cook, etc.: For references, consult Baker (SS).

396 Russian names: The conclusions are mostly based on study of the materials in Baker (SS); my colleague O. A. Maslenikov has kindly checked the Russian for me, and finds that whoever did the translations for Baker was well qualified.

397 Matanuska: Baker (SS).

398 Sumner: His famous speech had wide circulation as a government document, and is also to be found in Volume XI of his *Works* (1877). For this later history of the application of the name see again "The Name Alaska," cited above.

401 Nome: Davidson (SS).

402 Allen: *Sen. Ex. Doc. No. 125, 49th Cong. 2 Sess., 1887.*

406 Mt. McKinley: Belmore Browne, *Conquest of Mt. McKinley* (1913), pp. 6ff.

407 "the Alaskan . . . " Browne, *op. cit.,* p. 5.

408 "the Indian . . ." *Frank Leslie's Illustrated Newspaper,* lxxi, p. 286.

409 "to properly . . ." *ibid.,* lxxiii, p. 10.

409 Harriman expedition: See Volume I, pp. 63ff, of the expedition's publications.

411 Mt. Pillsbury: *San Francisco Chronicle,* July 18, 1956.

412 Hawaii: A place-name bibliography is given in J. W. Coulter, *Gazetteer of the Terr. of Hawaii* (1935). A more recent work to be noted is E. H. Bryan, Jr., "Hawaiian Place-Names," in Thrum's *Hawaiian Annual* (1947), and the fuller form of the same work as printed in the Honolulu *Star-Bulletin,* Jan. 2 to Feb. 7, 1947. Of older works the most extensive and useful is T. G. Thrum, "Hawaiian Place-Names," in Lorrin Andrews, *Dict. of the Hawaiian Lang.* (ed. 1922). Details on names, especially on generics, are to be drawn from the dictionary itself.

412 Menehune: This question is a hot potato, and no prudent scholar would go out of his way to touch it. P. H. Buck, *Vikings of the Sunrise* (1938), pp. 250ff, accepts the legend as having an authentic basis. Therefore I think that it cannot be lightly waved away. I believe, moreover, that I should not pass over this opportunity to consider the problem from the onomatologist's point of view.

414 Hawaii: See in particular, P. H. Buck, *op. cit.,* p. 19 and elsewhere.

417 Land divisions: On this and other traditional lore of the Hawaiians, see David Malo, *Hawaiian Antiquities* (1903).

422 Recent tendencies: I am indebted to a letter from E. H. Bryan, Jr. (Dec. 4, 1956).

423 Post-1944 changes: These are gathered from the Post-Office Guides and from the reports of the Board on Geog. Names.

425 Commemorative namings: Governmental practice, supported by the Board on Geog. Names, follows the generally commendable rule (see p. 200 for its suggestion even in Jefferson's time) that

nothing shall be named for a living person. Namings of towns, streets, privately-built dams, etc., cannot thus be controlled, but even these generally commemorate individuals who are safely hallowed by death. There has been, however, some naming for still-living war-heroes, e.g., MacArthur (see p. 380). Even national usage falters occasionally. Thus the Steese Highway in Alaska has borne the name of the army engineer who was chiefly concerned with its construction. Another example is Hoover Dam, a name which has given to the ex-president's political enemies an opportunity to make some unkind remarks about his status.

428 Dewyrose: The letter is undated, but came to me in January 1957; I have edited it slightly for publication.

430 Middlesex: *San Francisco Chronicle,* Aug. 15, 1953.

430 Gutter: Audrey R. Duckert, "Gutter: Its Rise and Fall," *Names,* iv, pp. 146–54.

431 Punxsutawney: Espenshade (SS) p. 191.

432 Two-letter names: Letter from F. T. Monroe, Dec. 15, 1953. For the compilation he also gives credit to E. C. Schallis.

433 American Name Society: The author has the honor of being its president for 1957. The dues ($5.00) include a subscription to *Names.* All interested persons are invited to join. Checks should be made out to the American Name Society and sent to 100 Codornices Road, Berkeley, California.

434 Avenue of the Americas: Use has been made of various copies of the *New York Times* located through its Index, in particular, of the issue for Oct. 3, 1955.

436 Bedloe Island: *San Francisco Chronicle,* Aug. 4, 1956: *N.Y. Times,* see *Index,* Oct., Nov., 1956; *Docs. Rel. to the Col. Hist. of N.Y.,* see Index; J. R. Brodhead, *Hist. of the State of N.Y.,* see Index.

437 Los Angeles: Personal information from E. G. Gudde; Stein (SS–S).

≫≫≫≫≫≫≫≫≫≫≫≫✲≪≪≪≪≪≪≪≪≪≪≪≪≪≪

George R. Stewart
A checklist by John Caldwell

ONE OF the most innovative and original of American writers, George R. Stewart published seven novels and twenty-five works of non-fiction. As the author of three reference books and many articles on names and naming, he was established as a major onomatologist. Although born in Pennsylvania he lived most of his life in California, much of it as a Professor of English at the Berkeley campus of the University of California. A large part of his work was about the overland migration and the people that settled and developed the West; but his interests were catholic, ranging from Classical antiquity to the twentieth century, from anthropology to meteorology, from covered wagon trails to transcontinental highway.

In 1938 Ben Ray Redman called Stewart a "novelist of major stature";[1] but, except for reviews of his books, there has been virtually nothing written about him. It is difficult to understand why a person who wrote so well about so many different things has not aroused a critical interest. This checklist is offered as one gesture toward acknowledging his place in American letters.[2]

---

[1]Ben Ray Redman, rev. of *East of the Giants,* by George R. Stewart, *Saturday Review of Literature,* 1 October 1938, p. 5.

[2]The collections and lists of Roy A. Squires, Donald Drury, and Robert Lyon have been very helpful to me in the preparation of this checklist.

George R. Stewart: A checklist

I. BOOKS

A. Non-Fiction

American Given Names, Their Origin and History in the Context of the English Language. New York: Oxford University Press, 1979. 288 p.

American Placenames; A Concise and Selective Dictionary for the Continental United States of America. New York: Oxford University Press, 1970. xl, 550 p.

American Ways of Life. Garden City, N.Y.: Doubleday, 1954. 310 p.; New York: Russell & Russell, 1971. 310 p.

A Bibliography of the Writings of Bret Harte in the Magazines and Newspapers of California, 1857–1871. University of California Publications in English, Vol. 3, No. 3. Berkeley: University of California Press, 1933, pp. 119–70; Berkeley: University of California Press, 1933. 52 p.; Folcroft, Pa.: Folcroft Press, 1969, pp. 119–70.

Bret Harte, Argonaut and Exile; Being an Account of the Life of the Celebrated American Humorist . . . Compiled from New and Original Sources. Boston: Houghton Mifflin, 1931. xi, 384 p.; Port Washington, N.Y.: Kennikat Press, 1964. xi, 384 p.

The California Trail, An Epic with Many Heroes. New York: McGraw-Hill, 1962. 399 p. (The American Trails Series); McGraw-Hill Paperback ed. New York: McGraw/Hill, 1971. 339 p.; London: Eyre & Spottiswoode, 1964. 339 p. (Frontier Library).

Committee of Vigilance: Revolution in San Francisco, 1851; An Account of the Hundred Days When Certain Citizens Undertook the Suppression of the Criminal Activities of the Sydney Ducks. Boston: Houghton Mifflin, 1964. vi, 339 p.; New York: Ballantine Books, 1971. 307 p. (Comstock ed.).

The Department of English of the University of California on the Berkeley Campus; An Informal Presentation of Some of Its Personalities and Activities During Its First Century. Berkeley: University of California, 1968. 67 p. (A Centennial Publication of the

University of California).

Donner Pass and Those Who Crossed It; The Story of the Country Made Notable by the Stevens Party, the Donner Party, the Gold-Hunters, and the Railroad Builders. With Old and New Illustrations Showing the Pass in Summer and Winter. San Francisco: California Historical Society, 1960. 96 p.; Menlo Park, Calif.: Lane Book Co., 1964. 96 p.

English Composition; A Laboratory Course. New York: Henry Holt, 1936. 2 vols.

Good Lives. Illustrated with Photos. Boston: Houghton Mifflin, 1967. xiii, 305 p.

John Phoenix, Esq, the Veritable Squibob; A Life of Captain George H. Derby, U.S.A. New York: Henry Holt, 1937. xiv, 242 p.; New York: Da Capo Press, 1969. xiv, 242 p. (The American Scene).

Man: An Autobiography. New York: Random House, 1946. x, 310 p.; London: Cassell, 1948. vii, 254 p.

"Modern Metrical Techniques as Illustrated by Ballad Meter (1700–1920)" Diss. Columbia University, 1922. 120 p.

N.A. 1: The North-South Continental Highway. Maps by Erwin Raisz. Boston: Houghton Mifflin, 1957. 2 vols.

Names on the Globe. New York: Oxford University Press, 1975. ix, 411 p.

Names on the Land: A Historical Account of Placenaming in the United States. New York: Random House, 1945. ix, 418 p.; New York: Editions for the Armed Services, 1945. 415 p. (Armed Services ed., 929); Revised and Enlarged Ed. Boston: Houghton Mifflin, 1958. 511 p.; 3d ed., Revised and Enlarged. Boston: Houghton Mifflin, 1967. xiii, 511 p. 4th ed., with introduction by Wallace Stegner and checklist by John Caldwell. San Francisco: Lexikos, 1982.

Not So Rich as You Think. With Drawings by Robert Osborn. Boston: Houghton Mifflin, 1968. vi, 248 p.; New York: New American Library, 1970. 176 p. (Signet Book)

Ordeal By Hunger: The Story of the Donner Party. With Drawings by Ray Boynton, Maps and Other Illustrations. New York: Henry

Holt, 1936. xii, 328 p.; London: Jonathan Cape, 1936. 352 p.; New ed., With a Supplement and Three Accounts by Survivors. Boston: Houghton Mifflin, 1960. xii, 394 p.; London: Transworld Publishers, 1964. 319 p. (Corgi Books); New York: Pocket Books, 1971. 320 p.; Historical Foreword by Marcus Cunliffe. London: Eyre & Spottiswoode, 1962. 394 p. (Frontier Library).

Pickett's Charge: A Microhistory of the Final Attack at Gettysburg, July 3, 1863. Boston: Houghton Mifflin, 1959. 354 p.; Introduction by Philip Van Doren Stern. Greenwich, Conn.: Fawcett Publications, 1963. 320 p.; Dayton, Oh.: Morningside Bookshop, 1980. 354 p.

"Stevenson in California: A Critical Study." Thesis (M.A.) University of California, 1920. ii, 100, iii p.

Take Your Bible in One Hand; The Life of William Henry Thomes, San Francisco: The Colt Press, 1939. 66 p.

The Technique of English Verse. New York: Henry Holt, 1930. x, 235 p.; Port Washington, N.Y.: Kennikat Press, 1966. x, 235 p.

To California by Covered Wagon. Illustrated by William Moyers. New York: Random House, 1954. v, 182 p. (Landmark Books, 42).

U.S. 40, Cross Section of the United States of America. Maps by Erwin Raisz. Boston: Houghton Mifflin, 1953. viii, 311 p.; Westport, Conn.: Greenwood Press, 1973. viii, 311 p.

The Year of the Oath; The Fight for Academic Freedom at the University of California, by George R. Stewart, in Collaboration with Other Professors of the University of California. Garden City, N.Y.: Doubleday, 1950. 156 p.; New York: Da Capo Press, 1971. 156 p. (Civil Liberties in American History).

B. Fiction

Doctor's Oral. New York: Random House. 1939. 259 p.

Earth Abides. New York: Random House, 1949. 379 p.; New York: Ace Books, 1959. 318 p. (Ace Star ed.); London: V. Gollancz, 1950. 334 p.; London: Science Fiction Book Club, 1953.

253 p.; London: Transworld Publishers, 1956. 384 p. (Corgi Books); Boston: Houghton Mifflin, 1969. 373 p.; London: Transworld Publishers, 1970. 316 p. (Corgi Science Fiction); Greenwich, Conn.: Fawcett Publications, 1971. 317 p. (Fawcett Crest M1551); Los Altos, Calif.: Hermes Publications, 1974. 374 p.

East of the Giants; A Novel. New York: Henry Holt, 1938. 478 p.; London: Harrap, 1939. 480 p.; London: Book Club, 1939. 480 p.; New York: Editions for the Armed Services, N.D. 509 p. (Armed Services ed. G-210); New York: Ballantine Books, 1971. 434 p. (Comstock ed.).

Fire; A Novel. New York: Random House, 1948. xi, 336 p.; London: V. Gollancz, 1941. 320 p.; Boston: Houghton Mifflin, 1971. 336 p.; New York: Ballantine Books, 1974. 246 p. (Comstock ed.).

Sheep Rock, A Novel. New York: Random House, 1951. 286 p.; New York: Ballantine Books, 1971. 243 p. (Comstock ed.).

Storm. New York: Random House, 1941. 349 p.; New York: Council on Books in Wartime, 1941. 317 p. (Armed Services ed.); London: Hutchinson, 1942. 240 p.; Washington: Infantry Journal, Penguin Books, 1944. 310 p. (A Fighting Forces-Penguin Special, S238); With a New Introduction. New York: Modern Library, 1947. ix, 349 p.; New York: Ballantine Books, 1974. 271 p. (Comstock ed.).

The Years of the City. Boston: Houghton Mifflin, 1955. 567 p.

II. EXCERPTS, ABRIDGMENTS, ADAPTATIONS

American Placenames . . . Dictionary: "What's That Again?" *American Heritage,* October 1970, p. 116 (excerpts).

American Ways of Life: "Naming America's Wild Animals." *Science Digest,* November 1954, pp. 68–71 (excerpt).

Earth Abides: Adapted and brought within the vocabulary of New Method Reader 3 (Alternative ed.) by Michael West. Illustrated by Peter Branfield. London: Longman, 1971. 89 p.

East of the Giants: Omnibook, April 1939, pp. 9–120 (condensation).

Fire: "Death of the Glen." *Current Thinking and Writing,* 2d series, ed. by Joseph M. Bachelor, Ralph L. Henry, and Rachel Salisbury. New York: Appleton-Century-Crofts, 1951, pp. 139–41 (excerpt); "Fire." *Ladies Home Journal,* March 1948, pp. 36–37, 157–99 (condensation); "Men Against the Flames." *Readers' Digest,* July 1947, pp. 141–76 (excerpts).

Man: An Autobiography: Readers' Digest, July 1947 pp. 141–76 (excerpts).

Names on the Land:"How Cities Get Those Funny Names." *Science Digest,* 19 May 1946, pp. 26–28 (condensation); "Melodrama in the Forties." *Esquire,* March 1945, pp. 100–2 (excerpts); "Names on the Land." *Life,* 2 July 1945, pp. 47–48, 51–52, 54, 57 (excerpts).

Ordeal By Hunger: "The Dry Drive." *Frontier* and *Midland,* 16 (Spring 1936), 206–11 (excerpt).

Storm: "Lineman" in *On Your Own,* ed. by William R. Wood. Philadelphia: J. B. Lippincott Co., 1953. pp. 350–55 (excerpt); "Man Is an Air Animal." *Heating, Piping, and Air Conditioning,* 14 (September 1942), 541 (excerpt); "Opening the Sluice Gates" in *Taken at the Flood: The Human Drama as Seen by Modern American Novelists,* comp. by Ann Watkins. New York: Harper, 1946. pp. 149–53 (excerpt); *Readers' Digest,* March 1942, pp. 123–44 (abridgement); *Weather.* Merit Badge Series, New Brunswick, N.J.: Boy Scouts of America, 1943, pp. 5–28 (Condensation); "When Your Electric Lights Go Out." *Readers' Digest,* November 1950. pp. 105–08 (excerpts).

To California by Covered Wagon: A dramatization, with music and sound effects, adapted from the Landmark Book of the same title by Elise Bell. Landmark Enrichment Records ERL 123, 1963.

III. EDITED WORKS, INTRODUCTIONS

Breen, Patrick. *The Diary of Patrick Breen, Recounting the Ordeal of the Donner Party Snowbound in the Sierra, 1846–47.* Introduction and notes by George R. Stewart. San Francisco: Book Club of California, 1946. 38 p.

Brewerton, George Douglas. *A Ride with Kit Carson Across the Great American Desert and Through the Rocky Mountains.* Introduction by George R. Stewart. Palo Alto: Lewis Osborne, 1969. 108 p.

Brown, James Berry. *Journal of a Journey Across the Plains in 1859.* Ed., with an introduction, by George R. Stewart. Book Club of California publication no. 135. San Francisco: Book Club of California, 1970. xvi, 72 p.

Bry, Michael. *This California.* Photos by Michael Bry, with accompanying text by George R. Stewart. Berkeley, Calif.: Diablo Press, 1965. 224 p.

Chiles, Joseph Ballinger. *A Visit to California in 1841,* as recorded for Hubert Howe Bancroft in an interview with Joseph B. Chiles. Forward by George R. Stewart, including his essay about Chiles written in 1920. Friends of the Bancroft Library Keepsake no. 18. Berkeley, Calif.: Friends of the Bancroft Library, 1970. 21 p.

Harte, Bret. *Bret Harte,* with a comment by G. R. Stewart, Jr. The Letters of Western Authors, a Series of Letters Reproduced in Facsimile, of Twelve Distinguished Pacific Coast Authors of the Past. Each with a Comment by a Contemporary Western Writer, no. 2. San Francisco: Book Club of California, 1935.

_____*The Luck of Roaring Camp and Selected Stories and Poems.* Ed., with an introduction, by George R. Stewart, Jr. New York: Macmillan, 1928. xx, 188 p.; New York: Book League of America, 1929. xx, 188 p.

_____. *San Francisco in 1886, Being Letters to the 'Springfield Republican.'* Ed. by George R. Stewart and Edwin S. Fussell. San Francisco: Book Club of California, 1951. x, 88 p.

_____. "Some Bret Harte Satires," ed. by George R. Stewart. *Frontier,* 13 (January 1933), 93–101.

Jefferson, T. H. *Map of the Emigrant Road from Independence, Mo., to St. Francisco, California.* With an introduction and notes by

George R. Stewart. California Historical Society Special Publication, no. 20. San Francisco: California Historical Society, 1945. xi, 23 p.

Reed, Virginia Elizabeth. *Across the Plains in the Donner Party.* Forward by George R. Stewart. Palo Alto, Calif.: L. Osborne, 1966. 55 p.

Shallenberger, Moses. *The Opening of the California Trail; The Story of the Stevens Party.* From the Reminiscences of Moses Schallenberger as set down for H. H. Bancroft about 1885; edited and expanded by Horace S. Foote in 1888; and now edited with introduction, notes, maps, and illustrations by George R. Stewart. Bancroft Library Publications, no 4. Berkeley, Calif.: University of California Press, 1953. viii, 115 p.

Stevenson, Robert Lewis. "San Carlos Day, An Article in a California Newspaper." With an introduction by George R. Stewart, Jr. *Scribners Magazine,* 68 (August 1920), 209–11.

Thomes, William Henry. *Recollections of Old Times in California, or, California Life in 1843.* Ed., with an introduction by George R. Stewart. Friends of the Bancroft Library Keepsake no. 22. Berkeley, Calif.: Friends of the Bancroft Library, 1974. 29 p.

IV. CONTRIBUTIONS TO BOOKS AND PERIODICALS

"The All-American Season." *New York Times Magazine,* 24 September 1944, pp. 18, 38.

"American Fiction"; "American Poetry"; "Belles Lettres and Criticism." In *The American Year Book . . . Year 1927,* ed. by Albert Bushnell Hart. Garden City, N.Y.: Doubleday, Doran & Co., 1928, pp. 712–16, 716–20, 720–21.

"And Adam Gave Names—A Consideration of Name-lore in Antiquity." *Names,* 6 (March 1958), 1–10.

"The Bad Old Summer Time." *New York Times Magazine,* 23 June 1944, pp. 20–21, 42.

"A Ballade of Railroad Folders" (verse). *Life,* 19 February, 1920, p. 307.

"The Basin and Desert," in *The American Heritage Book of Natural*

Wonders, by Alvin M. Josephy, Jr. New York: American Heritage Publishing Co., 1963, pp. 305–51.

"The Biography of a Winter Storm." *New York Times Magazine.* 26 February 1950, pp. 20–1, 46–7, 49.

"The Bret Harte Legend." *University of California Chronicle.* 30 (July 1928), 338–50.

"Bret Harte on the Frontier; a New Chapter of Biography." *Southwest Review,* 11 (April 1926), 265–73.

"Bret Harte Upon Mark Twain in 1866." *American Literature,* 13 (November 1941), 263–64.

"California Placenames." *American Speech,* 23 (April 1948), 136–37.

"The Careful Young Men: California." *Nation,* 9 March 1957, 208–209.

"Caribou as a Placename in California." *California Folklore Quarterly,* 5 (October 1946), 393–5.

"A Child's Tale of the Donner Tragedy." *Westways,* December 1934, pp. 22–3, 30.

"A Classification of Placenames." *Names,* 2 (March 1954), 1–13.

"Color in Science and Poetry." *Scientific Monthly,* 30 (January 1930), 71–8.

"Comments on Hoere (n)-kill." *American Speech,* 19 (October 1944), 215–16.

"The Drama in a Frontier Theatre," in *Essays in Dramatic Literature, the Parrott Presentation Volume, by Pupils of Professor Thomas Marc Parrott of Princeton University, Published in His Honor,* ed. by Hardin Craig. Princeton: Princeton University Press, 1935, pp. 183–204.

"The Drama of Spring." *New York Times Magazine,* 26 March 1944, pp. 12–13, 35.

"Dumas's *Gil Blas en Californie,* a Study of Its Sources." *California Historical Society Quarterly,* 14 (1935), 132–42.

"Each in Its Ordered Place; Structure and Narrative in Benjy's Section of *The Sound and the Fury,*" by George R. Stewart and J. M. Backus. *American Literature,* 29 (January 1958), 440–56.

"Early Missionary Life in California." *Presbyterian Advance,* 8 September 1927, p. 17.

"English Geography in Malory's *Morte d'Arthur.*" *Modern Language Review,* 30 (April 1935), 204–209.

"*Europe* and *Europa.*" *Names,* 9 (June 1961), 79–90.

"The Field of the American Name Society." *Names,* 1 (June 1953), 73–78.

"From Cape Cod to Dragon Rocks." *American History Illustrated,* July 1974, pp. 34–41.

"Fulbrighting in Greece." *Harper's,* October 1953,pp. 75–80.

"Further Observations on Placename Grammar." *American Speech,* 25 (October 19502), 197–202.

"George R. Stewart," in *There Was Light, Autobiography of a University, Berkeley: 1868–1968,* ed. by Irving Shaw. Garden City., N.Y.: Doubleday & Co., 1970, pp. 143–52.

"George R. Stewart on Names of His Characters" (interview). *Names,* 9 (March 1961), 53–57.

"Good Reading for the Road." *New York Times Book Review,* 7 June 1953, p. 10.

"Gunfire to Westward: The Pacific Coast in Wartime." *Mademoiselle,* June 1942, pp. 37, 80, 82.

"Heritage of Names." *Transatlantic,* October 1945, pp. 37–8, 60–3.

"Homer," in *Atlantic Brief Lives: A Biographical Companion to the Arts,* ed. by Kronenberger. Boston: Little Brown and Co., 1971, pp. 376–77.

"Iambic-Trochaic Theory in Relation to Musical Notation of Verse." *Journal of English and Germanic Philology,* 24 (January 1925), 61–71.

"An Interview with George R. Stewart," by Robert Van Gelder, in *Writers and Writing.* New York: Scribners, 1946, pp. 244–47.

" 'Iron-Hewer' or 'Man of Toft'?" *New York Times Magazine,* 20 April 1952, p. 17.

"It Pays to Watch the Sky." *Nation's Business,* November 1946, pp. 50–52, 83–84.

"John Sharpenstein Hager, Forty-niner in the Social Register," in *Lives of Eighteen from Princeton,* ed. by Willard Throp. Princeton: Princeton University Press, 1946, pp. 232–42.

"The Knights at Rhodes," in *A Book of Princeton Verse, 1916*, ed. by Alfred Noyes. Princeton: Princeton University Press, 1916, pp. 161–63; also in *Literary Digest*, 24 June 1916, p. 1858.

"*Leah, Woods,* and Deforestation as an Influence on Placenames." *Names,* 10 (March 1962), 11–20.

"McGinnity's Rock" (Fiction). *Esquire,* January 1947, pp. 102–3.

"The Meaning of *Bacheler* in Middle English." *Philological Quarterly,* 13 (January 1934), 40–47.

Men's Names in Plymouth and Massachusetts in the Seventeenth Century. University of California Publications in English, Vol. 7, No. 2. Berkeley: University of California Press, 1948, pp. 109–37.

"The Meter of *Piers Plowman*." *PMLA,* 42 (March 1927), 112–28.

"The Meter of the Popular Ballad." *PMLA,* 40 (December 1925), 933–62; also in *The Critics and the Ballad: Readings,* ed. by MacEdward Leach and Tristram Potter Coffin. Carbondale: Southern Illinois University Press, 1961, pp. 151–60.

"A Method Toward the Study of Dipodic Verse." *PMLA,* 39 (December 1924), 979–89.

"Mexico by Ear." *California Monthly,* April 1938, pp. 8–10, 24–5.

"Moral Chaucer," in *Essays in Criticism,* University of California Publications in English, Vol. 1. Berkeley: University of California Press, 1929, pp. 91–109.

"More on the Name California." *Names,* 2 (December 1954), 249–54.

"Mountains of the West: South Central Panarama." *Ford Times,* March 1949, pp. 31–6.

"Murder and Onomatology." *Nation,* 9 April 1960, pp. 313–16.

"The Name Alaska." *Names,* 4 (December 1956), 193–204.

"Names for Citizens." *American Speech,* 9 (February 1934), 78.

"Names of Wild Animals for Natural Features in the United States and Canada." *Revue Internationale d'Onomastique,* 12 (Decembre 1960), 282–92.

"Nomenclature of Stream-forks on the West Slope of the Sierra Nevada." *American Speech,* 14 (October 1939), 191–97.

"Notes on the Sleep-walking Scene." *Modern Language Notes,* 42 (April 1927), 235–37.

"The Novelists Take Over Poetry." *Saturday Review of Literature,* 8 February 1941, pp. 3–4, 18–19.

"On University Government." Berkeley: American Association of University Professors, Berkeley Chapter, 1960, 7 p.; also in *AAUP Bulletin,* 47 (March 1961), 60–62.

"One of 120,000." *Holiday,* November 1947, pp. 66–7, 69–70, 130–31.

"Ouaricon Revisited." *Names,* 15 (September 1967), 166–72. (Includes "The Source of the Name 'Oregon' ").

"The Overland Stage." *California Monthly,* March 1935, pp. 4, 7.

"Personal Names." *American Speech,* 26 (May 1951), 123–25.

"Placename Patterns." *Names,* 4 (June 1956), 119–21.

"Popular Names for the Mountain Sheep." *American Speech,* 10 (December 1935), 283–88.

"The Prairie Schooner Got Them There." *American Heritage,* February 1962, pp. 4–17, 98–102.

"A Proposal for Forestry Demonstration Areas Along Highways." *Journal of Forestry,* 48 (May 1950), 356–9.

"The Real Treasure Island." *University of California Chronicle,* 28 (April 1926), 207–13.

"The Regional Approach to Literature." *College English,* 9 (April 1948), 370–75; also in *Western Writing,* ed. by Gerald W. Haslam. Albuquerque: University of New Mexico Press, 1974, pp. 40–48.

"Report on the Nation." *New York Times Magazine,* 8 August 1943, pp. 14–15, 27.

"A Sidelight on History," in *A Visit to California in 1821* . . . Berkeley, Calif.: Friends of the Bancroft Library, 1970, pp. 19–21.

"The Smart Ones Got Through." *American Heritage,* June 1955, pp. 60–63, 108; also in *The American Heritage Book of Great Adventures of the Old West.* American Heritage, 1969, pp. 139–47; and in *Points of Departure; Essays and Stories for College English,* ed. by Arthur J. Carr and William R. Steinhoff. New York:

Harper, 1960, pp. 73–79.

"Some American Placename Problems" *American Speech,* 19 (December 1944), 289–92.

"Source of the Name *Oregon.*" *American Speech,* 19 (April 1944), 115–17. (Reprinted in "Ouaricon Revisited").

"Thoughts on the Donner Party." *California Monthly,* May 1936, pp. 14–15, 36–40.

"Three and Fifty upon Poor Old Jack." *Philological Quarterly,* 14 (July 1935), 274–75.

"Time's Petty Pace" (fiction). *Esquire,* November 1946, pp. 106–7.

"Travelers by 'Overland.'" *American West,* July 1968, pp. 4–12, 61.

"Truth Crushed to Earth at Gravelly Ford, Nevada." *Pacific Spectator,* 4 (Winter 1950), 46–48.

"Twilight of the Printed Book." *Pacific Spectator,* 3 (Winter 1949), 32–39.

"The Two Moby-Dicks." *American Literature,* 25 (January 1954), 417–48.

"Two Spanish Word Lists from California in 1857." *American Speech,* 16 (December 1941), pp. 260–69.

"United States Army Ambulance Service." *Princeton Pictorial,* December 1918, pp. 64–7.

"The West as Seen from the East." *Literary History of the United States,* by Robert E. Spiller. Rev. Ed. New York: Macmillan Co., 1953, pp. 771–77.

"The West as Seen from the East (1800–1850)." *Pacific Spectator,* 12 (Spring 1947), 188–95.

"What is Named? Towns, Islands, Mountains, Rivers, Capes," in *Essays and Studies,* University of California Publications in English, Vol. 14. Berkeley: University of California Press, 1943, pp. 223–32.

"What's in a Name?" *Children,* 2 (December 1927), 22–64.

"Whitman and His Own Country." *Sewanee Review,* 33 (April 1925), pp. 210–18.

"The Year of Bret Harte's Birth." *American Literature,* 1 (March 1929), 78.

Dictionary of American Biography. Ed. Dumas Malone. New York:

Scribners, 1928–37. Stewart wrote the following entries: "Derby, George Horatio"; "Harte, Francis Brett"; "McBurney, Robert Ross"; "Thomes, William Henry"; "Webb, Charles Henry"; and "Wells, William Vincent."

V. BOOK REVIEWS

A. Titled Reviews

"An Affair of Passion," review of *The California Oath Controversy*, by David P. Gardner. *Nation*, 19 June 1967, pp. 795–6.

"The Big Sur Country," review of *Deep Valley*, by Dan Totherah. *Saturday Review of Literature*, 25 July 1942, p. 5.

"Forty-niner," review of *Autobiography of Isaac Jones Wistar*. *Saturday Review of Literature*, 17 December 1938, pp. 10–11.

"The Good New West," review of *Westward Tilt*, by Neil Morgan. *Nation*, 6 July 1963, pp. 16–17.

"Land of the Mormons," review of *Mormon Country*, by Wallace Stegner. *New York Times Book Review*, 25 October 1942, p. 20.

"Lewis . . ." review of *I Remember Christine*, by Oscar Lewis. *Saturday Review of Literature*, 18 April 1942, p. 18.

"Railroad Boy," review of *Abel Dayton*, by Flannery Lewis. *Saturday Review of Literature*, August 1939, p. 12.

"The Rivers of America," review of *The Sacramento: River of Gold*, by Julian Dana. *Saturday Review of Literature*, 20 December 1939, pp. 12–13.

"San Francisco's Old Palace," review of *Bonanza Inn*, by Oscar Lewis and Carroll D. Hall. *Saturday Review of Literature*, 2 December 1939, p. 6.

"Seeing the Golden State," review of *Romantic Cities of California*, by Hildegard Hawthorne and *California, A Guide to the Golden State*, the Federal Writers Project. *Saturday Review of Literature*, 1 July 1939, p. 14

"Spotlight on the Pacific Northwest," review of *Swift Flows the River*, by Nard Jones. *Saturday Review of Literature*, 16 March 1940, p. 6.

B. Untitled Reviews

Ah Sin and his Brethren in American Literature, by William Purviance Fenn. *American Literature,* 6 (November 1934), 370–72.

The Big Four, by Oscar Lewis. *Frontier and Midland,* 19 (January 1939), 138–39.

Followers of the Sun, a Trilogy of the Santa Fe Trail, by Harvey Fergusson. *Frontier and Midland,* 17 (Autumn 1936), 56–7.

Joaquin Miller; Literary Frontiersman, by Martin Severin Peterson. *American Lterature,* 10 (March 1938), 107–9.

John of the Mountains, ed. by Linnie Marsh Wolfe. *American Literature,* 10 (December 1938), 502–4.

The Life of Riley, by Harvey Fergusson. *Frontier and Midland,* 18 Winter (Winter 1937/38), 118–19.

The Literature of the Rocky Mountain West, ed. by Levette Jay Davidson and Prudence Bostwick. *American Literature,* 11 (November 1939), 316–18.

We Lived as Children, by Kathryn Hulm. *Frontier and Midland,* 19 (June 1939), 291.

Western Prose and Poetry, ed. and selected by Rufus A. Coleman. *American Literature,* 4 (November 1932), 337–8.

VI. ABOUT GEORGE R. STEWART

Beeler, Madison S. *"George R. Stewart, Toponymist."* Names, 24, (1976), 77–85.

Caldwell, John, *George R. Stewart.* Boise, Id.: Boise State University, 1981. (Western Writers Series, no. 46).

Cogell, Elizabeth Cummins. "The Middle-Landscape Myth in Science Fiction." *Science-Fiction Studies,* 5 (1978), 134–42.

Egan, Ferol, "In a World of Creation." *Westways,* July 1980, pp. 16–19, 80.

"George R. Stewart on Names of His Characters," an interview conducted by Joseph M. Backus. *Names,* 9 (1961), 53–57.

Stegner, Wallace. "George R. Stewart, Western Writer: An Appreciation of a Remarkable Author." *American West,* March-April 1982, 64, 67–69.

INDEX

Transfer-names and cluster-names are included under one entry, e.g., under *Delaware* are included references to bay, river, colony, and state. Variant spellings and foreign-language forms since translated are listed under the now-established form, e.g., for Ouisconsin, see *Wisconsin,* and for Nouvelle Orléans, see *New Orleans.* Persons mentioned only in connection with places named for them are not separately listed. Names mentioned incidentally and not explained are not listed.

Index

Index

Index

Index

Index

Index

Index

Index

Index

Index

Index

Index

Index

Index

Index

Index

Index

Index

Index